Praise for *Johnny Cash:*

"Richly detailed . . . the amount of new archival material [Streissguth] unearths . . . is truly impressive."
—New York Times Book Review

"Streissguth has written a compelling and sympathetic life of the person at the core of the Man in Black persona . . . . This is a well-written evocation of a fascinating subject."
—Los Angeles Times

"[Streissguth] vividly shows how Cash's larger-than-life contradictions chart the fault lines in the American soul."
—Boston Globe

"The most well-rounded Cash book to date. Grade: A."
—Entertainment Weekly

"A welcome examination of this singular American character."
—Newsday

"Streissguth utilizes those who knew Cash best to paint the portrait of the man, husband, father and performer . . . an important and compelling portrait."
—Nashville Tennessean

"An exemplary music bio for fans of the man, the music, or the genre."
—Publishers Weekly (starred review)

"Streissguth dispels a few myths and offers an evenhanded, complete, and reliable look at Cash that has resulted from dozens of interviews with his friends, musical associates, and family members."
—Booklist

"*Johnny Cash* does a good job of revealing Cash as a person with larger than life passions . . . by documenting the sprawling, complicated man Cash was—at times confronting Cash's own self-mythologizing writings—[Streissguth] makes Cash a more compelling and real figure."
—Offbeat

"One feels in a theatre of sorts, so effortless the read and entertaining the tales . . . .The definitive biography to date."
—American Songwriter

"Many vivid and heart-rending moments . . . . Expertly researched."
—American Way

"Streissguth offers an impressively measured account of the man, one that's neither too harsh nor too fawning."
—Under the Radar

Also by Michael Streissguth

Johnny Cash at Folsom Prison: The Making of a Masterpiece
Ring of Fire: The Johnny Cash Reader (editor)
Eddy Arnold: Pioneer of the Nashville Sound
Like a Moth to a Flame: The Jim Reeves Story
Voices of the Country: Interviews with Classic Country Performers

JOHNNY
CASH

~

THE BIOGRAPHY

MICHAEL STREISSGUTH

DA CAPO PRESS | A MEMBER OF THE PERSEUS BOOKS GROUP

Cataloging-in-Publication data for this book is available from the Library of Congress

First Da Capo Press hardcover edition 2006
First Da Capo Press paperback edition 2007
HC: ISBN 13: 978-0-306-81368-9; ISBN 10: 0-306-81368-8
PB: ISBN 13: 978-0-306-81565-2; ISBN-10: 0-306-81565-6
Published by Da Capo Press
A Member of the Perseus Books Group
http://www.dacapopress.com

Da Capo Press books are available at special discounts for bulk purchases in the U.S. by corporations, institutions, and other organizations. For more information, please contact the Special Markets Department at the Perseus Books Group, 2300 Chestnut Street, Suite 200, Philadelphia, PA 19103, or call (800) 255-1514, or e-mail special.markets@perseusbooks.com.

1 2 3 4 5 6 7 8 9

For Leslie
and Cate, Emily, and Willie.

CONTENTS

ACKNOWLEDGMENTS

This book is the result of my interaction with the life, career, and legend of Johnny Cash. However, innumerable escorts ferried me over the fickle ebb and flow between my world and Cash's. I'm grateful to those who offered oars and skiffs and, when Cash's side of the river swelled and roiled at my approach, a life jacket.

As a form of gratitude, I list those who guided me, knowing that a nod alone is an insufficient expression of my sentiments. If I have omitted anyone, I beg forgiveness and freely blame the enormous legacy of Johnny Cash, which dominated my mind as Cash dominated the air around him in life.

I am grateful to the wonderful team behind me at Le Moyne College in Syracuse, New York, where I have taught since 1998. I could not have completed this project without Julie Grossman, a great friend and colleague, Linda LeMura, John Smarrelli, Wayne Stevens, Fr. Charles Beirne, S.J., Monica Sondej, Bill Hurley, Rita Bunis, Nancy Ring, Roger Lund (who cried when Don Rich died), and the Research and Development Committee, which granted me a sabbatical in 2004 to pursue my research.

Dan Roche, who also teaches at Le Moyne, thoroughly digested my manuscript and made innumerable recommendations; I know his review ate up a lot of his time, time away from his own writing and his family, which only multiplies my indebtedness to him. I am also indebted to Ed Brown, who spent many nights and early mornings at his kitchen table, sipping tea, the manuscript in front of him, thinking of better ways to tell the Johnny Cash story. My wife, Leslie Bailey Streissguth, also edited the manuscript, but she did so much more than that. She challenged my theories and suggested new paths of inquiry while continually providing encouragement, even during my long absences spent researching and writing.

My pursuit of the Johnny Cash story took me from the jagged outcrop on the American River in California known as Folsom Prison, to the astonishingly flat cotton fields of northeastern Arkansas, to the broad and majestic Shenandoah River Valley, to marshy riverbanks in south central Arkansas, to worn residential streets in Memphis, to bustling city blocks in Manhattan, and elsewhere. To write about Johnny Cash is to learn again about America and its people. Along the way, I met and spoke with dozens of patient and intriguing individuals who helped me. And I thank them: John M. Alexander; Ron Alexenburg; Joe Allen; Steve Andreassi and Cindy Baffa of the IUP Lodge and Convocation Center in Hoboken, N.J.; Dick Asher; Jane Bailey; John Bailey; Earl Poole Ball; Morley Bartnoff of the Cosmotoppers; Gene Beley; Steve Berkowitz; Ken Berryhill; C. Clifton Black; Rick Blackburn; Nesbit Bowers; Bobby Brenner; Donzil Burleson; B.J. Carnahan; John Carter Cash; Tommy Cash; Bill Craig; Bestor Cram; Joyce Criswell; W.R. Criswell; Frederick E. Danker; Don Davis; Hank Davis; Ramblin' Jack Elliott; Wanda Fischer; C.R. Fore; Freddie M. Freeman of the Air Intelligence Agency, Department of the Air Force; the late Denise Gasiorowski; Iris Chrestman Gattis; Glen Gibson; Kelly Hancock; Warnuel Hargraves; the late Burton Harris; A.J. Henson; Everett Henson; Walter Hettche; Mark Hoffman and James Segrest, co-authors of *Moanin' At Midnight: The Life and Times of Howlin' Wolf*; the late Saul Holiff; Mike Horan; Larry Hoyt; J.E. Huff; Stan Jacobson; Bruce Jenkins; Betty Johnson; the late Frank Jones; Leon Kagarise; Bettye Kash; Joey Kent; Sid King; Harvey Kubernick; Joe Lee; Sharon Livingston, who so capably transcribed many of my interviews; Hank Adam Locklin; Loretta Lynn; Andrew Male and Phill Kalli at *Mojo*; Jim Malloy; Jim Marshall; Alan Mayor; Bob McCluskey; Paul McCoy; Scott McCraw and Nick Spitzer of Public Radio International's *American Folk Routes*; Russ McDougall (USAF); Emily Mocete; Dwayne Mueller; Alanna Nash; Kenneth Nelson; Peter Nilles; Tom Noonan; Irby Pearson; Tom Perryman; Steve Popovich; Scott Radloff; Richard Ranta at the University of Memphis; Joe Reeves of the Shelby County (Tennessee) Register's office; Don Reid; Harold Reid; Lou Robin; Tamra Saviano; Jack Shaw; Harold Shedd; Hopeton Smalling; Milton Stansbury; Gayle Stelter; Mark Stielper; David Streissguth; Karl Streissguth; Meaghan Streissguth; Phil Streissguth; Valerie Streissguth; Teri Thall; William Thomas; Kent Underwood;

Hugh Waddell; Elijah Wald; Bill Walker; the late Billy Walker; Howard White; Ruth White; Robbie Witkowski; Michael Woods, S.J.; and Ginny Wright.

Particularly accommodating were Cindy Cash, Kathy Cash, Rosanne Cash, Roy Cash, Jr., Jack Clement, Marshall Grant, Marty Stuart, and Jimmy Tittle, all of whom sat with me for hours, answering difficult questions and doing their best to take me back through the years to Johnny Cash. Just as accommodating were Jonathan Holiff and Barbara Holiff, who, motivated by their respect for the Cash legacy and their father and husband's part in that legacy, kindly shared with me Saul Holiff's papers.

The staff persons of numerous archives around the country were kind and ingratiating: Eugene Morris, Joseph Schwartz, and David Pfeiffer at the National Archives in College Park, Maryland; Rodney Krajca of the National Archives in Fort Worth, Texas; Mary Evelyn Tomlin of the National Archives in East Point, Georgia; Michael Henry of the Library of American Broadcasting in College Park, Maryland; Dawn Oberg and John Rumble of the Country Music Foundation Library and Archives in Nashville, Tennessee; Chris Ratliff, Sharon Banker, and Edwin Baker in Special Collections at the University of Memphis, who guided me through the Mississippi Valley Collection and other resources; the staff of the Museum of Television and Radio in New York, New York; the staff at the Arkansas Historical Commission in Little Rock, Arkansas; and Kendall L. Crilly at the Yale Music Library.

I thank also Ben Schafer, my editor at Da Capo, whose enthusiasm for this project never waned, and Jim Fitzgerald for his work securing outlets for my writings about Johnny Cash.

INTRODUCTION

Johnny Cash and June Carter Cash's gravesite sits atop a small hill in Hendersonville, Tennessee. Perhaps when the celebrated couple chose the plot near their home outside Nashville it was a quiet place surrounded by rolling farmland and country blacktop. But in August of 2004, as I stood there waiting for Cash's second daughter, Kathy, and her husband Jimmy Tittle whom I was scheduled to interview in this unlikely location, the advance of suburban development and the unrelenting hum of nearby traffic distracted me. To the south, beyond the austere cemetery field filled with modest markers, a colony of new middle-income homes seemed poised to march in June and Johnny's direction. And to the north, on the other side of a four-lane highway, a large lumber and hardware store rose on the horizon.

Amid the encroachment of the sprawling world, the Cashes, whose roots were deeply rural, lie still under their simple brass plates. Next to them rises a black granite bench, looking like a giant anvil, which Cash ordered to be erected after his wife died in May of 2003. "I want a place to rest when I visit my baby," he told his daughter. But the balladeer, so feeble when he buried June, never used the resting seat. He died four months after June, before the bench was installed.

Side by side in the shadow of the bench, faded flowers and small gifts scattered all around, June's and Johnny's markers are cemented in the hub of what amounts to a posthumous family gathering. Buried nearby are June's parents, Mother Maybelle Carter and Ezra Carter, as well as Helen and Anita Carter, June's sisters and singing partners who died before her. Johnny's sister Louise is nearby.

When my interview with the Tittles ended, I walked with them through this sparse burial garden. Kathy lovingly gathered the old mementoes left by fans, friends, and family, and when she forgot the whereabouts of an extended family member's grave, she asked her husband for help. We zigzagged away from the black bench, Kathy pointing to the graves of Luther Perkins, Cash's original guitarist, and Rosey Nix, June's daughter from her second marriage.

After we returned to Johnny's and June's graves, I studied a few markers wedged into the family plot. They were not for Cash-Carter family members, or even for those who'd been close to the family like Perkins; they were former *Grand Ole Opry* members. Cash had kept the *Opry* at arm's length in life, but he had embraced those who dwelled in the *Opry*'s house and spared a few who died penniless the indignity of a pauper's grave. In life, I am told, he paid or helped pay for burials and markers all around Nashville.

As we turned toward the box-store lumberyard and my parked car, the Tittles pointed out one more curiosity. Just a few paces away from Cash was the Hurt family, claiming its own plot. The title of Cash's last single was "Hurt."

This cemetery appeared to hold its own biography of Johnny Cash.

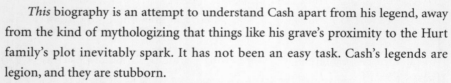

This biography is an attempt to understand Cash apart from his legend, away from the kind of mythologizing that things like his grave's proximity to the Hurt family's plot inevitably spark. It has not been an easy task. Cash's legends are legion, and they are stubborn.

To innumerable fans, his is the one face missing from Mt. Rushmore. So many would have the National Park Service make room for the famous American on the bleached outcrop that when I recently paired Cash's name with Mt. Rushmore's in a Lexis-Nexis search, the search engine spat out 125 articles. That's not counting the various magazine and newspaper articles outside Lexis-Nexis's grasp that have made the same claim. Songwriter, musician, and former Cash son-in-law Rodney Crowell issued a statement shortly after the singer died that appeared in many of those articles: "Johnny Cash will, like Will Rogers, stand forever as a symbol of intelligence, creativity, compassion and common sense. I'm thinking Mt. Rushmore." Crowell was obviously not alone, and he was certainly not the first to make the comparison. Somehow, over the years, Cash, like Washington, Jefferson, Lincoln, and Roosevelt, came to embody the American spirit. In our minds, he was a figure who fearlessly bounded for the frontier and kept alive our dying idealism and national pride.

Intrinsic to Cash's American countenance is the notion that he walked as a man among men, a lonely, battered, stoic soul. Irish rocker Bono, in his usual expansive tone, said after Cash's passing, "We're all sissies in comparison to Johnny Cash." Hundreds of grim songs and dark photographs could lead many to Bono's conclusion. In an age of metrosexual manhood, sexually ambiguous Calvin Klein models in glossy magazines, and changing male roles in society, Cash appeared unrelentingly male, indeed, mythically male.

His reputation as a man's man was in some ways embellished by his image as someone who seemed daily in touch with his loathsome side. Throughout the years, he sang, "I shot a man in Reno just to watch him die," and people took it as autobiography, perhaps because he sounded capable of it and his minor run-ins with the law over the years were so well publicized. (Cash's drummer W.S. Holland told me that men constantly stopped to brag that their uncles or cousins had marked time with Cash in a western penitentiary.) His final decade of recording (1993–2003) forcefully impressed the violent and brooding nature of Cash on the American public, this after more than twenty years (1970–1993) of Cash consciously distancing himself from this image in favor of exploring his faith and grooming a Christian appearance. In 1994, Cash and his albums with American Recordings set out to resurrect the man of "Cocaine Blues," who'd sooner shoot a triflin' woman than send her back to her mama. For the benefit of the young audience who may have only known Cash through his *Dr. Quinn: Medicine Woman* guest spots and his televised Christmas specials, the label's promotion engines cranked out black-and-white images of a man dressed in black who sang about murder and lived drug addiction, infidelity, and self-loathing. Again, Cash became the bad man of our vicarious experiences.

But this bad man could be good again, according to the rhetoric of Cash's career. "Redemption" might run a close second to "Mt. Rushmore" among words most closely associated with Cash. Although many took a secular view of his redemption, seeing it primarily through his ability to revive his career again and again, Cash staunchly viewed it through his regular efforts to find mercy in God's embrace. "I have unshakable faith," he declared weeks before his death. Throughout the years, Cash worked as hard on sharing his relationship with God as he did on plying his dark image. His appearances with Billy Graham, constant live and recorded performances of gospel music, and public battles with temptation conspired to make him something of a cleric. He seemed to have the authority of a minister or rabbi. But, of course, he was neither, even with the correspondence degree he earned in the 1970s from a Southern theological institute.

The myriad aspects of Cash's legend were cultivated over the years by Cash himself and by the marketing machine around him. In his lifetime, Cash took part in three books about his life: Christopher Wren's *Winners Got Scars Too* biography (1971), for which Cash shared in the advance monies; his own *Man in Black* (1975); and his *Cash: The Autobiography* (1997) written with Patrick Carr. All of these volumes gave Cash and his camp the opportunity to drive the discourse that forever buzzed around him. They elbowed aside, in effect, those writers who might have been more critical. If it was a deliberate tactic, it was shrewd. Independent writers were either scared away by the flooded market or learned to hew to the story as Cash had told it. Admirably, the books in which Cash participated spoke frankly about various aspects of his life, including his legendary substance abuse, but they also reinforced various myths and steered away from various complexities in the man's drama.

In part, perhaps, because of those books, Cash's legend has grown so bloated and unwieldy that in some quarters it has subsumed his art. Although the legend sprang from the art, the countenance of Johnny Cash is often strangely separated from the music. Cash is a saint to those who never heard him sing a gospel note, a bad man to college students who might not know "Folsom Prison Blues" from "Blue Moon of Kentucky," and a quintessential American to those unaware of his *America (A 200-Year Salute in Story and Song)* album of 1972 and "Ragged Old Flag" anthem of 1974. The disconnection was illustrated most vividly, perhaps, in the wake of Cash's death when the country-music industry launched a star-spangled (and profitable) appreciation after years of refusing to play his music or give him a Nashville-based recording contract. Astonishingly, the very institutions that so strenuously celebrated the late singer's iconic stature had for years ignored his art, suggesting, again, that the legend lives a fair distance from the music.

For many, though, the music will always trump the legend. I have run across men and women who care little for Cash's myths and instead relish talk of his early folk and gospel influences, marveling that one man could have absorbed and incorporated into his own repertory so much musical tradition by the age of thirty. Others whom I know, having little regard for the legend, rock their bodies to and fro when they hear Cash's "Rusty Cage" (1996), absorbed by nothing but the pulsing instrumentation and the urgent voice.

Yes, it is possible to know Cash simply for his art, just as it is useful (and fascinating) to put aside the myths and legend for a moment and consider Cash in his humanness. In plain light, his is the story of millions of Americans. He was seeded in the Great Depression's stagnation, fertilized by New Deal progressivism, and cultivated in the booming postwar opportunity outside rural life. Educated in the armed forces, as were so many young American men in the early Cold War era, he followed an all-too-common storyline of prosperity and indulgence, albeit in his case magnified by ten thousand. But aspects of his life were spectacularly anti-mythical, mundane even, like the daily paths of every man and woman. He gained and lost weight, enjoyed dips in the pool, shopped for antiques, fished, drove his own car, clung to his mother, recoiled from his father, peered at attractive women, gossiped, and planted tomatoes. Many said he magically filled a room whenever he walked in, yet it was our minds, fixated on the Johnny Cash legend, that permitted the illusion of massive presence. In simple terms, he was not the Homeric figure that he projected, although we wanted him to be.

He was, however, a man whose talent and drive were remarkable. His inherent ability to distill in simple and incisive verse complex feelings, historical drama, and real-life travail set him apart in the world, as did his magnificent powers of interpretation. His voice and his stage presence were big and unique. He wielded a razor wit, a biting sense of humor and irony, and a deep well of compassion. He stored hundreds of songs in his mind and could call them up at the slightest prompting. And he was a prodigious letter writer. When one might have expected his pen to be dulled by the demands of stardom, the fogs of drug addiction, or the inadequacy of rural education, he wrote long and thoughtful letters in hotel rooms, airplanes, at home, and in his office. In his rounded script or pecked out on a typewriter, his letters were about his faith, his love life, his anger, and ideas for his career. He wrote to air force buddies, his wife, his manager, and his daughters. He seemed programmed to write. His daughters estimated that hundreds of letters crossed the ocean to their mother when Cash served in the air force in the early 1950s.

Cash parlayed his desire and ability to express himself into a gilded body of American folk music and gospel projects. In time, his name and powerful symbolic presence resonated in every corner of the earth. And then in 1993, when it seemed it was all over, that his career had died, he melded his art to the young producer Rick Rubin and Rubin's American Recordings label. All of a sudden, college students became conversant on Johnny Cash, and I saw bumper stickers bearing his name plastered next to those of bands such as Particle and the Wharf Rats. It was reinvention, a second birth for Cash. And the world welcomed it.

Cash died in the prevailing winds of his American Recordings renaissance. Like director John Huston, whose last film *The Dead* drew wide critical praise and numerous awards, Cash's final recordings were received as triumphant caps on his career. We would have had Cash going out like this, the old gunslinger still deadly in his final duel. Indeed, even the end of Cash's story fed his legend.

ONE

~

COME HOME
1932-1955

1

DELIVERANCE

Farmers in Cleveland County, Arkansas, had heard little good news since skidding into Depression times, so the unusually balmy temperatures of January and February of 1932 were a promising sign for their early vegetable crop, and perhaps portended better days ahead. Each day the mercury rose into the sixties or the seventies, as if it were early spring. The farmers crossed their fingers and pulled up their coveralls, but they could not help but turn back to conversation about the alarming decline of cotton prices, the local bank failure, and the farm foreclosures that were denying many families around them the only living they had ever known.

One of those farmers was Ray Cash, a stump of a man whose face forever seemed on the brink of rage or tears. He sharecropped, so he owned no land for the bank to repossess. But sharecropping in 1932 was fast becoming a country boy's folly, as anybody who worked the land in southern Arkansas or anywhere else in the South knew. "Cotton went down to almost nothing," he told an interviewer in the 1970s. "A year before the Depression, cotton would bring $100, $125 a bale. In 1931 and 1932—they were the hardest years—I only got $25 for a five-hundred-pound bale." His truck patch near the house yielded plenty of food for his wife, Carrie, and their three children, but to buy what a garden couldn't grow—flour,

3

sugar, coal oil for the lamps—he often dropped his hoe to work assorted wage jobs. Cash had told the 1930 Census takers that he was a laborer for the state highway department, and he would report in later years that he often hopped trains to take work as far away as Mississippi. Closer to home, he also tended cattle and cut wood for his wealthy older brother Dave Cash.

Ray had lived under Dave's wing since adolescence. Their father had died in 1912, suffering from a disease that family members say resembled Parkinson's. During their father's prolonged illness, Dave had assumed responsibility for the family, in effect raising Ray until 1916, when at the age of eighteen the young man enlisted in the Army. Though grateful for Dave's benevolence, Ray would describe to his children and grandchildren a surrogate father as hard as cast iron and twice as cold. "[Dave] hated grandpa and he made no bones about it," says Kathy Cash, some weeks after meeting me at her father's grave. "I know it was rural Arkansas, but he raised him awful."

Perhaps to burn fear into the boy or teach him the prerogatives of Southern whites, Dave Cash once brought young Ray to view the corpse of a black man in whose lynching the elder Cash had taken part. There was something strangely routine in Dave's visit to the scorched body, as if he were merely surveying his land or checking a piece of fencing in need of repair. Ray was horrified: "We just stood there at the tree and kept looking up at him," he told Kathy. "You didn't say anything to Dave. If you didn't like it, you just kept your mouth shut."

Many decades later when Ray, who clung to his racism despite his distaste for the hangings, related such tales to his granddaughter, she'd say, "God, Grandpa. That is so weird."

"I was raised weird," he'd reply.

Dave Cash had built up something of a country empire in Cleveland County. On both sides of U.S. Route 79, which snakes through the county, he claimed abundant acreage and herds of cattle, and down in the southern part of the state near the Louisiana border he owned several sawmills. All of this he later leveraged to gain political power as a county sheriff and county judge in the 1920s and 1930s.

By the time Dave ascended to politics, Ray was already a veteran of a world war. Three years in the Army (1916–1919) had carried him first to the Mexican border and then to Europe, where he was part of a supply detail in France when the armistice was signed in November of 1918. He was back in Cleveland County with a wealth of worldly experience before the farmers finished hoeing the cotton crop of 1919. But he returned to a place bereft of possibilities; only odd jobs and landlessness awaited him.

In the midst of those odd jobs, Ray stumbled into a difficult courtship. While cutting lumber for a bridge that was to span the Saline River, he boarded with John L. Rivers and Rosanna Hurst Rivers, a Cleveland County farm couple who led music in the local Methodist Church. During the three or four weeks Ray stayed with the Rivers, their quiet, sweet-faced daughter Carrie caught his nervous eyes.

After finishing his cutting job and leaving the Rivers' home, Ray returned again and again to visit Carrie, but those visits at times proved to be a burden. Whether marked by his cocky nature or his kinship to Dave Cash, whom many despised for his wealth and cruelty, Ray was hassled by a corps of young men when he crossed on horseback or atop a wagon into the part of the county where Carrie lived.

"Men would stop him and try to keep him from coming in," explains Kathy Cash. "They hated him. They'd say, 'Where do you think you're going?' And he'd say, 'I'm going to see Carrie Rivers.' And they'd say, 'I don't think so.' He said he got into a lot of fights with people trying to keep him from coming to see her." For that reason, perhaps, Ray carried a gun when he courted his new love. But once inside her house, he'd unbuckle his holster and lay it on the mantle.

The rabble Ray encountered on his trips to see Carrie may have been of less concern to him than the question of his and her compatibility. Hardened by war and Dave Cash and rudderless in his home county, Ray seemed unlikely to ever be abreast of Carrie, who dutifully played the piano in church and clung to her father's cloak. They would make an unlikely pair. As she grew into womanhood, her height dwarfed him and her grace magnified his lack of refinement.

Ray married Carrie on August 18, 1920, when she was sixteen years old and he was twenty-three. If Carrie had hoped to continue in the kind of predictability she knew in her parents' house, she would have been quickly and continually disappointed. For the next fourteen years, Ray would chase, but not find, stability. Instead he moved his wife and their children from one tired house to another, often landing back with Dave Cash, the brother who provided.

During that warm winter of 1932, Ray and Carrie and their children, Roy, Louise, and Jack, were living in a small house in the Cross Roads community, a few miles from the town of Kingsland and not far from Carrie's parents. There on February 26, Carrie gave birth to a boy, weighing eleven pounds, whom they named J.R. Cash. As Cash himself later explained it, Carrie wanted to name him John while Ray preferred to name the boy after himself; the only compromise they could reach were the initials "J.R." Carrie and Ray's second eldest son, Jack, had the flu when baby J.R. arrived, and a few days later winter finally swept down from Canada. Temperatures plummeted to fourteen degrees, and snow blanketed the ground. Carrie draped blankets on the inside walls, but the cold wind still whistled in; she held her newborn close to warm him.

With the return of warmer weather in the spring and the Depression still snapping at his heels, Ray loaded his family and belongings onto the wagon and headed to his brother's place. In the early days of the Depression, Dave Cash and other land barons were buffered from the economic collapse by the sheer volume that their land produced. But by 1932, darkness had fallen over even Dave's gate, and he could only give Ray a brief respite.

Approximately ten miles separated Cross Roads and Dave's spread in the Draughon community, a lot of road to cover with four children on a horse-drawn wagon. The distance could not have pleased Carrie, who probably wished to stay closer to her parents. But more troubling for certain was her new proximity to Dave Cash, whom she had come to dislike as much as his other detractors around the county. Long after the Depression days, she would harrumph and bolt from the room at the mention of his name. Ray would protest: "That was my brother. He helped us."

"*Yeah*, he did," she'd say, with measured and uncharacteristic sarcasm.

In his new home in the Saline River bottoms, J.R. took his first steps and toddled through the groves of trees and nearby meadow grasses. Occasionally, a line of train cars lazily chugged by the family's splintered shotgun house, stirring the pudgy boy. His parents would recall that he'd stand on the porch under the low-slung roof and wave to the engineer. The youngster might also be on the lookout for his father, returning on a boxcar from some far-off job. After J.R. had grown to be a man famous around the world, a visit back to Cleveland County in 1976 inspired him to write "Ridin' on the Cottonbelt," a muse about his father's rail journeys: *The boxcar's cold and windy/And the dust goes around in circles in the air./But my hard times are behind me/And I'm returning home, so I don't care.*

But Ray Cash had many cares. Though little J.R. was perhaps still unaware, his parents and older siblings confronted the creeping specter of poverty. The Cashes were poor, and their moves among the farms and ramshackle houses of Cleveland County did nothing to help them overcome it. When local authorities published the list of those who had paid the poll tax—the tool that disenfranchised blacks and poor whites by inhibiting their ability to vote—Ray Cash's name was absent. He was among those left without political voice.

The extent to which poor farmers like Ray had any agency was thanks to their back-straining role in cotton's cultivation and harvest, but even that power was disappearing as the Depression chipped away at crop prices and finally all but shut down cotton cultivation. By the summer of 1933, the Roosevelt administration had paid more than twelve hundred landowners in the county to abandon some twelve thousand acres of cotton, shunting hundreds of tenant farmers and share-croppers from the source of their living. Since tenant families ran about eight of every ten farms in Cleveland County, the federal government's policy instigated a wide displacement of people. Many county folk, like the Okies to the west of Arkansas, packed their wagons and cars and lit out for California.

As the stream out of the county hastened, those who remained got more bad news. If they subscribed to the newspaper (which was now bartering subscriptions for corn and tomatoes), they read that the rolls of the so-called unemployable were growing with each month and that the desperate among them had taken to rob-bery, car theft, and kidnapping. Elsewhere in the papers, agriculture experts pleaded with stubborn farmers still grasping cotton's withering stalks to concen-trate on their home gardens and livestock. Home economists wrote about how wives could remove lettering from feed bags so the coarse material could be stitched into clothing; the empty bags were euphemistically called "thrift fabrics."

The Cleveland County Herald's report on John B. Lindsey must have seemed especially disturbing to Ray and Carrie. Married and a father of four, Lindsey had owned and worked a small farm in the county for most of his forty-five years. But he had been struggling with financial problems—growing debt and the fear of foreclosure, probably—and was drinking excessively to cope. One morning in mid-July he lost hope. The newspaper wrote that when his son came upon him, the boy failed to see that his father had consumed a bottle of tree poison:

> His son, who was preparing to go to the field to work, asked his father which field he wanted him to work when Lindsey replied. "I don't care if you don't plow anywhere. I have taken some arsenic and will be dead in an hour." The boy called a physician and some neighbors. Lindsey was carried to the house and is said to have asked the doctor for more poison in order that he might "finish the job." The doctor told him that he needed no more . . . as he would live only a short time. He died in a few minutes.

In Lindsey, Cleveland County saw the worst of the Depression's scourge.

In late 1934, Ray Cash's family was listed on the county relief rolls, which made them eligible for a host of federal government benefits, including subsidized jobs and the intriguing possibility of farm ownership in northeast Arkansas. Under a program funded by the Federal Emergency Relief Administration (FERA), county administrators recruited destitute farming families for resettlement in the Dyess Colony in Mississippi County. Interested Arkansans completed a lengthy application that queried them on everything from their debts to their church preference, and those whose applications pleased the local administrators met with a case worker who pressed husband and wife with additional questions about their farming experience, religious interests, and club affiliations. Any hint of physical defects, alcoholism, or radical beliefs was immediate grounds for disqualification. So too was dark skin: official policy excluded black farmers from the program.

Ray told an interviewer in later years that he learned about the resettlement program on the radio. "We heard that we could buy twenty acres without any money down, and a house and a barn, and they would give us a mule, a cow, and furnish groceries through the year until we had a crop and could pay it back, and we didn't have to pay until the crops came in." The thirty-seven-year-old father of five (daughter Reba had come along after J.R.) threw on his overalls and hustled to the courthouse in Rison to apply for his deliverance.

But deliverance, it initially appeared, would not be Ray's. When county officials named the two families they had selected for Dyess in November of 1934, the Cashes were not on the list. Instead, relief supervisor O.N. Eubank touted the Dosters and the Tatums. But in a development that begs speculation, the Cashes learned shortly thereafter that they would be resettled in March of 1935. State or federal authorities may have vetoed one of the families and named the Cashes in its place, or the Dosters or Tatums may have thought better of leaving their familiar, though ragged, home in Cleveland County. Either seems a plausible explanation of the Cashes' good fortune, but another—the intervention of Dave Cash—deserves consideration.

One week after Cleveland County administrators chose the Dosters and Tatums, a fire destroyed a barn on Dave Cash's farm. *The Cleveland County Herald* detailed the heavy losses: thirteen tons of cotton seed, fifty-four bushels of peas, and six hundred bushels of potatoes. One shudders to imagine Dave's reaction; even he could not so easily absorb such a loss. The blaze may have spelled the end of Ray's stay on his prosperous brother's land. The Cashes needed a next step, and Dave's political clout very likely could have helped them make it in the direction of Dyess, with or without the consent of local relief officials.

In the region where Dyess was hammered into the ground, ancient Indian tribes had once thrived and Spanish conquistador Hernando De Soto had led expeditions in the 1540s. The famous New Madrid earthquakes of 1811 and 1812 were centered in Mississippi County, although the temblor did little to upset the flat terrain that the Mississippi River had graded over the centuries. In recent years, the area had become the preserve of Lee Wilson and Company of Wilson, Arkansas, whose tens of thousands of cultivated acres made it one of the largest cotton planters in the world.

Wilson's fields rolled right to the border of the Dyess Colony, which in the early months of 1934 was little more than sixteen thousand acres of no-man's-land covered by swamps, thick brush, and felled trees. It was said to be home to wildcats and cottonmouth snakes. Years before, land barons had sought to claim the area for cotton cultivation and had begun stripping its timber, but they had abandoned their plans, leaving the massive task to more persistent souls.

Some years after those early attempts to clear the area, a team of men including W.R. Dyess took control of the land. Dyess, a native of Luxora in Mississippi County, was the state administrator of FERA. With his eye on skimming a ladle of government cream, he arranged the sale of the land to Uncle Sam for 2.3 million dollars. As Ray Cash understood it, the government would make plots of land from the Dyess tract available on easy terms to poor-but-able farmers who with other farmers would function as a cooperative, collectively selling their cotton and other crops. This would give them footing to compete with large cotton producers like the Wilson company, the only players able to make a go of it during the Depression. The potential for outright ownership of land was another possible benefit of the gambit, theoretically giving farmers a sturdier ship to navigate hard times.

With the government decommissioning so much land through the cotton-abandonment program, its purchase of a patch of Mississippi County jungle seems incongruous at first glance. However, the logic may have lain in the terrain itself. FERA, mindful of work-relief projects, could turn loose a corps of unemployed men to marshal the tangled land into lots and to construct modest farmhouses and outbuildings, not to mention the town hall, cinema, cannery, and other structures that would fill the town center. In fact, after Ray arrived in Dyess, he drew wages from FERA for work on land clearing and construction when he wasn't tending his own land during growing season.

Furthermore, if the farmers were to function cooperatively, there was sense in resettling them in the same vicinity (and on land so fertile). And the land could be had at such low prices that government officials in Washington could be persuaded to put aside practical questions about cleared land versus uncleared land, not to mention the ethical concerns of buying land from a government employee.

When the government acquired the land and installed W.R. Dyess as project director, fifteen hundred relief workers got the signal to bear down on the wild terrain. The men swarmed around their work and within weeks, roads were laid where a scramble of roots and soggy loam was before. The determined men's scythes and bulldozers advanced, and public buildings and homes rose.

Clearing and construction had begun on May 22, 1934; five months later, eighty-five new homes awaited their occupants.

In mid-March of 1935, a large truck hired by state relief administrators collected Ray, Carrie, Roy, Louise, Jack, J.R., and infant daughter Reba. The two-hundred-mile drive between Dave Cash's homestead and Dyess gave the Cashes plenty of time to ponder the changes ahead. As they trundled east, the hills and pine groves of Cleveland County gave way to expanses that seemed to have been flattened by a Bunyanesque roller. Large level tracts of land, many of them fallow, seemed to engulf the farm homes and outbuildings that stood by the road. As they pressed into Mississippi County, so named for the river that was its eastern border, the transformation was even more dramatic. They were coming upon flat, virtual wilderness.

The chill of late winter and the sloppy, rutted roads would remain each family member's sharpest memory of the day-and-a-half-long journey, even J.R's. Although he had turned three only weeks before the move, the arduous drive, as well as the fear and faith that he saw mingling within his mother, remained with him. "Sometimes Moma would cry and sometimes she'd sing, and sometimes it was hard to tell which was which," he said, describing the long drive in his second autobiography. "As my sister Louise put it later, that was one of the nights when you couldn't tell. It all sounded the same."

He must have been reminded of the journey in 1971 when he recorded Hal Bynum's "Papa Was A Good Man." Not far removed from the Cashes' own travail, a father struggling to make his way moves his family again and again, and his resilient wife and her faith are their cords of strength. It would be one of many songs in his catalog that romanticized his mother and father. *It rained all the way to Cincinnati/With our mattress on top of the car./Us kids were eating crackers and bologna,/And papa kept on drivin', never stopped once at a bar.*

The truck driver unloaded the Cashes in front of house number 266 on Road Three. Gleaming against the wet, clumpy earth around it, the white structure must have been otherworldly. After years in tired, neglected houses, they entered a home that smelled of newly cut lumber and fresh paint. The house with its two bedrooms, kitchen, living room, and dining room was palatial by Cleveland County standards, and the barn, smokehouse, and outhouse seemed worthy of a baronial estate. "It was a nicer house than any [we] had ever lived in," recalled Ray.

Indeed their house was pristine. But the land on which it sat humbled them. Although the relief crews had cleared land for houses, roads, and the town center, the families had to clear their own plots for farming. At 266, that task fell to Ray and his eldest son, fourteen-year-old Roy. As the spring heat dried the mud around the newly constructed home, they attacked the thick vegetation with saws and axes; somewhere under the massive snarl lay arable soil left first by centuries of submersion and then by periodic floods.

As Ray and Roy hacked and chopped, J.R., Jack, and Reba buzzed in play around their new home. Meanwhile, Carrie readied the family's new garden, the fruits and vegetables from which she preserved at the community cannery and stored for the winter of 1935–1936. To supplement Roy's wages until the first crops arrived, the colony advanced the Cashes a kind of script—which residents called "doodlum"—good for purchases at the Dyess general store.

The family delighted in this chance to strike a new covenant with the world, but the colony administrators knew that families such as the Cashes still needed help. Waving a banner of education and cooperation, government-employed home economists fanned out through the community to teach canning, cooking, and dressmaking, and to establish home demonstration clubs where wives and daughters could show off their home crafts and share their domestic skills. New arrivals in Dyess were rounded up and shown films about preventing malaria, a potential problem because of the swampy land around the community. Children received regular medical check-ups, although a few parents still reliant upon traditional folkways refused the care of citified doctors.

One colonist said that they were chosen people, plucked from poverty and dropped in a promised land. Another believed that Dyess colonists cut a sharper path through the world: down only because of a spell of bad luck, they represented the elite of the poor, eminently capable of hard work, ingenuity, and, indeed, success. They were bound to thrive in their new homes, and when they did, administrators quickly squawked about it in their single-spaced progress reports to Washington, D.C. Memoranda told of a woman who had canned prodigious amounts of blackberries, tomatoes, and corn; a man who had planted three fruit trees within fifteen days of arriving in Dyess; and a family that was quickly paying back its advances with honey from fifteen beehives. A Saline County native from near the area of the Cashes' former home grabbed headlines in the Washington-bound write-ups with his sixty-dollar cow: "Several months ago a cyclone struck the colony and while not much material damage was done a number of trees were uprooted. [The farmer] cut the trees into cord wood, with the assistance of his entire family, and from the proceeds purchased the cow. He sells the milk to the hospital and has paid $22.00 on his account in this manner."

Cleveland County natives steamed ahead, too. By April, about a month after moving in, Ray and Roy had sown three acres that would yield two bales of cotton, plenty of feed corn, and vegetables for the dinner table. With proceeds from the sales of his cotton and the excess feed corn, Ray also filled his barnyard with hens, pigs, and a cow.

Despite Ray's penchants for drinking and fighting, inclinations that would become more and more obvious as the years passed, his neighbors remarked on his diligent work habits, and colony records confirm those judgments. Not only did Ray Cash promptly make each of his annual payments of $111.41 for his house and land, he was also one of the few men who regularly repaid the annual advance he received on crops. In 1939, the books stated that Cash, along with nine others, was actually *owed* money by the colony. By 1940, Ray had mustered enough funds for a down payment on an adjoining farm, increasing his holdings from twenty to forty-five acres. Five years later, Ray owned his land and house outright.

As a worker, Carrie equaled her man. She hosted home demonstration club meetings, squeezed the most from the family's foodstuffs and doodlum, and played piano at the Central Baptist Church, which met in the town's community building, about an hour's walk from home.

Colony managers were pleased that families like Ray and Carrie's attended church, proudly pointing to the community's four Sunday schools that met in different homes, stores, and schools in the area. But they wrinkled their noses at families whose religious practices strayed from the mainline, an intolerance that, like its policy of racial exclusion, betrayed the colony's charitable and cooperative veneer. Like most communities in the South, Dyess consisted mostly of Baptists and Methodists; those not belonging to such denominations might expect a visit from a colony administrator. "There are quite a few Presbyterians and some Holy Rollers, especially among the more ignorant," reported officials. Those same officials reported sending one Holy Rolling woman back to her home county, charging that her rapturous outbursts "kept the colony more or less stirred up." And nobody knew what to do with the two Catholic families who lived in the community. Children passing their homes on the bus to school would whisper, "[T]hat's where the Catholics live," expecting that inside dwelled farmers whose straw hats covered blunt horns.

While colony officials and residents whispered about religion, they were far more vocal on race. They liked to boast that only one black—the school custodian—lived within the community's borders. Cleaning toilets and sweeping floors was about as much as any black man could expect to do in Dyess, unless he worked on the early clearing and construction crews. The Southern mores of the times simply did not allow for the possibility of blacks owning land and farming shoulder to shoulder with whites. "There are and will be nothing but white homesteaders on this project," declared officials. A farmer from Clay County to whom "race distinction meant nothing" was expelled from the colony when he took in black boarders, men who were likely working construction and clearing jobs in Dyess.

Just as Dyess accommodated no diversity of skin color or religion, it suffered little differences of opinion. A group known as The United Brotherhood of Dyess Colony was formed expressly to discourage dissenters, and it held the power to squash any challenges to the edicts and practices of the colony. By the end of the 1930s, though, colony officials were grappling with widespread disgruntlement, mostly from farmers bristling under Jake Terry, the bull-like farm manager who ordered colonists around like field hands and spat at their objections. When a number of farmers sought to organize as part of the Southern Tenant Farmers' Union (STFU), born up the road in Blytheville, the colony was clear and forceful in its disapproval. Some colonists complained that when they met to discuss their grievances, a deputy sheriff used force to break up the meeting. Although there is no evidence that Ray flirted with the burgeoning SFTU movement, it's certain that he hated Jake Terry so much, said Johnny Cash years later, that he named the family dog for him.

Many colonists left Dyess because they found its Orwellian aspects intolerable. Others abandoned their new spreads because of homesickness or in response to unfounded rumors that the colony planned to break its promise to transfer ownership of the farms upon the final mortgage payment. If the Cashes considered going back to Cleveland County, it could have been because Carrie often pined for her parents. Her loneliness stirred up angry debates between her and Ray. But where would they have gone? Lacking a good answer, they hammered their stakes deeper into the lumpy soil. With each year, Ray and Roy cleared more acreage for tilling, and the family folded more thoroughly into the community life of church, school, and home demonstration clubs. The memory of their Cleveland County poverty faded.

In January 1937, a persistent rain lifted water over the banks of both the Tyronza River and a drainage ditch that forged through the colony. The ditch was distant enough from the Cashes that its flooding was insignificant, but the Tyronza was little more than a mile away. It was close enough, in fact, for it to be a frequent site of summer frolicking for the Cash children.

Newscasters and wary farmers speculated that the levies buffering northeast Arkansas from the Mississippi River might burst at any moment, allowing the big river to release its muddy waters across the region's flat terrain and into the Tyronza. The feared wall of water from the Mississippi never came, but the Tyronza and the ditch were above flood stage from January 16 to 19, receded briefly, and then flooded again on January 20 and 21.

The flood inundated the northeast side of the colony, and by the evening of the 21st, many families abandoned their homes and farms for refuge in the town center. Rescue boats motored through the deluge, snatching up families who gathered on their porches clutching clothes and food. Carrie and the children were collected by boat and delivered to town, while Ray and Roy stayed behind to secure their house. By daylight on the 22nd, the Cashes were among fifteen hundred people huddled in town. Those like the Cashes, who had friends and relatives in the central and western regions of the state, were put on a westbound train, while others were dispatched to Memphis, Tennessee. J.R. was not yet five, but he would long remember the big train sloshing out of Mississippi County: "There was a man on the cowcatcher of the train with a long pole feeling in front to see for sure that there weren't any logs that had floated over the tracks that might wreck the train. And the next night we got to Pine Bluff, Arkansas . . . and we were safe."

Carrie shepherded her family to her parents', but she fretted about Ray and Roy. J.R. worried too, and wondered about what was happening back in Dyess. He found out one morning, weeks after the evacuation, when his father's voice awoke him. Ray was telling his father-in-law about the flood and the cow and beehives he'd lost. "He had opened all the doors and windows of the house—let the chickens in, even let the pigs in the house so we could keep them you know because the water had gotten right up to the floor but hadn't risen any further," remembered Johnny Cash.

"So he let all the animals in the house then he came on to the hills himself, but we stayed about another week. When the water went down, we went back home to the most terrible mess you can imagine. The couch was covered with eggs where the hens had laid. The pigs you can imagine what kind of mess they made all over the house, but we still had them."

The uprooting of his family in 1937 was another childhood event that nested in J.R.'s young mind and eventually tunneled into his adult artistry. Memories of the flood became "Five Feet High and Rising," which he recorded in 1959. "I got to remembering all these things," he recalled years after writing the song, "and the song just came out, you know. Just exactly how it happened."

In Cash's collection of childhood memories, the flood and its aftermath took their places next to the toil of chopping cotton, the fear and exhilaration of Baptist church services, and the strength of his mother's faith and love. In some form or another, many of those impressions and recollections found their way into his songwriting, or, at least, into his selection of songs written by others.

A few memories, too painful and embarrassing to share, never explicitly worked their way into his art. One memory in particular was so difficult to bear that Cash focused on an alternate reality to keep it at bay. In concerts, autobiographies, and interviews, he would tell of his father's faithfulness and bravery, as well as the admiration he had for him. But in public he mostly refrained from revealing the other side: the bitter man who reduced his wife to tears and sent his children cowering. His brother Roy weathered the worst of Ray's cruelty, as the eldest often do. Roy's mistakes or impertinent words in the fields could, and very often did, incite Ray to rip the leather reins off the mule and whip the boy. "He was a strict disciplinarian," observed one of J.R's pals. "He expected obedience from his children." Ray's hand and harsh tongue in turn embittered Roy, who (according to his own son) grew to be a harsh father and husband himself.

Stories of Ray's hard edge surfaced late in J.R.'s life. He revealed them to his children when they were grown and hinted at them in his 1997 autobiography. The reference to Carrie's sobbing during the move to Dyess was a subtle hint of the agony Ray inflicted upon her. Since the singer's death, the accusations have flown more freely yet remain muted in the official story. A 2004 biography of Johnny

Cash commissioned by the family cited Ray's short temper, but references to his blackest tendencies and abuse were stricken by the family before publication. They remain unspeakable among family members today, suggesting that the abuses went beyond the leather lashings Roy described and that they were meted out to every family member.

J.R. knew the sting of his father's beatings, but in adulthood, when he spoke with his children about his father, it was the psychological abuse that occupied him: guilt trips, belittling, and power plays. Publicly, Cash would go only so far in his indictments, trotting out relatively mild recollections of his father killing the dog Jake Terry to illustrate his father's cruelty. Knowing that he musn't embarrass his sisters and brothers with dark and public descriptions of their father's faults, Cash in his second autobiography probably made the dog a symbol of all his father's victims:

> It was a stray that I'd picked up on the road into the Dyess town center when I was five. . . .[Daddy killed it] after I'd had it about a year because he said it was eating scraps that could go to fatten up the hogs. He didn't admit it at first. I came home from school one day and called Jake Terry, but he didn't come, so Jack and I set out looking for him. We asked Daddy as we passed whether he'd seen him. He said no. Eventually we found him at the far end of the cotton rows across a shallow ditch, dead, with a .22 bullet in his head. . . . I was scared to say anything to Daddy, but Jack wasn't. He went straight to him and said, "We found Jake Terry down there across the ditch." Daddy looked up and said, "Yeah, I killed him. I didn't want to have to tell you boys, but we just didn't need another dog around here." We already had a dog called Ray, named after Daddy.

Ray Cash, of course, had winced at life's backhand since childhood. The death of his parents and siblings, the example of Dave Cash, war—each had taken a turn siphoning off his compassion. And who could count the toll of wounded pride? The short man had known failure after failure, been forced to turn to Dave Cash again and again, and resorted to relief in the early 1930s. Even Dyess had been a handout of sorts, albeit one he parlayed into prosperity. And then there was his fondness for booze, the match that often ignited his abuse. He'd use the few dollars from his army pension to buy pints of liquor, and neighbors recall seeing him zigzagging down the road, mumbling to the wind. The picture was often uglier when he woozily stalked into number 266.

~

For all of Ray Cash's anger and drinking, few in Dyess could name a harder-working man on Road Three than him. Ray made sure that people felt the same about his boys. J.R., like most children in Dyess, could hide in his childish play for only so long. A farming family survived only if everybody pitched in, particularly in October, cotton-harvesting time. From the moment he could lift a bucket, J.R. was carrying water to the fields for Roy, Ray, and Jack. By 1940, he joined the other boys as a regular in the fields. Carrie was out there, too. She would have been out there more often if she were not caring for Joann, born in 1938, and Tommy, born in April 1940.

The eight-year-old J.R. dragged a tar-bottomed cotton sack up the bushy rows of cotton, his doughy face grimacing at the pricks to his fingers from the sharp bolls. When he wasn't hoeing or picking, he chopped wood for the stove, milked the cow, helped to haul corn into town for milling, or tended to the home garden. Roy's graduation from high school in 1939 and subsequent marriage to the daughter of a Dyess farmer drew J.R. deeper into the working world.

But J.R. was still a boy and naturally slipped away for stick ball games in a neighbor's front yard, a swim in the Tyronza, or a snake hunt in one of the wide drainage ditches. More and more, though, his diversion was the radio. Shortly after moving to Dyess, the family had picked up a battery-operated console. Many nights after Ray's news program signed off, J.R. sat in the kitchen and commandeered the dials, searching for life outside Arkansas. While brother Jack studied the Bible by lamplight, J.R. cocked his ear to the speaker and traveled by the dim bulb that lit the radio dial. The live performances of the *Grand Ole Opry* and the *National Barn Dance*, the biggest hillbilly music platforms in America, crackled into his ear, as did the local live shows from stations in nearby Memphis and St. Louis. And when he wasn't listening to music, J.R. zeroed in on the closest NBC network station for the swashbuckling adventures of Jack, Doc, and Reggie in *I Love A Mystery*. "I . . . loved the stories over the radio," he'd say in later years.

As the broadcast dramas dissolved into late-night static, leaving his imagination hungry for the world outside Dyess, he could find inspiration in the paths cut by his two big brothers. In a community defined almost totally by farming, Roy and Jack—like the radio shows—showed J.R. other options. Until J.R. revealed his singing talents in high school, Roy was the artist among his siblings, distinguishing himself in music and high school drama. His pursuits, set against Ray's hard-boiled practicality, amounted to a kind of defiance on Roy's part, as well as a shock to anybody who assumed that no son of Ray Cash would ever look away from farming's coarse furrow. An honor student like his sister Louise, Roy enjoyed columns of local press about his supporting roles in plays such as *The Ambitious Guest*, an adaptation of a Nathaniel Hawthorne short story. He also played guitar in the Delta Rhythm Ramblers, a hillbilly band that J.R. once said got him thinking about playing music. The teens played on the radio in Blytheville, won a talent show in Portia, Arkansas, and competed in a state music contest in Little Rock. But the playing slowed in 1938 when on a winter's afternoon Roy lost the end of his thumb in an accident. Though he kept the band together for a few more years, the Second World War sealed its dissolution.

Roy also wrote ballads, mostly tales of western cowboys and rogues, the same themes that would show up years later in J.R.'s poems and songs. In 1936, Roy's "Wild Western Outlaw" made the Dyess newspaper:

> *I drifted into Santa Fe*
> *With "Banty Bill" and "Kansas Jake."*
> *We found that mining didn't pay,*
> *And looked for some soft stake.*
> *We picked the game of "Frisco Frank,"*
> *And after slinging lots of lead,*
> *We took five thousand from his bank*
> *And left two Hombres dead.*
>
> *We traveled north across the line,*
> *Taking fresh horses on the way,*
> *Then killed a guard at Gopher Mine*
> *And got the miners' pay.*
> *A posse trailed us day and night,*
> *They cornered us on Sandy Hill.*
> *Well, me and Jake got through alright*
> *But they got poor "Banty Bill."*

We headed for the U.S. Mail,
Watched the loaded train draw near.
We ditched it with a loosened rail
And killed an engineer.
This train had an extra guard
And they made it awful hot.
I saved my life by riding hard
But "Kansas Jake" was shot.

I robbed the bank at Silver Crown,
Raked in a dandy pile.
I hit the train for Denver town,
To blow my stacks in style.
I tried to get a brand new hoss,
Passing a sheep ranch late that day.
I was stabbed in the back by a Greaser's boss
Before I got away.

I am lying now in a herder's shack,
Watching the dirty wall.
Weak from the knife wounds in my back
Nobody hears me call.
Oh, I've shot it out with fighting men,
I've risked a life for a life,
And now I die in this dirty den,
Killed by a Greaser's knife.

While Roy's writing and acting turned heads, J.R.'s second role model charmed farmers in every corner of the colony with his piety. Jack's was not an arrogant piety: neighbors remember his bright greetings, his eagerness to help, and his humble concern for the needy. "He was one of the nicest, best people I have ever known in my life," says friend and neighbor Milton Stansbury. It was no surprise to those around him when Jack began to talk about life in a Baptist pulpit. Though only a young teen, he seemed ready to preach the Word, and had he taken it up one Sunday, it's likely many would have flocked to his congregation.

Roy impressed J.R. with his music, and he gave J.R. confidence by rubbing his head and telling him that someday he'd amount to something. But Roy was nearly an adult, and was therefore growing away from the young J.R. Jack, on the other hand, was accessible, a playmate, a local hero who in J.R.'s immature eyes was far closer to perfection than anybody he knew, and tougher and wiser and more Christian. J.R. adored him, finding in him a gentle father figure.

"Jack was my protector," he remarked thirty years later. "I was the skinny one and he looked after me. We were always together, always laughing. He taught me all those things a big brother teaches a little brother he loves. There was nobody in the world as good and as wise and as strong as my big brother Jack." Jack beckoned him to a higher purpose, but young J.R. never dreamed that his righteous brother would ultimately walk so far ahead of him.

2

GUILT

The year 1944 ushered in change for J.R. Just days after turning twelve, he publicly professed his faith at a revival in the Baptist Church. It was a decision no doubt hastened by Jack's example and the conviction, promulgated by the Baptists, that in order to receive salvation one must publicly declare acceptance of Christ into one's heart. Later he recalled the bald light bulbs and hard oaken pews pressing on his senses as he gathered up the courage to step in the aisle and respond to the preacher's altar call.

His spiritual house in order for the time being, J.R. observed furious reshuffling in his secular home. Roy was gone, married and working as an aircraft mechanic in the navy. Louise, too, had married, and was living with her in-laws in nearby Osceola. And the Cashes' spare days also appeared to be history. The family now owned a battered sedan, and the war had rejuvenated the price of cotton, moving Ray closer to paying off the note on his land.

The war and higher cotton prices were also changing the community in which J.R. had lived for most of his life. The paternalism that had marked Dyess in the 1930s faded by the 1940s as the government's focus shifted from domestic relief to winning the war. No longer were the colonists' hands held by home economists and farm managers. In 1943, the government ordered all new construction and renovations of existing buildings to cease, and then, a few months later, pulled out all together after Congress ordered the government to dispose of its financial interests in all resettlement projects. Many wondered if Dyess had any future at all; the war had sapped the colony of so many of its eldest sons.

Though many of those sons would return after the war, Dyess never would recapture its vibrancy of the 1930s and early 1940s. Its purpose was yoked to the Depression, and the Depression was over. Many of the small land owners sold out, realizing how impossible it was to sustain a family on twenty acres. Those who remained, like the Cashes, bought up land from their departing friends. But as the number of families dwindled, the colony's heart, its town center, faltered. Over the decades, its institutions shuttered their doors: the movie theater where the children saw their Gene Autry westerns, the cannery where the women brought their garden produce, and the restaurant where farmers bought a hot roast beef sandwich and Coke after milling their corn. By the 1960s, the center of Dyess would be well on its way to oblivion.

Men and women who grew up in Dyess return to the colony today and walk amid its sagging, weather-beaten buildings as if those buildings were cemetery markers. The former residents marvel that the town that once percolated with commerce, entertainment, and sidewalk gossip could now be barely clinging to the face of the earth. Ghosts from their youth cavort in the abandoned lot where their school used to stand and around the town center where they used to rendezvous. Those visitors, now well past retirement age, look back on accomplished careers as teachers, engineers, small-business owners, navy officers, and artists, and they know that Dyess enabled them to succeed. When their home counties could no longer provide in the Depression, the colony had been their families' refuge from hard times. Dyess was virgin land, its soil as dark and rich as coffee. In Dyess, crops could grow unfettered. In Dyess, the progressive policies of Franklin Delano Roosevelt offered a leg up. In Dyess, farmers could collectively sell their cotton, thereby regaining an economic standing that had been lost by the death of sharecropping. Dyess restored hope for the future, saving hundreds of families from less dignified possibilities. When the colony's progeny departed, caught up in the postwar abandonment of farming, that exodus tolled the beginning of the collapse and decay of their redemptive shelter. But, indeed, Dyess had saved them.

~

The transformation of post-war America would eventually take J.R. in its swell, but in 1944 more immediate change confronted him. Less than three months after his conversion, J.R. witnessed the death of Jack, an episode that he would say reaffirmed the faith he had pronounced at church but that also tortured him like taunts from the devil. Jack's death dragged the twelve-year-old J.R. from a relatively carefree childhood into a world often haunted by quiet grief and nagging uncertainty.

Jack had died slowly. On a Saturday morning in May, while J.R. ambled down to one of the ditches to fish, Jack and a friend walked to the woodshop in the high school's agriculture building, where students worked on school assignments or cut timber for colony projects. Jack had a job at the shop, but on this morning he was in charge. The agriculture teacher who normally supervised had gone on vacation and left Jack to oversee, hardly surprising given the trust and affection that the fifteen-year-old enjoyed in Dyess. In the plain wooden building dignified by tall churchlike windows, Jack and his friend were repairing tents that belonged to the colony. "Jack was trying to cut a board on a big Dewalt bale arm saw," recalls J.R.'s friend and neighbor Milton Stansbury. "And I don't know what kind of wood he had but, of course, he was just a kid, and someone had taken the guard off and put an oversized blade on it. And it just hit that wood and just come right to him and he couldn't get out of the way." The jagged blade sliced through Jack's stomach and abdomen.

Jack should have known not to use the saw without the guard, but colonists nevertheless couldn't help but think about who might have removed it. "Someone knows who did it but no one said anything and it really didn't matter then anyway," says Stansbury. "It was irrelevant. It wouldn't help anyone." The removal of the guard may not have been irrelevant to J.R. when in 1995 he theorized to journalist Nick Tosches that Jack had been murdered: "There was a neighbor that went down to the shop with him that day and disappeared after the incident. We couldn't prove anything, but I always thought of it as murder. My mother and daddy didn't. They never mentioned that boy. Nothin' was ever done about it."

J.R.'s eldest daughter, Rosanne, speculates that her father's claims of murder were probably dubious, a desperate effort on his part to explain the inexplicable. He may have also thought of murder in an indirect and general sense, a collective effort that placed Jack in a tragic time and place. With Tosches, he blamed one of Jack's chums. With Rosanne, he bitterly implicated his father Ray, whose tobacco habit, J.R. claimed, was sustained by Jack's wages from the woodshop. J.R., too, felt implicated and shouldered an enormous load of guilt over his brother's passing, much of it evidently imposed by his father who over the years told him it should have been him—the one who chose fishing over work—to die with the cut of a saw blade.

"Grandpa always kind of blamed Dad for Jack's death," explains Kathy Cash. "And Dad had this, just real sad guilt thing about him his whole life. You could just see it in his eyes. You can look at almost any picture and see this dark, sadness thing going on. Dad even told me one time, it was just the two of us in his Cadillac and we had left Grandma and Grandpa's, and he choked up. He said, 'One time when I was little my daddy—he'd been drinkin'—said something like "Too bad it wasn't you instead of Jack." I said, 'Oh my God, Dad. What a horrible thing to say.' And he said, 'Yeah. I think about that every time I see him.'"

In his first autobiography, published in 1975, J.R. dwelled on the guilt. He accentuated the regret he felt that Jack did not come fishing, even after he pleaded with him, as well as the sense of rejection when Jack, on his deathbed but conscious, failed to acknowledge him. "That was the one thing I never could understand—why Jack didn't look at me, and why he didn't have anything to say to me that Sunday morning in his hospital room." J.R. rationalized in his book that Jack's silence was a way of preparing him for the inevitable loss of a brother; still, it must have unsettled J.R. from that moment until his own death in 2003.

The one redemptive element for J.R. in the tragedy of Jack's death was a sense of God's presence. Jack lingered for several days, floating in and out of consciousness while friends gathered outside his hospital room to pray for healing. A faithful community comforted the Cashes. Numbed by morphine, Jack appeared peaceful, even while the doctors warned that death was imminent. And when words came, he spoke of seeing the Promised Land. In the Dyess hospital, there was a real conviction that Jack's next home was heaven. Such unanimous belief impressed young J.R.; back in school with his friends, he would speak of his "brother who is in heaven."

Jack died on May 20, 1944, and his body was brought to number 266 for viewing. When the time came to move Jack to the church for the funeral service, a corps of his fellow Boy Scouts arrived to carry the coffin. J.R. rushed to his closet, jumped into his own scout uniform, and rushed back to the sitting room to carry the coffin with the other boys. But his mother stopped him; relatives couldn't be pallbearers, she told him. "He was devastated," says Rosanne, who heard her father talk repeatedly about that day. "He never got over that."

Jack was buried in the sandy soil of a cemetery in Bassett, which sits off U.S. Highway 61, so close to the Mississippi River that one can smell it. As the disappointed J.R. and the rest of the grieving Cashes watched the coffin lowered into the earth, the first leaves of cotton were emerging from the patches surrounding the cemetery. The next day, wrote Cash in his second autobiography, father, mother and children were all back in their own cotton fields, hoeing away the weeds that could strangle a crop.

When J.R. turned out of bed the morning after Jack's funeral, his four-year-old brother, Tommy, stirred sleepily beside him. J.R. was now the eldest child at number 266. Five years earlier such status might mean an extra six inches of Ray's leather across the back of his legs. But it wasn't as bad being the eldest anymore. The hard work of clearing the fields had ended years before, and Jack's death had, for the moment, mellowed Ray. Though a night on the bottle could unleash one of his guilt-laden rants and a round of physical abuse, the loss of Jack had driven Ray to a mild sort of reflection. He showed up at church more often and even took a turn teaching Sunday school. "This is why I'm here," he announced one morning to the church boys gathered around him. "Jack had to die to bring me to this point."

As the Cashes learned to live without Jack, J.R. quietly slipped into his teen years. The puffy cheeks gave way to angular lines that followed his jawbone, and his stretching limbs and torso pulled his body toward the gauntness of his adulthood. Increasingly, J.R. showed his family and friends the somber and reflective dimensions of a dreamer.

There were few dreamers in Dyess. The practical Cash family never spoke about dreams, nor is it likely they even used the word itself. But J. R. didn't need to. In his teenage years, dreams made him conspicuous among his peers, his mind off in a distant place that nobody could fathom. "He fitted in well with our group, but he seemed to have more purpose," says his friend A.J. Henson. "And it seemed like he was going somewhere. He was on a journey. The rest of us were just there, having fun and enjoying ourselves."

Yet J.R. had fun too, and it was often mischievous: fisticuffs with pals in the school yard and playing practical jokes on schoolmates. A friend named Harvey Clanton deeply influenced that playful side, just as Roy encouraged music and Jack inspired religiosity. Pictures of Clanton show a boy who resembles George McFarland's "Spanky" from the *Our Gang* films, only Clanton appears more cunning than the celluloid rascal. "He was the best friend J.R. ever had, he was *the* best friend," says Stansbury. "Him and J.R. were built from the same mold."

Stansbury recalls that J.R. and Clanton were among the most troublesome boys in a history class; their one goal seemed to be harassing the teacher over his interest in a pretty female student. Interestingly, Stansbury's account of one of J.R. and Clanton's odd acts of rebellion in that class is one of the few clear and specific recollections of the young J.R. that I was able to garner from his childhood peers. It augured the kind of weird and extreme behavior that J.R. often exhibited in adulthood. It seems that the history teacher's Northern roots incited the boys' crude notions of Southern chivalry as well as their sexual rambunctiousness. "He was a really good teacher," explains Stansbury. "But, see, we were all from Arkansas. And he was from Chicago. And that didn't bode well for him. We should have been horsewhipped for doing him the way we did."

In my interview with Stansbury, he hesitates to disclose just what they—and more specifically J.R. and Clanton—did that was so heinous. "They just liked to have fun and tease other people and crack jokes and everything," he allows. "And they'd get there [behind] the desks, and they'd do all kinds of things in that history class. I won't tell you everything they did, but it was . . . ."

I interrupt him: "So something specific happened in that history class?"

"Yes it did," he replies. "The teacher didn't know about it, though. But they were back there acting like very mischievous boys. And they did about anything they wanted to, but they were having a lot of fun. But what they did he never did find out about it. He probably didn't want to know about it, anyhow."

I press further.

"Well, they were boys," he says. "And they were going through puberty, you know. . . . And I'll let you have it from there."

~~~

And then J.R. would inexplicably go quiet. Sister Louise, on visits back to help with the cotton crop, observed it: "When we'd be picking or chopping alongside each other, if I asked him something, very often he wouldn't even answer me. I'd ask him maybe a second time, and I'd look over at him and his mind seemed to be far away." What far-removed visions flashed in his mind as Louise studied him? When he finished hoeing a row, mustering the resolve for another, did he stare down the line of green cotton plants and see a runway that would lift him away? Or perhaps in the vast and empty sky where a daydreamer might spy the swinging hem of a giant's robe, he imagined bustling Memphis, Tennessee, the closest big city, or herds of cattle galloping out West, as in the movies.

Many may have been dulled by the rigid vastness of the Dyess outdoors or simply have recoiled from it, but J.R. saw in the eternal emptiness a picture of another place. "He was more visionary than the rest of us," remembers Henson. The youngster rarely spoke about his visions or aspirations, but if something more temporal caught his attention—like something a preacher said or the behavior of another student—he, above others, could and would articulate his observations. "He was the one who could express himself and his feelings more than the rest of us," says Henson. "He was sensitive. He thought a little deeper than the rest of us. He went way down deep inside and brought up feelings."

The dreamer's sensitivity on display when apart from Clanton roused the curiosity of friends, but it also cost him. Some thought the pensive boy a bit of a sissy. "We used to get him down and tickle him," says Stansbury. "We would get him down and tickle him and make him pee on himself, you know. But he was a good old boy." J.R. appeared to take such abuse in stride, but tacked to the guilt of Jack's death and Ray's harshness, it may have hurt more than was obvious.

J.R. found refuge in his dreams and in the comfort of knowing Jack was in heaven, and even in the schoolboy shenanigans. But he also found it in the stories that passed through Dyess like the shiny white clouds that sailed above him in the fields. In the evenings at the kitchen table, now in the painful absence of Jack and his Bible, his family could still find J.R. huddled next to the radio console, absorbing radio drama's mystery and mayhem. His father, too, breaking out of his silence, carbonated J.R.'s imagination with stories of his childhood and the Great War. J.R.

told the *Journal of Country Music* in 1997, he couldn't wait for the visits of a Texas vagabond whose yarns were as succulent as hot buttered sweet potatoes:

> He walked to our house—you could see him coming down the road. He had a dirty blue bandanna around his neck and old-fashioned clothes and a cowboy hat. Nobody knew how old he was—he smelled like a barnyard. We'd welcome him in and feed him. My mother would cook and offered him a bath. He'd sit in the living room and tell stories. His name was Jim George. The second time he came, my father said, "Here comes old man Jim George." He had this old blue bandanna around his neck and even when he took a bath he wouldn't take it off. My dad finally asked him after everybody'd loosened up a little, "Why don't you take that bandanna off and get some fresh air?" And Jim George said, "I don't want you to see the rope burns," and my daddy said, "What do you mean?" and he said, "I was hanged with some of the James Gang in 1882." And we didn't know whether to believe him or not. We didn't have any reason not to. The law was if they hanged you and you didn't die, you were set free. These were the kind of stories I heard coming up when I was a child.

To a boy obsessed with cowboy movies and visions of the western range, a Jim George was almost as good as a Gene Autry cavalcade rumbling into town. No wonder skepticism of the James Gang absurdity seemed in short supply. Even in adulthood, J.R. in a childish way remained enamored of the West, playing "bang-bang shoot 'em up" with like-minded buddies, dressing up like a cowboy, seeking roles in television westerns (often with little regard to their quality), and telling stories about the Jim Georges he knew.

The stories flourished also in the music he heard. Gospel songs he sang in church, at home, and in the fields, numbers such as "I'll Fly Away" and "Life's Evening Sun," told about Jack's destiny and Christ's promise of renewal and hope. Gospel music, more than revival meetings, preachers, and Sunday school classes, propped up the boy as he walked along. Dispatches from God, the songs filtered into his being where they remained for the rest of his life, never falling away from his repertoire. Few secular songs learned in his youth traveled so well.

The secular songs that stuck with him were likely to be country, or hillbilly as the genre was known in J.R.'s teenage years. Like millions around the South and beyond, he leaned toward the major artists of the day: Ernest Tubb, Eddy Arnold, and Hank Williams, the undisputed kings of Nashville. The Louvin Brothers hooked him, too. He often spoke of crawling into workers' trucks parked in the colony and switching on their radios to reel in Charlie and Ira Louvin's wailing harmony on WMPS from Memphis. The boy also listened to and liked pop music—it was all over the radio, more so than hillbilly—and, in moments incongruous with the image of a country boy's world, he unsteadily crooned Tony Martin and Perry Como hits while picking in the fields.

Because there was little live music around Dyess, most of the hillbilly music he heard was mass mediated, trembling on the airwaves over WMPS in Memphis, XERF in Villa Acuna, Mexico, WJJD in Chicago, and KCLN in Blytheville, Arkansas. "We weren't a musical bunch of people," says one former resident, explaining why Dyess—unlike so many Southern communities that spawned country artists—was bereft of homespun dance music and front-porch jam sessions. Colony administrators had assembled a fine community of workers with little time for sawing fiddles and strumming guitars. So one never heard about house parties such as those music history speaks about in the piney woods of East Texas or in the Mississippi Delta. A hillbilly band might have shaken up the community center every now and then, and Roy Cash's Delta Rhythm Ramblers, which if not for Roy's thumb injury and the death of the other band members in the Second World War, might have chalked the first line between Dyess and a recording studio. But Dyess was generally quiet, content with gospel, the music of the wind gliding through cornstalks, and crickets chirping in the August darkness.

Slouched against a grove of cottonwood trees outside the colony limits (tantalizing those who seek a Johnny Cash birthed from the panoply of American music) was a juke joint, where black men and women who worked the farms outside Dyess drank and danced. It could have been another vein of influence in J.R.'s artistic development, but the youngster never stopped there. Ray may have ducked in from time to time to buy whiskey. But J.R. and his friends—treading on their side of the age's racial boundaries—scurried by, hearing the pulsing sounds, muted by the distance between the shack and road. So there was no Arnold Schulz (Bill Monroe's black mentor) or Tee Tot (Hank Williams') in J.R.'s childhood to inform his nascent years with black influence. J.R. remembered hearing the radio performances of Sister Rosetta Tharpe, but the black gospel queen with spectacular verve would not redefine his interpretation of gospel music. He recorded jingly takes on her "This Train Is Bound for Glory" and "There Are Strange Things Happening Everyday" in the 1970s, but he rarely strayed from the standard Baptist hymnal and its arrangements when he turned to the gospel catalog for material.

Though J.R. all but ignored the juke joint's rhythms, there was other music on the colony's outskirts that he couldn't ignore. Drooping on a ditch bank on the northwest perimeter of Dyess was a ragged house where a destitute family lived. Squatters, they hunted, fished, and worked odd jobs to stay alive. J.R. knew the boy who lived there, Jesse Barnhill. Raised by his grandmother and grandfather, Jesse's right arm and legs were crippled by polio. And, like his grandfather who is said to have played guitar, Jesse knew something about music. A schoolmate remembers that the enigmatic boy could hold his finger against his nostril and conjure a squawking guitar sound. But few in Dyess High School knew that the boy who hobbled through the hall, slouched to one side, knew how to play a real guitar.

J.R. knew it, and after school, he often dashed off through the weeds to the splintered home, where Jesse cradled a guitar, gripping the chords on the neck with his left hand while his withered right hand pounded out the rhythm. The regular sessions with Jesse were J.R.'s first guitar lessons: "I was at Jesse's house every afternoon after school," he recalled, "and stayed until long after dark, singing along with him, or singing to his playing Hank Snow, Ernest Tubb, Jimmie Rodgers songs. Jesse taught me my first chord on the guitar, but my hands, being too small, I didn't really learn to play them."

Watching Jesse was like watching Roy: it nurtured in J.R. his own vision of one day picking and singing on the radio. In J.R.'s mind, his own guitar playing was always linked back to Barnhill and to his mother, who strummed a guitar early in the singer's life. None of his regular pals played instruments, and music was not taught in the schools. So slipping off to Barnhill's when there wasn't work to do around his own house must have seemed an exotic diversion to killing turtles and swimming in the Tyronza.

The mysterious Jesse Barnhill was another alter ego for J.R. Cash, the boy who dreamed quietly and grieved for his deceased brother. A lonely, brooding teenager, Jesse was a minstrel whose music likely helped him cope with his infirmity and the rejection that it engendered. Such a plight J.R. understood, living as he did with his father's repudiation but also with the knowledge that music could be a balm.

Barnhill's rejection, though, was almost complete: he lived on the outside of town and lurked on the margins at school. "No one would really take him under their wing," observes a classmate. "So, he just kind of stayed by himself." J.R. appears to have been one of the few to see beyond Barnhill's illness.

A photograph in the 1948–49 Dyess High School yearbook frames an unmistakable contrast between Barnhill and the other boys in school, even with his crippled limbs out of the picture. Amid passive faces, Barnhill engages the camera, poised it seems to take on something coming his way. Above him, also unlike the others boys, there is J.R., who virtually snubs the lens. But J.R is much like the others, too, wearing his starched white shirt with a flared collar, a hint of uncertainty on his face. Barnhill, whose head lists to one side, probably had no white shirt to wear. Rather, an eye-catching jacket climbs up and around his neck. Its collar is thick and black.

3

DREAMS

While J.R. and his classmates walked the halls of Dyess High School, they gave little thought to the fact that Dyess was slipping from under them, jarred by postwar prosperity and mechanization that would soon make farming profitable only on large tracts of land. The colony's success in caring so well for the Depression's refugees also had a hand in its own faltering; many of its inhabitants were poised to move on to bigger things. To stay would have betrayed Dyess's best aspirations: self-improvement, self-reliance, and formal education.

As never before in most of the Arkansas countryside, Dyess children received twelve grades of education in geography, science, math, and English. Their parents, entrenched in the fields with only limited schooling, never would have dreamed in their youth about the education available in Dyess. And whether those parents knew it or not, the lessons and new awareness of the larger world were ushering their children right out of Arkansas. "I don't know of hardly anyone who wanted to stay at Dyess and raise cotton," remarks one of J.R.'s peers who saw the changes. Most would not have to. The demand for manufacturing jobs that had bubbled during the war and boiled over in the years after 1945 shunted aside Depression worries and upset a generation-after-generation farming tradition. The times set free thousands of Arkansans from their centuries-old obligation to work the land.

At the same time, veterans back from the fighting in Europe and Asia brought home their stories of pretty girls, exotic cities, and battlefield valor. The ex-soldiers regaled their younger brothers with these tales, and those youngsters then passed them around outside the school building and cotton gin. A sense of romance rearranged many plans for the future.

For many teenagers in Dyess, the changes simply meant new ways to make a living: to Memphis to work in the lumber trade, to Detroit to man the automobile assembly lines, or to the armed services to stand watch against the Soviet threat. They saw in the newsreels and magazines and heard from those who had departed stories about the nice cars and homes available in Memphis, the cozy deployments on overseas bases, and the eight-hour factory shifts with overtime, if you wanted it. One need not have a University of Arkansas education to splash into the consumer wonderland of postwar America and rinse away the dirt of Mississippi County cotton farming.

In his senior year, the lanky boy whose low-grade pranksterism and dreamy seriousness impressed the Dyess crowd stepped up a rung or two on the high school social ladder. J.R.'s classmates voted him vice president, and he assumed an office in the school's chapter of the Future Farmers of America (FFA), an ironic position for a boy who'd soon abandon farming. Nonetheless, his rise to student leadership marked a coming out for the kid with average grades and with no apparent participation in sports, the typical route to popularity. Besides friends' memories of his swimming on a team and a stray photograph of J.R. in a basketball uniform, he appears to have avoided varsity athletics.

It's from this late stage in J.R.'s educational career that he comes into sharp focus to those outside his immediate circle of friends. With the politics, they say, came poetry—much of it about cowboys—and singing. "We didn't pay much attention to it," confesses Milton Stansbury. "But he used to like to write poems and things of this nature and I remember out in the ag building, I had a class there with him, he would write poems and he would sing them sometimes. But, us kids, as shallow as we were we didn't [say], 'Oh, man, you're going to make music.' You know, we wasn't thinking in that line. Looking back, you could see he had talent." Although he had not picked up the guitar after his evenings with Jesse Barnhill, and close friends from his primary school days don't recall him singing, he had evidently decided by his last year of high school that it wouldn't be so bad if the kids heard his warbling. His confidence was boosted probably by his mother's praises, exuberant recitals in the fields, and a brief set of voice lessons.

In adulthood, J.R. often spoke of those lessons and the voice teacher, who told him to go away and never come back because his sonorous style should never be tampered with. But more often he remembered and recited his mother's encouraging words. His father gave little thought to the boy's voice, but Carrie knew it was a gift from God. She'd told him so, he recalled, when she noticed one day after he'd come in from cutting wood that his voice had deepened.

"God has His hand on you, son," she said. "Someday you'll be singing on the radio, not just KLCN, Blytheville, not just WMPS, Memphis, but everywhere. Everybody will hear you sing, and the life you live will be a beacon. You'll have many followers. I pray that you'll have the wisdom to lead in the right direction. You have a special calling, a gift."

Cash again and again echoed his mother's words in his autobiographies, liner notes, and interviews, and the story most likely grew out of proportion to the truth with each telling. But the tone of it rings pure. Carrie valued music—she played piano, she played guitar, her parents were musical—so why wouldn't she encourage the son who carried on her family's tradition? Carrie also valued spiritual gifts, believing that God placed in man's possession certain talents that be used for His glory. Even if J.R. later exaggerated the effusiveness of his mother's vision, it's certain that Carrie would have encouraged an offspring, in whom she'd seen her musical self, to use his gift. He surely, too, would have welcomed her words.

And so he plied that gift. In school, he might pop up with an impromptu solo, as Milton Stansbury observed, or sign up for recitals and talent contests. Students remember seeing him stand up at assemblies in the dull cafeteria to earnestly croon "That Lucky Ole Sun," though they hardly shared Carrie's maternal enthusiasm for the boy's singing. Yet by the spring of 1950, his reputation was such that organizers of the high school commencement invited him to perform. On May 19, 1950, amid a program including "The Battle Hymn of the Republic" and prayers by the pastors of the Methodist Church and the Church of Christ, J.R. Cash intoned "Drink to Me Only with Thine Eyes," a 17th century ode by the English author and actor Ben Jonson:

Drink to me only with thine eyes,
And I will pledge with mine.
Or leave a kiss within the cup,
And I'll not ask for wine.
The thirst that from the soul doth rise,
Doth crave a drink divine.
But might I of Jove's nectar sup,
I would not change for thine.

Although J.R.s's friends observed welling within him a vision for himself, his steps after graduation were anything but certain. Sniffing around for some passage out of Dyess, J.R. traveled west to pick strawberries at the other end of the state, but he soon returned and decided to join the throng of Southerners taking to the North-bound roads and rails. There was nothing inventive about his choice. Many from Mississippi County had preceded him, first in a trickle just after the war, and then in a surge as the northern manufacturing engine turned white hot.

J.R.'s traveling companions were Frank Kinney, a Dyess barber with a wife and children (whose pockets were emptying as the number of male heads in the colony dwindled), and Milton Stansbury, the friend who observed J.R.'s antics in the history class. Stansbury had graduated from high school in 1949 to a carpentry job, but when he realized that he lacked the strength for such work, he took his father's advice and enrolled in a Memphis business school. He soon tired of the big city, however, and over the Christmas holiday before J.R. graduated, the two got to talking about Michigan: "We had already known several that had gone up there," says Stansbury. "And chopping and picking cotton the rest of your life didn't really appeal to J.R. and me. You know, we talked it over and everything. And so, we were getting feedback from the families of these other boys that had come up here so we decided, 'Let's go up there and see what we can do with it.' And we did."

The three gathered in the bus station in Wilson, a few miles to the west of the river and just up the road from Bassett, where the Cashes had buried Jack six years before. Outside the bus station, in front of the neat town square, stretched U.S. Highway 61, a road that reverberates in twentieth-century American folklore. Along its run through the state of Mississippi, before it jumps across the river to

Arkansas and continues north, America's greatest blues men and women were born, lived, performed, and rambled. Robert Johnson, killed some twelve years before J. R. left Wilson, bragged that he'd sold his soul to the devil on a lonely patch of the highway.

Whether they played the blues or not, many blacks saw Highway 61 as an escape route from poverty, semi-feudalism, and racism. For poor Southern whites, the road held a similar promise, and J.R. and his companions, who were twitching in anticipation, illustrated it.

The symbolism of Highway 61 was probably far from J.R.'s grasp in 1950; instead, his emotions roiled with the nagging mixture of uncertainty and grief that come with leaving home. For months before he left, family observed that he seemed to be present in body only. He'd often stomp in the door from school or the fields, barely a word for anyone, and melt into a quiet corner of the house.

Stansbury recalls that his own family, but not the Cashes, came the short distance to see them off. Kathy Cash tells me that her father recalled that Ray Cash barely acknowledged J.R.'s departure. "Grandpa just said 'bye' or 'see ya,' something like that. He said he just acted like he was walking to the store. They didn't know how long he was going to be gone. Grandma stood on the front porch and watched him and was crying."

So, carrying at least his mother's best wishes, J.R. stepped onto the bus. He headed first south to Memphis on 61, and then, catching another bus, traveled north by another highway. The bus ride was long—nearly twenty-four hours— and at the end was Pontiac, Michigan, a city of immense factories that cranked and rolled and steamed and stamped twenty-four hours a day.

In its march to supply the automobile-starved nation, Pontiac accepted any men, especially farmers whose work ethic was heralded across the industrialized North. Recalling neighbors' and friends' experiences, Stansbury, Cash, and Kinney suspected they'd be snatched up by the industrial machine as soon as they got to town, and they were right. "We got in about midnight," says Stansbury, "and some people we knew was in a rooming house over there and we went up there and hung around, messed around in the living room, you know, grabbed a few winks, and at eight o'clock that next morning, we were down at the employment office at Fisher Body on Baldwin. So, that afternoon at four o'clock we went to work, all three of us."

After joining the union and learning that they'd be making a dollar and a half an hour, the men spread out to their assigned jobs at Fisher, a General Motors operation. Stansbury took up a welder's torch, and Cash went to the assembly line where he stamped sheets of metal into hoods. Stansbury doesn't know what happened to Kinney after GM hired them, but he and Cash stayed a few more nights in the rooming house with the other Dyess men before they separated and found places of their own. Cash moved into a rooming house about a mile and half from the factory.

Stansbury adapted to the Northern industrial jungle, staying there until his retirement from Ford in 1991(except for a hitch in the Air Force and brief periods working in Kansas City and Memphis). Cash, though, quickly concluded that a future on the assembly line was too much to bear. He'd tell daughter Kathy that he'd been leagues out of his element. "Here I was, a country farmer kid who didn't know anything about any city," he'd say. "I was so out of my own. I was scared of everything. I was trying to be brave because I needed to get a job but I just didn't know what I was doing."

Fed up with the monotonous work that was supposed to be easier than cotton picking, as well as the long walk to work and bland food served in the boarding house, he was just waiting for an excuse to leave. And he found it, he told biographer Christopher Wren, after an accident at the press. "One day, I cut my right forearm on a hood. I went to the dispensary, and I quit that day."

Cash was back in Dyess before the end of June. He'd been out of school little more than a month. Carrie, Tommy, Reba, and Joann welcomed him back to number 266, while Ray likely saw in his son a little of the rudderless young man that he himself had been. Even Ray, though, could see that J.R. would have to find a vocation other than farming. Eldest son Roy had returned to Dyess and his own farm, but he was struggling, and Ray himself had been forced to take full-time work in a margarine plant down the road in Evadale, Arkansas.

Cash joined his father at the margarine plant, but it wasn't long before he took another route that was at least as popular among young Southerners as the hillbilly highway. On July 7, 1950, Cash visited the armed-services recruiting station in Blytheville and enlisted in the U.S. Air Force, a choice that may have had as much to do with the Korean War as with anything else. The outbreak of hostilities in Korea in June raised the real possibility that he'd be drafted to fight, so he (like many others) may have chosen the air force to avoid battlefield duty. It was no secret that the air force generally honored one's choice of posting, unlike the other branches, which would route a desire to serve in Oklahoma to an assignment in Okinawa. Many young recruits also believed the air force to be a lighter hitch, so light that some called that decision to fly off into the wild blue yonder "draft dodging." In later years, Cash cited the "wild blue yonder" part, the imagery of flying away. He'd been gazing at those blue skies after all.

The air force marked Cash's incarnation as "John." He said that the air force refused his initials and demanded a name when registering, so he had harked back to his mother's wish and recorded it on the application.

The air force was also John Cash's university, not only exposing him to parts of the world he'd never seen, but also forcing him to get along with the respectable and the raffish of air force personnel. Show business, he'd see later, was full of the nefarious types he'd meet in the military: slackers, addictive personalities, and opportunists. So his stint prepared him to negotiate with them, even if he didn't always do it well.

Later in the summer, Cash and his family drove to Memphis, where he boarded a train for Lackland Air Force Base in San Antonio, Texas, a bustling hub of men-in-blue activity. So many recruits processed through Lackland on their way to permanent assignments that tent cities rose to supplement the acres of crammed barracks. An air force base without an airstrip (the planes flew in and out of nearby Kelly Air Force Base), Lackland refined the young servicemen, teaching them to march, fire weapons, and respect authority. It also administered a battery of aptitude tests that pointed recruits to their destinations: cockpit, motor pool, bakery, or elsewhere.

In Cash, Lackland superiors saw an aptitude for radio work, the tedious job of manning a powerful receiver and recording transmissions, friendly or hostile, that darted through the skies. Thousands of servicemen monitored those transmissions during the early 1950s as the war in Korea intensified and the Cold War with the Soviet Union threatened to heat up into direct confrontation.

After two months at Lackland, the air force dispatched Cash to Keesler Air Force Base in Biloxi, Mississippi, where he learned Morse code, typing, and some electronics. Like the other airmen, Cash would have to interpret and peck out at least twenty words per minute before the air force assigned him to distant points. But Cash was an exceptional case. After seven months at Keesler, he reached twenty-six to thirty words per minute. As hard as his trainers tried to bamboozle him, by varying the tones of the scratchy dots and dashes or strengthening and weakening the signal at random intervals, Cash rarely paused. He absorbed the Morse code as if it were his own voice speaking to him. By the end of his stint in southern Mississippi in the spring of 1951, he was tagged for high-level security work and shipped back down to San Antonio, this time to Brooks Air Force Base. There he'd undergo sixteen weeks of specialized intercept training and finally receive his assignment.

Nobody back at Dyess High School would have called Cash a lady's man. With buddies at the swimming hole, he certainly chipped in a fresh quip or two about pretty young colonists. Once he hit his early teens, girls not surprisingly occupied more of his thinking time. Yet he only infrequently parlayed that interest into dates; he simply wasn't the guy with the girl on his arm. "He was nice looking and everything," allows one of his female classmates, "but I don't remember him going with anybody. I'm sure he must have, but it wasn't very much if he did. He didn't have a vehicle I don't imagine, you know, to go that far."

Cash did have his father's beat-up Ford sedan, though he recalled in his first autobiography that it hardly attracted the girls. But still, he dated. Biographer Steve Turner interviewed a number of women whom Cash had escorted when they were girls in high school. However, none of them felt left behind when Cash departed Dyess. He was free.

At Brooks Air Force Base, flush perhaps with romantic curiosity now that he was away far from home, Cash wasted little time finding a steady girlfriend. While out for an evening at a roller-skating rink, Cash met and immediately pursued a seventeen-year-old girl who would become his first wife, Vivian Liberto. Shy with a fawn's awkwardness, Liberto hesitated. She was interested in the tall, uniformed serviceman but feared her father, who was stingy in his approval of suitors (and especially those from the military who filtered through San Antonio with easy love on their minds). After a few circles around the rink, Cash badgered her, asking to escort her home. But she demurred, says their daughter Kathy: "She kept saying, 'No you can't walk me home. No, you can't ride on the bus home with me.' And

[Cash] just told her, 'I'm taking you home on the bus.' She was scared to death; she was so timid. She thought, 'My daddy's going to kill me for a guy walking me to the bus stop and getting on the bus with me.'"

Vivian was Italian, Catholic, and bathed in light bronze skin, more exotic than any girl Cash had probably ever known. Most Dyess boys might have dismissed her, if not for her dark complexion then for her Catholicism, but Cash persisted and evidently measured up in her father Roberto's wary eyes. The two dated until Cash left for his permanent assignment at Landsberg Air Force Base in West Germany. He and Vivian would not see each other again for almost three years. Amazingly, their bond survived the long separation as well as Cash's hunger for European women.

In late summer of 1951, Cash boarded a train for Camp Kilmer, New Jersey, and then a troop ship bound for Bremerhaven, in northern Germany. Traveling by train to Landsberg, in the Bavarian region of southern Germany, Cash and his fellow Americans (many of whom were still scraping farm dirt from their fingernails) observed wartime destruction that they'd only known from flickering newsreels. In the gloomy industrial regions, the train windows fleetingly framed rubble where bridges used to span, bombed out churches, and the charred skeletons of old houses. Only as the train sped into Bavaria did the pictures brighten. The rich countryside bloomed as if war had never soiled the region, and the buildings of Landsberg (which escaped Allied bombing) glistened in the fading summer sunlight.

However, what nature glossed over, Germany could not deny. Many pockets in and around Landsberg were the sites of Nazi atrocities. At least eleven concentration camps dotted the area, and in the city's prison where Americans in 1951 were still executing Nazi war criminals, Adolf Hitler had penned his *Mein Kampf*. Even the headquarters where Cash would be stationed remained haunted by Germany's Nazi past; it had been a Luftwaffe base during the war.

Stirring up an unsettling wind as the newcomers arrived were rumors that the recent hangings of seven Nazis at Landsburg were likely to provoke German protests. The airmen noted the resentment welling behind the polite faces of Germans who tended the gasthouses and worked jobs on the base. And they were disturbed by the eerie absence of men between twenty-five and thirty-five years old, so many of them having been killed in the war. Elements of their new home resembled a cheap noir film. The black market (virtually unheard of at home) thrived, and prostitution (well-hidden in the farming villages of America) burgeoned, fanned by the moribund economy and the availability of willing servicemen.

Underscoring everything German, whether good or bad, was the Soviet Union, the reason for the new recruits' mission. Cautious eyes were always trained on the east, "in case the Soviets tried to do something nutty," says one Arkansas man also stationed at Landsberg.

The air force had slotted Cash in the 12th Radio Squadron Mobile (RSM), a unit of intercept operators who eavesdropped on the transmissions of the Soviet Union and its satellite nations. Needless to say, the work of RSM was highly classified. Other radiomen throughout the armed forces merely passed messages among U.S. ships, bases, and platoons, but Cash and his comrades were cogs in a highly focused surveillance unit. One could call them spies on the Cold War front. They had passed rigid FBI screenings and received unrelenting instruction on maintaining the secrecy of their mission. Even today, when men who served alongside Cash describe their mission, they stammer and pause. They carefully consider their words, mindful of the days when such discussion could mean a court martial. During the almost fifty years between Cash's discharge and death, he rarely spoke in detail about his mission.

Cash was among the elite of the squadron. Bill Craig, a North Carolinian who rode abreast of Cash starting at Keesler Air Force Base, reckons that Cash was among the five most capable operators on base. It was a status rewarded by sexier assignments and supervisory duties. Cash monitored long-range Russian bombers, which were feared for their obvious capabilities, and tracked Soviet radar transmissions when American U2s sailed high over eastern territory. "Those planes would fly in over Bulgaria or some of the other satellite countries," explains Craig, who was often perched at Cash's side. "And the Russians didn't have a missile that would shoot them down at the time. So [the U2s] were impervious to the Russian MIGs, which would flame out trying to get high enough to shoot one of them down. That was exciting, and that was very interesting to us to monitor those types of things."

In the attic of the squadron's barracks, with a churning blanket of cigarette smoke hugging the ceiling, Cash and thirty-nine others on his trick surveyed the air eight hours at a time. Slouching over his manual typewriter, his ear cocked at attention, Cash was expressionless as he sorted out the competing noises in his headphones. Out of seven or eight different signals bleating away, he had to discern the one signal he wanted: a Russian plane's above Sofia or a Czechoslovakian radio operator's outside Prague. He almost always collared the sound he wanted, a talent Craig attributes to his evolving musical ability. Cash identified his targeted signal by honing in on its tone, the way a singer or instrumentalist keys into tone in order to meld with a band or imitate a song. Few could pick out the sounds he wanted to track better than Cash.

Short breaks from the stuffy room were often interrupted by cryptographers rushing to him with information about planes taking off from an eastern capital, such as Budapest or Moscow. Setting his cigarette in an ashtray, Cash would don his headset, quickly zero in on the radio signal, and furiously pound out his interpretation of the Morse code (data that he'd pass on to Landsberg security officials for further deciphering). Cash often boasted that he could rope a Russian plane's signal within seconds of the pilot switching on his transmitter. "We would catch [the pilot] warming up his key," says Craig.

The air force was also keen on determining the porousness of Cold War borders. In a high-tech game of cat and mouse, U.S. commanders often ordered their planes to cross into Russian, Hungarian, or Czechoslovakian airspace in order to gauge how soon enemy radar would latch on to them. It was Cash's and his comrades' job to spot that unfriendly radar signal as soon as it appeared. Should the Americans ever need to jet full throttle into Russia or another enemy land, they would know how long their element of surprise would last.

Those who shared Cash's Landsberg experience saw early in his stint a young man cautiously venturing into the world. Like a few of Cash's school chums, they sensed the gravity about him. He guarded his privacy and was often alone. It was nothing, says Bill Craig, to see Cash disappear by himself on a three-day pass.

Yet his self-assurance was also awakening, particularly in the radio intercept room where he was a leader of sorts, administering refresher courses to new arrivals and rallying the boys with wisecracks. Sauntering like John Wayne through the aisles of typewriters clutching transcripts, he'd joke about a frequent Russian transmission that transcribed to something like "goo-her." "Goober's back," he'd bellow to nobody in particular. "Ol' Goober . . ."

Speaking about Germany years later, Cash said that homesickness for Dyess soon faded from his mind but that he pined for Vivian. "All he could talk about was her," says Bill Carnahan, another fellow radio operator who also played music with Cash. When Cash arrived in Germany, he and Vivian commenced an intense exchange of letters that lasted until he returned to the States in July of 1954. Like a southern incarnation of John and Abigail Adams, the pair wrote each other almost every day. The farm boy from Dyess wrote with abandon (his daughter Kathy estimates more than one thousand letters), all in green ink that he reserved for the girl in San Antonio. "He'd write two or three times a day. And several of the letters I read were dated the same day, it'd be the same ink, it'd have the time at the top. It'd be like two hours later and he'd write her another one. You know, he was lonesome."

It's no wonder he so intensely pursued Vivian in San Antonio and then from far-off Landsberg. For the first time, Cash felt loving acceptance from somebody other than his mother and siblings; it was a new and irresistible feeling for him. In one of his letters, he proposed marriage, though he warned Vivian not to say anything to her father just yet. Hoping Vivian would eventually fly to him, Cash found an apartment attached to the Landsberg police chief's home. But her father nixed the plans, and Cash turned over the flat to his friend Bill Carnahan, whose wife would soon be arriving in Germany.

Vivian welcomed Cash's entreaties, despite the long wait she'd have until he returned home; time in which there would certainly be opportunities with other young men. She craved acceptance outside her San Antonio home, after having known a home life distressed by alcoholism. Her mother drank heavily and it often fell to her to cook, clean, and care for her father and siblings. "She became the mother of that house," says daughter Cindy Cash. "She said she was cooking meals by the time she could reach the counter." A troubled family life was the one certain thing the two sweethearts had in common.

Among many airmen, there were two standard military-issue diversions: booze and women. Cash was no different. Although his loyalty to Vivian and homegrown Baptist sensibilities initially kept him away from the carousing pack, he soon relented and found his tooth for mellow cognac and saucy German women. His appetite for both—in their various forms—remained strong for years to come.

Cash hinted in his first autobiography that debauchery defined his air-force social life, that he tried "most everything else" that grew from drinking. "And I guess I started to be a fairly profane person," he added in his book, "because for the first time in my life I got to seeing how good I could curse. The booze and the profanity began launching me into all kinds of other habits which soon became second nature."

Excursions to Switzerland, Italy, and France were educational, introducing him to exotic architecture, fine art, and new food. But they were also shopping trips, as were his weekly forays into downtown Landsberg. In Zurich on a three-day pass, mates from the 12th RSM stumbled into an empty bar one afternoon and spotted the tall radio man chatting up the barmaid. He was lining up, they supposed, his evening's recreation.

The promise of reunification with Vivian failed to quell him. During the last year or so of his Landsberg tenure, according to Bill Craig, Cash took a regular German girlfriend. She was a woman who'd been popular among the airmen in Landsberg, says Craig. Although Cash's comrades were surprised that he would get so serious about such a well-traveled woman, the men were blasé about Cash's move. Many German women (badly in need of economic support) courted the regular companionship of American servicemen and, says Craig, more than a few took them up on it.

Some airmen at Landsberg who didn't work the radio receivers went as far as to say that theirs was a delightful hitch, with abundant leave, easy access to buxom frauleins, frothy lagers, and light workloads. But Cash's stint was another story. The stress of his eight-hour shift, which often spanned the night, was enough to land a radio operator in primal scream therapy.

The job was imposing from the moment Cash showed up for work. He ran a gauntlet of steel doors and inquisitive air-force police, who issued him his identification tags and ushered him to a reception area for a security lecture. "This happened every day," complains Bill Craig. "At that time, they would tell you what they would do to you if you were caught divulging what you did or any military information to anybody, it was so highly classified." At the end of the shift, Cash sat for the same lecture, which must have seemed at once farcical and patronizing. Still, he had to be careful. One among them lost his stripes because he had left the attic with typewriter paper, planning to wrap sandwiches in it; the color of the paper was classified.

Cloistered away in an old brick building surrounded by fields of antennas, and forbidden from commenting on anything they did or heard on duty, mystery surrounded the members of the 12th RSM. Those who saw them in the commissary or mess halls thought they appeared drained, although they never knew exactly why. Word circulated at the base that the radio intercept operators frequently landed in the dispensary to decompress from the tension, rumors to which Cash could speak: "One night . . . I just got fed up. We were working on the second floor and, before I knew it, I picked up my typewriter and threw it plumb through the window. I started crying. They sent me to the dispensary and gave me a couple of aspirins. I got the rest of the night off."

Cash's outburst that night suggests something close to a mental breakdown, if not a full-fledged one. However, it was not severe enough in the minds of his superiors to remove him from his post. For almost three complete years, the man who stood tall and straight when photographed in uniform and who as a young cotton picker had hardly known walls sat hunched over radio and typewriter in a cramped room. Smoking cigarettes and gulping coffee, he waited for the sounds in his ears. And he paid a physical price. His family would notice a change when he finally returned home in 1954. His body was astir, aggravated by twitches and tremors that they hadn't seen before.

Cash also returned home with more refined musical abilities. Whenever air-force downtime had allowed, often with three days off after six days working, Cash attended to his music.

In childhood, singing had been kind of a lonely and sometime avocation, mixed up with school, church, field work, and play. However, in the air force, he enjoyed collaboration with an immediate musical community whose interests were almost identical to his. Southerners and Midwesterners all, the airmen rallied around country and gospel music, genres that encouraged their camaraderie and provided diversion that soothed the ache of homesickness and the minds dulled by radio work.

Cash joined the group sings, purchased a guitar, and learned two or three chords. From time to time, his gang gathered to play and sing in the dank barracks basement and once they performed at a squadron picnic. Feeling bold, they also switched on a Wilcox-Gay tape machine that Cash had purchased and recorded their rollicking versions of Hank Williams' latest and Roy Acuff's greatest. The sound may have been rough—as the tapes surely revealed—but around Cash in those amateur revels were capable players. Fellow airman Reid Cummins, from Arkansas, played a respectable guitar and coached Cash in his tentative strumming, and Bill Carnahan, from Missouri, could bring to mind Hank's and Ernest's singing and playing. The talent all around Cash motivated him, and he saw for the first time what it meant to perform music as part of a team. He saw how that team could inspire each individual member to produce something that was bigger than his own self.

Cash's guitar playing, improved as it was, was hardly the bulwark of the air force rhythm section, but the jamming encouraged his other talents of singing and writing. He knew he could sing in public—that much had been decided in Dyess High School—but his songwriting never before had received much airing beyond the school yard. Of the Cash family in Dyess, only Roy had been published. But in the air force, some remember that Cash's composition "Hey Porter," about a prodigal son returning to the South, appeared in a base publication.

Bill Craig, who roomed with Cash, can still envision the budding writer: sitting on his foot locker, clad only in boxer shorts, strumming his guitar, and scribbling down lyrics. "The other guys in the room said, 'John, you're wasting your time. You're never going to amount to anything. You just don't have it. Let's go to the airmen's club and drink beer.' He'd say, 'Okay, I'll be up there later.' And sometimes he would come and sometimes he wouldn't."

Hanging back in bed, a can of chili simmering on his hot plate, he might welcome another guitarist or a harmonica player for a little jamming, spin a few records on a turntable that one of his roomies owned, or record his new lyrics on his recorder. If his roomies returned from the airmen's club in a jolly mood, he'd move aside while they unsheathed their Chordettes and Mantovani records. "The three of us, [excluding] John, would lie there and harmonize to those songs," explains Craig. "And we wouldn't let Johnny do it. He just didn't fit. His voice was not a harmonic-type voice. We would give him hell if he tried to join in on the harmony."

So Cash returned to his verse, much of which would show up on discs early in his recording career, including "Run Softly Blue River," "Oh What A Dream," and "Belshazzar." The best known among that crop was "Folsom Prison Blues," which he'd penned after seeing Crane Wilbur's *Inside the Walls of Folsom Prison*, a Warner Brothers flick about a knot of disgruntled inmates out to topple a corrupt warden. It never gained traction in America's movie houses, but servicemen starving for entertainment gathered for any English-language movie. The film's theme of prison reform inspired Cash to write from the inmate's perspective. His jailbird dwells on his considerable crime—shooting a man "just to watch him die"—and the loss of freedom that came from it.

The young Arkansan could relate to loss of freedom. He felt that confinement in Landsberg, an assignment that he later compared to imprisonment: "I was locked there on that base, three years without a furlough to come home. The only way they would have let me come home was if there had been a death in my immediate family. I was not only isolated from my loved ones, but there was nowhere to go, no one to reach out to." In the stanzas of "Folsom Prison Blues," Cash is the inmate desperately wishing to jump the freedom train.

When he recorded "Folsom Prison Blues" in 1955, the ballad quickly became a Cash staple and proved also to be a model of Cash's writing style. Like many of his compositions, "Folsom Prison Blues" sprouted from his personal experience (in this case, loneliness and the emotional reaction to seeing caged men on film), incorporated the symbolism of trains, and dwelled on the lonely figure (not unlike Jim George who rambled through his town or the celluloid cowboys whom he'd seen gallop across the motion picture screen).

"Folsom Prison Blues" was also quintessentially Cash in that it fitted comfortably into the American ballad tradition. Obviously, the ballad walked like a ballad, and the references to violence, towering prisons, and iron locomotives gave it a western patina, like the standards "Streets of Laredo" or "The Bad Man from the Brazos." Moreover, in the style of most all balladeers, Cash borrowed freely from other songs to come up with "Folsom Prison Blues." He told his protégé Marty Stuart in later years that he had remolded Jimmie Rodgers' *I'm gonna shoot poor Thelma/Just to see her jump and fall* from "Blue Yodel #1 (T for Texas)" into the

"Folsom Prison Blues" line *I shot a man in Reno/Just to watch him die*. Not satisfied with appropriating only from the Singing Brakemen, the airman also borrowed from a copyrighted pop song of the day, "Crescent City Blues," which was written and recorded by Gordon Jenkins.

Jenkins, whose arrangement sweetened Frank Sinatra's "September of My Years" in the 1960s, had programmed "Crescent City Blues" on his 1953 concept album *Seven Dreams*, which followed a sleeper's nighttime fantasies in seven parts. Cash revealed later that he had owned the pop album in Germany. What Cash actually thought of the balance of the album is unknown, but he zeroed in on "Crescent City Blues"'s moaning, though stiff, lament. Cut from the same cloth as Harold Arlen's "Blues in the Night" and Kern and Hammerstein's "Old Man River," it was pure white-man's blues before Cash got hold of it and injected some soul.

A copyright lawyer would call Cash's appropriation plagiarism; a balladeer might be more forgiving. But whatever one might call it, in writing "Folsom Prison Blues," Cash had co-opted the rhyming structure of "Crescent City Blues" and lightly reworked many of its lines.

In interviews later in life, whenever "Folsom Prison Blues" came up in conversation with reporters, he rarely referenced "Crescent City Blues." He didn't really have to; most reporters wanted to talk about whether or not he'd really *shot a man in Reno just to watch him die*. Privately, he told manager Lou Robin in the early 1970s that he worried about Jenkins' reaction when Sun Records released his first recording of "Folsom Prison Blues" in 1955. Owner Sam Phillips, however, had told him that he had nothing to fear. Not until Cash re-recorded "Folsom Prison Blues" at California's Folsom State Prison in 1968 and saw stupendous sales did Gordon Jenkins confront him and draw a settlement that approached one hundred thousand dollars. "At the time," Cash said in 1996, harking back to when he wrote the song, "I really had no idea I would be a professional recording artist. I wasn't trying to rip anybody off."

The young staff sergeant—he'd been promoted—was in an intensely creative period, conceiving or adapting songs that his air-force group performed. Such performances validated his songwriting, as well as his talent for picking and singing, and marked a crucial prelude to the recording career that would soon follow his air-force discharge. Surviving Landsberg without the musical community that supported his art might have meant a dramatically different career path for Cash.

Although he often complained about the confinement of air-force life and would acknowledge that the stint nurtured more than a few of his troublesome character flaws, Cash could hardly deny that the experience had been in its own way liberating. It freed him to explore the gift that Carrie Cash had seen that evening when her boy had come home from cutting timber, sweating and singing.

4

MEMPHIS

In the wedding photos, Vivian Liberto beams. Her promised man is back by her side, and she is eager to commence married life, despite how little she knows her betrothed. The promised man's face tells another story. While Vivian has blossomed into young womanhood, the twenty-two-year-old Cash has for the moment lost his youth. For the first time, he is Ray Cash. Trepidation mutes his smiles, and the weight he has gained after sitting in a chair for eight-hour shifts and drinking copious amounts of beer gives him the jowly look of his father. His crisp uniform and his mother's height redeem him. A courtly groom, he appears resigned to any task, including, one presumes, marriage.

They married in San Antonio on August 7, 1954, and settled in Memphis, where many of Cash's friends and family from Dyess had gathered in the years since he had left Arkansas. Brother Roy, who had returned to farming after the war only to abandon it again to find work as a mechanic, and sister Reba, who had married in her teens, lived there too. Ray and Carrie soon followed.

Guessing that his interceptor work and love for music suited him for disc jockeying, Cash entered radio school on the G.I. Bill. But after spending some of his air-force savings on a 1954 Plymouth and plopping down a deposit for a small apartment on Eastmoreland Avenue in midtown Memphis, Cash needed a job. He inquired about police work but settled for a sales position with Home Equipment Company, which, according to its promotions, specialized in "home economy, insulation weather stripping, roofing, siding and appliances." The company, owned and operated by a kindly soul named George Bates, assigned him to appliances. He'd be selling them used in the store and door-to-door in the poor neighborhoods of Memphis. "When I went to work at Home Equipment, I really thought I'd be successful . . . ," he told biographer Christopher Wren. "But I hated trying to convince people they should have something they didn't really want. I felt dishonest."

Despite the disingenuousness he believed came with the job and his reluctance to traipse through Memphis knocking on doors, he was evidently making some sales. Within a few months, he and Vivian (who was now expecting) stepped up to a larger apartment in a one-floor duplex at 2553 Tutwiler Avenue, not far from his job on Summer Avenue and across the narrow street from a small Pentecostal Holiness church.

The anticipation of fatherhood's responsibilities failed to shake his lack of interest in working for the Home Equipment Company. On his lonely routes through tired Memphis streets, he'd stop to listen to blues guitarists on Beale Street or flip through the latest releases in record shops. Music, he said, diverted him from his monotonous chore: "I'd be at home and I'd see a guitar, and I'd sit and play and forget the business." He'd forget the business, too, whenever he met up to jam with Luther Perkins and Marshall Grant, two mechanics employed by the Automobile Sales Company at 309 Union Avenue. He had met them immediately after returning from Germany in July of 1954, the union brokered by his first inspiration in music, brother Roy, who also worked at Automobile Sales. Roy knew that Perkins and Grant liked to strum their guitars together and, while John was still in the service, he would tell them that his brother played too and that he sang just like Hank Snow.

Breaking away from work one day in July, Roy had hollered over to Grant that he was headed up the street to collect his newly discharged brother from the bus station. A few minutes later, Roy reappeared with John.

Grant, a stocky North Carolinian whose hair was sharply receding at the temples, looked up from his work as the two men stepped down the cement steps into the shop. Gazing past Roy, Grant studied John, who was slightly taller than his older brother. "I had this funny little feeling as he walked down to me," Grant later explained to folklorist and radio host Nick Spitzer. "It's hard to explain it. As a matter of fact, I can't explain it." As John neared, Grant's strange feeling crept up his back and straightened the hair on his neck. He shook hands with John, and they mumbled about their limited guitar skills. Then, Grant escorted the visitor across the noisy garage to meet his "pickin' buddy," who at the moment was deep into a repair. Grant kicked at the sole of Perkins's boot that was sticking out from under the car, rousting the lean mechanic from his work. The three men chatted some more about guitars and the pitiful duets Grant and Perkins performed in the Automobile Sales locker room. Within minutes, they had agreed to gather later and play.

Grant tells of meeting Cash in the same way the Samarian woman must have spoken to friends about her encounter with Christ at the well. She determined Christ to be a prophet, while Grant saw something prophet-like in Cash. If Grant, moved by his inexplicable chills, did instantly see greatness in his new friend, he is the third person, after Carrie and Roy, to divine J.R. Cash's destiny.

As soon as time allowed, Cash, Grant, and Perkins met up to compare their picking, which they found to be shaky all the way around. But they were undeterred and continued to play, hurrying out of work to one of their homes, where they ran through reams of gospel music and a handful of country songs they all knew. After a few weeks of strumming in unison with Cash on lead vocals, somebody suggested that they vary their instrumentation. "[Cash] had an old German guitar that he paid five dollars for," says Grant. "And I had a Martin that the wife had just bought me for my birthday, a really nice D-28 Martin, and Perkins had an old plug guitar that wasn't worth a nickel."

Setting down his dog-eared guitar, Perkins upgraded first. He stopped at O.K. Houck Piano Company on Union Avenue, where manager Sid Lapworth sold him a Fender electric guitar and amplifier. Perkins was a native of Memphis but had grown up in Mississippi, where he and his family hoed and picked cotton. In 1942, they had returned to Memphis where, a few years later, he married and became a father. After his electric guitar riffs became known worldwide, those who saw him grimacing and standing still as a statue onstage assumed him to be cagey and quiet. But to the contrary, Perkins could be charming, funny, and, as his visit to the music shop suggests, pioneering and energetic.

When Perkins returned with his new equipment, he told Grant that he'd seen a big stand-up bass in the store's back room. "You ought to go up and talk to him about it," suggested Perkins. So Grant drove down to Houck's on his next lunch break.

"We went back in his little room, and it's leaned up against the wall," continues Grant. "And it was ragged. And I said, 'Sid, what do you want for this thing?' And he said, 'I'll take twenty-five dollars for it.' And so I bought it and took it home. Put it in my car and took it back to the shop, went back to work, had to work it in my car and lay it on top of the seat, as a lot of bass people did. But anyhow, I called John, and I said, 'Luther's got this guitar, and I got a bass, and I don't know how in the hell you tune this thing.' So there was a person that worked at Auto Sales there, his name was Gene Steele, and he was a salesman there, and he had a little band. So I went to Gene the next day and said, 'Gene, how in hell do you tune a bass?' He said, 'I don't know, but we're doin' a little gig tonight with the band, and I'll ask the bass player.' He came back the next morning with a picture drawn in his hand, [showing] G, D, A, and E, just like the top four strings on a guitar. So I called John, and Luther was working on the other side of the shop, and I said, 'Look here Luther, this is how you tune this little sucker.' And I said, 'Let's get together tonight, tune it and make some music.'"

Grant scrawled the notes on pieces of paper and taped them to the corresponding spots near the strings until, he says, the instrument resembled a grey speckled bird. Relegated to rhythm, Cash caressed his old guitar, while Perkins patiently plucked notes that Grant tried to emulate. When they were ready to try it together, Perkins cautiously kicked off in the key of E, alternating between two strings, beckoning Grant who began slapping his bass like an angry father. Cash dove in with earnest strumming. "The sound of Johnny Cash," says Grant, "was born right there and then."

In Perkins and Grant, Cash found a nourishing community like he'd known in the barracks basement in Germany. Just when his musical pursuits might have petered out in the face of appliance sales, a new marriage, and impending parenthood, Grant and Perkins assumed care of Cash's musical aspirations, providing him a workshop to hammer out his vocals and rhythm-guitar playing. Yet it's misleading to look at the congregation only as Cash's forum. At least in the eyes of Grant and Perkins, theirs was a three-way collaboration.

It also was a traveling workshop. The coalescing musical group hopped among Cash's, Grant's, Perkins's and Roy's for practice sessions. Roy's son, Roy Cash, Jr., remembers that one of the first gatherings was at his Fairmont Avenue home. His father was the point person for the men and still fantasized about recreating the Delta Rhythm Ramblers. At the end of hot Memphis days in late summer, Roy Jr. opened his front door for his young uncle who appeared on the doorstep edgy and tightly wound from a day at Home Equipment. Toting his guitar, the frustrated salesman muttered greetings and asked his sister-in-law, Wandene, for coffee. "[He'd] sit down and just kind of start playing the guitar or tuning his guitar," says Roy Jr. "Not much small talk or anything like that."

Cash collared a stool from his brother's small breakfast bar and set it down in the middle of the living room, the only room large enough for the band and its audience of two or three. His one foot on the rail of the stool and other on the ground, Cash craned his neck over his guitar, picking at it while he waited for his mates. When Perkins and Grant showed up, they took their places on either side of Cash, and lurched into their songs.

During breaks from the music, someone would stack up records on the family's record player and they'd listen to Hank Williams, Ernest Tubb, Kitty Wells, Jimmie Rodgers, and Ray Price. The boys tried to match them, and, according to Roy Jr., they came pretty close. "Hey, you sing these better than them," he'd cry. "Why can't you be on records, too?" When the wives accompanied their husbands to Roy's for picking parties, they agreed that John and the band could put over a song every bit as well as the fellows on the records. "We had friends come listen," adds Roy. "They always commented on [their] distinctive sound."

Bolstered by these compliments, the band members poked around for stages beyond their front porches and basements. The first ones were modest: an evening set of gospel tunes at a neighbor's church, a benefit for a friend of Grant's who had been injured in a boat wreck, and a promotional appearance at a local car dealership. Roy Jr. recalls that Cash performed alone in a Christmas service at his family's church. Strumming his guitar, he sang "Silent Night." "It was very, very soft," says

Roy. "I don't think he even used a microphone. He had a voice that would carry. I can remember it just being very powerful."

With the boys, Cash found his biggest audience yet when he persuaded Home Equipment boss George Bates to sponsor the group on the West Memphis, Arkansas, radio station KWEM (which also had studios in Memphis). Despite Cash's ambivalence toward selling washers, Bates didn't seem to mind helping the boy to his destiny. Writing about Bates in later years, Cash seemed somewhat perplexed at his boss's generosity. But a survey of Memphis newspapers of the time reveals that he was one of the city's visionaries who pushed the urban community forward by merging its segregated worlds and encouraging young people toward their goals. A Catholic who was firmly among the city's elite, Bates served in meaningful civic organizations, organized citywide youth programs, and taught salesmanship classes to black Memphians through the Negro Chamber of Commerce. At the time Bates took Cash under his wing, he was part of a committee evaluating the city's zoning laws.

Crossing KWEM's threshold on Bates's dime, Cash was fulfilling something of an initiation rite for the region's promising musicians. Solid senders Howlin' Wolf, Sonny Boy Williamson, and Junior Parker had rocked its studio in the late 1940s, blaring their blues to the wilds of Arkansas, the streets of Memphis, and the cotton fields of Mississippi. And they were followed by white talent, such as guitarist Scotty Moore's hillbilly band, The Starlite Wranglers, the pioneering rockabilly group Johnny Burnette Rock 'n' Roll Trio, and Elvis Presley. The deal was this: find a sponsor, get some airtime. The arrangement lured dozens to KWEM's door.

The station's indiscriminate tastes hardly dulled Cash's and the boys' excitement at their new opportunity, a fifteen-minute slot on Saturday afternoons. At home, Cash dragged out his old recorder and calmly showed Vivian how to operate it so she could tape the show. Down at the studio, though, Cash was all nerves. Perhaps imagining Mr. Bates at home listening, or fretting about the band's tendency to veer off the rhythm, Cash tentatively introduced to their listeners the set of three songs they had worked up: "Wide Open Road," "One More Ride," and "Belshazzar."

When Grant claimed that the Johnny Cash sound was born back in his den when their electric guitar, bass, and rhythm guitar finally met, he was right in the sense that *a* sound, or the seeds of a sound, had been born. The boom-chicka-boom, that loping rhythm suggestive of a charging locomotive that became the band's trademark was still months away from perfection, and the first radio show bears that out. Cash's driving rhythm guitar distinguishes the performances, while Perkins's playing jingles in and out of earshot, hardly the alluring bell that it would become. Still suffering the jitters, Cash's breath all but eluded him when he launched into a stuttering plug for Home Equipment's Cool-Glo Awnings and asked for listeners to send in their musical requests on cards and letters. Cash recalled receiving exactly one reply.

The show aired for three months during 1954, until the band's live perform-ance schedule began claiming more of its time. "John needed the money [from the live appearances] dreadfully," says Grant, "and the radio show didn't pay anything, so it just sort of went away as our popularity gained a little momentum."

~

Grant's home at 4199 Nakomis Avenue, where the boys seem to have practiced more than anywhere else, was in almost every sense suburban and remains so today. Constructed with tan brick and a carport on the side, it was nestled in among leafy oak trees in east Memphis. It was far removed from the city's bustling downtown and even farther from the modest white neighborhoods northeast of downtown where Cash and his family members had settled. The Nakomis house sat a block away from the pastoral Audubon Park with its golf courses, tennis courts, and within a half-mile of the smart neighborhood where the newly-famous Elvis Presley would move his family in 1956.

But in 1954, Elvis was still conjuring his talents in an apartment across from the city's Lauderdale Courts housing projects, while bluesmen such as Bukka White and Furry Lewis were scratching out rhythm in splintered old shacks behind Beale Street. This diverse and wonderful music churned to life in the sweat and grit of a squat mid-South inner city, while the Johnny Cash sound—so associ-ated with the poor white experience—was nurtured and polished in suburban-like grace.

Such were the juxtapositions and contradictions of Memphis, Tennessee. It was a city of black and white, rich and poor, rural and urban, powerful and weak, refined and coarse. Yet the opposing worlds mingled, necessitating polite veneers of tolerance and planting the seeds of public integration. This was particularly true of the black and white worlds, which were pushed together by the postwar years' dynamic economic change and broader world view. Caught up in this convergence was Cash, whose move into the recording world cannot be fully understood without considering Memphis' uneasy interracial marriage.

From the moment the first wagon loads of cotton lumbered onto Memphis's cobblestone streets in the early nineteenth century, the city's reliance on a black underclass was sealed. Black slaves produced the white fluffy crop on behalf of the landed barons all around the mid-South, and Memphis profited immensely by distributing it to the world. Even with the end of slavery, the arrangement remained the same, although many poor whites elbowed into the flow as sharecropping burgeoned. Each spring, starting in 1931, while cotton leaves unfurled in mid-South fields, Memphis took on the air of Mardi Gras. The Memphis fathers proclaimed Cotton Carnival, beckoning whites to celebrate the bounty created on black backs. Businesses closed, children dropped their books and tablets, and parties abounded. "Black people were not entirely excluded, however," historians Margaret McKee and Fred Chisenhall wryly noted in their 1981 book *Beale Black and Blue*. "They were recruited to pull floats and to lead horses and mules that pulled other floats. Black women were hired to sit on cotton bales on Main Street, bandannas tied around their heads, looking like the 'aunties' and 'mammies' of slavery times. And well-built young blacks, dressed in scarlet breeches and naked to the waist, acted as attendants to the white man who was king."

In the wake of the First World War, black men and women in Mississippi, Arkansas, and other southern states began to tire of the aristocracy's collective heel digging into their shoulders. They dreamed of escape to the wage jobs of the cities, far away from the midday sun and the landowner who often cheated his sharecroppers with cooked books and unbalanced scales. Memphis was the first stop for many of those migrants, and between 1920 and 1930, they helped drive the city's remarkable population growth (162,000 in 1920 to 253,000 in 1930). One of those migrants was the black novelist Richard Wright, who arrived while still a teen in the mid-1920s. Like any country boy discovering the city, Wright was struck by the towering buildings and faceless crowds. Entranced at first by the "urbanity" of the white Memphians he met in his job, Wright soon stumbled hard into the white elite's utter blindness to the black spirit. The white man's cruelty and indifference privately enraged this new resident and foretold the racial violence that flared around the sanitation-workers strike in Memphis forty years later, a protest that was the backdrop for the assassination of Martin Luther King, Jr. Wright and his friends who worked in his building could only whisper their speculation about white lives and motives, he wrote in his memoir *Black Boy*. "But under all our talk floated a latent sense of violence; the whites had drawn a line over which we dared not step and we accepted that line because our bread was at stake. But within our boundaries we, too, drew a line that included our right to bread regardless of the indignities or degradations involved in getting it. If a white man had sought to keep us from obtaining a job, or enjoying the rights of citizenship, we would have bowed silently to his power. But if he had sought to deprive us of a dime, blood might have been spilt." Such resolve may have steeled many a black Memphian from the city's cruelty.

In the late 1940s, long after Wright had moved away from Memphis and while Cash was still in an Arkansas high school, Memphis still clung nervously to its rigid segregation. However, the rising tide of black economic prosperity began to blur those lines of division. Memphis had wandered along through decades of assumptions: that black smiles meant contentment, that rural immigrants cheerfully worked for dismal wages, and that the poor rarely aspired to worlds beyond their ramshackle city neighborhoods. However, when blacks acquired cash to spend and were lured away from menial tasks by the offer of higher-paying factory jobs in the North, white Memphis raised its eyebrow.

The city slowly awoke to black power, an awakening that deeply and publicly manifested itself in two institutions: radio and records. The implementation of an all-black radio format in 1949 by two white men who owned and operated WDIA was a deep public bow to black Memphis (as well as a way to sustain listenership as whites flocked to television). City broadcasters had earlier thrown crumbs to the black community in the form of one or two black-oriented shows during their programming week (including Dewey Phillips's rhythm-and-blues-infused *Red, Hot and Blue* program on WHBQ). But WDIA's owner John Pepper and manager Bert Ferguson sensed that advertisers and black listeners would follow the station *en masse* if it launched a day-long programming schedule for the black men and women of Memphis. Their station aired black-oriented public-affairs programs, black music and, perhaps most importantly, black voices. Educator and journalist Nat D. Williams, up-and-coming bluesman B.B. King, comedian and singer Rufus Thomas, and high-flying disc jockey Maurice "Hot Rod" Hulbert herded the black audience to WDIA. Within two years, it was the highest-rated station in Memphis, paving the way to black domination of the airwaves in Memphis, as well as black ownership in the Memphis radio market later on. Richard Wright would never have imagined elite white Memphis taking to the economic dance floor with black Memphis, albeit on drastically unequal footing.

If blacks actually bought detergent, mayonnaise, soup, and coffee, as WDIA's bursting advertising coffers confirmed, any entrepreneur could also see that they must be buying records too. The big record companies in the 1920s and 1930s had marketed cut-rate blues and jazz records to black buyers, but during the Depression that part of the business fell by the wayside, a victim of small profit margins. In the late 1940s, small independent labels such as King in Cincinnati, Chess in Chicago, and Modern/RPM in Los Angeles had emerged to fill the demand in the marketplace by recording black-appeal artists such as Muddy Waters, John Lee Hooker, and Bull Moose Jackson.

By 1949, when WDIA made its historic programming shift, no legitimate studio in Memphis had stepped up to record discs for the black audience. But when the station announced its preeminence among the Bluff City's radio outlets in 1950, a white man from Florence, Alabama, was thinking hard about it. Another postwar migrant to Memphis (though firmly in the middle class, unlike many of the sons and daughters of Dyess), Sam C. Phillips worked for radio station WREC, where he set up remote broadcasts of big bands from the terrace room of the Peabody Hotel, the *grande dame* of the city's hotels. Twenty-six years old in 1949, married, and the father of two sons, Phillips had lived and worked in Memphis since 1945, long enough to determine that the disparate classes and races in the city could make music together.

Phillips' penetrating eyes and measured confidence captivated women, and he could make men feel as if he saw inside them. Artists who recorded with him— even those who knew Phillips had fleeced them of their royalties—grudgingly admired him. They knew that if they intrigued him, he would push them deep into their own beings to find and retrieve the pure nucleus of their own music. Phillips was a believer in men and undoubtedly a believer in himself. But he was most importantly a wily and dogged entrepreneur. One did not need to possess divine vision to see in the late 1940s that black people in Memphis and across the South were underserved; one needed only the courage to breach the walls of segregation and serve them. Phillips knew blacks mobbed around WDIA; he knew blacks soaked up the hot rhythms on Dewey Phillips's show on WHBQ. He needed only to turn on WDIA to hear the live performances of B.B. King, Sonny Boy Williamson, or Bobby Bland or to peek into the weekly amateur shows at the Palace Theater on Beale Street to be assured that Memphis popped with riveting, though generally unrecorded, black talent. If blacks had their own radio station, Phillips may have wondered, why not their own studio?

He shared such musings with Marion Keisker, his right-hand woman during his early endeavors to record. "He would talk about his idea that he had," Keisker told Presley biographer Peter Gurlanick, "this dream, I suppose, to have a facility where black people could come and play their own music, a place where they would feel free and relaxed to do it."

It's not that blacks had nowhere to record in Memphis; black rhythm and blues artists had taped their stuff in bandleader Tuff Green's city home, at the YMCA, and at WDIA, where B.B. King recorded his first sides. But when Phillips pulled open the blinds of his Memphis Recording Service in January of 1950, blacks found opportunity in a proper studio in Memphis for the first time. Planted in his cramped control room, which towered above the studio floor like a pulpit, Phillips recorded the cream of Memphis's black talent (Howlin' Wolf, B.B. King, and others), sending their incandescent performances to Chess Records and Modern/RPM.

Now flourishing at 706 Union Avenue was a black-and-white collaboration not seen in the Memphis recording world since the big labels stopped lugging their lathes and microphones into town twenty years earlier. Phillips exorcized his artists' inhibitions, cajoling them, loving them, and berating them, all in order to capture the sound that came from the deep. At once their taskmaster and their cheerleader, he guided them toward their two-minute version of perfect soul. "You didn't get out of the studio until you got it right," noted R&B pianist Rosco Gordon. "He's the best, I tell you he's the best. He generated enthusiasm and energy."

Choosing finally to hold on to the music he recorded rather than send it to other labels, Phillips unveiled his own Sun Records in 1952. Burnt-yellow sunbeams, a circle of musical notes along the outer rim, and a bold notation of the record's hometown adorned the Sun labels. Those round stickers pasted on the gleaming black discs were virtual animation, a vibrant, startling contrast to the staid labels of RCA Victor, Columbia, King, and Chess. Sun's roster also proved dramatically different, studded as it was with the astonishing Little Junior Parker, Dr. Isaiah Ross, Little Milton Campbell, and others. It would become profitable, too, when Phillips began recording white artists with greater frequency in 1954. Of course, Elvis Presley, who embodied the musical Babylon that was Memphis, was Phillips's prize catch. But he also invited a mixed array of other white artists (Carl Perkins, Jerry Lee Lewis, Charlie Rich among them) who in time replaced black voices at Sun.

Cash soon followed Presley to Sun, but it's likely that neither he nor Presley would have had his first studio forum without Phillips's persistence in recording black talent. The black artists provided Phillips with the means to form his own label and then jump into the far more lucrative white market. And though Cash's music, unlike Presley's, was bereft of the tactile influence of black figures, he clearly inherited the legacy of the B.B. Kings, Bobby Blands, and Ike Turners of the mid-South who inspired Phillips to form Sun Records, and became among the first mid-South musicians recording in Memphis to achieve any sort of national notoriety in the 1950s. Without them, one could safely argue, no Sun label would have existed, and Johnny Cash, Marshall Grant, and Luther Perkins would have been just another Memphis trio pulling guitars at family reunions until their hair turned gray.

Grant claims it was he who suggested going to Phillips. Across the basement one evening, perhaps amid chat about approaching KWEM or their handful of public appearances, he told the guys it was time to think about recording. They all knew about Elvis Presley, "the kid" they called him, who had ventured from his Alabama Avenue home around the time of Cash's discharge from the air force to record "That's Alright Mama" for Sun Records. The black man's song in the cocky white boy's voice bounced around the Memphis airwaves all summer in 1954, tempting many young musicians around town to rattle the glass doors of the Memphis Recording Service.

If it was Grant with the idea to record, then it was Cash who seized upon that idea. Still attending radio school when he wasn't selling for Home Equipment, he often passed Phillips's storefront recording service on his way downtown for classes. Driving in his new Plymouth down the regal stretch of Union Avenue, past well-scrubbed storefronts, stately office buildings, prosperous churches, and nicely manicured homes, he began in late 1954 to stop at the plain brick building to seek an appointment with Phillips. But Phillips, now busy with the ramifications of Elvis, was never in his office. In a 1980 interview with Peter Guralnick, Cash said it was his challenge to worm his way into the studio.

"It became a fight," he said. "Finally one day I was sitting on the stoop just as he came to work, and I stood up and said, 'I'm John Cash, and I've got my guitar, and I want you to hear me play.' And he said, 'Well, come on in.'

"I sang two or three hours for him, everything I knew—Hank Snow, Ernest Tubb, Flatt and Scruggs (I remember singing 'I'm Gonna Sleep with One Eye Open from Now On'). I even sang 'I'll Take You Home Again Kathleen'—just to give him an idea of what I liked."

Cash told interviewers that he'd first cast himself as a gospel singer and that during that first meeting, he offered Phillips gospel, breaking out his composition "Belshazzar." But Phillips blanched, flatly telling Cash that gospel didn't sell. In later years, when Phillips took his turn to recreate his first meeting with Cash for interviewers, he recalled the young man's disappointment in his response as well as his obvious trepidation. "He was timid and afraid at that time," said Phillips, "and I am very certain very uncertain about himself. He said he knew I had recorded a young singer named Elvis Presley and he wanted me to do the same for him. . . . We sat around in my studio—it was so small that we had to move things around to get in—and discussed what he wanted to do. He mentioned the poems and other tales of his youth and promised to begin writing."

Outtake recordings released in recent decades confirm that Cash alone first gained entrance to Sam's sonic laboratory. Solo with his guitar, perhaps on the first visit or on subsequent visits by himself, he recorded at least five numbers of his own creation: "Wide Open Road" (which he recorded for release in 1955), "You're My Baby (Little Woolly Booger)," "Show Me the Green," and two takes on "My Treasure."

The vocals he laid down on Phillips's tape sounded much more mature than his twenty-two years. His range was limited to say the least, and he skidded off tempo from time to time, but his sonorous timbre and self-assuredness dominated those recordings. What he lacked in natural vocal talent, he made up for in attitude, an attitude that Phillips believed he could sell. "There was something about this guy that innately brought you closer to wanting to hear what he had to say to you," explained Phillips in 1997.

Phillips often said that he searched for the spirit in music, the magical and timeless essence of human emotion. He once summed up this quest so beautifully when he described Howlin' Wolf's voice as "where the soul of a man never dies." Never had he been so eloquent, not even in his sermons on Elvis. But he once said something that suggested he'd found Howlin' Wolf's kin in John Cash. Speaking about Cash in the late 1960s, when there were few solo artists as popular as him, Phillips touted the sturdiness of the singer's message in terms usually reserved for the Wolf. "It has borne out that the countenance of this man was right many, many, many years before most of us could believe it," proclaimed Phillips, reaching into his mystical bag for words. "Because . . . his message is possibly now more meaningfully accepted than it was in the beginning. In my opinion, the soul of the spirit of man never dies in his context." Phillips had spoken—with benefit of hindsight, of course.

When Cash returned to the studio with Perkins and Grant in the early spring of 1955, they meant to reel off something for commercial release. They'd been working up Cash's song "Hey Porter," one of his air-force specials about a man giddy with joy as his train glides back to the South. Rather like a character in a sequel to "Folsom Prison Blues," Cash's boy has escaped whatever chains confined him outside his native land, found his train, and shed his blues. "Hey Porter"'s spare, shuffling arrangement highlighted by Perkins's nervous guitar solo and Grant's steady train-a-rolling bass found a comfortable place next to the rockabilly that Sun was churning out with Elvis. But Grant recalls that its economical drama was almost spoiled in their basement sessions when they attempted to reach beyond their abilities and "improve" it. "We couldn't change it. And I'm just damn lucky and thankful that we couldn't. And as time went along, we tried to change it, and we couldn't change it. And why? We weren't musicians. We were two mechanics and an appliance salesman, and we couldn't change it."

As time would prove, Cash and his musicians were set free by their limitations. There was a phenomenal potency in their limited abilities. Grant's bass playing, learned in a matter of days, popped so hard you'd think he was slapping his towel on the back of your neck. And Perkins's electric guitar solos, albeit elemental and halting, pierced the brain. Together, Grant and Perkins created a second perform- ance that punched through a static-plagued AM radio or a scratchy 45-rpm single disc. Stated plainly, Cash needed that second performance. Although his voice was unique and cut through the rabble of Eddy Arnold–type crooners and nasally honky-tonk styles of the mid-1950s, it was ill-equipped to carry alone a recorded performance for an audience on the verge of selling its soul to rock and roll.

Phillips got a take on "Hey Porter" on March 22, 1955, but he didn't hear another useable cut to make a single. This time with the band, Cash had again attempted "Wide Open Road," but to no avail. Grant recalls that the men argued for "Belshazzar" or one of the other gospel numbers they knew, but Phillips told them where to go: back home to write another song.

Cash wasn't used to writing on demand, but back at the house on Tutwiler with Vivian's due date approaching, Cash labored at the kitchen table. He chugged his coffee and burned down cigarette after cigarette as if he were back at the radio intercept controls. Inspired by Memphis disc jockey Eddie Hill's trademark "we're gonna squall and ball and climb the walls," recalled Cash, he came up with "Cry, Cry, Cry" in two weeks. Back in the studio, Cash and the band turned in a mild, loping performance that seemed pedestrian next to the energetic "Hey Porter." But "Cry, Cry, Cry" nonetheless took the A side of the first single. Perkins never once ventured from his bass strings, denying the song his zesty flavor, so Cash enhanced the recording with a chucka-chucka percussive effect that he produced by thread- ing a folded sheet of paper between the strings up around the neck frets. The instrumentation was cautious and the lyrics cloying, but Cash's surging vocals redeemed the song. They were like murky river water cresting the banks.

Billing his new artists as Johnny Cash and the Tennessee Two, Sam released "Cry, Cry Cry" on June 21, 1955, and a corps of Memphis deejays (including Bob Neal on WMPS, Sleepy-Eyed John on WHHM, and Dewey Phillips on WHBQ), which Phillips had come to rely upon to debut his records, picked it up. By mid- August, they had wheeled it onto the Memphis sales charts, where it remained throughout the fall.

Cash had expected Phillips to release the single weeks earlier than he did, so he paced around home worrying that his chances for musical success were slipping away with every day of Phillips's inaction. Cash's late sister Reba often recalled that when Phillips finally moved, she saw her brother charging down the street to her home waving the record in the air. She and her husband, Donzell, didn't have a record player, so they knocked on the door of a neighbor who did. As the distinctive label rotated on the turntable, Cash caught his breath and grinned.

Cash probably knew little of it, but as his record poked around the Memphis charts, Phillips was negotiating a deal with Colonel Tom Parker and RCA-Victor that would turn loose Elvis Presley and bring Cash to the top of the Sun ranks. On November 22, 1955, Phillips accepted thirty-five thousand dollars for Elvis's contract. Within a week, "Cry, Cry, Cry" crawled onto the national country charts, symbolizing Cash's ascendancy on Union Avenue. The record vanished from the charts in a matter of days, but a torch had been passed in Memphis.

~~~~~

Sun scholars place the recording of "Cry, Cry, Cry" sometime in May of 1955, the same month that Cash and Vivian's first daughter, Rosanne, was born. Vivian was delighted with her new daughter, and judging by photos of Cash and little Rosanne taken in the mid-1950s, he, too, could not have been more pleased.

Although nobody knew it when Rosanne was born, or even after "Cry, Cry, Cry" flitted on and off the national charts in November, the life of the young Cash family would soon be dramatically rearranged.

~~~~~

TWO

~

A FIERY RING
1956-1967

5

FAME

When Sam Phillips released "Cry, Cry, Cry" in June of 1955, he introduced Cash to Bob Neal, a WMPS morning disc jockey and owner of the Bob Neal Record Shop located in the lobby of Warner Theatre on Main Street in Memphis. It's not enough to say that Neal was a disc jockey; he was a radio personality, one of the Bluff City's biggest. And when he dropped by Roy Cash's home one night to hear Cash and the Tennessee Two, the Cash family knew the boy was coming up on something big.

Always flashing a fifty-dollar smile, the portly Neal had started promoting and emceeing country-music package shows around Memphis in the early 1950s, a nice sideline considering he could plug the concerts on his country-music deejay show. Within about a 150-mile radius of Memphis, Bob Neal's name was golden and could guarantee a substantial turnout in the hamlets his artists visited.

In December of 1954, Neal had taken over the management of Elvis Presley, but with the coming of summer in 1955, Col. Tom Parker (Eddy Arnold's former manager) was elbowing in on Neal and Presley's relationship. Parker would soon pry the young sensation from the disc jockey's grip, but Neal had insurance. With Sam Phillips, he had established a booking agency,

Stars Incorporated, to exclusively book Sun Records artists. Cash and the Tennessee Two was one of Neal's first signings, and by June of 1956 he would also be the singer's personal manager.

In the summer of 1955, Neal dispatched Cash and the band to small towns where they peered out at audiences in high-school gyms, ramshackle clubs, and store openings. In conversation with Cash biographer Christopher Wren, Ray Cash placed one of the first shows in Etowa, Arkansas, just north of Dyess. "John came by our house in Dyess with Luther and Marshall, and I drove over with them in his green Plymouth . . . ," he said. "The show was in an old wood building, in a little old room next door to a crummy beer joint or café. I'd say there was forty people, maybe fifty, not more I'm sure. I think they charged fifty cents for adults and twenty-five cents for children.

"They put on a little funny act onstage. Johnny would pull out his comb and run it through his hair. And Marshall would throw the comb on the floor and pull out a blank pistol and shoot at it as if it had lice. The audience, they seemed to enjoy it. John would imitate Elvis too."

There were plenty of chances to perfect the Elvis imitation, a farce that would remain part of Cash's act into the 1960s. From the summer of 1955, Cash and Elvis were touring together frequently, and jostling playfully for the lion's share of the spotlight, says Roy Cash, Jr., who often tagged along on shows with his uncle. "Elvis would tease Johnny about being older than him, about him being the 'old man.' He was three years older than Elvis, and Johnny called him the 'shaky kid' or something like that. Looking back and thinking about it now, it was just kind of a surreal image: Elvis and Johnny on stage together poking fun at each other, in a little town of maybe ten thousand people where there was maybe two or three hundred people there watching the show."

In August, Neal dispatched Cash with Presley on a short mid-South package tour that Webb Pierce was supposed to headline, but the crowds demanded Elvis and for most of the tour he closed each show. The next time Cash took to the road with Elvis, in September in Texas, the Memphis Flash was headlining. It was Cash's first venture into the verdant fields of the Lone Star State, where fans had gone berserk over Presley earlier in the year. The reaction to Cash, whose first Sun release had been barely heard outside Memphis, was far more subdued: polite and appreciative, but never as calamitous as Elvis' audiences.

Enthusiasm over Cash swelled in early 1956 in the wake of "Folsom Prison Blues," his air-force chestnut. The band had auditioned the song at Sun with tape rolling the same day they produced the final cut on "Hey Porter," but the results had been ghastly. Perkins's fingers trampled over the strings, and Cash's vocals modulated between his solemn bass baritone and a frightful Elvis imitation. They revisited the song in July before leaving on the Webb Pierce tour, finally pulling out a take that Sam Phillips could sell.

It was Perkins's guttural introduction to "Folsom Prison Blues" (much improved on the final take) that told listeners that another unique sound was on the rise in Memphis. If a hangman hummed before his gruesome job, he would sound something like the deep throbbing of Perkins's opening. Cash's grim narration followed, bringing to mind a man who'd been imprisoned for fifty years.

There was nothing like it in popular music in 1956. Compared to Presley's exuberance, Perry Como's urbane whispers, and the Drifters crooning harmonies, Cash and the Tennessee Two's "Folsom Prison Blues" was rope burn. Even in country music, where the honky-tonk stylings of Porter Wagoner and Ray Price still fended off the rise of the highly polished Nashville Sound, it was more sorrowful and rougher hewn than anything heard in decades. "Cry, Cry, Cry" had leaned toward the rockabilly sound that Phillips was peddling with Presley and a herd of other minor artists on his label, but "Folsom Prison Blues," so jagged and raw, was an unflinching look at an ugly place.

Phillips plugged the disc in the country market, where the disc jockeys and their listeners apparently responded to the freshness of it, hoisting it up the *Billboard* chart in February of 1956. And the concert crowds, which in 1955 had saved their love for Presley, began to buzz, says Marshall Grant. "There was times that we were so different and awkward or whatever you want to call us in the first part of our career, especially after the first two records," he says. "We would go out on the stage, and people didn't know what to think about us. They recognized that style and sound we had, that boom-chicka-boom-chicka thing, but they were sort of mesmerized with us. There's been times when we'd do maybe a song or two songs that we'd recorded, and people would stand there and look at you with the mouth open because they hadn't never heard anything like us, because there hadn't been anything like us. A lot of that was our inability and not our ability. There's been times when we would finish the song, and there was no crowd reaction, and then maybe somebody would start clapping. I remember on a couple of dates when we'd do our last song—whatever that may be and at that point it was mostly 'Folsom Prison Blues'—and we'd leave the stage and there wasn't nobody clapping, but by the time we got off the stage and sometimes got to the dressing room, why they would start clapping and it would build and build and build and build as if they were saying, 'Well, we don't know what to think, but we like them.' They would literally call us back for an encore when we started with nothing, and [we] wound up with a standing ovation."

The Cash family fluttered over John's good fortunes, especially younger brother Tommy, who'd moved to Memphis with his parents, and nephew Roy, both of whom walked taller in their high schools with each new Cash release. "The family was ecstatic," recalls Roy Jr. "We were absolutely convinced that what did happen was going to happen. We were convinced that this was a major event. I can remember my dad [saying], 'He's going to be as famous as Ernest Tubb or Hank Williams.'" Roy Sr. of course, had never stopped believing.

On Tutwiler Avenue, Vivian wasn't so sure. She rightly feared Cash's rising fame, observing the snuff queens who gathered ringside hoping to catch her husband's eye and impatiently enduring the absences that lengthened with each tour. With little Rosanne crawling at her feet and pregnant with their second daughter, Kathy, Vivian had wept when Cash had left on an extended tour for the first time. Nervous and sad, too, he had tried to calm her as he walked through the apartment checking and rechecking every window lock. But she was inconsolable. Vivian would have traded away the tour's payday just to have him home that night and the nights that followed. But she couldn't, so she relied on Grant's wife, Etta, and her neighbor Pat Isom for company and help with the children. In the evening, Tommy and Roy Jr. showed up to play bridge and munch corn chips and bean dip with her. Their aunt never liked to be at home alone, so if Etta wasn't staying over, the teens bunked at Tutwiler for the night and scampered off to school in the morning.

Roy doubted Vivian would ever cozy to her husband's new career, even with the fame and fortune it promised to deliver: "She did not get all caught up in the entertainer's life at all," he says looking back. "She would have preferred him to be home working a nine-to-five job doing almost anything else. She was not one to let anybody know that she was Johnny Cash's wife or go out socially or do anything like that. She wanted an at-home husband to help her take care of her kids. She'd go to shows if they were local, but she didn't do any traveling."

Cash left home yet again in November of 1955, following another path that Presley had cut out of Memphis: to radio's *Louisiana Hayride*. Based in Shreveport's Municipal Auditorium and produced by radio station KWKH, the *Hayride* rode the station's fifty thousand watts of power straight on up the Mississippi River and as far west as California. From time to time, the Columbia Broadcasting System (CBS) and Armed Forces Radio picked up portions of the program and beamed it to even wider audiences. As Elvis Presley would attest, the program could be a launching pad.

Cash debuted on November 13, 1955, and a few months later, when "Folsom Prison Blues" took off, he began bragging that he'd soon steal Presley's top billing on the show. In letters to air-force buddies, he told of audiences that poured in from Louisiana and Texas and begged him for encores. Indeed, with every new appearance, the crowd stomped and hooted for this man, who to please them forsook the somber cloak he wore on records for a Presley-like swagger. Alas, he never had the chance to seize Presley's limelight: the rock-and-roll sensation soon rocketed out of the barn-dance world. Saddled with a one-year *Hayride* contract, Cash was left to bounce back and forth between Shreveport and Dallas, where he often appeared on KLCN's *Big D Jamboree*.

Though he'd never electrify an audience in the Presley tradition, Cash was nonetheless the next big thing on the Southern circuit. He must have sensed this status because he soon quit his job at Home Equipment, and the boastful tone of his letters to veteran airmen grew. "I'm fixin' to buy me a big Martin, nearly new with a heavy leather case both for $90," he crowed in one of those notes. "That's a right nice deal and see if it is. That's durn good for a newcomer like me. Right?"

"Folsom Prison Blues" had charged into country music's top ten by the spring of 1956, paving the way for Cash's next step up: to Nashville's *Grand Ole Opry*. The big daddy of country-music broadcasts, the *Opry* basked in a fifty-thousand-watt radio home at WSM and a National Broacasting Company (NBC) network hookup. Unlike its poorer cousin the *Louisiana Hayride*, the *Opry* hurtled into the populous Northeast and sat at the core of the bustling country-music business.

Artists who started on the *Hayride* coveted a move to the *Opry* and Nashville, where the promise of top-flight recording studios and big-time concert promoters awaited them.

It's hard to say how much Cash yearned for status in Nashville. He'd visited the *Opry* on his Dyess High School senior trip to Nashville in 1950, but in later years he never dwelled on the visit other than to recall his setting eyes for the first time on the 27-year-old Valerie June Carter. Cash told Ben A. Green of the *Nashville Banner*, who covered his first night performing in the Ryman Auditorium (July 14, 1956), that he was fulfilling a dream. But the encounter with the *Opry* was any-thing but dreamlike. He'd been uneasy with the show from the very moment he met *Opry* manager Jim Denny, who was one of the most powerful men in Nashville. Denny controlled who sang on the *Opry* as well as a powerful booking agency and the song-publishing company Cedarwood, which supplied many Nashville artists and labels with material.

Cash was understandably respectful of the man and dared not peep when he had to wait two hours for an audience with him. "Finally, he told me to come in," he told *Rolling Stone* in 1992. "He didn't even say, 'Sit down,' but I finally sat down across from him. He was busy with his papers, but finally he looked at me and said, 'What makes you think you belong on the *Grand Ole Opry*?' And I said, 'Well, I got a record that is in the bestsellers now, and I think those people know it and would like to hear me sing it.' And he said, 'Okay, be here Saturday night.' He didn't ask me, he told me. 'Be here Saturday night, I'll put you on for a song.'"

The *Opry* cast and audience were unaccustomed to the kind of show Cash brought with him. He had three instruments, which were two fewer than most country aggregations carried, and a throbbing, extroverted beat, while on the *Opry* the beat was more implied than anything else. With Nashville reporter Green, Cash was apologetic of his sound, fearful, perhaps, that he'd be branded rock and roll and cast out of the *Opry* realm. After all, plenty of the performers that night had felt the pinch of Elvis Presley, who seemed to be dampening country music's com-mercial prospects. Who knew how they would react to another Memphis tiger? Blinking with each camera flash, Cash pledged to Green that he was country all the way. "The fact [that] some of the songs have definite rhythm beat does not make them rock and roll songs," he argued. Nor, he added in earnest, should his imita-tion of Elvis on the road be construed as anything but parody.

That night Cash delivered his new song "I Walk the Line," and, according to the reporter, a "veritable tornado of applause rolled back." Cash would remember the torrential reaction, but he would also remember the night with pronounced unease. A conspiracy to trap Cash in the *Opry*, as if he were an unsuspecting groom, seemed to lurk behind each dressing-room door: "Don't follow Elvis down that road, don't break from the norm," the men and women seemed to be saying. "Stay here and we'll fix you up right." Cash could be the *Opry*'s Elvis.

"He'll be every bit as good as Elvis Presley," yelped an *Opry* source who wasn't identified in Green's article. "Probably better, and he'll last a whole lot longer. He has sincerity, he has bombast, he has a tone, and he carries to the rafters, the top row hears him. He'll be better than Presley because Johnny's a true country singer, and Presley isn't and never has been. Presley's a rock and roller and has sung only once at the *Opry* and that time as a visitor."

Walking out into the Nashville darkness after the show, Cash may have sensed his unease with the whole experience. "A lot of people supported me coming to Nashville . . .," he said in later years. "And then there were some who would make it a point to let me hear the remarks they were saying as I walked by. It was the same thing they were calling Elvis: 'white nigger.' And you know, when I left that night, I said, 'I don't wanna go back to this place anymore. I don't have to put up with that crap.'"

Cash, of course, returned to the *Opry* many times throughout the late 1950s, only he held the program at arm's length. He refused to grant it the central place in his career where many thought it should be. In 1948, Eddy Arnold, one of Cash's idols, had bid farewell to the *Opry*, to the utter amazement of fans, artists, and WSM staff. But Arnold's career had transcended the *Opry* at that stage. And Hank Williams' would have too, had his dependence on pills and booze not tethered him to the regular paycheck of weekly barn-dance broadcasts. Whether or not Cash was aware of Arnold's and Williams' relationships with the *Opry*, he quickly made up his mind not to let the radio show define his career.

Instead, the *Opry* enabled his encounters with June Carter, whom he had worshiped since glimpsing her on his high-school trip to the *Opry*. "I really liked what I saw of her from the balcony at the Ryman Auditorium . . . ," Cash would later write of seeing June on that school trip. "She was great. She was gorgeous. She was a star. I was smitten, seriously so." Now an emerging star himself, the

Opry gave Cash an excuse to engage her, and he wasted little time. On the night of his debut, he boldly marched up to June, who was resting backstage between segments, and proclaimed that one day he'd marry her. The entreaty bemused June, and before Cash left that night, she smiled girlishly while Cash crouched next to her for a photograph that somebody took of the two of them. Forty-four years later, June admitted that she, too, was smitten. "I can't remember anything else we talked about, except his eyes," she wrote. "Those black eyes that shone like agates."

Obviously, that first meeting wasn't the end of it. On subsequent visits to the *Opry*, while Vivian was back home in Memphis with one-year-old Rosanne and newborn Kathy, Cash continued to angle for June, whose marriage to country music star Carl Smith was breaking up. Don Davis, a Nashville steel guitarist who'd played on Hank Williams' first recording session in Nashville, was married at the time to June's sister Anita and figured out early that Cash was after his sister-in-law. Davis represented a West Coast publishing firm in Nashville and was pleased when the "Folsom Prison Blues" man expressed interest in a few train songs that he'd pitched to him. However, Davis clued in to Cash's agenda when Cash cheerfully asked to listen to the demos at Davis's house, where June could often be found.

June, despite the attraction she later confessed, brushed aside her married suitor and would soon wed police officer Edwin "Rip" Nix. But over the next five years, she never disappeared from Cash's radar screen; he was always happy to see her.

In 1956, Cash was much more successful at penning hit records than wooing June, as evidenced by the strong and steady rise of the very song he sang on his *Opry* debut, "I Walk the Line." Striding onto the country music charts just days before he took the stage at the Ryman Auditorium, it topped the countdown six weeks later. It was his first number one country hit.

The record was neither the most popular of his career nor the most popular country hit of 1956, despite its six weeks at number one (that distinction belonged to Ray Price's "Crazy Arms"). It wasn't even the first Johnny Cash classic, rolling into record shops and jukeboxes as it did on the heels of his mythic "Folsom Prison Blues." But "I Walk the Line" may well be for many the most memorable Johnny Cash song. And it is certainly the song that ignited the first of four distinct chapters in his epic career, spanning 1956 to 1967.

"I Walk the Line" washed him over the walls of country music and its *Grand Ole Opry* and carried him to the mass audience. Fans beyond the South took notice, pop disc jockeys picked up the record, and New York television producers (fearful that they'd lose another Memphis sensation to Ed Sullivan) began hiring him for guest spots.

Cash wrote the song, he said, the night after his *Louisiana Hayride* debut. He was riding the Texas circuit, where he and other *Hayride* acts filled their nights between Shreveport Saturdays. But like the other important songs he'd selected from his notebook thus far, this one originated in Landsberg, Germany. One night after a shift, the weary radio operator had returned to his billet to discover that someone had been messing around with his Wilcox-Gay tape recorder. When he punched the chubby rewind button and then pressed play, strange sounds moaned in his ear. An unearthly voice blurted what sounded like the word "father." "It just about drove me crazy for a year," said Cash. "I asked everybody I knew if they had fooled around with my tape recorder. I finally found out who did. He had put the tape on upside down and backwards. So when I played it, it was backwards. All he was doing was strumming the chords on the guitar . . . and anyway at the end of the chords, he said, 'Turn it off.' And as it happened, turn it off sounded like 'Father' played backwards. And it sounded like a religious ceremony or something. And it never got out of my mind and I never got that chord progression out of my mind—from E to A to D to A to E to B7th back to E. It broke all the musical laws in history, but I couldn't forget it."

Fast forward to a crisp late afternoon in East Texas during the autumn of 1955—Cash said Gladewater, while Marshall Grant placed the events in Longview. Killing time before an evening performance, Cash was noodling with his backward chord progressions and Grant was plucking on his bass. "I was making these little runs on this bass, trying to learn [the instrument]," says Grant. "I played with it all the time. Every minute I had, I played with this bass. I went 'boom, boom, boom, boom.' I did that three, four times trying to learn these, what I called, runs. And John came over with his guitar and said, 'What was that you was doing right then?' And I said, 'I'm trying to learn how to play this big S.O.B.,' and laughed about it. And he said, 'No, no, I'm not talking about trying to learn that, I'm talking about those little runs. Do that again. Can you do that again?' I said, 'I don't know. Forgot what I did.' He said, 'You know, you went with this "boom, boom, boom."' I said,

'Oh.' And I did it again. And I went through several chords and he said, 'Now do that again and come back to E. Just keep it going.' And he started slapping his old guitar. And he come up real close, and we just kept the rhythm going. He said, 'I keep a close watch on this heart of mine.' And he said, 'Don't ever forget that. . . . Tonight we're gonna write a song.'"

Cash and Grant had nailed the song's introduction, but its lyrics were inspired by Carl Perkins, their Sun Records *compadre* and frequent touring partner. Married men, they'd been talking about chasing women on the road, but Cash (just a five-month veteran of the concert circuit and still more than six months away from making a play for June) said he never ran around on Vivian. "Not me buddy, I walk the line," he said. The claim jarred Perkins. "There's your title," the rockabilly ace said. A paean to fidelity, "I Walk the Line" traveled from Texas back to Memphis with Cash and the Tennessee Two, where they worked it up for Sam Phillips, who recorded it in the Spring of 1956.

Whether Cash knew it or not, he had cooked up a song for Phillips's taste. It had the aroma of something he would gobble up; as elemental as a heartbeat and with a meaty hook line and a sentient human voice that would rise from the soda-shop din of the 1950s. And he hummed. Nobody with his bass baritone hummed in an introduction, yet curling from his gut, the hum accentuated the seriousness of his pledge: *I keep the ends out for the ties that bind/Because you're mine, I walk the line.*

Cash always said that he recorded a slower version of his composition, one he thought better conveyed his sentiments, and he complained when Phillips rushed out a more energetic take. "I heard it on the radio and I really didn't like it," said Cash later. "And I called up Sam Phillips and asked him *please* not to send out any more records of that song. . . . But he laughed at me. I just didn't like the way it sounded to me. I didn't know I sounded that way, and I didn't like it. I don't know. But he said, 'Let's give it a chance,' and it was just a few days until that's all it took to take off." Once again, Phillips heard what the singer could not hear himself: a spell-binding performance that many would place among the greatest popular songs of the twentieth century.

The record shot Cash's career down a gilded road, but it also confirmed for the moment Sun Record's resilience in the absence of Elvis Presley. With his belief in the marketability of the bare and the stark, Phillips carved out a niche in the country and folk audiences while the major labels placed their bets on polished pop appeal.

It was Phillips's art of "pickin' funk," as Jack Clement put it. A Memphis native, dance instructor, and recent veteran of the U.S. Marines, Clement had hitched up with Sun to help Phillips produce his growing roster, which by the summer of 1956 also included Jerry Lee Lewis, Roy Orbison, and Charlie Rich. Still feeling his way around Phillips' world after a failed venture recording his own artists for his own label, the young Clement couldn't deny that the Alabaman had ignited a powder keg in the Bluff City. But he wasn't yet convinced that Phillips really knew what he was doing. "It was the seat-of-the-pants kind of thing," says Clement. "I thought he was full of shit most of the time, and a lot of times he was. But then sometimes he's not. He was a lot more funky than I was. He wasn't a musician. He'd sung in some groups on bass a little bit and stuff like that. He could carry a tune, but he wasn't really a musician. So he didn't have to care about all that stuff. And he liked the big thumpy kind of sounds where you hear drums but you don't really hear rhythm guitar."

By the time Clement arrived in the midst of "I Walk the Line"'s strong ascent, he could see that Phillips was tiring of the day-to-day recording studio tasks. Burnt out from long days in the control room, he was injecting his Elvis Presley and Johnny Cash money into radio station WHER, an "all-girl" operation designed to net the female market in Memphis the way WDIA had grabbed the black market. With every new day that Clement spent on Union Avenue, Phillips was more and more often on the telephone sweet talking or swearing at distributors and promotion men or spinning big dreams with Memphis scion Kemmons Wilson. Wilson had also invested in WHER and would soon join Phillips in investing in the Holiday Inn motel chain. Clement saw that his boss was sometimes choosing to lounge by the pool rather than come to work, and he often had to send tapes home for Phillips' reaction. "It wasn't that he wasn't interested in what was going on in the studio," says Clement. "He just didn't want to have to be there. He had me by then. I was really the first guy that he sort of turned this stuff over to. He'd been looking for somebody like that, young fool like me, lot of energy." Little by little, Phillips turned over many of the artists to Clement, yet he always made time to listen for the soul that he felt made a record. "He was a lot more into feel than I was," admits Clement. "I was more into machines back then. The players were something to make the machines work."

Despite his pulling away from the grind of recording sessions, Phillips held on to Cash, remaining perched in the recording booth as Cash recorded three additional country smashes: "There You Go," "Train of Love," and "Next in Line." But by early 1957, Clement managed to edge in next to Phillips on Cash's sessions. He finally took sole control in the summer of 1957, supervising while Cash recorded "Home of the Blues," a kind of "Heartbreak Hotel" set to the boom-chicka-boom beat. It was then that Cash saw for the first time Clement's penchant for tinkering. On "Home of the Blues," Clement dubbed drums, piano, and another guitar. The producer was chasing the big sound just like Phillips had, only he employed instruments and voices whereas Phillips achieved his with reverb and emphasis on the beat.

Clement's formula gave Cash his next number one hit, "Ballad of a Teenage Queen." Clement had written the jingly number, about a girl who forsakes fame for her boyhood beau, hoping to record it himself and elbow in on Jerry Lee Lewis's, Johnny Cash's, and Carl Perkins's action. The Memphis papers had even splashed an adoring profile on him, heralding the next big thing out of Phillips' studio. When Clement played his version of "Ballad of a Teenage Queen" for Cash, however, Sun's current big thing asked to record it.

Decades later, Cash distanced himself from "Ballad of a Teenage Queen" and its chiming background vocals when it threatened to clash with his profitable dark image, but Clement claims that Cash was attracted to it from the beginning. "Cash loved it," says Clement. "And he knew the vocal group was going to be there 'cause it was on my record. Mine was kind of a work tape. It was close to being a record. It could have been a record. When Cash said he wanted to cut it, I started hearing numbers chinging in my head: 'Hey, I could make ten thousand dollars or something off that.'"

Phillips would make just as much from the record, but it was he—not Cash, says Clement—who disowned the song because the theme was so out of Cash's realm. "Everybody around the studio, all the girls and everybody was lovin' the thing," says Clement. "But [Sam] talked about that 'til he died. Every time I'd see him, he'd bitch about that. He said he went home and prayed about it. Said, 'Oh Lord, don't make it come to this.' It just wasn't his meat. Well, it was a whole, totally different record. It was a silly song in the first place, bunch of foo-foo singin' on it. But a totally bogus situation. I mean, when girls leave and go to Hollywood, they don't come back to a boy in a candy store. Fairy tale."

Cash's next number, "Guess Things Happen That Way," also spouted from Clement's pen as Clement was increasingly serving up his songs to Cash. In addition to providing repertoire and layering a pop veneer on Cash's records, though, Clement was also reorienting the group away from its reliance on Luther Perkins, at least in the recording studio.

From the beginning, while Cash's acoustic guitar and Grant's bass hammered out the group's trademark rhythm, it fell to Perkins to offer up the only lead picking, a task for which he was minimally prepared. But his licks were immediately recognizable and, in the minds of many, defined the Johnny Cash sound. As long as the people were buying Perkins's infusions, Cash had no choice but to work around him. "Everything was based around Luther Perkins, and a lot of it was his inability to do any better," observes Grant. "We had to fall back to what Luther did because John and I got a little better, but Luther didn't. And that's not taking anything away from him. We got a little better. But everything that we did in the studio was hinged around Luther's ability. But Luther's ability, so to speak, kept us humble."

Clement's addition of voices and instruments freed Cash from the ofttimes clumsy attempts to course his vocals and rhythm in and around Perkins' guitar playing. In Clement's arrangements, the halting Perkins solos often subsided next to tinkling pianos or insistent vocal groups or were eliminated altogether.

As the instrumental humility that Grant says encased Cash's recorded performances faded with Clement's increasing prominence, there was little indication that Cash protested. To the contrary, Phillips' assistant, Marion Keisker, recalled that Cash wanted an even more elaborate sound from the beginning. "Constantly, Johnny wanted to appear with a big brass band," she told interviewer Jerry Hopkins. "And there was constantly a knock down drag out fight to keep it simple."

The departure from the original sound accentuated Perkins' lack of expertise and sometimes engendered impatience with him. If Jack suggested a new lick on a session, recording could bog down while everybody waited for Perkins to learn it. On one outtake recorded toward the end of a long day in the studio, Cash himself scolded him while he fumbled through the introduction and break of "Always Alone," a song composed by Texas writer and singer Ted Daffan. As Perkins and a competing piano kicked off the number, Cash stopped the action. "Wait a minute," he remarked seriously. "You missed a note Luther." After a second muffed start, they made it to the break, but then Cash again interjected like an impatient father: "Luther . . . what are you doin'? . . . What are you doin'? . . . Key of A please . . . Key of A."

"Got it, got it, got it," squeaked Perkins, the chastened child.

Although a fissure developed in the studio between the Phillips sound and the Clement sound, any innovation stopped at the Memphis Recording Service's transom. At the barn dances, on concert stages, and on television, it was the same Johnny Cash sound: just Cash, Perkins, and Grant. But nobody seemed to mind that the shuffling and jingling that marked Cash's latest recordings couldn't be reproduced by the three men when they came through town.

Hank Davis, today a renowned Sun Records scholar, wrote about Cash's show when he saw him in 1958. Although Davis (then a teenager) was comparing each song with the records he had at home in his collection, he expressed no disappointment in the difference. He jotted down notes as he absorbed the show in White Plains, New York: "Finally Cash came out. Looked great. Watched the three of them carefully. Heard the sound but still couldn't see that they were doing anything special. Just playing in unison. Chigga-ching. Chigga-ching. Didn't sound quite as sticky as the records, but still definitely Cash. Luther Perkins looked frozen in place. A lifeless figure, no energy. . . . Marshall Grant was full of energy." Davis further noted that "The Rock Island Line," the folk song popularized by Leadbelly, churned in the three men's arms like a massive train engine and the performance of the gospel-influenced "I Was There When It Happened" came off just like the record. Nothing in Davis's eyes, however, beat the men's "Hey Porter," one song he had never heard due to its spotty distribution in the North. "The guitar lead-in sounded good and when we heard the opening two words we went berserk," he wrote. "'Hey Porter, Hey Porter . . . .' It was worth waiting for. Each of us tried to memorize it on the spot so we could hear it again in our heads later that night."

When Cash landed in communities such as White Plains (a suburb of New York City) it usually meant that Bob Neal had arranged a network television appearance in the Northeast, often on CBS-TV's *The Jimmy Dean Show* or ABC-TV's *The Dick Clark Show*. He and the Tennessee Two had made their first visit to New York in January of 1957 to appear on CBS-TV's *The Jackie Gleason Show*. The sojourn had been much heralded in the *Memphis Press-Scimitar*, framed as another Elvis Presley story.

Gleason, too, believed he was selling another Elvis Presley when Cash debuted on January 19th for the first of ten shows. After a series of comedic sketches (one with guest Jonathon Winters), the portly raconteur, a carnation stuck in his lapel, strutted on stage to introduce Cash. Gleason always gave the impression that the show was pulling him away from the golf course or the clubhouse bar, and despite his hearty introduction of Cash, there's no reason to believe he felt any differently that night with Cash waiting in the wings. "Ladies and gentlemen, I had the pleasure of being the one to introduce Elvis Presley to television," he announced. "And from then on you know what happened. Well, another guy who has just come up from the South . . . we think that he is going to be as big and perhaps maybe bigger than Elvis. He's already a riot down South and I know he's going to take the North tonight. Here he is! Johnny Cash!"

On the sparse stage, Perkins and Marshall struck up "Get Rhythm," which Cash later said he had written for Elvis but kept for himself. In the glare of the overbearing television lights, his greased-down hair shone and the fancy lapel of his black tuxedo jacket sparkled. Appearing utterly confident, his acoustic guitar led the charge of rhythm on a song that would be his closest stab at rockabilly during his entire tenure at Sun. Marshall was chewing gum. Perkins uneasily scratched out a guitar solo and nodded in relief when it is done. The camera panned back to Cash, who was now blinking feverishly. As "Get Rhythm" ended, his eyes rose up to heaven.

He thanked the crowd, shifting and bobbing like a radio operator just freed from an eight-hour shift. As he talked, his arms swung to and fro, his hands slid up and down the guitar, and he clutched at the strap. "Thank you very much folks," he bellowed. "Here's a song which, thanks to you, has been our biggest selling record to date. We hope you enjoy it tonight. It's one called 'I Walk the Line.'"

The stage darkened to accentuate the song's solemn oath. His opening hum expressed his seriousness and beckoned the viewer to listen closely. And although Grant's bass squeaked like a cheap mattress, Cash's face muted it. He stared at the

camera, pleading with it to believe in his sincerity. He would be true despite temptation's persistent clawing. Cash had been performing regularly for only little more
than a year, yet on the *Gleason Show* he showed that he had become an accomplished actor. He delivered the emotion of "I Walk the Line" so well, his eyes closing like a man in rapture, professing his love: *Because you're mine/I walk the line.*

Perhaps Vivian sat at home and wondered if her husband really was walking
the line.

It was a nicer home she and her daughters now occupied. Cash's popularity
meant they could leave the small apartment on Tutwiler for a modest brick house
on Sandy Cove just a few miles away. Situated on a cul-de-sac among young families like their own, Vivian and Cash (when he was home) often joined their neighbors in the middle of the circle after their children had gone to bed. They could
visit with adults, a brief escape from parenting, but still be close enough to watch
their home while the children slept. Very middle class, it must have been a dream
come true for Vivian, albeit a dream cut short by the next tour or a mad dash to a
New York television studio.

If somebody asked Vivian about Cash's whereabouts after he'd leave her for a
new calendar of dates, she'd just say he was off somewhere playing his music,
unsure whether it was Columbus or Cincinnati that weekend. She was weakly
resigned to her husband's career. "She knew that he was driven to do this and there
was not a lot she could do about it," asserts Roy Cash, Jr., who continued to keep
her company with Tommy after the move to Sandy Cove. "I do remember at one
point her saying something that kind of struck me because it was one of those
things that kids will repeat to other people. He had by this time made enough
money that he could retire and not ever have to go anywhere again. I could
remember her saying he could retire and not ever have to be on the road again. 'We
could live off of what he has already made.' What she was saying was that that's
what she really would have liked."

6

CALIFORNIA

Back home in Dyess, Arkansas, satisfaction meant slurping up a handful of peanuts floating in a Coke at the Saturday night movies, a little smooching in the tall grass near the river, or just the promise that tomorrow would bring the last day of cotton harvest. They were simple antidotes to the drabness of farm life. But a few who grew up and left Dyess equated such simplicity with deprivation. To compensate for the perceived want of their childhood, many overindulged in the fruits of their prosperous adulthood, only to face diabetes, alcoholism, obesity, and other maladies of consumer society.

But what Cash came to know after Dyess was far greater than mere prosperity. As fame crept up over his belt, he was free to explore the outer limits of his appetites. The tales are legion. One plate of biscuits and gravy couldn't suffice; he craved two or three. One romantic fling in San Antonio failed to please him; he needed one in the next town and the next. Sophomoric pranks that harked back to high school and the juvenile hijinks with Harvey Clanton never stopped with crank calls on motel phones or throwing a few firecrackers out the window of their rolling Cadillac. Cash and the Tennessee Two concocted elaborate capers and incendiary destruction, exploding homemade bombs in the desert, ransacking hotel rooms, and when the mood struck, shooting off a signal cannon that they carried with them.

In the late 1950s and early 1960s, their destruction occasionally made the news. Fellow country artists, who indulged quieter transgressions away from the confines of home and family, complained that Cash's antics ruined their reputations among innkeepers throughout the land. *Opry* star Billy Walker, who traveled on package tours with Cash, winced at his colleague's escapades. "He used to get crazy," he said. "I remember a tour way back there where him and Luther and Marshall bought five hundred baby chickens, and at this hotel in Omaha, Nebraska, they let a hundred baby chickens out on each floor of the hotel. There was another time when we were working this long tour together and we stayed in one location, and they took this hotel room and chopped all the furniture to Japanese style and painted it black. We was on one trip and they bought fifty or sixty cherry bombs and they'd flush the toilet and light the cherry bombs, which will go off underwater, and blow the pipe out underneath. It got to where we wouldn't stay where they were staying."

Cash's mischief flapped the tongues at the *Opry*. Increasingly, though, when the Nashville fraternity turned to the subject of Cash, it marveled at his considerable drug use. Alcoholism and substance abuse were hardly new to country music. They hung over the community like gnarled tree limbs, cursing artists such as Lefty Frizzell and Hank Williams, wrecking homes, and visiting layers of guilt upon men and women who'd been raised in strict evangelical homes where drink and drugs were demonized (if not always abstained from). Cash gave them plenty to talk about, for his drug use possessed him.

It was one appetite that was insatiable. When he first sampled amphetamines, those brightly colored capsules that agitate the nervous system, it was as if he'd begun snorting a decade-long line of pure cocaine. "It was a thing I did gradually," he said in 1975. "And it felt so good when I first started taking pills in '58 that I just kept trying things that felt better."

Cash frequently dated his drug use back to 1958, but Grant suspects that it began much earlier. "When John got out of the service, as I look back on it, he was doing some then, because he was strange," says Grant. "I loved him to death, everybody loved him to death, but he was strange and every day was different. Never questioned it. I just thought it was him. Then as a little success came along in '56 and '57, he got worse, and I didn't know what the deal was. I really didn't. And we were playing the auditorium in Milwaukee, Wisconsin, one day on a package show that everybody had been on. We were headlining the show, and I started looking for John, and I couldn't find him, which would have been unusual. This is in 1956. I started looking in dressing rooms, and I opened this little storage room right behind the stage, didn't know what was in there, and there he stood. Just as I opened the door, in went a handful of pills. And at that instant I said, 'Oh my God. That's what's wrong with him.' But I didn't say anything to him and went on the stage, and he did his thing. I started watching it, then I put it together that [it was] drugs. And it was all pills, these little things you get over in Mexico and so forth and so on. Benzadrine and one they called the Great Speckled Bird. You know, I didn't know what they all were, but he was getting his hands on them. Gordon Terry [a fiddler who often traveled with the Cash show as an added attraction] brags about the fact that he gave John his first pill, but I think he was taking some in the service. But anyhow, it started getting worse and worse."

One Benzedrine could have kept him alert for a day or two through the monotonous and grueling concert tours where Cash made his money, but he gobbled jars full of them. Obtaining the pills from shady Mexican suppliers when the tours dipped down into southern Texas and American physicians who were either starstruck or ignorant to the devastation of prolonged and copious consumption, he always had hundreds of the capsules within his reach. Guitarist George Riddle, who backed George Jones (another frequent feature on Cash shows), marveled at the singer's appetite and supply. "Like everybody else on the show we would observe Johnny taking handfuls of pills," he said in an interview. "I know one time he called us out into a back alley. We were in Des Moines, Iowa, and he was in one of these little pickup trucks with a camper on the top. He just got back from Mexico. He said, 'Boys, look what I got.' And he opened up a drawer. He had one of those candy scoopers like you pick up jelly beans with, and he said, 'How many do you want?' That camper was loaded down."

Although his drug use proved to be a lifelong habit, the most intense years stretched from 1958 to 1967, when he consumed the pills with little restraint. As son-in-law Jimmy Tittle observed years later, moderation had no place in Cash's vocabulary: "John had this thing, probably his entire life: If one's good, twenty's got to be really good."

In late 1957, Cash, Vivian, Rosanne, and Kathy moved from their Sandy Cove neighborhood to a brand-new spacious rambler on Walnut Grove Place. Situated on the quiet eastern edge of Memphis, they were near St. Andrews Fairway, home of patrician George Bates from Cash's Home Equipment days. Sitting among the city's established wealth, miles from the endless blocks of tiny homes in north Memphis where the pilgrims from Dyess Colony settled, Walnut Place symbolized the Cashes' new financial station.

As Vivian recreated a home in the new house, Cash was finding that his trail out of Memphis more and more often coursed through California. Through the offices of a young sandy-haired agent and promoter named Stew Carnall, he had spent four weeks touring in the Golden State during the first six months of 1957 alone. "Stew had a lot of connections out there with clubs," says Grant, "and when we would work for Stew that's all we would work was clubs, and that's all the way from San Diego to Vancouver, British Columbia." In addition, Cash and the Tennessee Two had begun appearing regularly on *Town Hall Party*, a jamboree featuring the Collins Kids, Merle Travis, Tex Ritter, and others that was televised every Saturday night on KTTV in Los Angeles. He also was showing up on *Western Ranch Party*, a nationally syndicated spinoff of *Town Hall Party*.

Cash saw that Los Angeles was musically and culturally a new world, far removed from Nashville's parochialism and Memphis's isolation. Though home to thriving jazz and rhythm-and-blues scenes and world-class orchestral music, the city unflinchingly welcomed rockabilly, western-swing, honky-tonk and cowboy styles. These additions were pleasing to the migrants from Texas, Arkansas, and Oklahoma who had flocked to the area during the Depression and Second World War. A country-and-western singer scarcely needed Nashville in Los Angeles. There was a host of recording and publishing companies, high-energy disc jockeys, and a growing movie and television industry which promised bit parts, movie-soundtrack work, and the hope of Gene Autry fame.

However, it was the goal of steady movie work, to follow in Elvis Presley's path, that caused Cash to linger in California. As early as 1956, Bob Neal had begun sniffing around for substantial film roles for Cash, attempting to sell the brooding young man as an actor in the John Wayne and Gary Cooper mold. The manager had turned down various spots in cheap film musicals, which would have had Cash appearing once or twice singing his songs, in hopes of receiving better offers.

But there were no immediate takers. So while Neal paraded his client through the offices of television and movie producers, Cash got to know the artists of *Town Hall Party*. He amorously pursued sixteen-year-old cast member Lorrie Collins, but appears to have spent more time under the artistic spell of singers Tex Ritter, Merle Travis, and Johnny Western, men who reawakened his interest in the Western balladry he'd read and mimicked in his youth.

Ritter, whose "High Noon" (from the movie of the same name) climbed the pop charts in 1952, was influenced by folk-song collector John Lomax while studying at the University of Texas in the 1920s and seldom recorded anything but traditional cowboy music. Ritter was the godfather of the Los Angeles country-and-western community, while Travis was trying to pick himself up from his career's long slide. An influential guitarist who boasted Chet Atkins among his followers, Travis had scored the megahits "Divorce Me C.O.D" and "So Round, So Firm, So Fully Packed" in the 1940s, but had failed to sustain his fortunes and was beset with devastating drug and alcohol problems. His folk credentials, though, turned Cash's head. In 1947, Capitol Records had released Travis's *Folk Songs of the Hills*, which included the modern coal-mining ballad "Sixteen Tons," but the album was fading from memory when in 1955 Tennessee Ernie Ford recorded "Sixteen Tons" and came up with a monstrous hit. Re-released in 1957, Travis's *Folk Songs* obviously impressed Cash. He recorded five of the original album's eight songs during his career. Two of them, "Dark as a Dungeon" and "John Henry", became as entrenched as "Folsom Prison Blues" and "I Walk the Line" in Cash's 1960s concert repertoire.

Johnny Western was the youngest of the trio Cash gravitated toward in California, and unlike Travis, his star appeared to be rising. Born John Westerlund III in Minnesota, Western's pseudo-cowboy credentials gleamed in the late 1950s as he toured with Gene Autry and the Sons of the Pioneers. He penned and performed "The Ballad of Palladin," which aired on every episode of CBS-TV's smash hit *Have Gun—Will Travel*. He would join the growing Johnny Cash road show in the late 1950s and remain on board for several years.

Western, Travis, and Ritter and their folk and western balladry gave Cash another reason to linger in California and brought him to reevaluate the Memphis country-and-rockabilly house where he lived. He was poised to open a new artistic chapter in his career.

Back at 706 Union Avenue, Sam Phillips was testing Cash's patience. Cash and the Tennessee Two believed that Sun was holding back royalty dollars, although nobody ever proved it. And to make matters worse, according to Jack Clement, Cash suspected Phillips was throwing him over for Jerry Lee Lewis. "Like I say, Sam loved Johnny Cash," says Clement. "He respected him more than any of them other characters. And I think he thought Johnny Cash understood that he was real busy promoting Jerry Lee Lewis. [Cash] came by wanting to go next door and have lunch one day. Sam was real busy on the phone calling distributors and stuff, so he didn't have time to do that. And I think that's what precipitated him wanting to leave." In later years, Cash blamed arguments over creative direction for the drift from Sun, not Jerry Lee Lewis. He believed that magical Memphis was stifling him. "There were so many things I wanted to do," said Cash. "I had all these ideas about special projects, different album ventures . . . , but I felt like at Sun I would be limited in what I could do, where with a major company I could do all that and reach more people with my music. I think I was right, too. Sam couldn't understand it back then. We had a little misunderstanding at the time, he couldn't see me wanting to go to another record company—*but I could.*"

Cash's disaffection must have rattled Phillips. Elvis was gone, and Carl Perkins, another heir apparent to Presley, had lost his footing after a devastating 1956 automobile accident in Delaware. Jerry Lee Lewis, the next big spark, would flame out in 1958 when his 1957 marriage to thirteen-year-old Myra Brown was chewed to pieces by scandal sheets all over the world. In 1958, Sun was not exactly the hot spot it had been in 1956. And as long as Phillips bowed to the teen market and discouraged albums, Cash concurred.

Out west, a more adult orientation prevailed in the recording industry, especially at Hollywood-based Capitol Records. The label's Tex Ritter recorded two concept albums for release in 1958, collections of western film songs and hymns, and lesser names, such as Capitol Artist and Repertory (A&R) man Cliffie Stone and *Town Hall* regular Skeets McDonald, were also recording albums of original material for Capitol. In Memphis, Phillips had permitted one Cash album, *Johnny Cash with his Hot and Blue Guitar,* almost half of which was stuffed with early hit singles. Cash yearned for the freedom within which his Capitol friends operated, and he soon found it with Don Law, the A&R man in charge of country-and-western music at Columbia Records.

One might have expected Cash to join Ritter, Travis, and company on the Capitol Records train. But the A&R man who would have signed him, Ken Nelson, says he never considered it, despite running into him frequently at an L.A. area doughnut shop. Prim in appearance and suspicious of artists who drank too much, Nelson may have been put off by stories of Cash's road antics and substance abuse. Earlier, he'd passed on George Jones, spooked by his insatiable thirst for liquor and his no-show reputation.

The white-haired Law, an Englishman known in part for drinking behind the control board, was perhaps more forgiving of a man's peccadilloes. What is certain is that when he began courting Cash after meeting him backstage at *Town Hall Party* in 1957, he immediately offered carte blanche, creative wiggle room. How could Cash ignore him? Law represented one of the biggest recording companies in America and had mid-wifed country classics with uncanny regularity: "Always Late (With Your Kisses)" by Lefty Frizzell, "Hey Joe!" by Carl Smith, "Crazy Arms" by Ray Price, "Singing the Blues" by Marty Robbins, "Honky-Tonk Man" by Johnny Horton, and others. Law cultivated most of those artists from his bases in Nashville and Dallas, so his courting of Cash marked a California invasion of sorts. The foray ultimately yielded few signings, but his netting of Cash was alone worth his efforts. The singer agreed in the fall of 1957 to join Columbia when his Sun contract expired in July of 1958.

Gossip about Cash's romance with Columbia drifted back to Sun Records in early 1958, but Cash feigned ignorance. Phillips didn't believe him. He wheeled out to Cash's shady street in east Memphis and confronted him. "I looked Johnny straight in the eye and I said, 'John, I understand that you've signed an option to go to another label at the expiration of your contract with Sun. I want you to look me straight in the eye and tell me, have you or have you not?' I knew when he opened his mouth he was lying. The only damn lie that Johnny Cash ever told me that I was aware of. That *hurt*. That hurt!" The lie only exacerbated Phillips's bitterness when his suspicions were confirmed. Sam exploded, threatened to sue Columbia for contractual interference, and finally demanded that Cash return to the studio to fulfill the obligations of his fading Sun contract.

Cash scoffed at Phillips, claiming his lost royalties more than compensated for any sessions he might still owe his old mentor. He only gave in when Sam began talking lawsuit over breach of contract. Cash grudgingly returned to Sun's studio in May of 1958, though he refused to record his own compositions (saving those for Columbia) and pouted from the time he walked through the door.

It was up to Clement to wheedle performances from Johnny Cash and the Tennessee Two. "I got as much out of him as I could," he says. "But his heart wasn't into a lot of it. One day we were there and he was ready to quit, and I was wanting to get some more stuff, and there was a Hank Williams song playing there on the speaker. I said, 'Why don't you give me five Hank Williams songs here. We'll do it in forty-five minutes. Just sing them, and let Luther and Marshall kind of be off mike. So I kept them way low and set out to overdub them and other [musicians] later. Well, that was okay, but it wasn't the best stuff we ever did. But that wound up being an album. And I wrote a bunch of songs during that time, and he cut a bunch of them. Some of them maybe he shouldn't have. They were good songs, and he liked them: 'Down the Street to 301,' 'Just About Time,' forget the rest of them."

Indeed, Cash also recorded "Life Goes On" and "Katy Too," both of which bore Clement's writing stamp. And the Hank Williams selections showed up later on a Sun album entitled *Johnny Cash Sings Hank Williams*, whose cover featured a model who resembled Cash turned away from the camera, gazing into the West.

The paint at Walnut Place in Memphis had barely dried and Vivian was coddling newborn daughter Cindy when Cash announced his future was in California. The extended Cash family understandably grumbled, and Vivian mourned the loss of her comfortable new home. But Cash, eager to make a film career and join the community of men singing in the American ballad tradition, was determined to go. He'd tell a *Los Angeles Times* reporter within days of arriving in town that the invasion of pop influences had chased him from Tennessee. "It used to be that practically every folk singer in the business lived within a 100-mile radius of Memphis or Nashville," lectured Cash. "That was one reason why the major recording companies set their country music headquarters there, and built fine recording studios. But then came rock 'n' roll. Suddenly country music singers were sharing the spotlight with pop singers. And we also found that these same 'popular' vocalists had begun to strum guitars—or were having background musicians strum 'em for them—you couldn't tell who was what without a record chart." Cash named no names and conveniently omitted reference to his own concessions to the teenage market, but he was clearly perturbed about the preponderance of rock and pop which he said was attacking the purity of country and western music. Los Angeles must have meant freedom to Cash, a place to liberate his music from the pressures of pop influence. It was an early disavowal of Clement's production, though Cash returned to him again and again for the rest of his life.

As much as Cash pointed to music as the impetus for his departure from Memphis, television was the primary and immediate reason. Bob Neal had been told by Bobby Brenner, a Music Corporation of America (MCA) agent who often booked Cash on East Coast television, that a Hollywood producer named Lee Cooley (who also happened to be a close friend of Brenner's) was keen to develop a TV show around Cash. This was exciting news. Cooley had produced *The Perry Como Show* on NBC-TV, and at the moment, was in charge of creating and producing musical programs for CBS-TV. His latest ventures were *The Big Record*, with Patti Page, and *Sing Along*, featuring Jim Lowe and Florence Henderson. Cooley's interest electrified Neal and Cash and immediately precipitated their move out west. They acted rashly, however, uprooting their families, not to mention Perkins and Grant, without as much as a verbal commitment from Cooley. The show never materialized.

The Cashes landed in an apartment in Hollywood and then, soon after, moved to a modern ranch home in nearby Encino. A magazine journalist who visited the Encino home not long after the family moved in seems to have thought he was on the set of a Fred de Cordova television comedy: Rosanne, Kathy, and newborn Cindy cawed, cried, and giggled while their parrot named Jethroe screeched at Vivian in her skin-tight pants. Cash, in "pointy Italian-leather loafers," stood apart, practicing his fast draw with a Colt .45 pistol, a new trick Johnny Western had been teaching him. This rare moment of family life, opened for a few minutes to the press, preceded yet another Cash tour. There were no movie roles yet, but recordings were another story. The reporter noted that the American public's thirst for them was unquenchable: "In four years, . . . Cash-composed songs have sold more than 6,000,000 records. The biggest Cash hit, 'I Walk the Line,' passed the million mark with ease; the latest, 'Don't Take Your Guns to Town,' is well on its way to repeating that performance."

The reporter called it right on "Don't Take Your Guns to Town." The ballad about an antsy young gunslinger was poised to equal the sales and chart action of Cash's most popular Sun hits. Recorded in the summer of 1958 during a spurt of sessions with his new label, Cash's composition fell right into the vein of songs that was defining country music and much of American entertainment at the time. Blaring from televisions and radios were programs and ballads set in the West some one hundred years earlier. One could scarcely turn on the television and drop on the couch without dodging the shootouts of *Gunsmoke* or tracking through the woods with Daniel Boone and Davy Crockett. The same was true at the nation's cinemas, where films such as *Rio Bravo* and *The Big Country* magnetized audiences. The Western themes infiltrated the panorama of American music too. Revivals of Copland's "Billy the Kid" and Grofé's "Grand Canyon Suite" sprang up in concert halls around the nation, while Marty Robbins's "El Paso" and Johnny Horton's "Battle of New Orleans" sold millions. Cash had told the reporter visiting his home that he was trying to sell "authentic folk music." It would be a profitable endeavor.

In "Don't Take Your Guns to Town," Cash sang about a young cowboy named Billy Joe who ignores his mother's plea to hang up his six shooters before an evening on the town, only to fall later that night in a mismatched shootout. The song returned Cash to his childhood when he composed verse set on the lonesome range. It recalled "Give My Love to Rose," a narrative ballad set in the West that Cash had adapted from the folk song "Give My Love to Nell" and recorded for Sun in July of 1957. "Don't Take Your Guns to Town" and the other numbers recorded on his first Columbia sessions were also a decisive turn back to the original Sun sound. Back in front of the instrumental mix were Perkins's simple, direct guitar runs, Cash's jingling rhythm guitar, and Grant's popping bass. Although Law decorated the sessions with the choruses of the Jordanaires and the steel guitar of Don Helms, a Hank Williams alumnus, the boom-chicka-boom sound again throbbed in the mix, boring deeply into the American ear.

"Don't Take Your Guns to Town" claimed the number one country music position for six weeks and climbed high on the pop charts as well. Backed with "I Still Miss Someone," the record was Cash's zenith in 1959, rising above eight other Cash single releases that year. Half of those releases had come from Memphis where Phillips kept plenty of Cash's Sun recordings in the pipeline.

The Sun releases must have irritated Cash as he built up his new catalog, but Columbia's indulgence surely soothed him. In 1959 alone, the label released three albums of new material: *The Fabulous Johnny Cash*, which contained "Don't Take Your Guns to Town," *Hymns by Johnny Cash*, and *Songs of Our Soil*. Nobody on anybody's country roster equaled such output. It was as if Cash were fulfilling the dreams that had eluded him at Sun: to record gospel music and create concept albums.

The Fabulous Johnny Cash and *Songs of the Soil* realized Cash's conviction to record American folk music. On the albums, Cash ladled out "My Grandfather's Clock," "Frankie's Man Johnny," and "I Want to Go Home," traditional ballads that Cash adapted and stamped his name on as writer, a practice that Cash continued for years to come. Along with "Don't Take Your Guns to Town," Cash indulged his fascination with the Old West by also adding "Old Apache Squaw," which looks at the travails of the American Indian through the eyes of an old Indian woman, and "Hank and Joe and Me," a story of three struggling gold miners that borrowed thematic elements from Bob Nolan's "Cool Water" and many other country and western saga songs of the day.

Amid the borrowed and rearranged folk songs on both albums were Cash's most important contributions to the folk canon, his own compositions that harked back to his childhood. Dredged from the Depression's hardships and the simple comforts that eased those hardships, Cash's songs documented a fast-fading American way of life. This choice to transform Depression stories into mass entertainment made Cash unique among the hitmakers of that time. This aspect of his music would influence many of the players in a new generation of folk singers who would emerge in New York in the 1960s.

The finest nuggets Cash mined from his past and included on the two secular albums of 1959 were "Pickin' Time" and "Five Feet High and Rising." A paean to the rhythms of rural life, "Pickin' Time" tells the first-person hopes of a farmer whose family scrapes by on beans and wears tattered shoes until the crops are ready. Harvest delivers them to better times, if only briefly. *It's hard to see by the coal oil light/And I turn it off pretty early at night/cause a jug of coal oil costs a dime/But I'll stay up late come pickin' time.*

"Five Feet High and Rising" is one of the jewels of the entire Cash catalog and one of his quintessential songs. Carried on the familiar loping rhythm of the boom-chicka-boom, "Five Feet High and Rising" watches the flood waters of 1937 grow around a farmer's feet. Again it's told in the first person; again it's the story of the Cash family. Cash was only five in the middle of the long winter of rain, but he recalled vividly listening to daily flood reports on the radio. Dyess farmers feared the Mississippi levee would break and lift the Tyronza River over its banks.

"We heard about the flood waters before we saw them," recounted Cash in *Country Music* magazine. "We heard that they were coming, but it was moving slowly, and there was no cause for alarm. And very quietly and calmly everybody packed up and got ready to go, except my daddy. I remember him taking a yard-stick and leaning over the edge of the front porch as the water had covered our field and was rising up on the steps of the house, and he was measuring how deep that water was. . . . I remember [daddy] saying one day that we just got word that the bus is going to be here in 15 minutes to take everybody to the train to take us to the hills and we've got to get ready in 15 minutes. That's what we did, and he put everybody in the boat—my mother and all of his children, but he stood on the porch and pushed us off toward the road."

The flood was real, and picking time was real. Both songs spoke with the simple eloquence of Hemingway and the Depression sensitivity of Steinbeck, conveying the hopes, rhythms, and hardships of rural life. Both spoke volumes, but when Law hit his stopwatch, each clocked in at well under two minutes. This dramatically underscored Cash's ability to mold his art to the demands of the modern pop-music industry, which required short singles and album cuts.

From 1958 to 1965, Cash's association with Columbia was defined by a commitment and focus unparalleled in the rest of his long career. During that time, he assembled a body of work that reflected his passion for interpreting in song American history and legends as well as the reality of rural folk, blue-collar workers, prison convicts, and American Indians. While much of the nation was punching into the 1960s on the strains of Brill Building pop, Philadelphia rock, surfing singles, and Beatlemania, Cash was digging up the country's thick and tangled roots.

Cash was also digging up every sort of amphetamine that he could find. His move to California saw a budding drug habit transformed into a full black blossom. A community of users and abusers in California only worsened Cash's addiction.

Fiddler Gordon Terry, who claims to have slipped pills to Cash for the first time, remained on the Cash touring show. And from time to time, Merle Kilgore, a buddy from the *Louisiana Hayride* days, joined the troupe. Both Terry and Kilgore were two of Cash's brothers in drug use. Another brother was Stew Carnall, who had parlayed his booking of Cash in California into a co-management deal with Bob Neal. While on the road with Cash, Carnall never missed a party. And although Grant looked on with concern and hid the drugs when he could, his efforts were futile. Even Perkins was following the boss' path into abuse. "I was fighting John on one end," complains Grant, "and Luther was supplying on the other end. It made for a bad situation."

Merle Travis, though, may be one of the unsung bad role models in Cash's career. His wild behavior, induced by rampant drug and alcohol consumption, presaged the miserable behavior that became so associated with Cash's own drug use. Through the years, the guitarist periodically found himself behind bars and locked away in mental wards because of drugging, drinking, and fighting. In 1956, he held his wife hostage in their own home, terrorizing her as police moved in to arrest the grizzled singer.

Travis' consumption intrigued Cash, and he became a gauge by which Cash measured his own pill consumption. In his second autobiography, Cash recalled a three-day drinking-and-drugging spree in the early 1960s, through which he was cognizant enough to observe the effects of various types of pills. "We all had our preferences in that regard—Merle was on sleeping pills while I was on amphetamines—but it worked out, more or less," he wrote. "If Merle could keep his dosage right, he'd stay in what he considered his mellow mood, not nervous, for long periods of time. In that state he could be hilarious, a wonderful conversationalist and raconteur. He took so many pills that eventually they'd start working like they were supposed to and put him to sleep, but sometimes that took three or four days. For me, the trick was to match my biochemical schedule, running on the fast track, to his. Sometimes it worked and great stories were told, great thoughts exchanged; sometimes it didn't and there was a lot of dead air." While he saw that the drugs could stimulate great conversation, he also observed that Merle more or less functioned as an artist while sponging up the drugs and booze. If Merle could, Cash might have reasoned, so could he.

At home, the drugs were dragging Cash's family into dysfunction. Now in yet another new home, this one in a lonely canyon in Ojai, Vivian and the children carved out a routine devoid of husband and father. At Cash's request, his brother Tommy and his nephew Roy traveled out West in the summers to keep them company as they had in Memphis when Cash first took to the road. But things were different. Nobody knew when Cash was coming home or what he'd be like when he did. In their few moments together, Vivian tried to be the anti-Travis. "She urged me not to take [the pills]," wrote Cash, "and of course that just drove the wedge deeper between us. I shrugged her off. Then, as my habit escalated, she actually begged me—'Please, please get off those pills. They're going to destroy us both!'—but I hunched up into myself and let it roll off my back." Though initially Vivian quietly tolerated Cash's drug use, her courage to speak grew with her desperation. What else could she do, even if her pleading sent Cash storming from the house? She wanted a husband and a father in her home.

During their second year in California, Cash's erratic behavior had become the norm. Vivian ceased to be surprised when Cash stumbled through the door in rumpled clothing, his hair a flattened mess. And on the road, the band was almost always braced for lethargy or nervous energy multiplied by ten. Either way, recalls Grant, Cash amazingly pulled off good shows. "You got to get him to the buildings," he says. "You got to get him on stage. You got to get him off stage. And sometimes this was a task. I have led John out on the stage where he'd be blowed out of his mind to where he didn't know where he was at. But lo and behold, there was something about him, that if you got him out there, and usually he'd walk out on the stage and the crowd would stand up screaming and hollering for five minutes, by the time that was over with, the guy could do a show. And do a good show."

Vivian, Grant, and Law knew the fitful lifestyle, but new entrants to the world of Johnny Cash never suspected that the balladeer who appeared so earnest on television and records could be so wild. Jim Malloy, a young Columbia engineer based in Hollywood, witnessed Cash's recklessness one afternoon while having a smoke outside a performance hall in L.A. The singer streaked into the parking lot driving a four-door Thunderbird, says Malloy, and rammed it right into an air-conditioning unit. "And I thought, 'Who in the hell is that?'" he says. "I walked back there to see if he was all right, and it was Cash. And he opened up the door, of course, and the damn wheels were laying [on the air conditioner], and he opened up the door and he got out, and he says, 'Boy, that son of a bitch is really a good horse. The only thing is, it's probably gonna get me killed.' John was really out of it at that point in time."

But Malloy had just seen the tip of it. In February of 1961, Law slated two Cash sessions in the Hollywood studios to record an assortment of songs that would appear on upcoming long-play and extended-play albums: "Forty Shades of Green," "The Big Battle," "He'll Understand and Say Well Done," and a few others. Cash missed a morning session, complaining of a sore throat, which was usually code for pill-induced dehydration. According to Malloy, Law went ahead and recorded the instrumental tracks with Johnny Western on vocals, and he was already nodding off after two fistfuls of whiskey when the rangy singer finally showed in the afternoon. Immediately, Cash eyed a bottle of cough syrup that Malloy was sipping to soothe his own throat. "He came in the control room and walked over to the console and he said, 'What's this?'" Malloy says. "And I said, 'It's a bottle of Vicks Formula 44. It's for your throat.' And he said, 'Can I use some of it?' And I said, 'Yeah.' He drank the whole damn bottle. Drank it and scared the shit out of me. And you know, when he got done, he couldn't talk, couldn't say a damn word. I remember as plain as day because I thought, 'It's going to go down that an engineer has ruined Johnny Cash's throat.' But he was like that. He would take any damn thing."

The session was Cash's first in Hollywood and first with strings and vibra-phone, which may have exacerbated his edginess. A few days later, when the singer had cleared the cough syrup from his system and laid down his vocals, Malloy tackled the job of mixing the songs. "Let me tell you something," says Malloy, "when I got done with that album and everybody had left, I said to John, 'I got it all done now. Do you wanna hear it?' He said, 'Yeah, let me hear it.' He tore his whole damn shirt off. Just tore it, all the buttons and everything. He was just so nervous and so out of it, you know. Scared the shit out of me because I had just been around John—probably with overdubbing and everything—maybe fourteen, fifteen hours, something like that. But anyway, he sat down and he loved it, just loved it."

Indeed, despite having been recorded under the pain of Cash's agitation, the songs from February 24th and 27th of 1961 were sterling. "Forty Shades of Green," Cash's tribute to Ireland, proved to be one of his classics. "The Big Battle," a sensitive portrayal of the Civil War and the healing of postbellum wounds, was one of the finest historical sagas he ever wrote and recorded. "I thought it was a good record, and I still think it is," said Cash in 1973, when all but the most ardent of fans had forgotten it. "The idea being that the big battle comes after the killing . . . in the conscience, in the hearts and grief of people that suffered the loss." Cash said "The Big Battle" was one of his proudest accomplishments.

As for the wide-eyed Malloy, eight years later he'd be called to Nashville to oversee the sound engineering of Cash's network television show. There he met a man whose mind and body had calmed.

7

J.R., JOHN, JOHNNY

The big sound of the small trio grew in 1960 when Cash hired drummer W.S. "Fluke" Holland for a series of shows at the Three Rivers Inn in Syracuse, New York. The club was one of the swankier stops on the northeastern country-music circuit in the 1950s and 1960s, a gig that got many country artists thinking about presentation. Tours in the Northeast usually took performers through the rustic music ranches (such as Sunset Park in Pennsylvania, New River Ranch in Maryland, Lone Star Ranch in New Hampshire), whose stages required little embellishment by the acts. But the prospects of a Vegas-like supper club with floor show, and a follow-up series of dates scheduled at the famous Steel Pier in Atlantic City, inspired Cash to fill out his sound and the group's stage presence. Holland, a tall beefy Tennessean who'd been a fixture in Carl Perkins's band since 1955, was more than capable of handling the job.

Grant oriented Holland to his new world while Cash spent the weekend in Syracuse kindling a quick romance with Maxine Brown, who with her brother Jim Ed and sister Bonnie shared the bill with Cash that August weekend. "He [Holland] just sat on the stool and, automatically he put that slap in there just like I was doing, and he was great at it," says Grant. "And [when I began playing] electric bass, his brushes and drums [brought] the sound back in full. And that's all he did for years." From then on, they were Johnny Cash and the Tennessee Three.

~~~~~~

Cash's recording-and-touring career remained in high gear in the wake of his relocation to Los Angeles, but two pieces of the California plan failed to drop into place: the movies and dramatic television. So Cash and the Tennessee Three continued their run of variety show appearances that had begun on *The Jackie Gleason Show* in 1957. They regularly soaked up the spotlight on programs such as *The Jimmy Dean Show* (CBS-TV), *Country Music Jubilee* (ABC-TV), and *American Bandstand* (ABC-TV). Beyond that, however, Bob Neal ran into closed doors at the major studios and television networks, lining up instead occasional guest spots on television westerns.

One of Cash's first appearances was on a pallid syndicated series titled *Shotgun Slade*, which was a rotating door for California celebrities such as pitcher Sandy Koufax, footballer Elroy "Crazy Legs" Hirsch, and singers Jimmy Wakely and Tex Ritter. Cash took his turn in line, hitching on for one episode: "The Stalkers." He stepped up considerably when the producers of ABC-TV's *The Rebel*, starring Nick Adams, invited him to sing the show's theme song, "The Rebel—Johnny Yuma," and to guest star in an episode titled "The Death of Gray," which aired in 1960 and drew critical praise.

In 1961, Cash attempted to parlay his small parts into a western vehicle of his own called *The Night Rider*. Its storyline was based on "Don't Take Your Guns to Town" and featured appearances by his California country fraternity: Johnny Western, Merle Travis, and Gordon Terry. The television networks and syndicators, however, left it alone. Although Cash persisted, his prospects seemed dim, particularly when his next filmed endeavor hit the screens.

In 1962, a film whose production had been delayed for two years finally wrapped. It was Cash's first feature role in a full-length motion picture, but his performance floundered. Anybody who saw *Five Minutes to Live* knew immediately why Cash had not followed Elvis Presley from Memphis onto the silver screen: he lacked the innate tools to make it. On the surface, Cash seemed a good fit for the role of a dark, amoral criminal. The part played to the brooding countenance he often projected on album covers and in television performances. A dreadful masochist, Cash's character terrorizes a banker's wife in her home while at the bank his partner in crime forces the husband to open the safe under threat of harm to his wife. The twist? The banker is planning to leave his wife. *Variety* found the film "clumsy" and fraught with "limp dialog, below par acting, and leisurely directing."

Briefly, Cash is believable, such as when he smashes a glass on the wife's fireplace mantel. He appears alarmingly natural wrecking the woman's living room. But his trademark sullenness alone was too little to carry the film. He was leaden, unable to bring much imagination to the role. All in all, the film came off like a poorly conceived *Twilight Zone* episode. And when Cash warbled the film's theme song over the credits, the message was unmistakable: he was a far better singer and songwriter than actor.

Cash could act in a song; there were few better in country music. But most of his screen acting, before *Five Minutes to Live* and after, was wanting. Over the years, there would be exceptions, like *A Gunfight* in 1970, when co-star Kirk Douglas inspired him to a commendable performance. But when Johnny Cash took to the screen on most occasions, it was primarily no more than Johnny Cash taking to the screen.

From time to time over the few years following his first film, there would be talk of Cash returning to the movies. His name was mentioned for the lead in a comedy romance titled "Cat's Keys" and for the part of Jimmie Rodgers in a biopic, the rights to which Cash had purchased from the Singing Brakeman's widow. Discouraged by his poor debut or unable to focus because of his increasing drug use, Cash settled for cameo appearances in a Hollywood folk romp called *Hootenanny Hoot* (1963) and the B-grade country-music *Road to Nashville* (1967).

Bob Neal had brokered the *Five Minutes to Live* deal with Flower Film Productions in 1959, but by the end of the year, he was discharged from the Cash camp, bought out, actually, by Stew Carnall. The break was probably inevitable. Neal had no interest in keeping pace with his client's immature and demon-paced lifestyle on the road, so he had gladly let Carnall own the touring component of Cash's career while he focused on managing the recording and video components. Carnall was only too happy to ride with Cash on the road where he found plenty of parties and the opportunity to gain more influence with the singer. Neal's amateurish handling of the CBS-TV talks that brought him and Cash to California in the first place, as well as his failure to find another television vehicle, didn't help his standing in Cash's eyes either. And not even *Five Minutes to Live* could redeem Neal. Cash had been forced to work on a percentage deal, receiving no monies in advance for his participation.

In 1960, after the firing, Cash's former manager relocated to Shreveport, Louisiana, where he struggled to revive his radio career by taking over the operation of KCIJ, a CBS affiliate. Neal would rise again, only he did so in Nashville, where a booking agency he established thrived in the 1960s and 1970s. Until his death in 1983, however, he remained bitter about Cash, complaining that he'd been left stranded in California after giving so much to his client's dream.

Neal may have grinned when he learned Stew Carnall's days with Cash were numbered, too. While Neal was trying to make his station come to life in Louisiana in 1960 and 1961, Cash was plotting to oust Carnall. Put off, perhaps, by Carnall's marriage to Lorrie Collins (whom Cash adored), or deciding there was only room for one unreliable character in his community, Cash dismissed Carnall in May of 1961.

At the time of the firing, Cash was already wooing Saul Holiff, a promoter from London, Ontario, whom he had met in the late 1950s. Holiff had booked Cash across Ontario since 1958, and when the need arose, acted as an unofficial adviser on the singer's treks through the north country, looking over wrinkled statements and contracts that Cash pulled out of his vest pocket. Self-educated in business (he'd sold fruit, newspapers, and clothes) and an aspiring actor with aristocratic desires, he had begun promoting rock and country concerts in the late 1950s, squiring artists such as Duane Eddy, the Everly Brothers, and Paul Anka across Ontario, New York, and parts of Michigan. A determined entrepreneur, Holiff also owned a profitable hamburger stand outside London, concocting crazy spectacles to lasso teen diners, such as a display of a woman frozen in an ice block and an invasion of men in ape costumes.

In 1959, as Cash worked another string of Canadian dates, Holiff persuaded the singer to visit his restaurant for an autograph session and a meal. The encounter, Holiff told me not long before he ended his life in 2005, was the seed of their management deal. "We had a terrible argument prior to getting to the restaurant," he said, "a misunderstanding of the way the contract was drawn up. It was a trivial thing, but, I mean, I was as hard-nosed as you can get. I don't even know where it came from. But they misinterpreted. They didn't understand the contract. It made a difference of about seventy or eighty dollars. It was just terminology. It's something about 'you take your advertising off the top before your percentage is calculated,' meaning they have to share the advertising [expenses] with me since that created the gross. They didn't understand that, and I made a statement to him. (I'd had Faron Young about two weeks earlier, who was one of the worst shit disturbers I ever had met in my life, and he gave me a dreadful time.) I said [to Johnny], 'You're just like all the rest of them, especially Faron Young.' And it piqued his interest, it really piqued his interest. I suddenly went from a slightly overweight nonentity to a slightly overweight guy who was rather outspoken."

Stunned, Cash refused to eat Holiff's hamburgers that night, so the impresario led him up the road to a steakhouse where the promoter figured he scored his second point with Cash. By the time he arrived at the restaurant, the star was worrying about Vivian and the kids and whether some mountain lions were creeping down from the canyons to skulk around their home in Ojai. When the nervous father told Holiff that he had promised to telephone Vivian to reassure her, Holiff unveiled his car phone and offered it to Cash. The futuristic novelty impressed Cash, as did the fairly deep conversation that Holiff said the two shared later that night. Holiff recounted, "So I guess you put all those things together and the fact that I was articulate enough to be challenging to him, and he was smart enough and well read enough and interested enough to have a conversation other than crap. And that's how it started."

The unlikely couple, the tall Southern Baptist and the short Canadian Jew, began a private courtship. As if to demonstrate goodwill, Cash attempted to sabotage Carnall's dealings with Holiff whenever the two businessmen discussed Canadian tours. Cash would feed Holiff information about the fees Carnall paid to artists such as Rose Maddox and Bob Luman (who often toured with his show), which allowed Holiff to rebuff Carnall whenever he padded his asking price for the two artists.

Soon Cash and Holiff were dealing in the light of day. By the summer of 1961, with Carnall a memory, Holiff was hustling to prove his mettle as Cash's new manager. Thinking big, he first extracted two thousand dollars from Cash to travel to Asia to investigate concert opportunities. Holiff returned excited about the possibilities there and contacted Col. Tom Parker about a Presley-Cash tour of Japan.

Parker politely declined. But if Cash had any doubts about Holiff in 1961 over the failed overture to Presley, they soon dissipated as Holiff browbeat Columbia Records into offering a better contract to Cash. Holiff pulled off the trick when he and Cash met in New York with the debonair president of Columbia, Goddard Lieberson, whom Cash had dubbed "The Great White Father."

"I'm like a mystery guest, like a complete unknown entity," said Holiff. "And to Goddard Leiberson, I'm the equivalent of an irritating mosquito. Goddard Leiberson was an aristocrat married to a ballet dancer of considerable fame, and an elegant looking guy, and a classical music fan to the *nth* degree. But he either did, or pretended to have, great interest in Johnny."

Holiff figured Cash was tossing him into the lion's ring to test his worthiness to manage. "I decided that I had to move from being a spectator to this interrogation of deciding about me, to an active role.," said Holiff. "I had to suddenly become not good old, nice and mild mannered dumb-ass guy. I had to become assertive. So I picked the meeting with Goddard Leiberson where I was completely, totally out of my element. And here I am in his rather spacious office with this handsome-looking, rather elegant guy talking to Johnny about [the] contract. And I decided it was now or never; I either said something or it was over. That's how I felt. I became abrasive. I said, 'You're going through the motions. Actions speak louder than words, and so far it's all words. You don't appreciate your talent. You're not doing what can be done for him.'

"Goddard Leiberson gets very angry and he gets up and he storms out of the office. And he doesn't come back. And that's when my relationship with Johnny became an actual reality. I think he realized that I was either one of the world's best actors from a small town that ever existed, or else I rose to the occasion. I never dreamed I could, but I made my point. I got him sufficiently upset. The renegotiation took place."

Holiff rarely renegotiated for Cash again. Strung out and hungry for cash, the singer routinely appeared alone in Columbia's New York offices in search of advances and alterations to his contract. This frustrated Holiff, for his charge was no negotiator.

On the other hand, Holiff did play a central role in a 1961 merger that would define Cash's path for the next forty-two years. He hired June Carter to join the

Johnny Cash Show for a December performance in Dallas. Doing so, the manager brought into Cash's close and regular proximity the long-held object of his desires and secured for him a lifetime duet partner, show opener, lover, booster, seamstress, caretaker, and nemesis.

Everybody in country music knew June Carter. Daughter of Maybelle Carter of the seminal Carter Family, she had toddled out on the road with her mother and sisters Helen and Anita when the original Carter Family (with Maybelle, Sara, and A.P. Carter) broke up in the 1940s. Little Junie banged away on her autoharp with the new Carter Family as they futilely sought to reclaim the family glory, darting to dates in the Southeast or serenading audiences on one of the many regular radio broadcasts they called home over the years. In 1949, the band picked up the fledgling guitar wizard Chet Atkins in Knoxville hoping he would rejuvenate its sounds. Sadly, though, not even Atkins could enliven them. The electric honky-tonk age of the late 1940s and early 1950s drowned their old-timey sound, and by the time June joined Cash's package show, Mother Maybelle was working in a nursing home, relegated to the *Opry* on Saturday nights.

In the late 1940s, June had worked up a comedic routine, in which she cast herself as Aunt Polly, who was something of a Minnie Pearl, Jr. The skit may have spiced the Carters' show on the road, where rube humor rained down like corn spitting from a combine, but back at the *Opry*, next to veterans such as Pearl and Rod Brasfield, Aunt Polly seemed half-baked. June peaked early in her experiments with her comedic alter ego, when she recorded a hilarious take on Frank Loesser's "Baby, It's Cold Outside" with Homer and Jethro in 1949. With Cash, she'd always be a capable and funny stage foil, but Aunt Polly never gelled.

In 1952, June married country superstar Carl Smith, with whom she had daughter Carlene, but the union fractured not long after their child's birth in 1955. Shirking Cash, who surely wished to replace Smith (at least behind closed doors), June married again in 1957 to Nashville police officer Rip Nix, and with him she had another daughter, Rosey. But June never settled into family life. Torn by her traditional duties as a wife and mother as well as a dogged and genetically coded desire to perform, she clung to her career. She studied acting in New York and picked small television parts, not unlike those Cash himself was getting in the late 1950s.

By 1962, when June and the Carter Family had become regulars on Cash's road show, she had set aside acting for the time being and, for the sake of her children, was only playing ten country-music shows a month. However, the tide of Johnny Cash, which had first risen before her in 1956, eventually consumed her. By and by, she drifted from her home commitments, making every show, dodging the pranks, ironing the clothes, patching the holes, and falling for the star despite her marriage to Nix and Cash's to Vivian. She worried after Cash when they were off the road and worried after him when they were on the road. Where only Grant had dared to take on Cash's drug habit and erratic behavior, now there was June too. "It was a terrible shock when I found out John was taking pills," she wrote in a memoir published in 1979. "He dropped a few in front of me in Macon, Georgia, one afternoon, and I could hardly believe it. I knew he didn't sleep much at night. You could hear him roaming around his room if you were anywhere near. I could remember how it had been with Hank Williams a few years before when Hank took so much medicine for his bad back, and how my sisters and I had worried about him."

June welled up the courage to confront Cash about his pills and the poor behavior that accompanied them, and Cash seemed to appreciate in a meek way, just as he'd appreciated Holiff's rebuke of him in Ontario. "Once we were in Albuquerque, New Mexico, and we were all in the car waiting for John," continued June in her book. "He just wouldn't come out of his room. He wouldn't get out of bed, and we were going to miss the show in El Paso. He must have had a bad night, and bed was the only sensible place to be. . . . I looked at Marshall, Fluke, and Luther, gritted my teeth, went back in the motel, flung open his door, and hollered at the top of my lungs, 'Lay there, star!'"

Cash bolted after June, tailing her all the way into the car, which then screeched off to the airport. She wrote, "I sat there knowing I'd never get to work with the group again—a girl just doesn't holler things like that at her boss—and trying to figure out how I'd get new booking dates for the months ahead. Later at the airport, when I had my head in my coffee cup, Johnny handed me an Indian peace pipe he had gotten in the souvenir store, and we made El Paso on time."

Despite the rage June incited in Cash, described in her book's Holly Golightly tone, there was little chance that Cash was going to fire her. He'd been waiting for her to land nearby for years. Picking up where he left off when June married Nix, Cash's romantic pursuit of her must have begun immediately. And he must have been met with some success, because by the end of 1962 (June's first full year with the show) she was thinking and talking and writing about the torment of a mar-

ried woman loving a married man. It was the retreaded theme of a thousand coun-
try music songs, but when June sat down with Cash's friend Merle Kilgore to write
a song about tortured love, the verses that they created were unique and mysterious as the others were formulaic. "Ring of Fire" framed Cash and June's relationship as a question of love or death, prompting one *New York Times* writer to call it
many years later "probably the most complicated popular love song in country
music." June's sister Anita recorded the song first, but on March 25, 1963, Cash
gave the song a grave reading. With Jack Clement producing and a smart chorus of
mariachi horns added for zest, the country star turned "Ring of Fire" into one of
his standards. It also became an ethereal memorial to his and June's conflicted, celebrated love.

June's nascent affair with Cash raised eyebrows among the musicians on his
show, but her refusal to look the other way while Cash popped pills encouraged
Grant. After a few tastes of Cash's drug-induced anger, ill will, and hysteria, Grant
had concluded quickly that there would be no pleasant endgame for Cash if he
kept up his habits. So he thwarted Cash's suppliers whenever he could and, with
June, redoubled his efforts. "She and I fought a lot of battles through John's drug
years to keep him alive, keep him going," says Grant. "We stayed up night and day
to keep him alive and keep him going. We fought battle after battle after battle, and
as somebody said one time, jokingly, but it was the truth, 'We fought battle after
battle with John but we lost every one of them.' In a matter of speaking we *did*. But
I think in the long run we won out, we kept him alive."

There must have been times when Grant would have been happy had Cash not
survived his bouts with drug and alcohol consumption, for the burden of cleaning
up after him was taxing. He pulled him out of stupors, answered to promoters
whose shows Cash missed, and weathered Cash's criticism that stormed down
when his mood blackened. Unlike Cash, Grant prided himself on his self-control,
resisting many of the road's temptations (save for juvenile pranks) and scoffing at
Cash's gluttonous appetites. The notion of Cash as boss was ironic in Grant's eyes.
Cash was above him only because the band needed a front man. Indeed, Grant recognized Cash's gifts, not the least of which was his public charisma, but he always
believed Cash and the Tennessee Two had risen on the equal strength of three men.
As each year passed more quickly than the last, however, recognition of Grant's

role faded until most knew him only as a sideman—and often Cash treated him that way. The slight infuriated Grant, while the drug battles frustrated and drained him.

In front of Grant, and now June, emerged two Cashes: the one they called "J.R." or "John," the angel, and the one they called "Johnny," the demon. Perhaps we will never know the amount of grief that the demon in Cash rained down on Grant and June over the years, but it's clear that nobody would have blamed him or her for leaving him. So why did they stay? Was it fame and a meal ticket for June and fortune for Grant? Grant dismisses such speculation. It was, he says, the promise that the sober Cash, the one he and June both could love, would return. "We'd go out with him and he'd act like an animal and you just hoped and prayed for the time that he would come back and be the old J.R., the great, great, great man," he says. "No matter how he had treated me or how he had treated June, if you showed up for the first day of a tour and he was straight, immediately, it was all forgiven. You forgave him for everything that he did to you. You just forgave him for it. And that's what I did, always did."

Back in Nashville, June's brother-in-law Don Davis saw the fallout of her growing attachment to the increasingly erratic Cash. He'd watch June return home from tours, crippled with sadness, moaning, and taking to the bed. There was "slight physical abuse," recalls Davis, along with "harsh words and arguments." During June's split from Carl Smith in the 1950s, Davis had nursed her, taking her to the hospital during fainting spells and sitting up with her in the night reassuring her. So, naturally, he objected when Cash's treatment of her became so debilitating. Acting the big brother, he confronted Cash but, like Grant, discovered there was no single Cash to confront. It might be the contrite apologetic man or the unremorseful one. In any event, despite the interventions of Davis (or Grant), Johnny and June's clashes became a defining characteristic of their relationship.

On the road, June often shrank from confronting Cash, leaving it to others to hide the pills or push him onto the stage. One night in Ontario, June passed the cattle prod to Loretta Lynn, who was new to the business and on her first concert tour. "June got mad at him for some reason, I don't know," says Lynn. "(I know, but I'm not going to tell it.) I went in his dressing room and said, 'Johnny, get your overcoat on, you're going on stage.' Nobody else was doing it. They was mad at him. I went and helped him get his coat on and I said, 'You're on stage, boy.'"

Lynn observed a man that evening who needed Carrie Cash and her mothering, or June Carter and her mothering. "And that's all he needed," Lynn exclaims. "He wanted somebody to care enough to tell him."

~

8

BALLADEER

When Johnny Cash died in 2003, many reflected on a man who seemed to embody the American frontier spirit. Some remembered other Cashes: the troubled sinner, the redeemed Christian, the voice of social consciousness, and the premiere name in country music. Other voices of appreciation harked back again and again to a man majestic and courageous whom they said belonged on Mt. Rushmore with Washington, Jefferson, Lincoln, and Roosevelt. Certainly, he looked the part: his grim dented face and dark garb so Lincolnesque. With each day of mourning, a rising disjointed chorus of midnight chatters and Nashville stars elevated their man in black to that grand perch until it became the most hackneyed Cash cliché. In the call's increasing dullness, though, is the truth that Cash was their quintessential American, the last of the frontiersmen.

The image emerged in the late 1950s and early 1960s, seeded by various elements in Cash's presentation: the voice that was as deep and worn as a dry river canyon, the constant allusion to trains (those mighty engines of the westward expansion), and his compositions rooted in the American soil ("Give My Love to Rose," "Pickin' Time," "Five Feet High and Rising," and others). If Cash had done nothing but sing about trains and the rural life in a deeply American voice, the image would have thrived on its own. But Cash and his conspirators in the mass media and record business nurtured the image.

In 1959, amid his failed attempts to find a space all his own on television and movie screens, Cash appeared in a celebration of the West on NBC-TV's *Bell Telephone Hour*. It both exemplified and fortified Cash's link with the American past. A recent immigrant from radio, where it debuted in 1940, the *Bell Telephone Hour* was one of the gilded variety shows in the broadcast media, showcasing the best of classical music and Broadway show tunes. The cast changed with every program, but the featured artists were always culled from the establishment of American popular culture. The selection of Cash affirmed his status in entertainment and was one of the building blocks of the balladeer image that would soon come to shroud him. Hosted by the avuncular Burl Ives on October, 23, 1959 (only the third broadcast since jumping from radio), the program featured Coplandesque musical arrangements, the solos of Broadway stars Edith Adams and Dolores Gray, and a hefty slice of the American Ballet Theatre's performance of *Billy the Kid*. At first it seemed an odd fraternity for Cash, who normally consorted on television with the rambunctious *Town Hall Party* clan in Los Angeles. But the directors skillfully cast the young singer in the role of lonely troubadour, striding through town unsmiling to tell a story or two before leaving at dawn. When Ives introduced the cast, Cash sat on a barrel, leaning back, hand wrapped around his raised knee. His face deeply ambivalent, he refused to play to the camera. He seemed the rogue drifter feared by the fathers of the town's daughters. The mood around Cash lightened when he dished out Stephen Foster's "Camptown Races," as American a song as any on the show that night. But Cash stood alone throughout a program of intricately choreographed scenes from Broadway. He was the grave figure of the West. At show's end, when the cast belted out a corny yet rousing chorus of "Ta-Ra-Ra-Boom-De-Ay," Cash retreated into the crowd, discomfited by the big closing.

Many of Cash's appearances on television in the era of the *Bell Telephone Hour* took the show's cue: Cash in black, standing alone, growling the songs of his fabled catalog, cast in the past. An *Ed Sullivan Show* broadcast, also in 1959, was a companion to the *Bell Telephone Hour*, placing Cash's performance of "Don't Take Your Guns to Town" among a reenactment of the Lincoln-Douglas debates and Frankie Laine's sung rendition of the Gettysburg Address. Hosts rarely introduced him as hillbilly or country and western. He was always the folk singer, America's number-one folk singer. A visit to Los Angeles television's *Star Route USA* was just another that echoed the *Bell Telephone Hour's* presentation of Cash. Hosted by Charlie Williams, a friend and cowriter of Cash's hit "I Got Stripes," the entire program was dedicated to Cash. It featured his and the Tennessee Three's own versions of his songs and covers of his songs by the show's cast of regular singers. Cash appeared hidden in shadows throughout, as if encased in another time. He sidestepped "Ballad of a Teenage Queen" and "Guess Things Happen That Way," opting instead for the songs that linked him with the natural landscape and the hard times of rural life: "Pickin' Time" and "Five Feet High and Rising." When Cash and the Tennessee Three launched into his "Big River," which used the Mississippi River as a metaphor for elusive love, Perkins's steely introduction slashed through the studio, marrying the electric guitar's audacity to the ancient river's power and omnipotence. In the television variety-and music-program world, there was no figure more suited than Cash to deliver the echoes of the past. He was palatable to the audiences of the emerging television age: seasoned in voice and orientation yet patently modern (like western television's Fess Parker and James Arness), his hair slicked back like Elvis's, and a riveting electric guitar behind him.

While television cast Cash as the bard of American living rooms, Don Law and Columbia Records were making sure that record turntables and radios resonated the theme. Along with popular songs like "Ring of Fire" and "Understand Your Man," recorded with the teen market and his core country constituency in mind, Cash released a collection of concept albums from 1960 to 1965: *Ride This Train*; *Blood, Sweat and Tears*; *Bitter Tears*; and *Johnny Cash Sings Ballads of the True West*. They delved into the West, American history, and the working experience and cemented his reputation as popular music's chief historian. In country music, thematic albums were nothing new. But few artists hung their career on albums that echoed the anguish of the American Indian (*Bitter Tears*) and the common laborer (*Blood, Sweat and Tears*) and the struggles of the fledgling American nation (*Ride This Train* and *Johnny Cash Sings Ballads of the True West*). The albums' modest sales must have disappointed Law's bosses at Columbia and diminished the singer's bargaining power at the label, but Cash was undeterred. "I got a lot of credit for it among the other artists," he remarked in the 1970s. "A lot of other people openly admired them, but some people didn't want to accept the fact that a country artist was doing things like that. I had a few people tell me that it wasn't country and that it wasn't right for me to do it. They said it wasn't commercial and all that jazz." In later years, he cited *Ride This Train* and *Bitter Tears* as among his best works.

Some have speculated that Cash paid tribute to commoners and outcasts to deal with the guilt he felt as his fame and prosperity frayed his humble moorings. But the albums must also be viewed in the context of Cash's aspirations for his music. He was determined to focus on the balladeer's burden, to become the link in a chain forged by stories about people and their lives. The roots of this endeavor lead back to his childhood, where he mused on western themes in poetry and absorbed the stories of the radio and country raconteurs around him. He had sought to claim his link when he moved to California and enlisted with Columbia Records in the late 1950s.

The hit singles paid the bills and satisfied the accountants; the concept albums fulfilled his dreams. Of all of Cash's recordings, they remain among the truest reflections of Cash's artistic vision.

Saul Holiff liked to claim credit for his hand in packaging Cash as the nation's troubadour when he gave his client the title "America's Foremost Singing Storyteller." "He liked that," said Holiff. "It hadn't been used. It was used and abused later on. Everybody became a Singing Storyteller at one time or another." What the appellation lacked in zing, it made up for in plain truth. For the most part, Cash was telling stories, not simply repeating verses of heartbreak and romance like many of his contemporaries across pop music.

Holiff pasted the new appellation to Cash's concert program for the singer's May 10, 1962, appearance at Carnegie Hall, a night that Cash must have hoped would perpetuate his troubadour image. Lumbering on stage dressed as his hero Jimmie Rodgers, carrying a train lantern and wearing denim coveralls, he aspired to bring to the audience the heritage of his music. Like Columbia A&R man John Hammond's fabled Spirituals to Swing concerts of the late 1930s, which gathered the range of jazz influences, Cash attempted to present the panoply of country music, where it had been and where it was going. On the bill with him were, of course, the Carter Family, Texas honky-tonker George Jones, bluegrass vocalist Mac Wiseman, and the young country-folk trio the Glaser Brothers.

As the ticket holders paged through their programs and nestled in their plush seats, they might have been anticipating a night that would be akin to the resurrection of Hank Williams, but Cash disappointed. Though he was well up to the task of expertly acting his music when his pill use was reigned in, on that night, Cash was helplessly in addiction's grip. Many audiences across America had suffered through Cash's croaking performances when no amount of soda, coffee, and water could replenish him. Carnegie Hall was one of those nights. "I could only whisper," wrote Cash. "And as hard as I tried, song after song for an hour, I couldn't sing. The audience was disappointed, but accepted with reservation the M.C.'s explanation that I had a bad cold and laryngitis. I found a dark corner backstage and sat there in deep depression. Mother Maybelle Carter and her daughters Helen, Anita, and June came back to try to cheer me up."

The review in the next day's *New York Times* memorialized the embarrassment. Reviewer Robert Shelton discerned Cash's potential for greatness but little else. "Mr. Cash came highly endorsed by reputation and a series of successful recordings," he wrote. "He is known as a song-writer and singer in the vein of some of the late country greats, such as the late Jimmie Rodgers and the late Hank Williams. But the hoarseness of his voice and the incohesiveness of his performance suggest that another hearing is needed before his name can be mentioned in the company of such reputable country minstrels."

What might have been a major recommendation of Cash's folk-music credentials became yet another lost night on his tortured road. On the concert circuit anyway, it was back to the parks and ranches to play "I Walk the Line."

Save for June, who daily honored her family's musical tradition in concerts, Cash was alone in pursuit of his musical visions. The artists he toured with generally ran in the honky-tonk vein. He was spending less time with his Western-oriented California clan as he sought to avoid his family, whom he now considered stifling. Grant and Perkins couldn't see the vision. They'd been reduced to sidemen and were happy to lope back to their Memphis homes between tours, the days of creation in their basements long over.

One evening in Las Vegas, though, Cash thought he found a lifeline. Listening to *The Freewheelin' Bob Dylan* album of 1963, he heard a voice that siphoned waters from the past, protested the status quo, and sounded as good as any country-music performer's he knew. Impressed, he dashed off a letter to Dylan, who also recorded for Columbia, initiating a halting correspondence fueled by Cash's curiosity and Dylan's obvious respect for a man who had recorded modern electric folk since the 1950s.

"I invited him to come see me in California," said Cash, describing the early letters, "but when he came to California later he couldn't find my house. I got another letter that was written in Carmel and by the time I answered it, he'd already gone back to New York. When I was in New York not long after that John Hammond told me that Bob was in town. So he came up and we met at Columbia Records. We spent a few hours together, talking about songs, swappin' songs and he invited me up to his house in Woodstock."

Dylan's invitation amounted to something of a welcome to a scene that balladeer Utah Phillips called the "great folk scare." Cash's exploration thereof is somewhat elusive. Dylan, not surprisingly, has never talked about it much and refused an invitation to talk about it for this book, and Cash in later years distanced himself from his 1960s fascination with Greenwich Village minstrels. In the throes of the Nashville music establishment by the mid-1970s, perhaps he thought his dalliances with the folk scene might rupture his image for the mainstream country-music audience.

It's undeniable, though, that Cash found kinship among the young men and women of the Northeast who were reviving the American ballad and using their roots-based music to question authority. On his first visit to the Gaslight nightclub on MacDougal Street, probably in late 1963, Cash must have worried that a few of the locals would question the presence of the network-television, big-label star. Indeed, a few men and women murmured about it when the razor-thin man sauntered down the steps into the well that was the Gaslight, but he was in good company; Peter La Farge and Ed McCurdy escorted him.

Word of La Farge had reached Cash earlier in the year. Nashville promotion man Gene Ferguson had shown him La Farge's "The Ballad of Ira Hayes," about the Pima Indian who helped raise the flag at Iwo Jima, only to die impoverished, alcoholic, and forgotten on a reservation. La Farge himself claimed Indian blood but was probably just carrying on like many of his peers who reinvented themselves as bluesmen or children of the Dust Bowl. La Farge performed in rodeos in the late 1940s, boxed, and acted in Shakespearan plays. Lately he had turned to writing about the Indian experience, and he lived near Ramblin' Jack Elliott in the Earle Hotel in Greenwich Village. "He was pretty suave," recalls Elliott about his friend. "He always wore very beautiful tailor-made rodeo clothes."

Like La Farge and Elliott, Ed McCurdy was a regular at the Gaslight, crooning his ballads in a rich baritone voice. He was an elder statesman of the scene, having recorded since the early 1950s and achieving some fame on the college-campus circuit.

Together, La Farge and McCurdy licensed Cash in the Village, and although some in the small subterranean room might have scoffed at Cash, he was a bona fide curiosity. Elliott, who'd learned at the side of Woody Guthrie in the early 1950s, was startled at the sight of the singer. "It might have been a Monday night, I guess it probably was," says Elliott. "I walked in there one night and there was this big tall fella standing there. He had to duck his head, and carry his head sort of bent over to the side because the ceiling was so low and he was so tall. It was Johnny Cash." The crowd, it turned out, was only too happy to welcome him. He was a star whose voice had thundered above the teenage rock and pop of the 1950s, communicating an agrarian sensibility and vision. His rural background gave him an authority that resonated with the suburban pack that had traveled to the city to play its music.

In an impressionistic *Sing Out!* essay published in 1965, La Farge reckoned that Cash had been searching when he entered the Gaslight. "He wasn't looking for much," wrote La Farge, "just himself." The months after his appearance at the club would bear out La Farge's observation, as Cash latched onto La Farge and Elliott and recorded their songs, as well as Bob Dylan's.

In March of 1964, Cash first turned to "The Ballad of Ira Hayes," which was probably the first straight-ahead protest song Cash had ever recorded. He spat the lyrics, imbued them with impatience and disgust that the nation would allow to languish one who had fought nobly for its cause. When he brought "Ira Hayes" to the Newport Folk Festival on Saturday, July 25, 1964, he was more subdued. Leaving his intensity in the Nashville studio where he recorded it, Cash performed the song with caution, even joking about its commercial prospects. Perhaps he thought the folk audience would question his credentials to sing protest music, but he had nothing to fear. A lonely hoot shot up from the audience when Cash mentioned La Farge's name, and the audience offered up a sturdy applause when he finished the ballad.

Robert Shelton of *The New York Times*, who had dismissed Cash's Carnegie Hall debacle two years before, was much more generous at Newport. He praised the singer's balladry and credited him with building a bridge between the folk revival and commercial country music.

Cash closed his set with the Carter Family's "Keep on the Sunnyside" before scampering into the night with Bob Dylan.

～

There's little evidence that Cash and Dylan spent much time together after the meeting in Hammond's office that Cash later described. But the 1964 festival, which Dylan hung around for all three days leading up to his headlining performance on the final day, gave them some time to compare notes. After Cash's set, he and his troupe had to shove off for Nashville for a session before commencing a tour through the upper Midwest, but before he left, Cash and Dylan set up at a local motel. They spent the night taping songs with Joan Baez and her sister and brother-in-law, Mimi and Richard Farina. Writing about the evening years later, Robert Shelton said that Dylan and Baez's embrace of Cash invigorated him: "To find Newport so warm made him feel even taller than he was. It touched him to find that the two young stars of the folk world, Baez and Dylan, cared enough about him to spend the whole night taping him. To show his appreciation, he gave Dylan one of his own guitars."

Cash and Dylan continued to communicate on a number of subjects, including the Dylan's romantic woes. His girlfriend at the time, Susan Rotolo, had angered him by going off to Italy for a year. When she returned, she ran into Cash, who had taken Dylan's view that she'd deserted him. Spying Cash in the Gaslight, Rotolo was excited to meet the star; they had never met before. But Cash just stared at her. "I just said, 'You know, I really like your music,'" she remembered, "and I said who I was, and he just nodded. But he didn't say, 'Sit down.'" Rotolo quickly determined that Cash didn't like her, and she crept back into the club's shadows.

Just as Cash's relationship with La Farge and McCurdy paved his way into the Gaslight on that first visit, his burgeoning association with Dylan freed him in folk circles. And the association had become very public. Just forty-eight hours after his guitar pull with Dylan and Baez in Newport, Cash and his band crowded into the Nashville studios to record a first take on Dylan's "Mama You've Been on My

Mind" (he eventually got a final take in December of 1964). By summer's end he'd also waxed a duet with June Carter on Dylan's "It Ain't Me Babe," which climbed to the top five of the country charts late in the year and crossed over to the pop side.

When he wasn't trading verses with Dylan or recording his songs, he courted La Farge and Elliott. Cash was just building another community, like in the air force, or in mid-1950s Memphis, or in Los Angeles. He seemed to know that traveling and picking with fresh voices would feed his own music. In the winter of 1965, a day after a show in Boston with Ramblin' Jack, Cash, Jack, and June clambered into a rental car to visit Dylan near Woodstock, New York. The young artist was there enjoying solitude, picking guitar on benches along the quiet streets and writing in the Café Espresso. Elliott's wife followed behind them in her small car.

"John wanted to go over to Woodstock to retrieve an old Gibson guitar that used to belong to Gene Autry, and he had loaned it to Bob Dylan," explains Elliott. (Could this have been the fabled guitar that many assumed Cash, in a gesture of respect, bestowed on Dylan at Newport? If it was, he didn't mention it to Elliott.) "He wanted to go get it back from Bob. We rode over there with June drivin' and John ridin' shotgun, and me in the backseat. We stopped to have a little bite to eat on the Mass. Pike. I don't know if we really ate anything, but John went to a machine that dispensed all kinds of little plastic doo-dads and gifts and things, and he bought a bunch of them and gave them out to everyone. Then my wife couldn't start the car. It was an English car. And John looked at it, we lifted the hood and he removed a spark plug and he cleaned the spark plug with a pocket knife. I said, 'You're a mechanic. Where'd you learned that John?' He said, 'When I was a boy, I grew up on a farm and I had a neighbor who had a car and I used to watch him.'"

Cash's handiness with a car engine only fed Elliott's belief that Cash was "the real thing," the kind of man's man absent from the folk scene, who lived a "real" life and sang what he lived. The car restarted, although it would run out of gas later. June, Cash, and Elliott, who were so immersed in chattering about songs and life that they had not noticed Elliott's wife's flagging car behind them, sped back along the Turnpike to find her. Evening had fallen when they reached Dylan's refuge. He'd been living at Albert Grossman's house, but mindful of waking his manager, he received his tired guests at the Café Espresso.

"Bob played us a couple of his brand new songs that he had just written, one of which was "It's Alright, Ma, (I'm Only Bleeding),'" says Elliott. "John got the

Gibson back from Bob and after an hour or two of conversation and singing and picking, we got back in the car and headed down towards New York City, and John and June must have dropped me off in Greenwich Village where I was living. They were headin' to Virginia."

Besides the guitar, Cash left Woodstock empty-handed, unlike Newport when he'd walked away with Dylan's blessing to record "It Ain't Me Babe" and "Mama, You've Been on My Mind." Bob reserved "It's Alright, Ma" for his album *Bringing It All Back Home*. Still, Cash was hard-pressed to squander a long day spent with the folkies. He turned to Elliott on the drive out of Woodstock and asked him to sing something he'd wrote. Elliott recounts, "I said, 'I never wrote nothing, but I've been trying to write a song lately.' He said, 'Well, sing me that,' I said, 'Okay' I only had one verse [from] 'Cup of Coffee.' I sang the first verse and that was it. It just ran dry. He laughed. He thought it was very funny. I didn't realize it was funny. I just thought it was a song about a tired trucker. I just had the one verse. His laughter egged me on, and I soon made up a second verse to it. And some speech talking thing . . . some of that got written right in the car. John memorized it. He liked it an awful lot. A week later, I got a letter from John. He had sung my song a few days after [the drive] on a TV station down in Virginia." In his note, Cash invited Elliott to Nashville to help him record his "Cup of Coffee."

When Cash turned to Elliott's song in Nashville in March of 1965, he was deep into his communion with the folk world. Beginning in late 1964, as "It Ain't Me Babe" scaled the charts, and continuing for the better part of 1965, he routed his Newport inspiration into virtually every recording, eschewing the commercial singles which had subsidized his concept albums. In December of 1964, he had taken another shot at "Mama, You've Been on My Mind" and tackled a raft of material that may well have appeared on a Vanguard or Arhoolie album: "The Long Black Veil," a neo-folk song brushed with artificial patina by Nashville's Marijohn Wilkin and Danny Dill; "The Wall," a prisoner's song by Harlan Howard; "Wildwood Flower" by A.P. Carter; and "You Wild Colorado," his own homage to one of the great rivers of the West. In this flurry, he unveiled his most unapologetic protest song yet, "All of God's Children Ain't Free." *I'd whistle down the road but I wouldn't feel right/I'd hear somebody crying out at night/From a sharecropper's shack or penitentiary/All God's children ain't free.* Before the year was out, he also dusted off

Johnny Horton's "When It's Springtime in Alaska," the country chestnut "Orange Blossom Special," and the Irish ballad "Danny Boy."

Law released "Orange Blossom Special" as a single. When it roared from the roundhouse on its way to the country and pop charts in February 1965, Cash was preparing to record his most ambitious concept album to date, the two-disc *Johnny Cash Sings Ballads of the True West*. According to Cash's notes for the album, Law had urged him to record an album of Western songs in 1961, and then in late 1964, the dapper producer (mindful, probably, of his singer's new folk influences) reiterated the idea. As Cash told it, to find content and perspective he cracked open volumes of American ballads and he interviewed Tex Ritter for three hours. Ramblin' Jack Elliott offered up the decades-old "The Ballad of Charles Guiteau," about the man who shot President Garfield in 1881. Elliott learned the aged narrative from his banjo-playing friend Darrell Adams who had learned it from Bascom Lamar Lumsford, a folklorist and musician from North Carolina. Not to be bothered with the song's rambling history, Cash gave Elliott writer's credit and retitled it "Mister Garfield."

June Carter delivered "The Road to Kaintuck," about the bloodied way to the West; Mother Maybelle produced "A Letter from Home," a lament for a homesick cowboy; and Peter La Farge gave up "Stampede." The songs came easily enough, but when Cash sought to channel the Western spirit to touch the songs' essence, he embarked on a torturous odyssey. Whether it was just a bad drug trip in his back yard or a lonely sojourn in the Arizona desert, we'll never know. "I followed trails in my Jeep and on foot, and I slept under mesquite bushes and in gullies," he wrote in his liner notes. "I heard the timber wolves, looked for golden nuggets in old creek beds, sat for hours beneath a manzanita bush in an ancient Indian burial ground, breathed the West wind and heard the tales it tells only to those who listen. . . . I walked across alkali flats where others had walked before me, but hadn't made it. I ate mesquite beans and squeezed that water from a barrel cactus. I was saved once by a forest ranger, lying flat on my face, starving. I learned to throw a bowie knife and kill a jack rabbit at forty yards, not for the sport but because I was hungry. I learned of the true West the hard way—a la 1965."

Cash often strayed off into the desert, to commune with God or hash out his guilty feelings over June and Vivian, but the incredible accuracy of the knife-throwing hunter weakened by starvation and dehydration (not to mention the residue of amphetamines), says that Cash was learning more than folk tradition from his new cronies. He had also picked up the art of myth making. If Dylan could jaw about vagabond journeys out West when he'd really been sitting in a high-school math class in Hibbing, Minnesota, and Jack Elliott could cook up a cowboy personage out of his Brooklyn childhood (as Elliot Charles Adnopoz), why couldn't Cash reinvent himself as the authentic messenger from the West, as burnt and beaten down as the desert floor? After all, Cash might have reasoned, wasn't that the folk singer's job, to be the vessel of emotions and experiences observed along the way? Channeling the aura of the desert was just a slight exaggeration.

Released in 1965, the double-album set of Cash's Western world was too much for most consumers' wallets, but a single-disc version released in 1966 sold much better, reaching number four on the country album charts.

The flirtation with Dylan and company never remolded Cash as a folk revivalist, but it did encourage and redirect his pursuit of music associated with the pleasant and the pitiful of the American legacy. The mass audience, ignorant of Cash's traipses through the Village, probably saw the product of his explorations as nothing more than another spin on the American ballads he'd been recording since the 1950s. Certainly, he grew artistically from the intersection with the folk revivalists, and his association with Dylan sporadically continued throughout the 1960s. But the lasting public legacy of his folk visitation seems to be its part in swelling Cash's quintessential American image, which became fully realized in the 1970s. The concept albums, western ballads, traditional country numbers, and neo-folk songs recorded in the heart of the 1960s were part and parcel of Cash's later public role as America's American. He would be the man whose music was shot to the moon in a capsule, who played Abraham Lincoln in a blockbuster mini-series, who was a major actor in America's official celebration of the bicentennial, who came to be the voice of American rail history, and who led many to claim that he deserved a space on Mt. Rushmore.

There is one videotaped moment that encapsulates (like no other readily available source) Cash's relationship with the folk world, his fascination with the scene, and the scene's fascination with him. It is his appearance on Pete Seeger's *Rainbow Quest*, a program which aired on educational television in the New York City area. Seeger, the father figure of the folk revival, hosted artists with ties to the ballad tradition, sitting them down on a spare yet homey set and drawing out the music from their repertoire that he found interesting.

Appearing in 1965, Cash was frightful on the show, yet the program freed him to chortle out about songs he loved. It was a rare public opportunity. Sitting in a circle with June and Seeger, talking about his music and childhood, he lurched about like a heroin addict, squirming in his chair, hugging his stomach, and heavily rocking his chair back and forth. He scratched his neck, roughly massaged his chest, and twirled the toes of his boots. He sucked down cigarettes as if they were chocolate sticks. He interrupted his host, talked over June as she meekly attempted to tell stories about Sara, A.P., and Mother Maybelle, and dropped his lighter on the floor. Seeger and June, the sober friends, gave Cash his distance so as not to be elbowed by his thrashing about or engulfed by his agitated and overflowing personality. When the three fell into the Carter Family's "Worried Man Blues," June appeared to embody her own worry, wondering perhaps if Cash would tip over in the chair and collapse into a pile of long bones.

There was only one tranquilizer for Cash's edginess, the songs. Like a direct flow of Valium to the veins, the singing calmed Cash's tics and jerks and violent spasms. The songs were his fiber; he could recall them at the mere suggestion, from seldom-heard Carter Family tunes to ancient spirituals. He sang them without hesitation.

Even in his agitation, Cash seemed at home, showing enjoyment that one supposes he experienced whenever he communed with Dylan and other folk revivalists. Where else could he share his love for traditional music? And Seeger was captivated by the tightly wound spring in front of him. Despite his apparent discomfort with Cash's strange twisting in his chair, Seeger was unstintingly polite while he fawned over Cash's popular success and rootedness in the soil. "I was never a cotton farmer," confessed Seeger in his introduction of Cash. "I never walked behind a mule. Never drove a truck either. . . . But this fella . . . came out of a family of hard working people in Arkansas. Done a lot of hard work himself. He also liked to pick a guitar and he liked to make up songs. And his songs touched the heart strings of all kinds of people around the country." In Cash, Seeger found the authenticity that was largely absent from the folk movement. In Seeger, Cash found the sustenance and inspiration of community.

Motoring through New England with Ramblin' Jack, traipsing through the wilds in search of Indian spirits, and hanging out at the Gaslight while keeping up a breathless touring pace took Cash away from home for months at a time. And yet "months at a time" actually sounds too regular for Cash. There was no regularity to his reappearances in California. He was simply gone indefinitely. His intensifying affair with June, as well as his invigorated interest in recording led him to camp in Nashville, if he stopped at all, rather than return to Los Angeles.

His negligence frayed Vivian's endurance and puzzled his children, who were growing up with an unusual notion of fatherhood. Cash certainly was cognizant of his fatherhood, as Saul Holiff recalled when he was touring Ireland with Cash in the summer of 1961. "We were heading towards Waterford, and we were going through a small place called Tara. And it was a horrific storm, thunderstorm and lightning. And we stopped for shelter in this old, five-hundred-year-old monastery that was falling apart with no roof. And Vivian was pregnant, expecting in about a month. We were in Tara, and that's when he said, 'That's what we'll name my daughter.' I don't know if he knew it was a daughter. That's how Tara got her name. But that was an amazing narrative of gloom and doom, and stuff worthy of old 18th century English literature."

Cash had divined a name for his child in the Irish mist, yet in later years, Vivian told eldest daughter Rosanne that Tara escaped his mind when he arrived home several days after Tara's birth on August 24, 1961. "He came off the road and they sat talking for a few minutes," explains Rosanne. "And she said, 'Don't you want to see the baby?' And he said 'Oh, I forgot we had her.' She also told me something Dad said once that having four children made him feel trapped, and she said, 'Why?' And, he said, 'When there's three, they can form a circle around you and you can still get out. If there's four you can't get out.' Now, that is so Dad. That is so something he would say."

Taking his cowboy philosophy of child rearing with him, Cash departed a few days after meeting Tara. When September came, he was in Iowa, back on stage. Kathy Cash asserts that virtually nothing could pull him back. "Dad quit coming home," she says. "I remember one year Mom went an entire year without knowing where he was. Their anniversary came, didn't hear from him. Christmas came, didn't hear from him. Birthdays came. It was awful. We didn't even know if he was alive, except we'd see something on the news saying he'd performed here or there. He had the office send his schedule. He was down there in New York with Bob Dylan, hanging out with him.

"I'll never forget on their anniversary, Mom sitting in the living room by herself just crying and smoking and drinking coffee and, you know, standing in that picture window. She stood in that picture window, it seemed like our entire childhood waiting for him to drive up. And I'll never forget our housekeeper, sweet lady, felt so bad for Mom that she brought her in a little plant and something else, I forget. I didn't know whether to say 'happy anniversary,' to acknowledge it or not. But [our housekeeper said] 'I just want you to know I'm thinking of you.' And Mom just burst into tears."

Kathy says Christmas was no better. She remembers that in 1964 Vivian and the girls celebrated without him. And then early in the new year, after another prolonged absence, Cash appeared. "All of a sudden we wake up one morning and Dad's there," says Kathy. "And he's brought each of us a combination radio and turntable with tons of records, and the whole thing is spread out in the living room where our Christmas tree would have been. I remember walking in there and going 'Hi, Daddy.' He said 'Hi, baby. Merry Christmas.' And I just looked at him and looked at all the presents and walked out. He said, 'Wait a minute, I got you a present.' I said, 'I'm too sad. Where were you Christmas?' And I know it hurt his feelings, but I couldn't help it."

Cash gazed down at his daughter's big brown eyes and apologized.

9

SELF-DESTRUCTION

Cash's family and bandmates witnessed firsthand the scourges that drugs had brought upon him, and only the more gullible concert fans bought the claim of a bad cold whenever the singer wobbled and whispered through live shows. But the general public who knew Cash only from his TV appearances and hit songs was ignorant of the singer's troubles. Robert Shelton of *The New York Times* had politely ignored the chemical elephant lurching around the stage when he panned the Carnegie Hall show in 1962. And many who saw Cash fence-post thin on television in those days before Woodstock and the rise of the drug culture were probably too naïve to suppose that it was addiction gnawing away at him.

America woke up to Cash's self-destruction in early October of 1965, when newspapers, television, and radio reported his arrest on federal drug charges in El Paso, Texas. It was the culmination of a bad week. A few days earlier, he'd been in New York where he was to anchor the elaborate finale of a "Nashville in New York" edition of CBS-TV's *Steve Lawrence Show*. He and the Tennessee Three were to open the routine with "I Walk the Line," out of which would grow orchestral accompaniment followed by interjections from Eddy Arnold, Minnie Pearl, and Steve Lawrence. The conductor and arranger Bill Walker, a native Australian only recently settled in America, wondered during dress rehearsals whether the dark-garbed star was fit for the job. "The whole thing hinged on Johnny starting this whole thing off," says Walker, who would join the *Johnny Cash Show* on ABC-TV in 1969. "I'd rehearsed the orchestra part, and we seemed to be okay there. And so Johnny gets on stage, and he's out of it." Luther Perkins thumped out the deep intro to Cash's 1956 hit and Cash stumbled in with his ponderous hum, but there he stopped. "He never, ever started the song," continues Walker. "He just started and looked at the audience. Well, the producer came over to me and said, 'What is going on here?' Now, I'm the new kid in town . . . and I'm ruined." While Cash droned his opening for the twelfth time, Walker rushed over to Saul Holiff who was watching an all-too-familiar scene. "So, Saul went over and just took him off the show, took him completely. And these guys got in their bus and left."

Walker stayed up all night in New York writing Cash out of the number while the Cash troupe darted South for a short tour of Texas. The conclusion of that tour would mark Cash's undoing. In the hours after the last show in Dallas, while the rest of the musicians scattered for a few day's rest, Cash skipped his flight back home to Los Angeles, scampered down to El Paso, and hailed a cab to Juarez, Mexico. There he purchased socks full of amphetamines.

While he was sitting on a plane on Monday, October 4th, waiting to fly out of the El Paso International Airport, two narcotics agents nabbed him. They believed the singer had bagged some heroin in Juarez, a misimpression that relieved Cash after they confronted him. He told them he'd never tried heroin. Nonetheless, the pills were controlled substances that Cash had illegally obtained. The agents arrested him and threw him in jail. When Sam Phillips called the jail to offer help, Cash knew that the wire services were tapping out the dreadful news, but he was afraid to ask his old mentor how he knew his whereabouts, ashamed that his children and parents now knew the sad truth.

Recounting his brief incarceration in his first autobiography, he wrote about the pain of disappointing loved ones and recoiling from his cell's filth. "The plumbing didn't work. There was no mattress, no pillow—just a dirty blanket over the springs. The light stayed on all night. I watched the roaches crawl across the floor. Some of the others were laughing and cursing each other. I heard a boy crying and another one praying. I tried to pray and couldn't. The pills wore off about sunup, and I finally slept. At noon they brought me a bowl of black-eyed peas and a piece of bread, which I ate." Cash's autobiographical account suggests that peace had fallen over him as he woke and ate his jail-cell rations. In reality, he was agitated. Dressed in patent-leather slip-ons and a rumpled grey gabardine suit for his bond hearing, he hissed at reporters who gathered in the courtroom and threatened to kick a photographer's camera from his hands.

Marshall Grant, always the fixer, found an El Paso lawyer who arranged bail for Cash, and in the end, got him off with a one-thousand-dollar fine and a stern lecture from the judge.

Two months after being bailed out of the El Paso jail, Cash returned to the city for his arraignment, where he pleaded guilty to the drug charges. Vivian accompanied him, to garner sympathy for the singer, one supposes. When they emerged together from the courthouse, an Associated Press photographer snapped a shot that, when reproduced in the nation's newspapers, gave Vivian the appearance of a light-skinned black woman. The image presented a dilemma in January of 1966, when white supremacist groups in the South, angered at this apparent miscegenation, began calling for a boycott of Cash's shows and records. The National States Rights Party, a racist organization based in Birmingham, Alabama, skewered the singer in its newspaper, *The Thunderbolt*: "Money from the sale of [Cash's] records goes to scum like Johnny Cash to keep them supplied with dope and negro women."

The charges naturally alarmed Cash and Saul Holiff, as they faced the threat of canceled shows throughout the South. In defense, Holiff scrambled to mount public relations and legal efforts to defuse the rumors about Vivian. "And that meant contacting newspapers to get the story out about what was correct to offset articles that were repeating these hate things," said Holiff in 2004, "to offset the picture of them standing in front of a courthouse in El Paso, where she did definitely look very dark. And I spent days and weeks and months." What was at stake, of course, was the core Southern audience that pumped life blood through Cash's career, a demographic that was likely to condemn interracial unions.

Newspaper articles defending Cash, many of which Holiff instigated, pitted the star as a hero fighting the Ku Klux Klan, even though it wasn't the Klan *per se* crusading against Cash. But even momentary reflection on the conflict reveals a thorny question about the singer's sentiments on race. In denying that he was married to a black woman, what was he saying about black people, men and women? Was it a slur to be linked to a black woman? Cash and Holiff's battle, tailored to win white support, suggested as much.

In the months after *The Thunderbolt* article appeared, Cash pressed on with his Southern shows, weathering mild protests and harassment, including a leaflet campaign in Knoxville, Tennessee, and a loud call for a boycott of his show in Mobile, Alabama, in October of 1966. In the end, however, the charges evaporated, having had little effect on his tour grosses. In fact, press accounts of Southern shows in 1966 show that ticket sales in Dixieland capitals remained brisk. The only cancellations appeared to be linked to indignation over the singer's drug arrest.

Although the singer may have picked up sympathy among progressive audiences, who may have counted Cash's self-defense as a strike against racism, eldest daughter Rosanne saw the battle as another Cashian smoke screen. "He wrote me a letter from the road during the height of his drug use and during the height of the Ku Klux Klan episode," she says. "And he said something about why he couldn't come home at the end of his tour because he had to stand up for what he thought was right and fight the Ku Klux Klan. And I must have been nine maybe, something like that. And I had literally torn the letter in half. And put it back in the envelope and saved it. I remember it was my way of saying, 'That's not true. You're just staying away because you want to stay away.' I was angry."

The regret and shame that weighted down Cash immediately after his arrest melted away as the weeks passed. Back in Nashville to record Bob Dylan's "One Too Many Mornings" before traveling with Vivian back to El Paso for his arraignment on December 28, 1965, he sat down with journalist Dixie Deen. Deen was a friend of his who had recently married Nashville singer-songwriter Tom T. Hall; she had also co-written "Troublesome Waters" with Mother Maybelle Carter and her husband Ezra Carter, which Cash recorded in 1964. Defiant for a man on his way to meet a Texas judge, Cash's response was memorialized in one of Deen's regular features for *Music City News*, a Nashville monthly.

"I don't pretend to be anything I'm not," protested Cash in Deen's presence. "I've seen the bad publicity, the horrible pictures of me in the papers within the last couple of months, and I don't even read what it says, because I know exactly what the papers want to do. . . . They want to make [this arrest] sensational, and prove that they are heroes by tearing down an image, or an image which they think has been built up. I am guilty of as many sins as the average person, but I don't say that I am guilty of any more than the average person. I may have a few different ones, but certainly no more."

Quoting Frank Sinatra's credo about no performer owing his audience anything more than a good performance, Cash condemned those whom he believed lounged around Nashville sizing up his and others' foibles. "They say what is wrong with them, and what they should do or shouldn't do, and then they turn around and borrow a quarter from somebody to pay for their coffee. I think they would do a whole lot better for themselves if they would be out working at what they sound like they're believing in, rather than putting somebody else down, because they're really not accomplishing anything. I do not say this because it's bugging me, I couldn't care less, really. I'm glad they're calling MY name. It's a pretty easy name to pronounce, and I understand it's been called quite often around here."

Away from Nashville, Cash was soon making light of his arrest in front of concert audiences and, according to Grant, was consuming pills as if he'd never been arrested. "He stayed in pretty good shape for about a month," Grant told biographer Christopher Wren, "and then slowly he drifted back into pills. Two weeks after he started again, he was back in, head over heels, worse than ever."

~

Cash ended the interview with Deen in an upbeat and playful mood, joshing her about stinging worms around his California home, bemoaning his daughters' love of the Beatles, and thinking about recording in Israel. He was, he told her, also looking forward to a three-day stand in March of 1966 at the O'Keefe Center in Toronto. "I think they're billing it as the Johnny Cash concert, or something like that," teased Cash. "We'll have June Carter, the Statler Brothers, the Tennessee Three and myself and we'll have another act added. It will be presented as prestigiously as any show that has played there."

Canadian Saul Holiff anticipated the show too, always happy with victories large and small on his home turf. Infatuated with style, Cash's manager identified more easily with the grand O'Keefe Center in the heart of Toronto's financial district than, say, Buck Lake Ranch in Angola, Indiana. After Toronto, Soliff had slated a swing through the slushy winter of upstate New York, a trip he dreaded, so he relished the thought of the O'Keefe's elegance and its general manager who carried himself with appealing old English airs. But Cash was in a dramatically different frame of mind when he arrived for the Toronto date; the anticipation he had uncorked with Dixie Deen had drained away.

"He was very, very, very strung out—terribly so," said Holiff. "And he had lost his shoes somewhere along the line backstage. Johnny had smashed a bottle [and] he came out on the stage in bare feet. The seating capacity of the building was thirty-three hundred, and there may have been about three-thousand people there. And the manager of the building . . . he's contending with what he considers a primitive savage. I mean, I'm not introducing words that don't apply. I'm pretty well quoting what he said."

Barefoot and befuddled, Cash just wobbled amid the sparkling shards of glass. Ticket holders stared in silence. The curtain fell. Holiff cancelled the show.

But the New York dates remained a go. Cash had long been able to bounce back from mindlessness to make the next show, but this time Grant, Perkins and Holiff didn't believe the boss would make it. Holiff thought he might be slipping into a coma. Like actors in a recurring bad dream, Grant and Perkins loaded Cash into their Dodge motor home, and as the singer lay deep in senselessness, they wheeled out for Rochester, New York.

"There were pills that were hidden on the bus," said Holiff, "and everybody thought that we would be intercepted at the border, and we'd all be arrested. And, somehow, that never happened. I don't know how. And somehow or another we arrived, it's a two-show deal at Rochester, seven o'clock and nine-thirty. And we arrive at the parking lot around six o'clock, and the motor home is sitting there. [My wife and I] were in our own car, separately, staying at a separate place. We arrive at the parking lot. We walk up to the motor home. We step into the motor home and looked down on the floor to see if Johnny was there. And he's at the table, and he's drinking coffee and he's full of beans. He had made—what no one has ever understood—a full recovery from what appeared to be entering into a coma, and he went on to do two terrific shows. And they were both sold out."

~

Few around Cash believed he could survive so many deep falls into unconsciousness. And even if he continued to emerge time after time from his self-made abyss, there was the real possibility that he'd die from his almost-monthly car wrecks or be found frozen to death behind a club somewhere in Saskatchewan. But Cash cheated death.

As Grant attests, his mainline fans remained loyal despite the corrosion in his life, crowding the auditoriums, fairs, and country-music parks despite the haphazard performances. "There was something about him that when he got his guitar on his back and he walked up to a microphone, didn't matter how bad of shape he was in, he always came around," says Grant. "I won't say one-hundred percent, but two-hundred percent from where he was when I woke him up. But people looked over that. They saw him, heard those familiar songs, they heard the sound and there was so much hollering and screaming that people couldn't even hear him anyhow. It was like being part of Johnny. They accepted it. Main thing is, he was there, he was on stage, and he was trying. And they accepted it and didn't fault him for it. Absolutely amazing."

But the men who promoted his shows, who put up the front money to pay for marketing and the venue, were not so forgiving. Grant estimates that by 1967 they were canceling half of their dates, which kept Holiff busy rescheduling missed shows and fending off lawsuits brought by disgruntled promoters. When Holiff struck a deal with Nashville agent Lucky Moeller to book Cash into some of the better fairs around the nation (larger state fairs, for example, rather than the small county fairs that were now often Cash's stages), Moeller found only four takers. Most potential buyers, reported Moeller in a letter to Holiff, were interested in Cash, but they feared he wouldn't make the show. The news infuriated Holiff, who dashed off a terse telegram to Cash, blaming him for Moeller's failure to secure gigs: "Your professional behavior is totally reprehensible, showing a complete disregard for the rights and feelings of every one around you."

From time to time, when the ringing phones and the certified letters from angry promoters overwhelmed him, Holiff himself would take a page from Johnny Cash's book and disappear. In May of 1966, the manager vanished in a huff when the singer skipped a Paris concert to hang out with Bob Dylan, who was on tour in England (a moment filmmaker D.A. Pennebaker captured on film as the two sang a jagged version of "I Still Miss Someone"). Back in North America, Holiff again abandoned his charge. "We were on a tour of Canada," said Holiff, "and we were playing places like Winnipeg, Calgary, Edmonton. We were in Edmonton and he was on a rampage of pep pills, and he had a Martin, an expensive guitar, very expensive guitar. And he was in a darkened room, and he hadn't slept for a couple of days, and he's already missed one of the dates. And they're all my dates that I'd set up because nobody wanted to book him. You know, they couldn't trust that he would be there. He took the guitar and smashed it against the wall. I had said things to provoke him. And I guess he just didn't have the nerve to hit me with the guitar so he hit it against the wall and smashed it." Holiff vanished and cancelled the remaining dates in Canada.

Holiff recalled that after he finally left Cash's employ in the early 1970s, people in the Cash camp derided him for disappearing every once in a while in the 1960s when the ground turned soppy. In fact, regulars on Cash's touring show, such as members of the Statler Brothers and Grant, echoed such criticism in interviews with me. "He was as unique in his world as John is in his, whatever world that is," says Don Reid of the Statlers. "[Holiff] loved the title but didn't like any of the work. But anyway, he would fly first class and just wait until all the work was done; then he would arrive. He was one of those kinds of guys." There were charges among those in Cash's world that Holiff seemed more concerned with his sun tan than managing Cash and that he never did anything but book shows. Although there is an element of truth in the claims, in Holiff's defense, Cash was virtually unmanageable. Clearly, Holiff had tried to push Cash's career into new dimensions, arranging international tours, booking Carnegie Hall and the Hollywood Bowl, and seeking out expansive television stages and endorsement deals. But it was next to impossible to make headway with Cash often swerving off the planned course.

By the mid-1960s, Cash and Holiff bickered constantly, as the manager's reprimand of Cash over the Moeller fair bookings illustrated. The cordial tone of their early correspondence, as Holiff was entering the picture and Cash was doing his best to undermine Stew Carnall for Holiff's benefit, wore away as Holiff attacked Cash's immaturity and disregard for others. Cash, in turn, irrationally accused Holiff of theft and threatened to break up their relationship. Holiff also threatened to leave many times, but he stayed until 1973. Cash was fortunate that Holiff did; the manager was part of the thin glue holding together his disintegrating career.

In addition to jeopardizing his relationship with Holiff and various concert promoters, Cash's hit-or-miss consistency on the road was also squeezing his bank account. Monies lost from skipped shows and flubbed television appearances, not to mention bills for ransacked hotel rooms and smashed vehicles, often meant that his supporting musicians (which in 1967 included the Statler Brothers, Carl Perkins, and the Carter Family) were short-changed. His parents, who had moved to California to manage a trailer park that Cash had purchased, went without their son's financial support. Ray wondered if he'd been wise in hanging his dependence on Cash, but breathed a little easier when he filled out the paperwork for Social Security. Grant sweated when he realized he was making less than his mechanic's wages of the 1950s.

Other financial burdens were even more daunting to Cash. Former manager Carnall was suing Cash for back royalties, and the federal government was seeking $125,000 from Cash for his part in sparking a fire in California's Los Padres National Forest that destroyed more than five hundred acres of land. In June of 1965, Cash had rambled into the part of the forest near his home to fish, and when his camper truck got stuck on the road, he gunned the motor, spewing sparks and gas fumes that ignited the fire. Legal fees gobbled more of his money, but having to pay the full amount could have busted him. The final settlement cost Cash eighty-two thousand dollars.

Further tightening the vise was his impending divorce from Vivian. She had finally asked for a divorce in 1966, which meant Cash would have to surrender half of his future royalties from songs recorded before the divorce, other property and assets, and child support. While he waited for the divorce to become final, he rashly increased his debt load by purchasing a large home that Nashville developer Braxton Dixon was building for himself on Old Hickory Lake in Hendersonville, just outside Nashville.

Wishing to be closer to June, he'd already taken an apartment near Nashville with the firebrand singer Waylon Jennings and become a regular visitor at Mother Maybelle's home. He was determined to set down stakes in the town he'd abhorred for so long, and he persuaded Dixon to surrender the Hendersonville home to him. But Cash's financial burdens mocked the deal. He struggled to come up with cash for a down payment and only succeeded when a Columbia executive acting as an agent of the label stepped forward and guaranteed the loan.

Panicked by his mounting financial woes, Cash wrote Holiff asking him to reduce the commissions he charged against Cash's earnings, but Holiff fired off a letter in response chastising his client for overextending himself. Holiff took Cash to task for buying the house on the lake along with antique furniture to fill it and a fence to go around it. He also noted Cash's purchase of a new Cadillac, the $70,000 annual expense of having Carl Perkins and the Carter Family on his road show, and the singer's refusal to make investments that would reduce his tax bill.

Holiff ultimately agreed to cut his commissions, but Cash still needed to scrounge dollars elsewhere, so he continued to call Columbia Records seeking advances on his cooling record sales. This frustrated Holiff because he knew that Cash's requests for money were eroding the singer's own bargaining position. Even so, Cash was still selling enough to warrant those Columbia advances, and royalties from earlier hits replenished his bank account twice a year. But the money drained away almost as soon as it poured in. A big record would have helped the situation, but in 1967 none seemed forthcoming.

Grant recalls that by the fall of 1967 Cash had stopped trying to record. "John had gotten to where we couldn't get him in the studio. He just wouldn't go. Then when we'd go to the studio, he wouldn't have anything to record. He always blamed it on somebody else for not recording a hit record, and lot of times it was me for whatever reason. But we couldn't get him in the studio."

Some three years had passed since Cash scored his last number-one country hit: "Understand Your Man," which spent six weeks at number one. And although he and June had recorded "Jackson," their career song and seen it pop up to number two in 1967, Cash watched his "The Wind Changes" single limp to number sixty that year, his worst showing ever on the country charts. On the album scene, the story was similar. He'd not seen an album of newly recorded material reach number one since 1964. His most recent release, *Carryin' On*, a collection of duets with June (including "Jackson"), sold moderately and garnered tepid reviews. "This is a nice album, and a very nice display by Cash of his lighter material," Peter Reilly stiffly wrote in *Hi Fi/Stereo Review*. "Miss Carter assists him more than ably."

Even with Cash's flagging marketability in 1967, he remained among the top marquee names in country music and stood in no danger of losing his Columbia contract. However, Eddy Arnold, Buck Owens, Merle Haggard, Glen Campbell, and even Loretta Lynn had elbowed him out of the highest echelon of country-artist sales. A winded runner, Cash lagged behind with no immediate prospects of catching up. The confusion and sense of desperation wrought by his addiction and mounting financial problems only pushed him farther back in the pack of recording artists. One Columbia executive says that he and many of his associates mourned over (and resigned themselves to) Cash's squandered talent in the 1960s. "The thing about Johnny Cash, I think so many of us felt so strongly that he had such potential," says Wornall Farr, "that we were heartsick with what he was doing to his career and his physical person. We just ached to somehow get him to straighten up and be the person he could and should be."

As Farr's observation implies, financial and professional woes weren't Cash's only worries. Physically, he had been scratched raw by his amphetamine and barbiturate consumption. And his emotions were crawling with fears that June would leave him and the show and squash his hopes for marriage.

Throughout their tempestuous relationship, which seemed to come directly from the stormy lyrics of "Jackson," Cash repeatedly asked June to marry him, but she put him off. She was unwilling to drive the final wedge into Johnny and Vivian's marriage, wary of his volatility, and fearful of Cash's drug use (although according to Grant, she, like Luther Perkins, was now popping pills right alongside Cash, just not as many). She finally told Cash that she would marry him if he kicked his habit, and by October of 1967, he was weakly resolving to do just that.

Whenever Cash spoke of finally subduing his hunger for drugs, his account was often shrouded in myth. He alternately described two different low points: an attempted suicide in Nickajack Cave near Chattanooga, Tennessee, and an arrest in Lafayette, Georgia, after a sheriff found him pounding on the door of a rural home. Although Cash was indeed arrested in Georgia (after wheeling an Eldorado Cadillac through the woods as if it were a Jeep and then, as he described, banging on the door of the home), the cave story founders under scrutiny. Grant is one of the story's detractors. "That did not happen," he flatly declares. "He knew some people down there, a couple of musicians: Norman Blake and Bob Johnson. And he'd go down there and hang out with them a little bit. He didn't take all those cave adventures and all that. It did not happen."

As dramatic and potentially transformative as the Nickajack Cave and Lafayette, Georgia, experiences may have been, a growing fear of losing June Carter was most likely the real impetus of Cash's scaled-back drug use. On October 21, 1967, he wrote a ten-page letter to Holiff, who seemed to have become a sounding board as well as the fix-it-all manager. In it, Cash's tone of desperation over June was unmistakable. He wrote that June had threatened to leave him and the show effective November of 1967 because he had not met what apparently were two of her conditions for marriage: that he bring her to California so she could get to know his daughters and that he seek medical treatment for his addiction. Furthermore, Cash expressed fear that the failure to finalize divorce proceedings with Vivian would be the final blow to his hopes of marrying June. The dream he held for so long, he moaned, appeared likely to die. In a fit of anger, Cash put words to his and June's mercurial relationship, lashing out at what he believed were her chaffing demands and complaining that she had dominated him as she had dominated every other man who had ever loved her. Nevertheless, by the close of Cash's letter, his dire need for June was clear. He craved her. And he pledged to seek medical help when his current tour ended.

In actuality, Cash put the matter of his recovery into June's hands, assenting (at her urging) to meet with Nat Winston, a psychiatrist who was at the time Tennessee State Commissioner of Mental Health. The Carters knew Winston from his hometown of Johnson City, Tennessee, where Mother Maybelle had played regularly with Bonnie Lou and Buster Moore, a veteran country music duo who starred in a local television show in the 1950s. Winston picked the banjo and often jammed with Maybelle. As Cash dwindled, June brought Winston to Cash's bedside in his new Hendersonville home. Cash was "in obvious distress," wrote Winston decades later. "I immediately saw the need for help. He was a large man, I knew, and he looked like he didn't weigh more than 150 pounds. He was anxious and nervous and lying on the round bed in the master bedroom. June had told me that he had been taking massive amounts of amphetamines. Indeed, Johnny said he had been taking twenty and thirty at a clip, three and four times a day, then taking a tranquilizer, Equanil, twenty or so at night, to try to get some rest. He was indeed quite ill."

Extracting from Cash a shaky commitment to reform, Winston commenced a rigorous campaign to help Cash stem his desire for drugs. He met frequently with Cash for one-on-one counseling and with June's help blocked the couriers and old friends who arrived with fresh supplies of Cash's pills. Still, Cash was relentless, slithering around his cavernous home scratching for pills he'd hidden under sinks and carpets. Before one counseling session that fall, Winston and June arrived to find Cash high again, soaked and shivering in bed after driving a tractor into Old

Hickory Lake. "We could still see the wheels of that upside-down tractor in the lake just below the home in the cove," wrote June in her first autobiography. "And for once I didn't know where the strength would come from to continue. Nat and I had a long talk, and I went home."

Despite the tractor incident, Cash emerged from his sessions with Winston with a dramatically scaled down appetite for pills. But he was not free of drugs. The 2005 Cash biopic starring Joaquin Phoenix and Reese Witherspoon, like countless retellings of his life, has Cash riding with June into the sunset, the drugs left behind. But it was a pale rendering of the truth. "They kept him off them for thirty days," says Grant. "About the fiftieth day, he was right worse than it was before he stopped." Cash probably didn't set aside drugs until 1970, when his and June's son John Carter was born, and then he remained drug free for about six years. By the late 1970s, he was back to feeding his habit. "There wasn't five days from 1976 until he came down with his disease that he was straight," argues Grant. "They did a good job of covering it up. [Rehabs in] Betty Ford three times, several in Tennessee, some in Texas. People around him will still say that he kicked the habit in the 1960s."

THREE

~

SLOW AND FREE
1968-1972

10

FOLSOM

While Cash struggled to banish his addiction in a bedroom outside Nashville, a massive wave of change in American society that had been rising for at least twelve years was crashing down and taking in its roiling flood millions of men and women. Freedom and new social awareness rode the swell, but there was also death at the hands of drugs and urban rioting. And among Nixon's silent majority, there was skepticism of the tide as well as a desire to return to the comfort and security of Eisenhower's 1950s.

The modern civil rights movement, instigated on a bus in Birmingham, Alabama, during the same year Cash released his first records, had been the initial ripple of unrest. It was a clear sign that social activism still pulsed in America, even in the wake of post-war docility and McCarthyism. Saving America from its penchant for benign neglect, civil-rights workers in the 1950s rallied a long march into the 1960s, winning important legislative and moral victories. More importantly perhaps, they provoked social activism among many who never suspected they were capable of it.

That spirit of activism, in part, defined the 1960s. Slowly, long-held assumptions cracked and fell to the ground. Impassioned blacks, including the sons and daughters of those in 1940s Memphis, lunged for their American birthright. Simultaneously, many whites questioned their exclusive ownership of opportunity and sought to reform their purpose in the nation by protesting war, joining freedom riders, volunteering for workers' rights, or merely reexamining privileges that had been long taken for granted. This notion of redefinition or reinvention, often with a greater good in mind, infused the tumultuous and fertile decade.

Redefinition also characterized much of the decade's music. Whether inspired by a political objective or the pure desire to experiment, musical innovation coursed through the 1960s as in no decade before. Musicians in the folk revival of the early 1960s, many of whom dumped their given names and middle-class identities in favor of more romantic guises, rejected corporate rock and pop by reaching back for ballads rooted in the early American experience and beyond. At the same time, bands such as the Beach Boys and the Beatles evolved from their original teenage pop orientations to create incisive personal statements and the sonic collages that were *Pet Sounds* and *Sgt. Pepper's Lonely Hearts Club Band*, respectively. As we've seen, even Cash was swept into the tide of experimentation as he wrung what he could from his encounters with Ramblin' Jack Elliott, Peter La Farge, and Bob Dylan.

The enigmatic Dylan also fed from Cash as he sought reinvention a second time, edging away from the folk-singer designation to embrace a wider folk-rock-country orientation. By the winter of 1966, Dylan had landed in the Nashville studios, where he and his new producer Bob Johnston came up with the classic album *Blonde on Blonde*. His flirtation with Nashville, during which Cash flitted in and out of his life, culminated in *Nashville Skyline* of 1969, a homage to the home of country music and a gentle invocation of the music's simple rhythms and themes. Dylan's awakening to country music dropped him in the thick of the folk-rock trend, where a coterie of paisley-clad followers (like the Byrds and the Lovin' Spoonful) found tremendous success in marrying their love of Dylan's folk to country and rock. Robbie Robertson, whose rockabilly-and-blues band, the Hawks, backed Dylan on his 1965–66 world tour, believed he'd been blessed to be part of the ever-shifting musical geography of the mid-1960s. "The Beatles were making very interesting records," he once said, "there was a whole wave of amazing music coming from Motown and Stax, and Dylan was writing songs with much more depth than what had come along before. Everything was changing, all these doors were being opened, and it made you think, 'I could try anything, right now.'

Revolutionary times are very healthy for experimenting and trying stuff—and for being fearless in what you try."

Reawakened rock fans, folk revivalists, folk-rockers, and others demanded more from their music: recordings that challenged society's status quo, violated instrumental assumptions, stretched technological limitations, and amplified their generation's voice.

The electricity charging through music naturally blew fuses in the recording industry, upsetting old ways of doing business, particularly at the major labels. Columbia Records was home to many of the innovative musicians of the era (including Cash, Dylan, the Byrds), but its corporate culture was slow to follow its artists' lead. Many in positions of power, who still defined the label by its long-time association with artists such as Ray Conniff, Andy Williams, and Mitch Miller, clashed with the new guard who sought to reorient the company toward Dylan, Simon and Garfunkel, the Byrds, and other unconventional musical acts of the late 1960s. In earlier years, the company had relied upon the wisdom of seasoned impresario Goddard Lieberson and his underling John Hammond to make room in its house for refreshing innovators, but by 1967 the aging Lieberson, at least, had been marginalized, signaling the end of an era at Columbia. He surrendered power to Clive Davis, a graduate of Columbia's legal department. Davis admitted to knowing more about contracts than about music, but he astutely realized that if Columbia Records was to remain among the giants it had to move away from crooners and bandleaders. Standing in his way, though, were old-line A&R men and entrenched sales and marketing people who grinned smugly in their knowledge that even in 1967 the veteran pop artists often outsold the newcomers. Bob Dylan may have deeply and distinctively branded American culture, but Andy Williams outsold him by tens of thousands.

It fell to Davis to convince skeptics that Dylan and artists like him represented the future of Columbia Records. He succeeded, and the word went out around the company to sign the experimental artists, or the underground artists, as they were becoming known. Spurred on by the label's incentives, even promotion men got into the act, peering into the clubs and haunting the festivals searching for anti-establishment musicians for the establishment label. One of them, based in San Francisco, found Moby Grape.

Led by songwriter and Jefferson Airplane graduate Skip Spence, Moby Grape was the kind of electric, LSD-tinged sound that Columbia could sell to those who had tired of AM radio's Top 40 and were now tuning into free-form underground formats on the FM band. So Columbia courted on Moby Grape's behalf the FM disc jockeys, flying them to Frisco days before the Monterey Pop Festival for a faux flower-child blow out, replete with Moby Grape Wine, invited hippies, and plenty of reefer (as well as the more traditional bikini-clad hostesses serving flutes of champagne).

The idea was to cast the band into the anti-establishment scene and watch those who craved something different take the bait. Columbia released five Moby Grape singles at one time (quite unusual) and exploited in the press the arrest of two band members shortly after the San Francisco bash—anything to emphasize unconventionality. Ultimately, Moby Grape shriveled on Columbia's vine, but Clive Davis' signings of Janis Joplin, Santana, and Blood, Sweat and Tears invigorated the label.

The transformation at Columbia, so concentrated on the West Coast scene, soon spread to Nashville. And its first victim was Cash's producer Don Law. Citing a mandatory retirement policy (which had conveniently spared John Hammond and Goddard Lieberson), Columbia forced Law from his country-music perch and replaced him with Bob Dylan's producer Bob Johnston, a Texas native with the verve of a tonic salesman. New York reporter Michael Zwerin, who met Johnston in 1968, figured that the shirttails flapping around the producer's waist were just a small indicator of his colorful pedigree. "Bob is middle aged, stocky and talks about his winners a lot," he wrote. "His head of straight blonde hair fights the tonic slicking it down. He might be a big shot sheriff. . . . Eight gold records hang on the wall of his study in his sprawling, six figure house: *Highway 61*, *Blonde on Blonde* and *The Sound of Silence*."

Don Law, who boasted his own collection of gold records, pleaded with Columbia's brass to leave Johnston alone and name instead Frank Jones, Law's co-producer. But he did so to no avail. Although Law would continue to independently produce a handful of Columbia artists, he could only collect his pension and a lot of well-earned sympathy. The dismissal seemed disrespectful to some, particularly in light of the major roster of talent he'd compiled and the fact that aging executives Lieberson and Hammond were immune from the retirement policy. As for Frank Jones, he went on to lead the Nashville operations of several major labels, but many say he never recovered from Columbia's slight.

The immediate aftershocks of Law's removal permeated the Nashville establishment and made it difficult for Johnston to negotiate the town. Marshall Grant sized him up and deemed him a grandstander, and Don Reid of the Statler Brothers agreed. "He was a wild man," observes Reid. "He produced some records on us also, in the late sixties. He was one of those wild, unorganized, near-bohemian types that I don't know how he ever got it all put together as a record producer. The only thing I remember about him is, no matter what song he was doing, he'd flip the switch on and tell the drummer to lay a wallet on the drum. He wanted to mute that drum so he'd always say, 'Lay a wallet on it.' And the drummer would pull his billfold out and lay it on the drum and he'd say, 'Okay, that's it.' That was the sound he was looking for."

In Clive Davis' 1974 autobiography, the music executive documented the Nashville uprising against the bombastic new presence. He wrote, "Rather than go about his work quietly, building up a record of imposing artist signings, [Johnston] kept giving interviews saying how he was going to shake up Nashville; how things had gotten encrusted and fossilized and how he was going to create waves and change everything. This must have scared the hell out of the ruling establishment, and Minnie Pearl was apparently chosen as the person to tell me. She casually walked over to see me at an annual dinner given by Broadcast Music, Inc. . . . Then she got to the point. Bob Johnston wasn't the kind of person who succeeded in Nashville; he was shaking up established ways of doing business and rubbing a lot of people the wrong way. The town was . . . *noticing* this. What a terrible thing it would be for Columbia's great name if the company became known as a . . . disruptive force on Music Row."

But Johnston was supposed to be a disruptive force in Nashville. He'd been elevated to energize Columbia's country music, which Law had presided over for almost two decades. Although charges of bizarre studio behavior and self-promotion plagued Johnston's reign in Nashville, he justified his ascent in just one important move. He green-lighted the album *Johnny Cash At Folsom Prison* and pushed the recovering singer into 1968's formidable tide of change.

Cash had long wanted to record a prison album, ever since he and the Tennessee Two first appeared at Huntsville State Prison in Texas in 1957. He wrote in his liner notes to *Johnny Cash At Folsom Prison* that Columbia had refused him the opportunity since 1962, when he first raised the idea. Cash co-producer Frank Jones denied that Cash had ever asked when I asked him about Cash's unanswered pleas, but that doesn't mean Cash hadn't asked. It's possible that Cash hit Don Law's brick wall or that he met resistance from executive management when he went over Law's head (as he often did).

When Cash raised the idea with Johnston, Johnston immediately saw the potential. Newly ensconced in Nashville, the producer saw Cash's vision. "Bob Johnston believed me when I told him a prison would be *the* place to record an album live," wrote Cash in his liner notes.

In retrospect, the concept of a live prison album at Folsom seems so natural: the man with the face and voice like your mind's image of a convict would bring home his hit song "Folsom Prison Blues." The hook was so undeniable that one wonders why the album hadn't been recorded years before.

Cash had visited Folsom for the first time in November of 1966, after an inmate named Earl Green (who'd killed a man with a baseball bat) asked a visiting pastor if Johnny Cash might be inclined to bring his show to the prison. That pastor was Rev. Floyd Gressett, who led the church Cash sometimes attended in Ventura, California. When Gressett delivered Green's message, the singer immediately agreed. Cash believed that prison shows were a fulfillment of his Christian obligation. Hauling the Carter Family with him, including Sara Carter from the group's original line-up, Cash performed in the prison yard, while Earl Green handled the sound. The raucous crowd's reaction got him thinking once again of bringing recording equipment into a prison. "While we were there," Cash told a writer in 1968, "I asked the Folsom entertainment director . . . about the possibility of doing another show and having it recorded for an album release. He said, 'Anytime.'" After a year of negotiations involving Cash, Johnston, and the California Department of Corrections, the date was set for January 13, 1968, a Saturday.

Under gloomy skies, Cash and his troupe walked through the gates, leading an entourage of reporters and photographers, along with Gressett, Bob Johnston, Ray Cash, and a handful others. They passed the dirty imposing outer walls of Folsom, pulling their dark coats close in the morning chill. Photographers snapped pictures of them, but nobody smiled. Cash seemed to be steeling himself for the show, coming on tough for the small group of paparazzi, or resolutely trying to contain his concerns about whether or not the recording would come off according to plan.

Inside, the mood lightened. Quartered in a kitchen near the cafeteria where Cash's two shows were to be recorded, the musicians nibbled sandwiches, sipped coffee, and traded licks. The first show was scheduled for nine-forty in the morning, and as the time approached, inmates who'd been up since the mandatory waking time of seven o'clock sauntered into the cavernous dining hall and took seats around hexagonal tables bolted into the floors. Down in front, near the wooden stage, a tall lean inmate named Glen Sherley leaned forward on his bench, cigarette in hand, waiting for Cash.

Inmates whom I interviewed decades after the show talked about the simple pleasure of seeing top-brand entertainment; it was almost like being on the outside. They also observed that once Cash stepped up on stage, he seemed to understand their loss of freedom and labored intensely to strike a bond with them. Sherley, perched nervously in the front row, probably felt Cash's entreaties more acutely than any of his fellow prisoners because one of his own songs had reached Cash's music stand the night before.

Gressett again had interceded with Cash on behalf of a Folsom resident, handing over the song to Cash at rehearsals in nearby Sacramento. He had slipped Sherley's "Greystone Chapel" out of Folsom some weeks before, after Sherley and Earl Green had put it on tape. "He was a terrific writer, songwriter," recalls Green. "He was one of the best lyric men I ever heard. He wrote that 'Greystone Chapel' in about thirty minutes. I told him, you know, Johnny was coming to Folsom and he ought to write something and we'll try to get it to him. And he wrote that in about thirty minutes and the next morning he come out and said, 'Listen to this,' and he sang it to me."

Dwelling on the power of mercy and faith to defy prison walls, "Greystone Chapel" sealed the bond between Cash and the inmates that day. Sharper than the bloodiest ballads or grimmest hanging song that Cash fired at Folsom, "Greystone Chapel," the prisoners knew, was their voice. And when Cash took it on, they cheered him as if he were one of their own. Those on the outside who bought the album months later heard crazed yelps when Cash uttered the famous *shot a man in Reno* line of "Folsom Prison Blues," but that reaction was actually added by a Nashville engineer in post-production; the prisoners saved their most strident applause for "Greystone Chapel."

The Folsom show appears to be the birthplace of Cash's well-known introduction, "Hello, I'm Johnny Cash." For years, Grant had dramatized the star's concert entrances, but according to Johnston, Cash's brief self-introduction proved far more dramatic. Before the show, says Johnston, when he asked the band how the opening would go, Grant piped up that he'd bring Cash on like he always had. "He said, 'I'm going out and introduce Cash. Ladies and gentlemen and all. . .,'" recalls Johnston. "I said, 'Bullshit.' I said, 'Johnny, that's goddamn ridiculous.' I said, 'We're going out and hold our hands up [to quiet them]. All you gotta do is walk out there and jerk your head around and say 'Hello. I'm Johnny Cash.' And then you don't have to worry about even fucking singing. You can wave at those people for the next two hours and leave, and you'd have a giant album.' And [Cash] said, 'Get out of my goddamn way.' Never heard him say that, and he walked out on stage and turned around and said, 'Hello. I'm Johnny Cash.' And that was the end of it."

Indeed, the men exploded, and as Cash led them through "Give My Love to Rose," "Busted," and "Dark as a Dungeon," the level of adulation remained high, spiking whenever Cash blurted an obscenity or taunted Johnston or a prison guard. Cash's set was inspired; songs of confinement such as "Dark as a Dungeon" or "I Still Miss Someone" portrayed the men's prison confinement, no matter that the lyrics were literally set in coal mines or in the throes of love's loneliness. And when Cash's confinement songs dragged the men to the depths of their imprisonment, draining them, stilling them with a mirror on their fate, Cash lifted them again, reeling off two silly Jack Clement novelties that he'd recorded in 1966. He also roused them with "Orange Blossom Special" and "The Legend of John Henry," both jarring and rhythmically insistent.

June Carter, though, snapped the men to attention like no other diversion in Cash's arsenal. She floated onto the stage in an attractive black skirt suit and black stockings, her flowing brown hair collected regally on her shoulders. The men couldn't help but come alive. Singing "Jackson" with her man, she quelled the intensity that had crept into Cash's performance.

When the first show closed in the gust of "Greystone Chapel" applause, Cash hustled back to the kitchen to wait for the next show. Moments later, Glen Sherley,

with a clutch of guards around him, burst into the room. Giddy over Cash's performance and the singer's talk about releasing "Greystone Chapel" as a single (idle talk, as
it turned out), he clasped the singer's hand. Hope burned in the prisoner's eyes.

~

In the first days of 1968, in that sour-smelling kitchen of Folsom, reinvention
stirred the air. Sherley continued writing and would in time gain release from
prison thanks to Cash and "Greystone Chapel." And Cash was to feel a rush of popularity that was unprecedented in his career. *Johnny Cash At Folsom Prison* was
released in the spring of 1968 into the undulating confluence of political activism
and musical experimentation, and there it found a home.

The album's initial spark in the marketplace was hardly organic. The Columbia
promotion engine suspected the underground audience might lap up the record
with its bleeped-out cussing and roaring prisoners, so it bored a few holes into the
young, anti-establishment market (as with the Moby Grape campaign). "See, that
album appealed to the underground because of the nature of it," explains Tom
Noonan, the label's head of promotion, "because it was made in a prison and the
prison was in California, and that's where the underground broke from. So, we had
an advantage." In advertisements placed in May and June of 1968 in upstart week-
lies, such as *The Village Voice* and *Rolling Stone*, Columbia worked the rebel angle.
The ads suggested that Cash was a former inmate, and his liner notes on the album
were vague about his time behind bars. A scar on the right side of his face, the
result of a botched dental procedure some years before, was taken by some to be
the reminder of a knife wound and highlighted the dangerous image. Cash found
the mistaken and persistent belief that he'd been in prison tiresome in his later
years, but he was surely aware that the misperception was partly his and
Columbia's own doing. Although he wouldn't have gambled on the possibility of
anybody reading the ads and liner notes, both were successful in building intrigue
among those in search of an anti-establishment voice, many of whom had approvingly watched him consort with Bob Dylan a few years earlier.

The alternative press seized Columbia's cue, hailing an album whose sound
wildly deviated from the current pack of albums in any genre. Richard Goldstein
of *The Village Voice* pointed his readers to a "deeply moving 'live' concert" spiced
with steely echoes of crashing doors and jangling keys. Goldstein continued:

Cash's voice is as thick and gritty as ever, but filled with the kind of emotionalism you seldom find in rock (for all the hue and cry about passionate intensity, white pop singers don't often let go, do they?). His songs are simple and sentimental, his message clear. But those who expect to find an expanded, concerto version of "I Walk the Line" here, will be stunned by this album, and its chilling sense of just what it means to be imprisoned, here and now. You can feel the rapport as the audience responds to Cash's hard-luck ballads, his accounts of futile attempts at escape, and his inevitable equation of separation from loved ones with death. The feeling of hopelessness—even amid the cheers and whistles—is overwhelming. You come away drained, as the record fades out to the sound of men booing their warden . . . . Talk about magical mystery tours.

In a few sentences, Goldstein bottled the uniqueness of the album. *Johnny Cash At Folsom Prison* lay far from the work of those rock bands that had turned individuality into a formula with their eight-minute psychedelic jags and circular lyrics. And by invoking the Beatles' *Magical Mystery Tour*, the critic was either saying that the album had far more to say than the Fab Four's 1967 romp, or that at least *Johnny Cash At Folsom Prison* was in its league.

Goldstein also touched on the album's social message, its communication of "what it means to be imprisoned, here and now." Undoubtedly, Cash's implied statement that prisoners deserve America's compassion was part of the album's appeal. Legions of artists in the 1960s sang about the plight of the disenfranchised, but Cash met society's orphans on their own turf, rolled tape, and released the results. In the midst of national mourning over the assassinations of Martin Luther King, Jr. and Robert F. Kennedy, the album was perhaps a reminder of their shared vision of accommodation for those on the fringes.

Little more than a year later, Goldstein would up the ante for Cash, implying in a *Vogue* essay that Bob Dylan was merely following in the Arkansan's footsteps. *Rolling Stone* editors appeared to be in the same frame of mind. In a prominent space a few weeks before Columbia launched *Folsom*, they wondered if Dylan, who had emerged from exile in Woodstock, was a "little like Johnny Cash." The pairing of the two in the quickly rising journal may have had as much to do as any force in the 1968 burgeoning of Cash and his new album. Weeks later, as the album rolled out of the factories, the magazine splashed a dramatic photograph of Cash on its front page and set the country troubadour and the folk-rock minstrel next to each other in an article inside. "Johnny Cash, more than any other contemporary performer, is meaningful in a rock and roll context," observed editor and publisher Jann Wenner. "At the end of the Newport Folk Festival in 1964, Cash, who had just finished a compelling set of story-telling songs gave his guitar to Bob Dylan, the traditional country singer's tribute to a fellow musician. They are both master singers, master story-tellers and master bluesmen. They share the same tradition, they are good friends, and the work of each can tell you about the work of the other."

And so began the second chapter in the saga of Johnny Cash's art, 1968–1972. As the news of Cash's very different album cut like lightening through the anti-establishment press, and the new single "Folsom Prison Blues" as well as other album cuts blared on underground radio, the mainstream audience quickly got hip. His trusty base in the country audience, which never needed much prodding anyway, propelled the single and album to the top of the country charts. And the pop audience, who never paid much attention to the alternative press, joined the dash to the record stores once establishment sheets such as *Life*, *Time*, and *Look* clanged their bells for Johnny Cash. By October, the album had reached five hundred thousand in sales, enough for a gold record.

Johnny Cash At Folsom Prison had met a moment in time. Its intersection with audiences who demanded a credible spokesman, identified with rebellion, and valued social messages made it not only one of the most popular albums of 1968, but one of the more important albums of the 1960s. For Cash, the album was a turning point. His subsequent releases sold millions, network television courted him, and his name more than anyone's came to symbolize country music.

The album, the marketing of the album, and the intense press coverage redefined Cash's image as well. He was no longer just America's Foremost Singing Storyteller. Cash had now fully developed two other aspects of his legend: spokesman for the disenfranchised and the brooding bad man who perhaps had killed a man but, like the formidable Leadbelly, had escaped a life sentence.

When Cash and June left the Folsom compound in January of 1968 under shining skies, they knew that year would be like no other since they had begun working together. Just days before the Folsom concert, Cash's divorce had become final. In February, the newly single man impulsively proposed to June on stage in a hockey arena in London, Ontario. They set a March date, but before they sped up to Franklin, Kentucky, for the nuptials, the two collected a Grammy for best country-and-western performance by a duo for "Jackson."

Cash continued to stumble through his recovery from addiction, but his marriage and the loud affirmation of his work in the wake of *Johnny Cash At Folsom Prison* kept him farther away from amphetamines than he'd been for more than a decade. He was farther away, but not completely away. Grant observed that Cash was not clean for his proposal or for his wedding. "When he proposed to her on the stage in London, he was not straight," says Grant, "on a scale of one to one hundred, fifty percent maybe. When we walked off the stage and [June] was standing at the back of the stage, there in that old ice hockey arena, I said, 'June, you've made a mistake.' She said, 'Well, Marshall, I got caught.' I said, 'Well, you've made a mistake. If you go through with it, you are in for one hell of a life.'"

At the wedding reception in Hendersonville, Grant confronted June again: "I told her, 'June you got a hard row, you got a hard row.' She said, 'Well, Marshall, we're just going to have to face it day by day.' And that's exactly what we did."

After the wedding, Cash exhibited something of a spiritual reawakening, not that he'd ever really let go of his faith. "The times when I was so down and out of it were also the times I felt the presence of God, . . ." he told an interviewer. "I felt that presence, that positive power saying to me, 'I'm still here, Cash, to draw on whenever you're ready to straighten up and come back to life.'" When he could, he began attending a Baptist Church in Hendersonville, and after the marriage, he and June embarked on a journey to Israel that became the basis for *The Holy Land* album, his follow-up to *Johnny Cash At Folsom Prison*. In Israel, the two carried a tape recorder, which they used to capture their reflections on faith and impressions of Bethlehem, Jerusalem, the Sea of Galilee, and other sites that he and June had sung about since childhood. Their narrative and a passel of new gospel songs mingled on the album. "The main reason for doing this," he explained at the time, "is that I have recorded two hymn albums in my career, and every so often I want to do one when I have decided that I want to look for something new in religion—a refresher. I want to do a classic in religious albums."

Unlike Tennessee Ernie Ford's *Hymns* (1956) or Mahalia Jackson's *Live At Newport 1958* (1958), *The Holy Land* never became the classic that Cash hoped it would. But the album accentuated a recurring trend in Cash's recording career; whenever he enjoyed the authority of spiking popularity, he frequently spent his capital recording sacred music. In 1957, after selling enough "Walk the Line"s and "Get Rhythm"s to please Sam Phillips, he recorded his own "Belshazzar" and Jimmie Davis' "I Was There When It Happened." A highly coveted prize at Columbia when he signed in 1958, Cash's first album with the label featured gospel singer Dorothy Love Coates' "That's Enough," and his second album was composed entirely of hymns. In the years after 1968, following his dedication to network television, he poured himself into the multimedia project *The Gospel Road*. And, again, in the last year of his life, as he relaxed in the afterglow of his rejuvenating American Recordings years, he offered the world *My Mother's Hymn Book*, a set compiled from the sacred songs that Carrie played and carried with her throughout his Dyess childhood. "The songs in that old book mean more to me than I can tell you," said Cash in his liner notes, "so I'll just sing 'em, me and my guitar, simple, no adornment, knowing that God loves music and that music brings hope for a better tomorrow."

In a letter he wrote to himself on January 1, 1969, Cash admitted that he was "still pretty carnal" and dwelled on small personal setbacks, despite the major victory of *Johnny Cash At Folsom Prison*. Heavy on his mind also must have been the death of Luther Perkins.

Back in early August of 1968, after a day spent working on the roof of his new house in Hendersonville, Perkins had lit a cigarette and fallen asleep on the sofa of his small brick home in Hendersonville. Cash's psychiatrist Nat Winston recalled later that the guitarist had been drinking. Flames sparked by the cigarette engulfed Perkins, scorching more than half of his body. Around dawn, Perkins's second wife, Margie, and his adopted daughter Kathy discovered the guitarist in the smoke-filled den. But by the time fire and rescue teams arrived in the early hours of August 3rd, Perkins was unconscious. An ambulance rushed him to the burn unit at Vanderbilt University Hospital, but he died two days later.

Perkins' final guitar work for Cash was recorded in July for *The Holy Land* album, but his slashing licks at Folsom remain the most memorable of his last performances. "If you listen to Luther's work that he did, especially on 'Folsom Prison Blues,' the guitar breaks and everything, Luther was a star that day," claims Grant. "Well, they all loved the Tennessee Three, all of them did, but Luther [was irresistible] with his old dry-panned look and everything. And you know, he never changed his expression, never moved his eyes. The only thing he moved while he was on stage was his fingers of his right and left hands, and the prisoners took to that very, very well."

More than a decade after the triumph of *Johnny Cash At Folsom Prison* and Perkins's death, Cash reclined on a chunky chair in Grant's Memphis home and explained his relationship with his original guitarist to a reporter. He was like a brother, said Cash, as he patted down his unruly hair and brushed lint from his pants. "A part of me died with Luther," he said. "He gave me a lot and I never will forget it."

There was more that Cash could have revealed that day in Memphis. According to Winston, Perkins had called Cash before he fell asleep, begging him to come over, that he needed help. Cash lived close by, but he could tell that Perkins was drunk. He said he'd be there in the morning, but by morning Perkins was at Vanderbilt. In the years that followed, Cash repeatedly claimed responsibility for Perkins' death, not so much because he'd ignored his friend's plea that night, but rather because he believed he'd led Perkins into chemical abuse. "The two of them were sort of hand in hand with the drugs," says Grant. "It's like Carl Perkins said, 'If John would have went to Luther at any time and said, 'Luther, let's stop this crap,' Luther would have stopped. John had tremendous power over Luther. He would do anything that John wanted him to do, unfortunately."

To Cash, losing Perkins was like reliving the episode of his own brother's death. The guilt over Perkins, like the guilt over Jack, haunted him.

11

OVATION

Carl Perkins stepped into Luther Perkins's place on stage and might have remained there had Cash not believed, in an indication of the respect and affection Cash held for him, that it was below the rockabilly pioneer's dignity to be a mere sideman. The two had lived through dark times over the previous ten years. Perkins with his alcoholism and lost opportunities and Cash with his drugs, guilt, and recklessness. Now, they were emerging from the darkness together, but no mass audience awaited Perkins: It had disintegrated back in the 1950s, in the last strains of his "Blue Suede Shoes." The Beatles had aired their admiration for him in the thick of their 1960s popularity, and he'd been right beside Cash on the golden stage of Folsom, but none of that translated into popular demand for the humble man. "John was trying to help Carl and Carl knew that," says Marshall Grant, who'd known Perkins just as long as Cash had. "Carl didn't resent that; he was very appreciative of it. But Carl was going to be the next Elvis, and all of a sudden the bottom falls out, and now he's leaning on John for survival. That was a little uncomfortable for Carl. But they were such great friends that they sort of set it aside. You know, we were like brothers with Carl."

Perkins remained at Cash's side into the 1970s when a substantial reawakening to rockabilly in America and Europe finally gave him his own modest stage. From time to time in the ensuing decades, they reunited for concert appearances and recording projects, and then Perkins was steady on his own feet.

By late September of 1968, Carl had been picking in Luther's place for more than one month, but a delayed airplane flight to Fayetteville, Arkansas, would soon relieve him of his duty. Perkins and Grant had been trying to get out of Memphis to meet the Cash show, which was slated to appear at a rally for Arkansas governor Winthrop Rockefeller, but stormy weather had grounded them at the airport.

In Fayetteville, Cash was looking at the possibility of going on with Fluke Holland only, but then a rangy young man up from Oklahoma offered to fill out the Cash sound in Perkins's stead. Robert Wootton played country music seven nights a week in Tulsa and had learned every electric guitar part of every Cash hit. That day, he recalled later, he'd ridden shotgun on a pick-up truck to Fayetteville after telling everybody back in Tulsa that he was going to play with Johnny Cash.

When he reached the big flatbed truck on which Cash was to perform, he pushed to the front to watch the forlorn singer with his out-of-tune guitar and his eager drummer. "One of the girls I was with went around behind the truck," recalled Wootton in a 2004 radio interview. "She saw June back there and she said, 'Do you think John would like to have someone play guitar?' And [June] said, 'Do you know somebody?' She said, 'See the guy over there with his chin on Johnny's foot?' I was looking straight up at him. I was in awe. I couldn't believe I finally got to see him."

When June summoned Wootton over to her, he scampered under the flat bed truck and confirmed that he could play guitar and, more importantly, do it like Luther Perkins. "So she called John off stage and told him so," continued Wootton. "The first thing he said to me was, 'Tune my guitar.' I got to use Carl Perkins's guitar and Luther Perkins's amplifier. While we were waiting, they asked if anybody in the audience could play bass and this guy came up. Everybody thought I was from Fayetteville, so I was the hometown hero for the night. But when I walked on stage, it was magic."

Nobody remembered the bass player who filled in for Grant. On the other hand, except for a few gaps after spats with Cash, Bob Wootton revived the sound of Perkins for almost thirty years.

At first glance, the *Johnny Cash at San Quentin* album of 1969 seems to bear the mark of a Columbia marketing executive flogging a good idea into the ground. Why stop with *Folsom*, he might have reasoned from a swivel chair in New York, when so many other prisoners around the nation would be willing to scream and shout on a Cash album recorded for the anti-establishment crowd?

But Columbia got a pass on this one. The *San Quentin* album sprouted from dealings with Granada Television in the United Kingdom, which hoped to get Cash back to Folsom as part of a film documentary on the psychology of prison inmates. Saul Holiff and Cash initially snubbed the idea, and Folsom State Prison wasn't too interested either, but when the filmmakers agreed to shoot a scheduled appearance at San Quentin State Prison, the men flashed the green light and brought along Bob Johnston and his recording equipment. Filming and recording at the maximum-security facility near San Francisco were scheduled for February 24, 1969.

Little more than a year and a hundred miles separated Cash's Folsom gambit and the San Quentin show, but the motion-picture cameras and the pressure of besting his first prison album cast a contrived feeling over the 1969 concert. The two events lived in different worlds. Constrained by Cash's self-consciousness and an overwrought bad-man routine, *San Quentin* seemed to be more of an act than *Folsom* was. Nonetheless, he had the men in the palm of his hand.

As winter rain lashed outside in between intervals of cold moonlight, even June was more at ease. Wearing a white skirt hemmed just above her knees, she stirred whoops and cries when she hiked it higher and gently thrust her hips, a tease she refused to try at Folsom. This time, Mother Maybelle and June's sisters, Helen and Anita, packed the stage too. At Folsom, Cash had crept on stage like a puma after brief rehearsals in Sacramento; at San Quentin, he had hours of practice and sound checks on the prison stage, fine tuning the sound for the engineers and the film crew. There was another "Greystone Chapel," "I Don't Know Where I'm Bound," written by an inmate in the audience. And Cash's "San Quentin," a sort of "Folsom Prison Blues" custom-made for this institution, addressed the bitterness of prison life, damning the institution and herding the cheering prisoners to his side. Those prisoners and their cacophony were probably the most genuine elements of the show.

In later years, Cash recalled many times how his encore of "San Quentin" possessed the inmates, pushing them toward total riot and giving him a perverse sense of power and pleasure. Producer Johnston was startled. "It was surprising," he says, "because Johnny said [later], 'When I sang it again and all of a sudden I looked around and I knew that if I wanted to let those people go all I had to do was say "The time is now." And all of those prisoners would've broken.' Johnny said, 'I was tempted.' Now that puts a different light on how wonderful Mr. Cash is, and what a great man he is, and shit like that. Power corrupts so much that he turned around and said, 'Wow. I'm tempted right now to say "Let's do it." All of the guards were backing up towards the doors. I went and got in the back of a bunch of guards there because I figured when it broke, I wanted to be the first one out that door. They'd already clicked their guns. They're looking down with their [scopes] on and shit, and all of these people, when you go in, you sit down at a table and you applaud, you clap. You don't get up. You don't stand up. Those people were on top of the tables. They were going 'WUUHHH, UUHHH.' They couldn't get them to stop it." A Navy veteran and self-styled rebel, Johnston had seen nothing like it anywhere. "All he had to do was say something," he continues. "It would've been a huge riot, and Johnny and all his family would've been dead out there. I think I would have made it because I was back there with the guards by the door."

It's not that Cash planned to shatter the peace with his second take on "San Quentin," no matter what he said about it in later years. After its first performance, as the men clamored for it again, he paused. It was the concert's edgiest moment. Sipping a cup of water, he let the audience calm down, trying perhaps to douse the threatening flames, and then launched into a tempered version of it. Cash had growled the lyrics of "San Quentin" the first time he sang it, and Bob Wootton's guitar had rattled the hall like a billy club against steel bars. The second time, though, they took one step back. But it didn't matter. The prisoners stomped and shrieked. A black man raised the fist of black power. The cameramen took cover, and the guards squirmed.

The fans gobbled up the album. Members of the underground who enthused over *Johnny Cash At Folsom Prison* may have sneered at the obvious exploitation of the 1968 concert and left *San Quentin* in the record bins. But *San Quentin* vanquished its doubters and easily outpaced its predecessor's run in the marketplace. It was a new world, and *San Quentin* enjoyed marketing advantages that seemed unimaginable just one year earlier. *Folsom* had gingerly stepped into a marketplace where Cash was a peripheral figure, but in 1969 Cash was an emerging cultural force, the focus of intense media scrutiny, the subject of a major documentary, the center of clanging speculation about his relationship with Bob Dylan, and the star of his own television show.

Major magazines splashed profiles on Cash as the new album appeared in June, and Robert Hilburn of the *Los Angeles Times*, finding a purity in *San Quentin*, crowned it the superior of the two prison albums. "The new *Johnny Cash at San Quentin* is every bit as exciting [as *Folsom*] and, no doubt, a lot more representative of the mood of convicted men," he wrote. "Since it was the first of its type, *Johnny Cash At Folsom Prison* will probably remain the more discussed album in future years. But the new one is a classic. It offers a fascinating look at the rebelliousness of man."

The album that Hilburn heralded also boasted "A Boy Named Sue," the stupendous hit single that *Folsom* never had. It was a record promoter's dream, the big single that beckons people to the album. The comedic ditty about the explosive reunion of a son and his father who named him Sue (written by Shel Silverstein, the *Playboy* cartoonist, children's book author, and folk singer-songwriter) shot to number one on the country charts and number two on the pop charts, making it Cash's biggest single ever.

The many stories of the journey of "A Boy Named Sue" to Cash's hands outnumber lines in the song, but it appears that the actual route was through Don Davis, the music publisher who'd been married to Anita Carter and witnessed Cash's wooing of June in the late 1950s. Silverstein, a gangly man with a massive shaved head, wanted to become a partner in the publishing company that Davis owned with Harlan Howard, but due to his abrasive personality, Davis and Howard had passed. Davis, however, offered to take "A Boy Named Sue" to Cash, a day or two before Cash left for San Quentin.

Cash was intrigued and attempted to learn the song on his flight out to San Francisco. Holiff recalled his client examining the lyrics at a coffee shop in Chicago's O'Hare Airport while waiting for their connection: "By that time he had spilled a lot of coffee all over [the lyrics], because he had a thing about carrying a jar of Chase and Sanborn instant coffee. He would take spoonfuls of that and put it in the coffee that we got [in restaurants]." As the coffee sloshed about in Cash's nervous hands, spilling on Silverstein's lyrics, he learned the words and decided they would do for San Quentin. On the record, the prisoners' raucous cheers and the bleeped out word or two gave "A Boy Named Sue" an underground edge *a la Folsom*, but the song was so laden with irresistible hooks and the formulaic country elements of beer, brawls, and busted relationships that it pierced the popular and country markets without needing the initial underground interest.

In addition to "A Boy Named Sue," a major factor in *San Quentin's* healthy sales was *The Johnny Cash Show*, which was airing as a summer replacement on ABC-TV when the album was released. Columbia's marketing people estimated that the television show added tens of thousands to the album's sales tally.

However, beyond its obvious boon to the marketing of Cash's records, the TV program proved to be a monumental career achievement and a sparkling conclusion to the performer's turbulent public life in the 1960s. No doubt a few in the nebulous underground market considered the show a concession to the dark forces of the establishment. And it was, but it nonetheless was a canvas for Cash's art and communicated his social messages like no other medium had. Cash was often criticized in the late 1960s for being silent on civil rights, and his handling of the white supremacist boycott in 1966 may have raised questions about his position on race. But *The Johnny Cash Show* spoke loudly and decisively on race, at least as loudly as *Folsom* and *San Quentin* had spoken on class and compassion.

ABC-TV had invited Cash to fill its summer schedule in place of the vacationing *Hollywood Palace*, a musical variety show often hosted by Bing Crosby. Cash bit because that's what you did in American entertainment when your reputation ballooned, host a TV show. "I never liked television," he grumbled as the show went into production. "But now I have decided I am going to like it. I mean, if I'm going to have to do it every day, I might as well enjoy it. I don't like being so confined, but I like my guests, and it's my show, and it has to be good."

To strike a comfort with the medium, he and Soliff enumerated a number of conditions with Columbia Screen Gems, the production company that would deliver the show for ABC. Primary among them was that the show be staged in Nashville at the Ryman Auditorium. Beyond the city's obvious place at the heart of the music he hoped to emphasize, country, it kept him close to home, where he was sincerely trying to establish roots. The producers would have preferred Los Angeles or New York, but he chose Nashville, he said, "because this is my home. If any real country show is going to go, it's going to go from here."

There is irony in Cash's waving so heartily the banner of country music as his television show inched toward its debut. For so long he'd evaded the country label. After the unsettling experiences that surrounded his *Grand Ole Opry* initiation in 1956, he had returned to Nashville only for his obligatory *Opry* appearances, recording sessions, and trysts with June. He had done his best to avoid the city's definition of country music. He had cast himself as a folk singer in the late 1950s, a label viewed with suspicion in Nashville by the early 1960s, and his work for the next ten years reflected such aspirations. He was country only in his strong identi-fication with the genre's progenitors (including Jimmie Rodgers, the Carter Family, and Hank Williams) and the music industry's need to match him with a clearly identifiable audience. He almost never referred to himself as a country artist, and if his 1966 interview with Dixie Deen (the one right after his drug arrest in El Paso) was any indication, he still despised Nashville even after ten years of coming to town.

Yet by 1969, he was anxious to have his show be an outlet for country music, and it's hard to pinpoint a reason. Perhaps because he was living near Nashville, he hoped to gain acceptance in its community. Maybe now that his mind was clearing of chemical influence and he was free from his first marriage, he'd simply lost the fuel for his fights with the city that gossiped about him and insisted on defining his career. Commercial considerations, too, were probably at work. His show needed to attract his core audience, which despite his best efforts to alienate it was the country audience, those who flocked to the ranch shows and county fairs and gob-bled up those tiny single records with the cherry-red Columbia label. It's likely that Cash was playing up his show's identification with country to attract them as well as the progressives on the coasts who had decided that, for the moment, country music was all right. In any event, the show marked a turning point in Cash's self-identification. For more than twenty years after the show went dark, Cash proudly shook hands with the world as country music's top ambassador.

Another one of the concessions that Cash and Holiff sought from the produc-ers was the hiring of Bill Walker to coordinate the music and conduct the orchestra that no network variety show could be without. Walker was considered Nashville's top arranger and conductor after handling the music for Eddy Arnold's best-selling albums and tours during the previous five years. But Arnold and Walker had fallen out, leaving Walker free. Despite Walker's disastrous encounter with the drug-addled Cash on the *Steve Lawrence Show* some years before, he signed on for the Cash show.

Finally, Cash's deal also imported Canadian writer and director Stan Jacobson, who would take over as producer after one year when veteran Bill Carruthers left the show. In 1967, Jacobson had produced a Canadian Broadcasting Corporation program on Cash from Toronto, where a lot of people still didn't know what to make of Cash after he'd stumbled off the stage of the O'Keefe Center in 1966. Cash and Holiff were not easily persuaded to return. "I finally convinced them to do the show," says Jacobson, "and I called it *The Legend of Johnny Cash*, because that's what he was to me. And my production assistant and I went down to some place in Maryland, just outside of Baltimore where he was performing, to watch a show to see what songs he did, before I started writing the show. I remember on the bus back from after the performance, he was nervous and scratching his face. I turned to my production assistant, who was a woman, and we were having a drink in the hotel. I said, 'What have I got us into?' Anyhow, he showed up in Toronto, and we started shooting on the Monday. I brought him to the studio Sunday night. And he looked at the set, and he said, 'Where'd this come from?' I said, 'We built it for you.' He said, 'You mean you built this for me only? What do you do with it after?' I said, 'Well, it's taken down and destroyed.' He couldn't believe that this was done for him. The show went on the air [and] it was the number one show of the week during the National Hockey League playoffs."

In Nashville, as production on *The Johnny Cash Show* commenced in the spring of 1969, several glitches plagued the operation and sent the crew and Cash scrambling for answers. The sound was miserable, which would soon prompt Jacobson to hire Jim Malloy, the engineer whose Vicks Formula 44 Cash had downed in 1961 in Hollywood. Malloy had since joined the studio engineering staff of RCA in Nashville and would soon jump over to record production, where he would be responsible for a clutch of Nashville hits.

Worse than the initial sound, though, was the business of producing a network program in the ancient Ryman Auditorium. Bill Walker recalls rats scurrying across his shoes in the make-shift orchestra pit. Cast and crew shivered in the winter and melted in the summer. Everybody recalls vividly that on the day of the Apollo moon landing (July 20, 1969), the old hall's floor buckled and crashed under the weight of a large production crane.

The star, too, may have been crashing. In the pilot episode, Cash's face drooped as if he had an upset stomach or was missing a fishing trip on Old Hickory Lake. His frequent blinking, shifting, and fiddling (the plain nervousness that had followed him back from the air force) marked the entire summer replacement run, subsiding only in the second season. While making the first few shows, Jacobson feared that Cash might tumble over, although not because of drugs or booze. "The opening number was Johnny walking down these stairs beside these palm trees that seemed to have died about four years ago," he recounts. "And he's looking very uncomfortable because he wore high boots coming down the stairs. That's the opening number. And I said to Bill Carruthers, 'With all due respect, you can't do that to him.' 'Well, how do we open the show?' [retorted Carruthers] I said, 'The same way he did *San Quentin.*' And I asked John about 'Hello, I'm Johnny Cash,' and he said Bob Johnston, his record producer told him to say 'Hello, I'm Johnny Cash.' So I said, 'I want to steal a page from Bob Johnston.'" Jacobson played the San Quentin record for Carruthers, and they carted away the steps and palm trees. Cash retaped the opening with his simple introduction.

The first edition of *The Johnny Cash Show* brightened tubes across America on June 7, 1969. It was much anticipated, primarily because of Cash's featured guest, Bob Dylan. The balladeer had only rarely appeared on network television and had only briefly greeted the public since a motorcycle accident sidelined him in April of 1966. One underground columnist quipped that the Fillmore East in New York was dark that Saturday night so everybody could stay home and gawk at Dylan.

But there were plenty gawking at Cash, too. Despite his nerves, he was resplendent in a black jacket, ruffled white shirt, and meticulously coiffed hair, as he pulled aside the curtain on his new show with a riveting medley of his hits. One suspects the applause lights were superfluous at that moment.

The audience roared, rising as if to assume its own part in the show. And Cash was surely glad they did. He knew a live audience; a television audience was too abstract to play to. So he fed on those who had stood in line outside the Ryman. Not even Elvis Presley had played so well to a studio audience. On his televised comeback that aired in December of 1968, Elvis sat virtually in the lap of the audience, many of whom had been collected on the street outside, but he still was on a pedestal, an unapproachable god who had given up live performances eight years before. Cash, on the other hand, dove into his audience, whom he'd never left.

Saving Dylan for later, in case anybody at home was tempted to turn off the television, the producers slated Joni Mitchell as the first musical guest. She was an unmistakable symbol of Cash's conviction that the actors in the folk revival were welcome on his show. Over the run of the show, in Mitchell and Dylan's wake, followed Ramblin' Jack Elliott, Arlo Guthrie, and Pete Seeger.

Cash's desire to host Pete Seeger tangled him in the network's conservatism, which squirmed at the sight of Seeger, that old Communist and anti-war voice. In a room at the Ramada Inn near the Ryman, which functioned as an annex for the show, Cash confronted Carruthers about Seeger. "I wanted [the network] to call me and tell me why Pete Seeger can't be on my show," he said. "Pete Seeger is a great American; he's sold the Appalachian Mountains in Asia. Why can't I have my friends on this show?" Cash eventually got his way, but the battle to host Seeger (and repay to the invitation to Seeger's show in 1965) accentuated the uneasy arrangement over bookings that settled between Cash and the network: Cash could welcome his favorites, although they might not be ratings winners, as long as they weren't too controversial or esoteric. But he also had to accept the networks desire to feature stalwarts of the variety show circuit: Bob Hope, Phil Harris, Al Hirt, Patti Page, and the like.

The premier episode was perhaps the most quintessentially Cash of all of them. Free for the moment from the variety-show-circuit riders, he bowed to folk roots by including Dylan, Mitchell, and the Cajun fiddler Doug Kershaw, who shook like a toy puppet and beamed with a gap-toothed smile. The first show also presented a video montage of Folsom Prison scenes over his performance of "Greystone Chapel," an obvious nod to the success of his recent live albums and his belief in the redemption of the imprisoned. Even the commercials rang of the Cash experience; one of them hawked Vivarin (a stimulant) and the other Nytol (a sleep capsule).

The men and women erupted when Dylan took his turn in the spotlight, but the audio problems that had gnawed at the show in effect cut him off from his audience. He ambled into "I Threw It All Away" from his newly-recorded *Nashville Skyline* album, but the audience could barely hear him over the shuffling drums, although the tape picked him up. Dylan also sang "Living the Blues" and saddled up next to Cash in a recreation of the host's Hendersonville living room to sing their duet "Girl from the North Country," the opening cut from *Nashville Skyline*.

"Well, Dylan got a standing ovation," says Jacobson, who from his perch near a camera had observed the performance of Cash's friend. "And he left the stage, and he wouldn't come out. He was so nervous. So I went backstage to this cockamamie dressing room. I said, 'Bobby, you're coming with me.' He said, 'Where?' [I said] 'On stage. Those people aren't leaving until you come out.' He says, 'Stan, I'm scared.' I say, 'They love you.' I grabbed him by the hand and I led him out on stage, and they just freaked." Dylan obliged them by repeating his songs, this time with stage amplification.

It had been Dylan's favor for his big-star friend, enduring the clawing reporters, nosy fans, and unwanted spotlight in Nashville to call attention to the new show. The ploy had worked. His contribution garnered space for previews of the show in newspapers and magazines across the country. *Vogue*, *Rolling Stone*, and *The Village Voice* used the TV show as a backdrop for speculation on Dylan's direction, which many presumed was hopelessly pointed to Nashville. "Another thing I entertained," wrote James Stoller of the *Voice*, "was that Dylan's entire down performance was a none-too-expert imitation of glum Mr. Cash."

Dylan's appearance spread out some television traction for Cash, but the show had much to overcome, particularly the hammered-together ambiance and the host's occasional uneasiness. "The show on the whole was a disappointment," complained Louise Sweeney of the *Christian Science Monitor*. "It looked as though ABC hadn't spent nearly enough time or money on packaging the showcase for this formidable talent. The sets were really bad: a series of some of the tackiest trees, roots, and trunks ever seen. Except for the [prison] footage, the camera work was dull. The pace of the show lagged badly, too . . . ."

Cash's stiltedness in the first shows attest to his role in the production's initial look of malaise, but ABC overlooked it and agreed to buy a new patch of shows that would begin airing early in 1970. At a press conference announcing the renewal, Cash promised to continue in the vein of the summer run: "I'll continue to do it the way I feel it, the only way I know it, with the Tennessee Three. I've worked up that background for 15 years and I see no reason to change. When they buy Johnny Cash they buy my style and the Tennessee Three is part of my style."

Moving to Wednesday nights in the new season, Cash dealt out episodes that strayed little from the original summer-replacement shows. His guest list was wildly eclectic, including acts such as folk singer Eric Andersen, singer-songwriter James Taylor, country father Roy Acuff, country-pop star Eddy Arnold, rock band Derek and the Dominoes, and soul powerhouse Joe Tex. Cash also continued using his music to proffer his vision of America. In a weekly segment he called *Ride This Train*, which was co-written by Merle Travis, Cash's singing narrated a video tour of some slice of American history or society. Exploring the West, the life of the American Indian, or the prison system, it was like adding video to *Bitter Tears*; *Blood, Sweat and Tears*; and his other 1960s concept albums. The only segment of the show not taped in front of a live audience, it was Cash's favorite.

The Johnny Cash Show also offered his first clear statement on race in America. In 1969, a *New York Times Magazine* article that Cash admitted to reading chastised him for ignoring the violence in the black ghettoes and the freedom marches in the South. "Perhaps many of the down-South country folk who buy his platters would rather not hear about those subjects," writer Tom Dearmore proposed. Cash had certainly said plenty on discrimination against the American Indian, but with the advent of his own show, he now assertively turned to black and white relations.

In one of his first broadcasts, Cash delighted in introducing O.C. Smith, the pop and R&B sensation from Mansfield, Louisiana. He beamed and entwined his hands with Smith in a soul shake. It was as if Cash were saying, "Accept it; the world's changing." A year later, he made way for the soul star Joe Tex, whose explosive imitation of Elvis on the show couldn't be more emblematic of the racial confluence that dwelled within rock and roll. Elvis had borrowed from black music, and here was Joe Tex taking it full circle. The message of racial unity rolled out even more determinedly in the summer of 1970, when Ray Charles and his Raelettes appeared on the show. Charles grooved through "Finders Keepers, Losers Weepers," and then Cash walked over and sat next to him on his piano bench. It hardly seems radical from the vantage point of thirty years later, but a white man and a black man sharing a bench in some Southern towns might have found themselves on the run. Probably thinking of Charles's best-selling *Modern Sounds in Country and Western Music* of 1962 and his other sporadic country recordings,

Cash praised the black singer's role in the commercialization of the genre Cash was now so vigorously promulgating. "On behalf of the Country Music Association," announced Cash, "I want to say thanks to you for bringing country music around the world." It was another great anti-bias moment. Country music and Ray Charles? You better believe it; the music of the white South could be the music of the South, period. And when Charles belted out "I Walk the Line," with Cash looking on approvingly, some of those millions watching may have gotten the message.

There were other social messages. He ended the shows with essays speaking out on war and peace, drugs, and religion. In a meditation on the Civil War to introduce "Battle Hymn of the Republic," he spoke not of North and South, slave or free, but in what appeared to be a thinly veiled plea for unity of "both sides" in a nation torn by Vietnam.

On a pure entertainment level, the show was a patch of sweet strawberries. The veteran star Phil Harris, so cool and ambivalent, almost stole the show from a fawning Cash. Roy Orbison, the only figure darker than Cash, reeled off a haunting take on his "Oh Pretty Woman." Cash, Carl Perkins, and Eric Clapton jammed on Perkins's "Matchbox." And Stevie Wonder pumped out Cash's "Get Rhythm" and his own protest classic "Heaven Help Us All."

While not a ratings champion, the show was holding its own in its time slot and spreading the news about Cash. Holiff saw the dividends of the show's ascent as his asking price for a live show doubled and tripled and the venues were less and less county fairs and now included Madison Square Garden in New York and Maple Leaf Gardens in Toronto. Heretofore untapped slices of society came around, too, as Holiff observed when he and his star strolled by a group of older Jewish men and women in a Rhode Island hotel lobby: "We walk out," explained Holliff, "and the people, they're elderly, look up and see this big tall guy dressed in black, and they stand up and start applauding him. Now, this is after the first [TV] show that he did. And I swear that these people from Brooklyn, the Bronx, Queens, and Staten Island, you name it, never even heard of the name of Johnny Cash ever before. He had so suddenly grabbed the attention of so many people. It was astounding."

By the fall of 1970, some six months into the the show's renewal, Cash was obviously improving. He had slicked himself up for TV; he was hipper, wittier, more sophisticated, and more articulate, the result perhaps of fewer pills and more experience. He was not as cowed by his celebrity guests, as a burning duet with Peggy Lee revealed. It's one of the riveting moments of the entire series. Lee and Cash duetted on "I'm A Woman, " a jazzy, demure number in which Cash should have been entirely out of his element, but he was a capable suitor, playing to her smoldering persona. They held hands, Cash inches from the sexy chanteuse. He seemed to want to clutch her. The lights dimmed, and they reclined in "For the Good Times." If only there were more such sublime moments the show might have lasted forever.

But the show's flame was dangerously flickering as it entered the 71–72 season. Perhaps the show was faltering because Cash and his producers had never figured out which audience it was trying to serve: the silent majority or the rock and folk crowd. In any case, ratings were tumbling. "Screen Gems-Columbia Pictures got nervous," says Jacobson. ABC got nervous. "And they said we have to do these mini-specials. And one was a western special, which we did out West at Tucson, at great cost, and Kirk Douglas, God bless him, was a guest star. And they wanted me to do a circus show, because circus shows get big ratings. And I told Johnny, 'This is what they want you to do.' He said, 'Well, you tell them I'm not doing it.' I said, 'I work for them. They're going to fire me.' I remember when I told him 'They're fixin' to fire me.' He said, 'If you go, I go.'"

The production company fired Jacobson for refusing to take Cash to the circus, but Cash went to the circus anyway, in a program that aired in early March of 1971. The show failed to survive through the month. In a wholesale purging driven by the program's declining ratings and a federal government order reverting early prime-time hours back to local stations, ABC ended *The Johnny Cash Show*. The country star was in good company; the network also axed *The Lawrence Welk Show*, *That Girl*, and *Let's Make A Deal*.

Cash was touring Australia when he learned the news. Bill Walker, who was along playing piano, recalled that ABC's pullout infuriated Cash, primarily because the singer had made plans around future taping schedules. NBC invited him to move the show to its network of stations, but Cash refused. "I'm declaring a moratorium on television," he was heard to say.

The effect on the generation that spent a small part of its adolescence glued to *The Johnny Cash Show* is probably the program's greatest legacy. Recently, a baby boomer I know in Los Angeles named Morley Bartnoff, who happens to lead a pop band called Cosmo Topper, told me he watched the show every week. "That show had an amazing effect on me because not only did I realize this was some kind of left-of-center character that they actually gave his own television show to, but it was the first time that, I think, most anybody got to see Joni Mitchell and Bob Dylan and Kris Kristofferson and Derek and the Dominoes with Eric Clapton on TV." Bono of U2 claims to have watched in Ireland, like thousands of others. Cash was a licensed host among the young, a draw that brought many to see the strange and beautiful chords of American music.

The show also encapsulated the major themes of Cash's art: rural life, Christ's teachings, the West, common struggle, and America's virtues and failings. In his mind and on his television stage, America's soul lived in a heartland where dreams rode on trains, God saved men, and the disenfranchised enjoyed a shot at justice and reward. Such beliefs were never so clearly stated by Cash as when he expressed them on *The Johnny Cash Show*.

12

THE GOSPEL ROAD

The shock and anger that Cash felt at his show's cancellation rapidly dissipated as he and his troupe toured the cities and countryside of Australia. "A burden had been lifted," he would say. When a reporter asked him if he had enjoyed network TV, he replied that the first year had been fun but he soon realized that he was merely a cog in the network machinery, and an expendable one at that. He had tired of the grueling production schedule, battles with the network and producers, and the gaggle of feature writers traipsing through his hotel rooms and back stages at the invitation of network publicists. "I began to feel as if every part of my personal and family life was being merchandised and exploited," he said. "I felt as if they were stealing my soul. To get ratings, they immediately started putting guests on my show that I couldn't—if you'll pardon the expression—relate to. People about whom I felt nothing, and that just made me uncomfortable. Eventually I was walking around thinking, 'I don't have to do this. What am I doing this for?'"

There was no reason to continue if he wished not to. In 1971, Cash could do just about anything he wanted to do, for his image and marketing power were unequaled in country music. He could fill rock arenas such the Forum in Los Angeles and Madison Square Garden in New York and expect his every record release to scale the country charts and dent the pop side, too. He'd also revisited his earlier cinematic aspirations, starring in two movies that wrapped production before the demise of the TV show: *Trail of Tears*, about the forced march of Cherokees to Oklahoma, and the triumphant *A Gunfight*, a dark western costarring Kirk Douglas and Karen Black and financed by the Jicarilla Apache Indian tribe. A victim of limited distribution, *A Gunfight* nonetheless offered Cash a role suited to his persona and abilities. He played a reluctant gunslinger drawn into a showdown with Kirk Douglas's character. "The Cash performance . . . is a fierce and towering one," noted critic Louise Sweeney. "He has an almost epic presence—so strong on camera sometimes that he looms above all the other characters like some dark cliff."

For Saul Holiff, who admitted that Cash's renaissance took him by surprise, the event that defined the singer's new stature was his booking at the Canadian National Exposition in Toronto in August 1971. "The [venue's] typical season would be Bob Hope, Jack Benny, the Rockettes—grand, big spectacles plus very big names, Lambert, Hendricks and Ross, stuff of that sort," he said. "So here we are with Johnny. It's late August, and the grandstand is sold out. The ticket prices had gone a long way from two, three and four dollars. They were like eight, ten, and twelve. So we had a dressing room set up in the middle of the track, like out in the field, out behind the stage that was put up each year facing the grandstand. And we would be taken by golf cart to the stage for each of the acts. The trailer was very comfortable and everything done really nicely. We're sitting out there and looking out at this crowd, and we had no idea that we had sold out. So, the general manager comes back and says, 'The demand is so enormous that we're going to ask you to do something that we've never asked in our history of presenting shows. Would you be willing to do a second show?' We did. We had an enormous gross. I mean, my end was more than I ever expected to earn probably in my lifetime. That day was spectacular. The weather was perfect. Just everything came together, just turned out to be perfect. And the Cashes were in good humor. And they were being interviewed about me [for a newspaper profile], and they were complimentary. They were very complimentary. I remember that vividly."

Holiff, who admitted to continually underestimating Cash, had been ill-prepared for the rising popular tide that embraced Cash in 1968. Major television offers, movie deals, and big concerts dates inundated Holiff, who could just about handle negotiating the occasional television appearances and concert dates in mid-sized theatres, county fairs, and country music parks that pretty much had defined the parameters of Cash's work before *Johnny Cash At Folsom Prison*. Holiff and Cash needed assistance, so through a Los Angeles disc jockey who had helped promote some of Cash's shows they met Lou Robin, a partner in one of the nation's top concert-promotion firms. Robin batted in the big leagues, promoting shows for Crosby, Stills, Nash, and Young; Blood, Sweat & Tears; Simon and Garfunkel; Creedence Clearwater Revival; and Bill Cosby. At the time, Robin and his company Artist Consultants were looking to move away from rock acts because their drug use and wild audiences created more headaches than Robin wanted to bother with. Cash, whose drug binges were settling down in 1969, promised Robin less craziness plus concert revenues that almost equaled those of the rock acts.

Raking in nightly grosses that reached tens of thousands of dollars, Robin gained prominence in Cash's world. When he began handling logistics beyond those related to concerts and brought on West Coast agent Marty Klein to identify other ways to market Cash, Holiff might have felt the squeeze and embarrassment at the possibility that he was becoming redundant and that Cash was keeping him around out of mere loyalty. However, Holiff betrayed none of those feelings in his interviews with me. In fact, a review of his correspondence from that time reveals that he seemed to be enjoying the fruits of Cash's revival, which perhaps he had earned after the hell of the 1960s. In letters, he badgered Klein for complimentary hotel accommodations and tickets to various events for family, friends, and himself, regardless of whether these happened to coincide with a Cash appearance. Holiff was comfortable, he said in interviews with me, until the summer of 1973, when he and the Cashes were encamped for a string of shows at the Sahara Tahoe Hotel in Nevada.

Holiff characteristically was there for the luxurious stretch in Nevada, but was under Cash's scrutiny for having missed a less glamorous evangelical appearance Cash had made with Billy Graham some months before. "I was probably at the highest point in my life," said Holiff. "I was jogging five miles a day. I was wearing Brioni Italian suits that are now selling for thirty-five-hundred dollars, and everything that Johnny had . . . I requested and got almost the same. Like the date at the Sahara, he got a house with staff, and a couple blocks away, I got a house with a staff. I had everything you could possibly want. I was making tremendous money, and I was in tremendous shape. It just couldn't be better. So I go over to his house in the morning after my mandatory jog, and I start to become criticized for not being at

1942

1. J.R. Cash at age 10.
(Mississippi Valley
Collection).

2. Jack Cash (left) with J.R. Cash. Sister Reba is peeking
between them. (Courtesy of Cindy Cash).

3. Jack Cash's tombstone in Bassett, Arkansas. (Photo by Michael Streissguth).

4. Roy Cash in the early 1940s. (Courtesy of Roy Cash, Jr.).

5. J.R. Cash (top row, second from right) and his alter egos, Jesse Barnhill (bottom row, second from left) and Harvey Clanton (bottom row, second from right). A.J. Henson, another friend, is in the third row, second from right. (From the 1949 edition of *The Keepsake*, the Dyess High School yearbook).

6. The air force veteran and his new bride Vivian (Liberto) Cash in San Antonio, Texas, 7 August 1954. (Courtesy of Cindy Cash).

7. George Bates, the guardian angel. (Mississippi Valley Collection).

8. Johnny Cash on the *Grand Ole Opry*. (Saul Holiff Collection).

9. Sun producer Jack Clement.
(Mississippi Valley Collection).

10. Vivian and Johnny. (Courtesy of Rosanne Cash).

11. Vivian and Johnny in California with (L to R) Kathy, Cindy, and Rosanne. (Saul Holiff Collection).

12. Cash in his home studio of sorts. Note the photograph of his mother Carrie Rivers on the shelf. (Saul Holiff Collection).

13. With Saul Holiff in Holiff's Hollywood apartment. c. 1962. (Saul Holiff Collection).

14. Dueting with Joan Baez in the height of Cash's folk adventures. The Statler Brothers are on the left. W.S. "Fluke" Holland is on drums. Luther Perkins is to the right. (Saul Holiff Collection).

15. With June Carter in 1966 on a tour of U.S. military bases in Europe. (Saul Holiff Collection).

16. The first visit to Folsom Prison.
November of 1966. (Saul Holiff Collection).

17. June Carter.
(Saul Holiff Collection).

18. With Ray Cash, Reba Cash Hancock and Carrie Cash in early 1968.
(Courtesy of Gene Beley).

19. Luther Perkins at Folsom, January 13, 1968. (Copyright Jim Marshall).

20. Jamming with Carl Perkins at Folsom. (Copyright Jim Marshall).

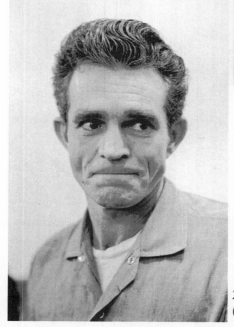

21. Glen Sherley at Folsom. (Copyright Jim Marshall).

22. Signing another Columbia contract with Don Law, standing, and Goddard Lieberson. (Saul Holiff Collection).

23. With Mother Maybelle Carter in Memphis, 1970. (Mississippi Valley Collection).

24. With Marshall Grant in Memphis, 1970. (Mississippi Valley Collection).

25. The changing of the guard. Lou Robin (l) and Saul Holiff. (Saul Hollif Collection).

26. Baptism in the Jordan River with Jimmy Snow (l) and Larry Lee (r). (Saul Holiff Collection).

27. With June and John Carter at the American Music Awards, 1977. (Author's Collection).

28. With (l-r) June, Dorothy Ritter and John Ritter in 1981. John Ritter died a day before Cash in September 2003. (Author's Collection).

29. Taping a Christmas special for CBS-TV with members of the children's choir at the church of St. Marks in Edinburgh, Scotland, 1981. (Author's Collection).

30. With Steve Popovich at the Polygram signing ceremony in Nashville, August 21, 1986. (Photo by Alan Mayor).

31. With brothers and sisters. L-R, Tommy Cash, Joann Cash Yates, Johnny, Louise Cash, Roy Cash, Sr., and Reba Cash Hancock. Jack—in an old photo—looks down from the wall. (Courtesy of Roy Cash Jr.).

32. With Roy Cash Jr. at his commissioning in 1985. (Courtesy of Roy Cash, Jr.).

33. With daughter Rosanne and Waylon Jennings at a Nashville awards ceremony, February 11, 1988. (Photo by Alan Mayor).

34. Cash's daughters Kathy, Cindy, and Tara at a B'nai B'rth ceremony in Nashville, March 30, 1989. (Photo by Alan Mayor).

35. Jimmy Tittle in 2003. (Photo by Alan Mayor).

36. Recording with Tom T. Hall and Jack Clement in Nashville, February 26, 1988. (Photo by Alan Mayor).

37. Back in black. On a session for a Willie Nelson tribute album with Waylon Jennings, left, and Austin singer-songwriter Jesse Dayton, center, 1995. (Photo by Alan Mayor).

38. With (l-r) Marty Stuart, June, and Connie Smith in Nashville, October 8, 2002. (Photo by Alan Mayor).

the Billy Graham crusade. And this is gentle. This isn't harsh. And I'm being told that all I'm really interested in is money. Now, that always strikes me as kind of hilarious because the Cashes were always interested in money, too. I didn't have the market cornered on money. But then that's part of our history that somehow or other the Jews are the only ones who are really after money. Somehow or other, the rich people of the world like the tycoons in England, they aren't interested in money. So I objected vehemently and said I wasn't there because it wasn't feasible to be there and I didn't need to be there. And I objected to being portrayed this way. And out of the blue I said, 'You know what? I think it's time that I gave you nine months notice.' And they looked shocked. And then—this is the strangest part of it all—from that time on, for months, there was never one ill word, never ever a suggestion that I would be leaving. Never. On the contrary, I think they had looked upon me—I'm positive of it—as a good luck [charm]. Like, that I brought luck to their situation. Like I was some sort of medallion. It had something to do with being superstitious, I know that. And then I probably might've felt a similar way. And we went right through when we were in Scotland, and it was like [September], and there was a Muhammad Ali bout on somewhere in the world, and I bet Johnny five hundred dollars, and I won. You couldn't find a better relationship going on. And I still left in November. That's the truth. That's what did happen."

~

Lou Robin's ascent to Cash's management was just one of the changes filtering through Cash's life in his early 1970s heyday; the other was the birth of his and June's boy, John Carter Cash, in March of 1970. In contrast to his daughters' quiet births in Memphis and Los Angeles, John Carter's arrival was heralded like a prince's. He was the son of country music's first couple and a symbolic victory in Cash's climb back from the abyss. "The past couple of years have been the happiest of my life," Cash announced to a magazine writer shortly after John Carter's birth. "I'm a human being again; I've got the right wife, I'm working steady, and I finally got a son."

Judging from his statements and actions in the early 1970s, Cash was clearly determined to be a better parent to John than he'd been to his daughters. He carved out more time for home life and, recalled Holiff, Cash and June took John Carter with them on the road as often as they left him home. "He started traveling with a nanny, and we went everywhere," said Holiff. "New Zealand and Australia, Tasmania,

Scandinavia, he went everywhere. And everywhere we went, as John Carter became two and three, Johnny would take off with him and take him to a museum or take him to a zoo, or take him to some spectacular gardens, say in Hawaii or in Australia, and talked to him and looked at things and pointed them out, had a dialogue with him. It was our opinion that John Carter was going to either turn out to be a genius or the world's greatest artist. He had enrichment that was extraordinary. I mean, aside from care and protection, it was like carrying a series of mobiles hanging above the crib, only there was no crib."

As Cash and June enriched their boy, their boy was obviously enriching them, particularly Cash. According to Marshall Grant, when June gave birth to John Carter, the drugs vanished. "Starting in late '68, '69 and '70," says Grant, "John got ninety-percent straight, not a hundred percent but he got ninety-percent straight. And he come around, and he looked like a million dollars, but there was always just a little there, not a lot, but just a little. And then the day that John Carter was born he quit cold turkey, period. From 1970 until 1976 he was as straight as any man that has ever lived, and there was a great, great, great, great human being for all those years."

Rosanne Cash concurs. Fourteen years old when John Carter was born, she and her sisters were permitted to spend more and more time in Nashville once Vivian was convinced of Cash's changed ways. "From the time John Carter was born there was a turn-around, definitely," says Rosanne. "It was exciting to be with him then. It was just fun. He was into everything, and he was so happy to have this baby and, you know, I put all my shit aside about him having . . . the golden child."

Many out in the world may have grumbled over the crumbling of the prisoner/bad-man mantle, but Rosanne welcomed it. "The man who was clean, happy and religious? I enjoyed him," she says. "That was such a good period. I loved being with my dad then. I think that's when I got my real dad back, the dad I remembered from when I was five or six years old. I loved him. He was great and so much fun and we'd go to sometimes three, four movies a day. We'd go in the Jeep out in the fields, get out and pick blackberries. He'd play guitar on the porch. He'd set off firecrackers in the front lawn. He made ice cream. He'd take us fishing. I did gardening with him. We planted cotton and vegetables, hands on in the garden. But it was a great period. He was present. He was in his body."

Invigorated by his freedom from drugs and escape into family life, Cash at the same time was refocusing on his religious convictions, which seemed to have been dormant for so long. *The Holy Land* LP of 1968 had been the first tithe that he paid to God after the *Folsom* success and then he frequently injected his television show with gospel music, but many more gospel projects awaited.

Cash's recommitment to his faith slowly took form in the weeks, months, and years following his troubled showdown with addiction. He and June revisited the Baptist Church in Hendersonville from time to time, and on the road, they often slipped into local churches for Sunday morning services.

Even at San Quentin, wedged between his cussing and carrying on, Cash reeled off three gospel numbers, including Carl Perkins's "Daddy Sang Bass," a number one hit from *The Holy Land*. The television show was no different. The producers may have blanched as every third show, it seemed, reverberated with gospel songs, such as "Peace in the Valley," "The Old Account," "How Great Thou Art," and "He Turned the Water into Wine." In 1971, Cash dedicated an entire program to gospel music, featuring Mahalia Jackson, the Blackwood Brothers, the Oak Ridge Boys, and the Edwin Hawkins Singers, and the preaching of Billy Graham. The extravaganza could not have been a ratings winner and surely turned off a lot of people who had initially switched on their sets to see acts like Bob Dylan and Joni Mitchell. But Cash was clearly tickled to have collected so much gospel talent in one place and to have given a stage to Billy Graham, the foremost evangelist of his time. He beamed throughout the show.

Graham had courted Cash in late 1969, after witnessing his own son Franklin's enthusiasm for the singer. Seeking common ground with his son and alliances with public figures who could help him bring the Gospel to young audiences, Graham contacted Cash and initiated one of the most visible aspects of Cash's gospel career. Throughout the decades, Cash and June regularly appeared on Graham's crusades, and from time to time, Graham or his name wandered into Cash's recorded repertoire. Graham's preaching was interspersed with Cash's singing on the "The Preacher Said, 'Jesus Said,'" a cut Cash wrote for *Man in Black*, the first album released after the TV show was cancelled. And a few years later, in 1974, Cash inserted Graham into his survey of evangelicals "Billy and Rex and Oral and Bob" from *The Junkie and the Juicehead Minus Me* album.

"I have never known a greater man among men . . . ," wrote Cash of the spiritual giant in his life. "As a friend of mine, he is one of those in the inner circle, those four or five friends you will only know in a lifetime of friends that come and go." Aside from Cash's father, Graham was the one man on earth who could humble the singer, although it's apparent that he (who so enjoyed the company of presidents and kings) was himself starstruck by Cash. The man's man veneer that so defined Cash melted away in the presence of the honey-voiced man from North Carolina. Cash sought Graham's approval, and he measured his growth against Graham's spiritual messages.

Evangelist Jack Shaw, whom Cash hired in the 1990s to counsel those in his concert audiences who needed help, recalls watching an eager Cash become puppylike as the singer introduced Graham and his wife, Ruth, to him. By then, Cash was appearing for long stints in Branson, Missouri, and so was hard-pressed to break away for the crusades, but Graham sent a jet to fetch him and ensconced him at the hotel until it was his time to appear with Graham. "When it came time to leave," says Shaw, "we came out of the room and John, three times, said, 'I have this minister traveling with me, Billy and Ruth. This is Jack Shaw.' [This was] in the hallway, we were walking down. He got in the elevator, he told them again. We got downstairs, he told them again. He was so glad that he was doing something that would affect peoples' lives with the gospel of Jesus Christ, which is why I think he was telling him that." And Cash was pleased that Graham would be pleased. Shaw begins to say that Cash "idolized" Graham, but he stops and corrects himself. "He was really impressed with Billy Graham," says Shaw. "He felt so good about his relationship with him."

Of course Graham was far too busy to be daily counsel for Cash as the singer endeavored to grow in the faith. For that, Cash found a church home not far from Hendersonville, the Evangel Temple, a small Assemblies of God congregation pastored by Jimmy Rodgers Snow, the son of country music star Hank Snow. The church's embrace of baptism of the Holy Spirit (believed to be a special infusion of spiritual power experienced by some after receiving salvation) and its manifest speaking in tongues conflicted with the comparative restraint of June's Methodist upbringing and Cash's Baptist raising. The couple was ultimately lured by his sister Joann, who attended the church; by their own earnest desire to find a church home; and by the witnessing of members Dottie and Larry Lee, friends of Luther

Perkins', whom they had gotten to know while grieving after the guitarist's death. On May 9, 1971, Cash, with June by his side, made a public profession of faith at the altar of the tiny church. For the time being, he immersed himself in the church, leaning on the fellowship of Snow and other Evangel Temple members.

Cash had long understood that Christianity demanded his witnessing to others on behalf of God, which is one of the big reasons he recorded so much well-known gospel material in the years before and after his spiritual and commercial reawakening in 1968. But in the wake of joining Evangel Temple, his public association with Billy Graham, and the cleansing power of John Carter's birth, divine obligations were mingling with pure artistic inspiration. Just as a film about Folsom Prison, friendships with California musicians, and his allegiance with Bob Dylan had sent him dashing down paths of creativity, the reemergence of religion in his life electrified his artistry.

His first meeting with Graham, a lunch in Hendersonville in early 1970, was just one of the morsels that fed his gospel energy. Within twenty-four hours of the minister's departure, Cash had written "What Is Truth?", which implores us to resist the temptation to judge the young: *Yeah, the ones that you're calling wild/Are going to be the leaders in a little while/This whole world's wakin' to a new born day/And I solemnly swear that it'll be their way.* Released in the spring of 1970, the song proved to be Cash's biggest pop hit since "A Boy Named Sue." But Graham's visit also stirred a far grander vision. The Cashes' desired to produce a film and album about Jesus, which had first entered their minds after finishing work on *The Holy Land.* "We'd thought about making a kind of travelog," said Cash in an interview, "walking the steps that Jesus walked and telling His story and then we talked about taking some contemporary, country-style Jesus songs, having songwriters write them and telling His story with them. As it turned out, that was a rough concept of what the film was actually going to be. We didn't know it at the time."

Graham inspired them to revisit the idea that would evolve into Cash's most ambitious project ever, *The Gospel Road,* a cinematic rendering of Christ's life that was Cash's own. Few people talked about multimedia in the early 1970s, but that's what Cash gave them in *The Gospel Road*: a 90-minute dramatic film, with a double-LP that was really more of an audio version of the film than a mere soundtrack album. Cash would call it his and June's "proudest work."

From the beginning, the project was all Cash. Working from a rough script he had written with Larry Murray, a writer from the ABC-TV show, he assembled a sparse cast in Nashville. In November of 1971 they departed for Israel, where they met a local film crew that Lou Robin had hired. The U.S. cast reflected either Cash's limited budget or his noble resolve to do the film his way, without the interference of outside influences. Director Robert Elfstrom, who also portrayed Jesus in the film, had gained Cash's trust a couple of years earlier when he directed a documentary on the resurgent star, and much of the remaining American cast were selected from Cash's circle of family and friends. June played Mary Magdalene, Cash's sister Reba Hancock played the Virgin Mary, Larry Lee played John the Baptist, Jimmy Snow played Pontius Pilate, and Saul Holiff (who was still with Cash at this point) played the high priest Caiphus.

Holiff, draped for the role in crisp, glistening vestments, delighted in playing a character who was something akin to the capo of the Jewish Mafia. Really along for the ride (his role was minor as Lou Robin had made most of the arrangements), Holiff was sobered by the festering Arab-Israeli tension that he observed as he and the crew stepped over rusted shrapnel and studied bullet-pocked walls, remnants of the 1967 war. "Everyday we went through places that were all hostile and angry," he said. "Soon after, the war broke out again, and you'd never dream of going through there, places like Napolis and Jericho, and into the mountains where the movie was done. That was all Arab territory, totally."

Sublimating their fears, the crew persisted in their work. They assembled the actors who played Christ's twelve disciples from a group of European backpackers, filmed panoramic scenes of the Jordan River and the countryside of Nazareth, and reenacted scenes such as the marriage in Cana, the Last Supper, and the crucifixion.

Although Cash noted the political heat simmering in the Holy Land, he was more interested in the witness that the project itself was for the crew, particularly Elfstrom's technicians, whom the director had called "a bunch of blackguards." Initially, Elfstrom himself, who objected to organized religion, had blanched at taking part in a religious film. But Cash convinced the director that Christ transcended the church, and in basic terms, was a "reformer and revolutionary." He then turned to Elfstrom's crew who, according to Cash, had rumbled into the East Jerusalem base awash in drugs and profanity. Cash described the encounter in *Country Music* magazine:

I had about a 30-minute meeting with this crew the evening we got to Tiberius, Israel. We sat around the floor, and I told them that whatever they'd done before, it didn't make any difference to me. Some of them had pretty tough reputations; they'd been in the riots in Mississippi; some of these people that worked on this film had been in South American revolutions. I said, "We're beginning a film about a man that is my Lord, and you're working for me, and that's all I want you to remember, that we're making a film about my Lord. There's not gonna be any orders given; there's not gonna be any rules laid down." And I said after the first day of filming, "I think you're all gonna get into the spirit of the thing and believe in what we're doing." And the second day of filming, everybody was up at 3:30 a.m. cleaning equipment. We drove 20 miles and were on location when the sun came up ready to start shooting. It was that way every morning. This was the most devoted bunch of people that anybody could ever hope to have.

Cash and Elfstrom spent almost a year editing the film, as Cash filled scenes with his songs and those of a variety of songwriters, including Larry Gatlin, Kris Kristofferson, Joe South, John Denver, and Christopher Wren (a journalist who had been approved by Saul Holiff to write the first serious biography of Cash, *Winners Got Scars, Too*). The soundtrack music was gospel set to boom-chicka-boom. The movie itself proved a compelling personal statement and a credible interpretation of Christ's days on earth, if one could look past the sharp Southern accent of Mary Magdelene and the preponderance of comb-overs among males in the cast.

An amalgamation of the four gospels' portraits of Jesus, Cash's Christ is divine, loving, fatherly, and, most important perhaps, human. He gently walks among the men and women of His world and trods over the rocky landscape as if He were of it, not above it. Even His anger at the scribes and Pharisees who permit commerce in the temple is convincingly of this world. Some critics of Cash's creation may have found the Christ of *The Gospel Road* to be too human in light of the film's portrayl of His interaction with Mary Magdelene, which, though ambiguous, was altogether sensuous. In one of the artistic highpoints of June's career, she plays a Mary Magdalene whose utter submission to and admiration for Jesus casts Him both as Lord and lover. As Cash narrates, "Mary was the kind of woman that Jesus had a lot of love and compassion for, *a lot* of love and compassion."

A minimalist production, in keeping with Cash's own storytelling fashion, *The Gospel Road* was also modern and impressionistic, employing experimental camera shots and linking Christ with the 1970s. One of the most startling moments is in the crucifixion scene. The image of Christ on the cross is transplanted from Golgotha to the smoggy, faceless cities of 1970s America, suggesting either that we continue to crucify Him or that the promise of His death lives with us even in modern times.

And certain through it all is Cash. Invoking his "Ride This Train" vehicle from the 1960 album of the same name and from his television show's regular feature, he invites the moviegoers to "come along with me in the footsteps of Jesus." He's a dramatic and authoritative storyteller, striding along the banks of the Sea of Galilee explaining Christ and Mary Magdalene's relationship or straddling a rock on a high peak reciting the Lord's Prayer. They were scenes that must have immensely pleased Carrie Cash and made Cash himself feel that he was fulfilling the mission that brother Jack had been unable to pursue.

A chilly winter's rain pelted Charlotte, North Carolina, on the night of *The Gospel Road*'s premiere. Hundreds of fans and curiosity seekers jammed the theatre lobby, many hoping to spot their Man in Black. They weren't disappointed. While Instamatics popped and a cleaning woman clutched his shoulder as if it were a fold in Christ's garment, Cash pressed tall through the crowd. Distracted by an earlier bomb scare and the absence of Billy Graham, who was honorary chairman of the screening (which was a benefit for nearby Gardner Webb College), Cash had fidgeted and drummed his fingers through a press conference before cutting it short by some twenty-five minutes. But if he worried about the audience's reception, he shouldn't have. They would have cheered home movies of John Carter. The president of Gardner Webb, who also emceed the evening, was so moved after the film that he considered asking people to approach the front and pronounce their faith. But, according to a newspaper account, he "decided it was neither the time or the place." Plastic buckets for contributions to the college floated through the audience.

Despite the promising opening in Charlotte, Cash feared that his filmed testimony might never ascend from the South. "We were really trying desperately to get it distributed beyond the conventional places," said Holiff, "and we succeeded. I think I had a little something to do with that. Maybe it was more than just a little. But we did get into theaters, but getting that out of basements of Baptist churches in the South was quite an achievement. That was something that wasn't considered for a minute commercial, but it wound up being in theaters in lots of places, including even my hometown of London, in a first-run theater on main street. So once again, when I was willing to write it off as a basement thing somewhere in Mississippi, [Cash] proved me wrong again."

Twentieth Century Fox stepped forward to distribute *The Gospel Road*, but with muted enthusiasm. Showing it around the South throughout 1973, it wasn't until December, some ten months after its Charlotte premiere, that Fox scheduled a New York date. It was hardly a launching pad, however. Despite widespread media coverage and a hearty endorsement in a *Newsweek* magazine review, the company promised only to schedule the film where they received requests for it. It wasn't long before *The Gospel Road* settled into the church basements of America, where it flickered for many years on white painted walls and portable screens.

The album version of *The Gospel Road* also stalled before rising to the general population. It ascended to number twelve on the country charts, the worst showing of any album release of new Cash material up to that point. And the only single release from the album, the infectious "Children," toddled to number thirty. *The Gospel Road*'s half-hearted reception in the marketplace could have been predicted given the limited success of similar projects by other artists. Film and record promotion people rarely get excited about material that strays from an artist's tried-and-true formula, and the media promotional engine, uneasy about religion, would rather talk up the secular. In the era of *The Gospel Road*, only *Godspell* and *Jesus Christ Superstar*, both of which had put forth Christ as a pop-culture figure, had broken the mold. Cash's simple film never stood a chance against such lavish productions and certainly failed to return Cash's five-hundred-thousand-dollar investment. But Cash never blinked, despite the financial loss and Holiff's warning to him that he'd lose pockets of his secular audience over the film. Cash would unflinchingly say that the film was his witness, and that he and June never felt like they had lost a nickel on the project.

The tragedy of *The Gospel Road* that Cash never discussed (though he may have dwelled on it) was that critics, historians, and the public never appreciated the unique and artistic statement that it was. He had taken his deeply personal convictions about Christ and turned them into a multimedia expression. He had never done anything like it. The concept albums of the early and mid-1960s had merely pulled him into libraries, discussions, and desert sojourns as he researched songs and stories; *Folsom Prison* and *San Quentin* had been high-voltage versions of his regular shows that had required little preparation. On the other hand, Cash poured years of his life into *The Gospel Road*, first lending his name to advertisers such as Amoco and Lionel Trains in order to raise money for the project, and then doggedly pursuing the concept in recording studios, atop rocky peaks outside Jerusalem, and in editing suites with Elfstrom. Few, if any, of his peers had stepped from their regular recording careers to pursue a new genre, and the fact that Cash did so is a tribute to his continued desire to challenge himself by reaching for new spheres. Many secular artists had recorded spiritual music from time to time (Elvis Presley, Eddy Arnold, Red Foley, and virtually every country music artist), but nobody had made such a rich, faith-based statement and then followed it up with extensive public interviews expanding on his beliefs. Cash's testimony rang with sincerity, while gospel recordings by other secular artists seemed tailored to the niche market for gospel music that existed within the country audience.

Ultimately, *The Gospel Road* receded into the background of Cash's career because America's arbiters of chic rejected it. The image proffered by the film clashed with the dark countenance that fascinated them. Tellingly, *Rolling Stone* ran an extensive profile of Cash shortly after *The Gospel Road*'s release, but omitted any mention of the film or album. In the ensuing decades, darkness in Cash's image overcame the spirit of *The Gospel Road*. The film and album marked the beginning of a long and arduous third chapter in Cash's career, 1973–1993.

～

Oddly, the prison albums that did so much to construct Cash's dominant bad-boy image in their own way reinforced his Christian profile by accentuating his role of protector of and voice for the disenfranchised. In appearing before crowds of caged men, outcasts from society, Cash was living Christ's golden rule. He'd seen the moral lesson at work in Dyess, where cooperation among farmers could mean the difference between baled cotton and rotten cotton. He had also lived it, as his childhood friendship with the outcast Jesse Barnhill could attest. Despite the carelessness and cruelty that marked many of his relationships during the 1950s and

1960s, he had never entirely let go of the spirit of charity. He harbored Patsy Cline in his home when the country star arrived beaten and bruised from a skirmish with a partner, he coughed up five thousand dollars in 1965 for Jimmy Rodgers Snow when the evangelist sought to build his church, and he wrote another check for five thousand dollars in Saul Holiff's name when the manager, forever feeling unappreciated, was chairman of an Easter Seal's campaign.

The impulse to sympathize with the other fellow and to go further by offering his hand came as naturally to Cash as a rhyming couplet. A despondent serviceman named Conrad J. Ward never forgot meeting Cash outside the *Louisiana Hayride* in 1959 and pouring his woes to the black-clad singer as he scrawled his autograph on a scrap of paper. Suicide must have burned in Ward's eyes because when Cash handed him the autograph, he set down his guitar case and led the 22-year-old a few paces away to a quiet spot. "Try to remember something, son," implored the singer, staring into the young man's eyes. "Life has corners, corners you'll find you have to turn even when you didn't know they were there. And though things may seem terrible at the time, around every one of those corners is a new story and a new friend. Life is a challenge. There's always something to look forward to." Cash stopped a moment before refocusing on the young man's eyes. "Suicide is a dead-end street," he said, just above a whisper.

Twenty-five years later, when Cash's daughter Cindy had moved to Nashville to live with him, she witnessed another example of Cash's compassion. On a cold December morning, she and her father had stopped by his office to pick up some cash for an upcoming tour and then dropped John Carter at school. On their way back home, they spotted a lonely figure on the side of the road. "This guy was sleeping under a bridge with no blanket, only his coat over him," says Cindy. "I said, 'Look at that Dad. He's just got to be freezing.' He pulled the car over without saying one word, and got out of the car. I thought, 'I have got to hear this.' So I just kind of got out of the car and stood up by the car and stayed there to hear what he was saying to this man. This man just kind of sat up and was just waking up. Dad said, 'What are you doing under this bridge, son?' He said, 'I'm headed to Kentucky to spend Christmas with my kids. I got three kids.' [Dad] handed this guy a thousand dollars and said, 'Get you a bus ticket. It's too cold to hitchhike. On your way home, be sure to buy those kids some Christmas presents.' And we drove off. I turned back around to look at this man. His mouth was hanging open. [Dad] was always able to put himself in someone else's shoes. He was under that bridge sleeping in the cold with that guy."

In the late 1960s, Cash had reached out to Glen Sherley, the convict whose "Greystone Chapel" Cash had recorded at Folsom and whose future seemed as uncertain as that of the suicidal airman or the man under the bridge. In 1971, Sherley walked free from the California penal system thanks to Cash's advocacy. The authorities had agreed to release Sherley on Cash's promise to employ him, and within weeks of departing the Golden State for Nashville, Sherley was writing for Cash's publishing company and performing on his touring show.

By the time of Sherley's parole, Cash had become an insistent and highly visible voice on prison reform. He had spoken out in countless media interviews and continued to perform well-publicized prison shows. In 1972, after Sherley's release, he lobbied President Nixon and addressed a U.S. Senate subcommittee working on reform legislation. In front of the senators, he declared that reform was critical in order "to give a man some hope in prison, to give a man some encouragement to be a better citizen while he is there and if he is a better citizen, while he is there, he is going to come out a better citizen."

Prison reform was one of the most visible manifestations of Cash's Christian beliefs, and his interest in Glen Sherley was proof that his dedication spanned beyond words. A man could be transformed in caring hands, insisted Cash, and he held up Sherley as an example in concerts, interviews, and the Senate testimony. Sherley sat next to Cash in the Senate hearing, and when called upon, he trumpeted Cash's theme of concern for humankind and praised his new boss for taking an interest in him when nobody else had.

"But it was a mistake, a bad, bad mistake," says Marshall Grant of Cash's good deed for Sherley. "But John didn't know that. John's a very caring person. He had a very soft spot in his heart for prisoners, no matter what they did, because they're human beings. And to lock them behind bars, he just feels is the most dreadful thing that could ever happen to a human being. It probably is, I don't know. But that's just John, and John got him out. He didn't really do a lot of research to see what kind of dude Glen was, but believe me, it didn't take us long to find out."

Sherley's prison stories were like tales from the crypt, and Grant loved to hear them when they traveled on the road, but it seems that one night the ex-con sidled up to Grant and told him that he'd sooner cut his guts out than live peacefully with him. Grant, a sturdy man in any group, trembled. It was hard enough keeping the Cash road show on track without looking over his shoulder at Sherley, who frequently said he'd rather be back in prison anyway. "I said to John, 'Hell, he wants to kill me. He wants to be my friend and everything, but he wants to cut me apart.' I said, 'I can't deal with this guy no more. And I'm not going to deal with it. My life is important, and I fear for everybody on this show. Because if he wants to cut me up, he probably wants to cut you up and everybody else on the show, and I'm not too sure that under the right circumstances he might not do it. So you do what you want to with him, but I'm through with him.' And I think that John probably took that to him in some way, and he and Glen, away from everybody else, had some words of some sort. And John just told him he couldn't travel with the show anymore. But John had a place, a house there that he was letting him use and all that stuff, and he told him you can do this, that, and whatever you want to do. We just can't take you anymore. And so with that things really started falling apart in Glen's life, really started falling apart."

Sherley descended into a lurking drug addiction and squandered any gains that he'd made under Cash's wing. Bouncing from friend's house to friend's house in a battered old car, he grew so scraggly that the chiseled, clean-shaven face that had burst with hope when he first met Cash was scarcely recognizable. By 1978, he was living with a brother in California, where one spring morning he rose from bed, walked out to his brother's porch, and shot himself dead. Sherley's death must have devastated Cash. It was, in a way, the death of his passion for prison reform.

Years later, after Cash had put to bed his 2000 album *American III: Solitary Man*, actor Tim Robbins interviewed the ailing singer for a promotional disc that was meant for radio airplay. In the course of the gentle interview, Cash turned to his prison concerts and brought up Sherley: "He lived a very good productive life for many, many years until he had a tragic ending from . . . ." Cash hesitated, then continued, "well . . . actually . . . cancer."

~

FOUR

~

A COLD, WILD WIND
1973-1993

13

LEGEND

While *The Gospel Road* was failing to reach a mass audience during the spring of 1973, Rosanne Cash was graduating from high school back in California. Immediately afterward, she set out for Nashville, beating a path that her sisters Kathy and Cindy would follow when age allowed. Fourth sister Tara would keep her distance from the clatter of her father's world, shunning the music business and Nashville for the familiarity of the West Coast and, later, the Pacific Northwest where she resides today.

But Rosanne was courting the music business, and by February of 1974, she was in the House of Cash studios (a facility in a small office building that Cash had built in Hendersonville), recording solos, duets with her father, and background vocals for his albums. Her take on "Broken Freedom Song," written by Kris Kristofferson, landed on her father's *Junkie and the Juicehead Minus Me*, a poor selling album released in 1974 that Cash had essentially given over to the aspiring singers in his family. June's daughters Carlene Smith and Rosey Nix joined Rosanne in singing lead and background vocals.

Rosanne also hit the road with her father, crooning behind him with the Carter Family and stepsisters who might occasionally drop in to embellish the show. The tour dates that Rosanne joined were wedged between major commitments that

191

exploited Cash's broad entertainment appeal: he appeared as a conniving evangelist on NBC-TV's *Columbo*; hosted the Country Music Association awards broadcast; and spent one month shooting *Ridin' the Rails*, a television documentary that he narrated on the colorful history of trains in America. It was as grueling a year as ever for Cash, and it was the first Rosanne had witnessed up close. The demanding pace, she observed, was sapping her forty-two-year-old father. "The tour was relentless," she says, "and it was really long and all of us were exhausted, but we hadn't done half of what Dad had to do because, as well as the performances, there were all these other demands on him: interviews, television, meet and greets. And he just kept going and kept going and kept going. And when [the tour] was done, we were in the airport going to Jamaica [for vacation]. It was over, and he broke down and cried. He just kind of walked off and put his hands over his face, and he started to cry. What I remember most is, 'Wow, he waited 'til the end.'" When Rosanne glanced over at June, she must have expected her to either collapse with him or hide her husband's sobbing from airport gawkers, but she was amazed to see instead June's unflustered response. "She was so calm, she just accepted it," she says. "She went over and patted him, told him it was going to be okay. He could do it, it was done, we're going home."

Anybody standing by as Cash purged his fatigue and frustration might have questioned his dedication to the road. But Rosanne knew. He was the same man who had confounded her mother with his compulsive need to be gone, even, as Vivian would say many times, when he didn't need the money. The tapping foot, the twitching face, the incessant picking at his guitar, Rosanne had seen, were the tics of a man for whom motion was life. "He loved [touring]," says Rosanne. "He loved it. It was his own addiction. I mean he always said—he's home for three days, four days, he'd start getting so restless—'Where are we going next?' When do we start again?'" Cash pined for the rumbling of the bus, anticipated the amenities that awaited in each new hotel room, and hungered for the next audience. "He wanted to be in motion," continues Rosanne. "He wanted to be in motion all the time. It was like an engine, you know, it just didn't stop."

Even as Cash pressed forward like a man with no tomorrow, he couldn't ignore the fact that, since *The Gospel Road*, the popularity of his work declined with each new release. *The Junkie and the Juicehead Minus Me* album, weighted by his family singers, stumbled in 1974, and its two singles never entered the country charts.

Columbia thought it might arrest the slide when it asked Cash to lend his vocals to songs by young songwriters, to be recorded over canned instrumental tracks laid down in Los Angeles. But the experiment, released in 1975, only accelerated the slippage. *John R. Cash*, named to suggest a back-to-basics approach, fared worse than any album to date, hampered by Cash's unenthusiastic vocals, flaccid instrumentation, and a clutch of songs that were by and large ill-suited to the singer. "My Old Kentucky Home," written by Randy Newman, was one such song, a moonshine cocktail of hillbilly clichés (drinking, spousal abuse, and idleness) that Cash had previously been too dignified to touch. Cash's take on Billy Joe Shaver's "Jesus Was Our Savior," though closer to his own *oeuvre* than "My Old Kentucky Home," was another misstep. Following a major Cashian theme, it was a simple song about faith and rural struggle: *Jesus was our savior/Cotton was our king*. But Cash had written the diamond of rural struggle songs, the elegant "Pickin' Time." Next to it, "Jesus Was Our Savior" was uninspired, cluttered with superfluous narrative. The saving grace on *John R. Cash* was Tim Hardin's "The Lady Came from Baltimore" about the redemptive power of an adoring woman, a theme Cash knew something about. It hit number 14 on the country charts in 1975, his best in two years, and confirmed that Cash could handle the material of modern songwriters, if it was the right material.

Despite "The Lady Came from Baltimore," the album fell to the wayside. The country charts snubbed it, and Cash almost immediately disavowed the album in the press. "[Columbia] thought it was the way to go, and I didn't know for sure at the time," he said some eighteen months after the release in an interview with *Country Music* magazine. "So I went along with it, and I let them select most of the songs—which was a mistake, because if I'm not personally involved in my music, it ain't going to be right. I'm not going to have a feeling for it when I go into the studio. So that whole scene . . . was a wrong scene for me."

As Cash indicated in the interview, only one song on the album, "Lonesome to the Bone," was his. The album marked a distance from songwriting that had grown every year since the *Johnny Cash At Folsom Prison* popularity roared into his life. Dogged by a growing list of professional commitments (TV, commercials, and interviews) and intent on dedicating more time to family, he had less time to write.

And as he rocketed toward the center of the Nashville universe, he found that he didn't have to write. He employed a clutch of young songwriters in his House of Cash publishing company (which was also housed, along with the new studio, in the House of Cash office building). But whether the most talented writers were his charges or not, they all clamored for his attention.

Kris Kristofferson, an air force veteran and Rhodes Scholar, was one of the new guard in Nashville determined to reach Cash. After country artists Roy Drusky and Roger Miller turned his songs into hits in the late 1960s, Kristofferson (who was not a House of Cash writer) was on the cusp of prosperity when he pitched "Sunday Morning Coming Down" to Cash. The first-person ramble of a lonesome wayward man confronted by the purity of an ideal Sabbath day, the song had already been cut by Ray Stevens who took it to the country charts in November of 1969.

But Cash would not be put off by Stevens's success with "Sunday Morning Coming Down," remarking later that it was so close to him that he felt like he'd written it himself. Developing a friendship with the Texas native whose dangling locks gave him the look of rock god Jim Morrison, Cash carried Kristofferson to the 1969 Newport Folk Festival for a July 18th performance. A few days later, he recorded "To Beat the Devil," his first stab at a Kristofferson number. A year later, he finally recorded "Sunday Morning Coming Down." The Columbia engineers captured Cash's version live as he performed it for his television audience at the Ryman Auditorium, and it became the centerpiece of his number-one *Hello I'm Johnny Cash* album, which featured choice bits from the TV show. "Sunday Morning Coming Down" rose to number one on the country singles charts, ultimately proving to be the 1970s hit most closely linked to Cash. For the rest of his life, Cash never went too long without dipping into Kristofferson's well. He would record "Help Me Make It Through the Night," "The Loving Gift," "Me and Bobby McGhee" and others, but none were as popular nor as compelling as "Sunday Morning Coming Down."

Following Kristofferson's lead, Vince Matthews, another emerging bard in Nashville, served up to the magisterial singer "Wrinkled Crinkled Wadded Dollar Bill" (1969) and "Melva's Wine" (1972). And other sought-after writers joined the line: Billy Ed Wheeler (who co-wrote "Jackson") gave him "Blistered" (1969), a top-five hit; Jerry Chestnut came up with "Oney" (1972); and Dick Feller wrote one of the most under-appreciated numbers in the Cash canon, "Any Old Wind That Blows" (1972).

There's no question that some of the most memorable Cash hits of the early 1970s were of Cash's own creation ("What Is Truth?," "Flesh and Blood," and "Man in Black"). But in the years marching up to the misbegotten *John R. Cash* and soon thereafter, chances were that if Cash scored a hit, it bore another writer's stamp.

As Cash retreated from writing, the rock and folk audiences who had dashed to his feet in the wake of *Folsom* and *San Quentin* were backing away from him and taking with them their significant buying power. These converts had zeroed in on the rebellion and protest that boiled in the prison albums and unwittingly laid the bricks for his path to establishment celebrity. These *Folsom* and *San Quentin* fans would not have chosen such celebrity for Cash, and when some of them saw him take to his ABC-TV show dressed like a riverboat gambler and loudly endorse Richard Nixon's Vietnam policy at a Madison Square Garden concert in December of 1969, they began to grow wary.

At the Garden, in front of thousands, he'd proclaimed himself to be "a dove with claws," and many groaned. *The New York Post* dismissed as Wallace-ites the thousands who had cheered Cash's pronouncement, and *The Village Voice* saw the moment as driving a wedge between "rock and revolution." Appreciative articles on Cash in the tabloid-sized pages of *The Village Voice* and other alternative week-lies dwindled with every appearance of fawning profiles in the pages of supermarket journals such as *Life*, *Reader's Digest*, *McCalls*, and *Redbook*.

The pages of *Broadside*, the folk-music periodical which had once run a letter from Cash defending Bob Dylan, now were menacing woods to Johnny Cash. A disgruntled reader who saw Cash sing "This Land Is Your Land" on his television show complained in the magazine that Cash had transformed Woody Guthrie's chestnut into something akin to a Nixon campaign commercial. "Cash made everything into beautiful pictures of flowers, clear water, clouds, birds—but no people!" protested the reader. "When the hell did Woody Guthrie ever write a song that was not basically about and for people? Johnny Cash turned this song into a squishy flag-waving statement."

Although Cash recorded some of his most blatant protest songs in 1970 and 1971, "What Is Truth?" and "Man in Black" respectively, the rock audience barely stopped its evacuation to notice. His performance at the White House in 1970 and a public meeting with Nixon in 1972 (even though Cash was pressing him on prison reform) only fueled the separation, as did his unabashed allegiance to evangelical Christian leaders Billy Graham and Rex Humbard. Such connections consolidated Cash's mainline country-music audience, but even so, it was apparent that by 1973 none of Cash's political associations nor, for that matter, his artistic endeavors held much interest for those who had turned on to Cash in the late 1960s.

Nashville, too, tainted Cash. For a brief time in the late 1960s, it had been the object of national fascination as writers of all stripes pondered Bob Dylan's encampment there and trade magazines marveled at the millions of dollars generated by its recording studios. Of course, as Cash became one of the most intriguing figures of 1968 and 1969, his choice to live and make TV shows in Nashville transformed it into a mecca in the eyes of some. But very quickly, after Dylan abandoned Nashville and Cash's fire dimmed, Nashville and its prime export, country music, lost their luster among the voices of rock culture. Country artists who reached the international audiences thanks in part to Cash (Merle Haggard, Charley Pride, Loretta Lynn among them) enjoyed huge record sales as Cash's slipped, but nobody filled Cash's profile in the eyes of the audience outside country circles. Nobody was as rebellious nor as interesting as Cash had been. Nobody else appeared to be an authentic voice of the nation's downtrodden as Cash had been.

Critic Richard Goldstein, who had held Cash on a pedestal in the late 1960s, concluded in 1973 that the genre of music that the singer represented was rooted in bigotry and a "musical extension of the Nixon administration." His belief may have found credence in 1974 when Nixon, his presidency in ruins, received a hero's welcome at the opening of the new Grand Ole Opry House outside Nashville. While the fading leader banged out "My Wild Irish Rose" on the piano, Alabama Governor George Wallace, the symbol of white separatism, sat looking on in his wheelchair, an honored guest of the *Grand Ole Opry* management. Cash had appeared at the *Opry* the evening before for the legendary show's last performance at the Ryman Auditorium, but wary perhaps now of Nixon, Cash had not taken the stage on Saturday night.

Dragging Nashville and those invested in it down lower was Robert Altman's film *Nashville*. The 1975 drama recognized the city's rightful place as an entertainment capital, but scorned the egotism, knee-jerk patriotism, and religious fervor of its music community. The movie's characters seemed to exploit rather than reflect the simplicity of rural life where country music traced it roots. Although none of Altman's characters resembled Cash, the film unflinchingly cast doubt on those country musicians who would publicly profess faith and patriotism.

Not until the fleeting Outlaw movement of 1976 would Nashville again snag the interest of the urban tastemakers. Its ambassadors Willie Nelson and Waylon Jennings (who were taking their rough-hewn music to audiences in hip venues like Max's Kansas City and Soap Creek Saloon in Austin, while Cash was doing supper clubs) brandished their independent streak after watching the Man in Black do it in the late 1960s. But the Outlaw movement was on a track that diverged from Cash's. He had inspired them all right, but the music he was making in the years of their advent was anything but outlaw.

So Cash enjoyed moderate country hits, still-faithful concert crowds, ongoing television appearances, and the growing mantle of legend. He was the face of country music, but had slipped from the creative vanguard where the innovators remolded and propelled the genre.

America's bicentennial year arrested Cash's commercial decline, if only temporarily. His image as one of America's patriots had by then subsumed the Folsom rebel veneer and was just what celebration organizers in Washington, D.C., and Hollywood producers were looking for as they courted audiences possessed by national pride. During 1976, Cash hosted an NBC-TV program that wove the story of the circus into America's two-hundred-year history; guest-starred with June on NBC's historical drama *Little House on the Prairie*; served as grand marshal for the federal government's official July 4th parade in Washington; and performed a benefit for the American Freedom Train, a red, white, and blue steam locomotive carrying historical artifacts for public display that snaked across the nation that year.

This mad dash to exploit Cash's image probably explains his brief return to regular television in 1976. Shot at the new Grand Ole Opry House, *The New Johnny Cash Show* aired on Sunday nights during CBS-TV's late summer prime-time schedule. Spangled with glitter, in dramatic contrast to the subdued set of the original *The Johnny Cash Show*, the program showed Americans a Cash who was much more comfortable with television than he had been in the late 1960s. You always knew Cash was reading cue cards when he spoke to the camera, but in 1976 he paced along his stage with the air of a land baron. His hair was feathered back in the fashion of his young friends Kris Kristofferson and Larry Gatlin who appeared on one show, and the old scar that dug into his face now seemed more jowly than menacing.

Cash's hunger had diminished, the need to sell himself and his songs had long since subsided. When he turned to "I Walk the Line," the severity that sharpened it in 1957 when he performed it for the first time on television had vanished. It had ceased to be a pledge and was now but a standard to be trotted out on necessary occasions. Regular spots featuring comedians Steve Martin and Jim Varney spiced the show, as did Cash's swaggering duet with the greasy Waylon Jennings and a sweet performance with daughter Rosanne. But Cash mostly played it safe, falling back on the old hits and playing the straight man to June's impish prodding. "Around our house," he'd announce to the audience (as if a small bungalow with fires burning awaited him back in Hendersonville), "you're watching what is known as the Johnny Cash, June Carter, all-American, God bless mama and daddy, gather 'round the children, family singing show."

And that's pretty much what viewers got, with liberal helpings of June, gospel music, and a forty-second feature on bicentennial moments. From time to time, the "old Johnny Cash" reared up. He still preached on an America where the little guy enjoyed dignity and the train still drove commerce and inspired dreams, and he concluded the show with poignant social messages.

Cash was at his best during that four-program stand when he championed equality, still an elusive concept in the two-hundred-year-old nation. Every show featured the Baptist Catholic Methodist Choir, a black musical congregation that in its very name spoke about inclusiveness and whose regular role on the show symbolized black America's rightful place at the table. Cash relished introducing the group, the words "Baptist Catholic Methodist" rolling off his tongue like a shot cannonball, ridiculing divisions in Christianity and rejoicing in African-American culture. Rosanne, who served as a production assistant, watched her father from the control room or the side of the stage and thought he was firing his enthusiasm at his father Ray, whose mind was still mired in racism.

By late September, *The New Johnny Cash Show* had reached the end of its run, but Cash was gaining momentum. He toured the upper Midwest, Texas, and the

Northeast, and he appeared again on television's Country Music Association awards (which he hosted), the *Tony Orlando and Dawn* show, and his own Christmas special.

~

The heavy bicentennial exposure also fueled Cash's first number-one hit in six years, "One Piece at A Time," a naughty ditty about a General Motors worker who constructs a gawky automobile from parts swiped from the factory. Wayne Kemp, a prolific songwriter and singer on the United Artists label, came up with the song after hearing a tall tale about an Oklahoma airman who stole enough parts from his base to make a helicopter. Kemp planned to record the song himself, but Don Davis, who had brought Cash "A Boy Named Sue" and had been producing Cash's sessions since February of 1976, persuaded the songwriter that he'd make bundles of money if the Man in Black ran with it. The only problem, according to Marshall Grant, was that Cash showed little interest when he finally began noodling around with it in March.

"We were at the House of Cash doing a session, and John, he was in good shape, but he was tired," says Grant. "And he come up and set on the stool a little bit and sang some songs, because he was notorious for coming to the session not knowing what the hell he was going to do. But that was all right. That didn't bother us. So I knew he was very, very tired, and I was just sitting there in a chair, and he was sitting on a stool, and he was singing a few songs, and then directly he set his guitar down. And he said, 'You know Marshall, I'm going to go to school, get John Carter, and take a nap. You do whatever you want to do, and I'll be back here later on this afternoon.' I said, 'Okay John, [but] that song you was singing there about the automobile. What was the name of that song?' And he said, 'That "One Piece at a Time?"' I said, 'If that's the name of it, before you leave, just put that down on your tape with just you and your guitar and let us work on it a little bit while you're gone. We don't have anything else to do.' He said, 'You like that song?' I said, 'Well, yeah. I do.'" Suspecting that Grant's days back at Automobile Sales in Memphis warmed him to the song, Cash nonetheless went ahead and put down a scratch vocal before leaving for his nap. When he was gone, Grant and the rest of the musicians worked up an instrumental track. "About six o'clock that night he showed back up, and he sat down on his stool, picked up his guitar. And I said, 'John I want you to hear a track on "One Piece at a Time," and I'd like to put your

voice on it.' He said, 'Did y'all do a track on that?' And I said, 'Yes, we did.' And so
we rolled the track, and I said, 'I want to sing a little harmony with you here.' And
so he did it. And I walked up and sang 'One Piece at a Time' with him, and we listened back to it. He said, 'You like that?' I said, 'John, sure I like it. Everybody likes
it. It's a good song.' He said, 'I don't know about that thing.' I said, 'Well, let's do it
right one time.'" So we recorded 'One Piece at a Time' and it was released at a time
when we were going to Europe for three weeks. Almost on the same day that we
left it was released, Columbia shipped it out. And before we come back home, it
was the hottest song in the States."

"One Piece at A Time" played on radio stations during the spring and summer
of 1976, jostling with country hits such as Elvis Presley's "Hurt," Marty Robbins's
"El Paso City," and Crystal Gayle's "I'll Get Over You" on its way to number one.
Like a horse fan at the races, Cash peered at his song's position on the countdowns.
He relished the drama. "It's like everyone shared in the excitement of 'One Piece at
A Time' being number one," he observed in an interview at the time. "Everybody
in town would be calling the office or the studio, saying, 'It's number seven this
week,' and somebody would get a tip that it was going to be number four next
week, and they'd call. So I started looking at the trade magazines. I still don't read
'em, but I look at the charts and see who's doing what and what's happening in the
business . . . who's selling, who's not. It's kind of interesting—again." "One Piece At
A Time" camped at number one for two weeks. But in the Top Forty arena, beset
then with disco and increasingly uninterested in country music, the novelty song
about a car stalled at twenty-nine.

Many hoped the hit would usher in a new day for Cash, but it was just an
anomaly. Within months, he was casting about for another way to encourage
record sales. At first it seemed that the 1950s-brushed "One Piece At A Time" was a
back-to-basics strategy that just might work. Cash spoke to journalist Patrick Carr
about his planned follow-up, a take on the old Presley piece "I'm Left, You're Right,
She's Gone" ("got a sneaky feeling about that one"), and talked about his next
album reaching back for more from the Sun closet. The singer predicted more
Presley stuff, a Carl Perkins chestnut, and something by Roy Orbison. But it never
happened. "I'm Left, You're Right, She's Gone" languished in the vaults, and the
Sun-oriented album was just talk.

By foregoing a Sun-influenced album, Cash seemed to have decided that if he were going to click in the late 1970s, his music would have to be rooted in contemporary times. Yet he harked back in time again when he recorded *The Rambler*, an album that recalled the radio shows of his childhood. He and a hand-picked cast mostly from his family acted the story of a man (maybe a Glen Sherley) wandering the highways. A program of boom-chicka-boom songs interrupted the dialog at various points. The album flopped.

In pondering his recording fortunes, Cash would often talk about "Cowboy" Jack Clement, who had settled in Nashville in the 1960s after leaving Memphis and setting up camp in Beaumont, Texas. Since "Ring of Fire" and the Clement novelties that Cash had recorded in the 1960s, his and Clement's paths had diverged. Clement followed Charley Pride, directing most of the star's early sessions, started his own record label, and opened three recording studios in Nashville. Cash and Clement crossed paths when Cash reunited with Waylon Jennings in 1976 to record "I Wish I Was Crazy Again" and "There Ain't No Good Chain Gang," two songs that wouldn't see the light of day until 1978. Clement had recently produced Jennings's Outlaw classic *Dreaming My Dreams*, which must have gotten Cash thinking about what Clement could do for him. "Jack Clement is always around," said Cash in 1976, "and I feel like I am, too, and sooner or later Jack Clement and I will do something together again. We didn't do too bad on 'Ring of Fire' and 'Ballad of A Teenage Queen' and 'Guess Things Happen That Way,' some of those—and we'll have some ideas that gel perfectly sometime, and we'll get back in the studio together eventually."

"Eventually" would be some time in coming. Clement would not receive producer credit on a Johnny Cash session until 1980, but in the meantime they edged closer and closer together, reigniting their creative relationship on a middle-ager's wild weekend in New York in July of 1978. "He called me one Friday," recalls Clement, "and said that him and June and Jan Howard were in New York, and they were going to see *The Best Little Whorehouse in Texas* that night. And they had voted me as their favorite person that's still around or something. They wanted me to come join them. So they talked me into flying up there, and I went. I got there after act one, and from then on, I loved that play. I loved the music and everything. When I walked out, I bought a cassette of it, and then we went to eat. So everybody kind of walked out of the theater singing. And then we walked across the street to some restaurant, one upstairs; a lot of people from the theater were in there. And we walked in, and everybody waved at him. We go over and sit down, then I started singing, 'The Whippenpoof Song' or something. Pretty soon the whole room's singing along. And it was great. That whole trip was great. Then we went to some club, and I got drunk. There was this couple sitting next to us and I was picking on him, telling the girl, 'You ought to dump him and go with me,' whatever. It was all in fun."

Cash had already been working on Clement's "Gone Girl" back in Hendersonville, but he perfected it in New York, belting it out with Clement and Howard in his hotel room. Clement and Howard also taught him Mick Jagger and Keith Richards's "No Expectations," which, according to Cash, they sang forty times for lodgers in the next room who banged on their walls to demand an encore. By the time they left New York, Cash had decided to take the album that would be titled *Gone Girl* to Jack Clement Studios, although Clement would not claim producer credit on the album.

Clement also lent his devilment. Set free in his own studio, Clement was the jester to Cash's musical court, bringing back the prankish elements of Cash's early tours and, as Cash saw, corralling everybody into his circle of merriment. "It's awfully important to the musicians," said Cash, "to feel that the artist is not acting like a star and not acting like the boss; he's acting like somebody that you're having fun with. That's what my guys felt in that studio. . . . They were talking and laughing and cutting up and kidding Jack Clement about this and that, trying to make him balance a glass on the top of his head and do different kinds of dances. So we just had a lot of fun. Everybody was loose and laughing, and that's what helped to make it work."

For the next twenty-four years, Cash returned again and again to Clement, knowing that he'd find a comfy sofa, bowls full of chocolate bars, a fridge stocked with Cokes, and at least the promise of a hit. "He got to where he'd come over here a lot," says Clement. "He had a key to the place one time. He lost it, and I never did give him another one. Well, you know, sometimes you'd hear somebody walking around upstairs. 'Somebody's walking around upstairs,' [a visitor would say]. 'No, that's just Johnny Cash.' He'd come over and hang out, walk around, and leave."

Cash would come by for the sophomoric shenanigans, too, as video footage that Cowboy shot from time to time can attest. In one video, Cash sings "Come along inside Jack's brain" to the tune of "Come Along and Ride This Train," leading a camera through the inner sanctum of Cowboy's offices and studio. In another clip, Cash wheels into Clement's backyard in a new low-sitting European sports car. Demonstrating entry and exit strategies, he plops down on the driveway, shuffles next to the car on his bottom, and swings his legs inside. To get out, he turns himself on his stomach, drops his hands on the cement, and crawls from the car. "Here's my Tom Selleck look," he deadpans as he cruises away from the camera.

In 2003, one of Cash's last visits to the Clement amusement hall was also caught on video; he's wearing a paper crown and a pig snout. Somebody says off camera, "Sir Francis Bacon, ladies and gentlemen." Laughter ensues. Cash replies, "I had a dog named Sir Francis Bacon." Disease had parched his voice and hollowed his eyes, but Cash played it up for the camera, acting the idiot, knowing that when you visit Jack Clement, you fool around.

The first foray into Clement's world would have been complete had 1978's *Gone Girl* album reflected Cash's excitement at being around the songwriter and producer, but the album settled into the stack of lackluster artistic efforts of Cash's 1970s. Although Cash's rendition of "No Expectations" was a credible country song and his own "I Will Rock and Roll with You" was like riding back to Memphis in a 1955 Chevy, they failed to redeem the album's dullish veneer and poor set list. Cash had illadvisedly covered "The Gambler," a mega-hit for Kenny Rogers, and when he tried out Jo-el Sonnier's "Cajun Born," he sounded like a stockbroker calling a bayou square dance.

A majestic photo of Cash dominates the cover of *Gone Girl*. Chin gently perched on his folded hands, he is draped in an enveloping black wool shirt. A painting of a pastoral eighteenth-century scene fills the background, framing his formidable body. He is in a sense Mark Twain comfortably seated on his porch in Elmira, but Twain sat more easily in the days of his middle fame. There is angst in Cash's appearance. His mildly contorted face is like wind-beaten ridge on the verge of falling into the sea; his jaw pulls his face to the left while his nose droops to the right. Listlessness possesses his eyes, illustrating a resignation of some sort. "Take me from here," they seem to plead.

These were years of resignation in Cash's life. Despite occasional victories and the affirmation that legend bestows, he despaired over a career that was sustained by his past rather than by his present. The focus that new fatherhood brought in 1970 and the excitement of the *The Gospel Road* challenge had long since drifted away. To take their place, Cash surrendered again to his addictions. According to Grant, the drug-free life that had begun with John Carter's birth ended in 1976.

"We were playing this show in Hartford, Connecticut, and when we got to the building, he was there, which is totally out of character," says Grant, "and I knew something was wrong because the backdoor man said, 'Y'all come on in. Your boss man's already in there.' Well, I knew something was wrong. And so I started to the stage carrying [my bass], and he was coming off the stage down a little hallway, dressing rooms on both sides. And when he saw me, he darted in one of those dressing rooms. And I went out on stage, and I put my bass down, tuned it up a little bit, and come out there and went in that room. I said, 'John, tell me one thing. . . . Why? Just tell me why, if you can John, tell me why after all these good years. Why? Just tell me why.' And that was just about the way I said it. And he looked at me like he could run completely through me and out the other side. He said, 'Let me ask you something Marshall. Have you ever been through the change of life?' I said, 'Well, no, I haven't. I don't think.' He said, 'That's all that's wrong with me, and you're going to see that's exactly all that's wrong with me.' I said, 'John there's more than change of life here. You're back. The ol' Johnny's back, and there's problems down the road.' This-hundred-and-eighty-degree man came back. Now all of his buddies that was getting [the pills] for him—and we could talk years about this—they suddenly become his best friends. People like June Carter Cash and myself were the worst enemies. And starting in mid '76 it escalated every chance he could get, with no withdrawals, with no turning back."

Grant claims the next few years with Cash, until Grant was fired in 1980, were "a living hell," worse than the 1960s. When I asked him for an example of how bad it got, he cited a gig in Cohasset, Massachusetts, when Cash showed up with a broken nose he had suffered in a car accident in Jamaica.

"I always gave this little countdown before show time: four minutes, two minutes, one minute," recounts Grant. "This is for the sake of the entire show, to let the people know what was going on. I gave that in Cohasset one day, and he sent Lou Robin up to tell me to come back, that he needed to talk to me. [Cash] said, 'Marshall, I never want to hear that again. Never do I want to hear a countdown on a show. I will send you word when I want to start the show. You don't say one thing on the microphone until I send you word.' And he said, 'We're going to start all of these shows twenty minutes late and probably thirty minutes late. And today it will be thirty minutes. Don't ever give another countdown as long as you live.' I said, 'Okay, John if that's what you want.' He was in terrible shape. And so I walked back out and told the band, 'Guys, it's going to be a little while. I'll let you know.' The people were very restless. He sent me word, and we got all of us in synch, and we got a big round of applause. When he walked on the stage, he had his whole head wrapped in gauze. He had him a bunch of gauze, roll after roll after roll. The only thing that you could see were his lips and his eyes. He looked like a mummy. The band when they saw him, we all just fell out of synch, even me. I said, 'God almighty what's going on here?' He fumbled around and did the whole show for about an hour and then went back to the hotel after the show. And then I come back to the hotel, and he's sitting there on the balcony. And I walk out there. And he said, 'I want to tell you one thing: These doctors in Jamaica and Boston know nothing about broke noses.' He said, 'I rebroke my nose. If you want to know what is wrong with me, I rebroke my nose and all the stuff that you see on my head'— and it was still on there—'that's just to hold it into place until tomorrow morning, and it'll be all right.' I said, 'Well, John, I certainly hope so because you look in pretty bad shape.' I was talking to him like a child. The next morning—he didn't go to bed—when he came out he took the gauze off and said, 'See this nose?' I said, 'Yeah.' He said, 'Straight, huh?' I said, 'Well, John, no it's about like it was.' He said, 'It's straight enough isn't it?' And I said, 'It's straight enough. It's straight enough.'"

14

ADDICTION

Gone Girl was the second album in 1970s that had fallen short of the country charts. It hardly seemed possible. How could a Johnny Cash album suffer such rejection? Rosanne, who continued to occasionally appear on his records and shows as her solo career grew, saw that her father's search for the answer was frustrating him. "There was this element—I want to say desperation but that's not quite it—of concern and restlessness," she says. "Like, where is it? He was really looking, exploring, and then he would really talk up what he was doing right then, and then that wouldn't be it. And he'd go on to the next thing, and he'd really talk it up: 'This is great! This is great!' And that wouldn't be it. I saw him do that for a lot of years."

Cash's projects for 1979 and 1980 were at once touched with brilliance and pocked by formula. *Silver*, recorded for his twenty-fifth anniversary in show business and produced by Emmylou Harris's husband, Brian Ahern, unfurled an imposing take on "Ghost Riders in the Sky" as well as an accompanying set of cuts that were joyous, poignant, and inventive. His follow-up album *Rockabilly Blues* found Cash expertly handling Kristofferson's "The Last Time" and Nick Lowe's "Without Love." Ironically he flailed about in the bland songs of his own creation: "Rockabilly Blues (Texas 1955)," "She's A Go-er," and "W-O-M-A-N."

It's hard to imagine that Cash could have turned in anything better than *Silver* or the shining cuts of *Rockabilly Blues*, so it's no wonder that feelings of concern and restlessness plagued the singer. His dwindling songwriting abilities and the rekindled drug use surely discouraged sales, as did Columbia's waning interest in the singer. Pianist Earl Poole Ball, who'd begun playing in the studio and on the road for Cash in 1975, produced *Rockabilly Blues* and saw that in the absence of an obviously hot single, the record company had virtually ignored the album. In fact, Columbia's inattention was not especially new. The origin of its disinterest in Cash stretched as least as far back as 1978, while *Gone Girl* was struggling.

In late 1977, Willie Nelson had informed Columbia Records that he wanted to record in Memphis, Tennessee. The musical outlaw had an album of pop standards on his mind to be produced by Booker T. Jones, the muscle behind Booker T. and the MG's and a major player in the soul-music revolution at Stax Records in the 1960s. Columbia balked, all but ordering him back to the Waylon-and-Willie formula that produced gold with "Good Hearted Woman" in 1975. Any executive should have known that such demands clashed with Nelson's ethos of unpredictability. So the grizzled singer lugged the great American songbook to Memphis and churned out an album that promptly sold one million copies. The country music scene, accustomed to and satisfied with fifty thousand in sales per album, had seen few albums like it since Cash's *San Quentin*. Nelson's *Stardust* changed everything. While *Gone Girl* and every other Cash album sputtered on the sales charts, *Stardust* would glide on the dance floor for ten years.

Nelson's 1978 success raised the stakes in Nashville. Rick Blackburn, who was vice-president of marketing at Columbia-Nashville at the time, says Columbia's corporate parent in New York, CBS Records, saw dollar signs. If *Stardust* could sell millions, the brass reasoned, why couldn't their folks down in Nashville find a way to make it happen again and again? Executives in New York appeared to see the Nashville operation as nothing more than a line on a sales chart because there's little evidence that anybody in New York cared about the music. In fact, Walter Yetnikoff, who presided over the label from 1975 to 1990 (while brushing cocaine off his lapels), makes no mention of country music or its musicians in his 2004 autobiography. This is in contrast to Clive Davis, who, although no big champion of art over money when he ran the label just before Yetnikoff, at least acknowledged

Cash and his CBS roster mates Tammy Wynette, George Jones, Lynn Anderson, and Charlie Rich in his 1974 autobiography.

Yetnikoff's command in the late 1970s became thirty-five percent profit and twenty-percent growth. In other words, if the company invested one million dollars in Nashville, it wanted $350,000 back in profit and twenty percent more profit the following year. "That becomes a very tall order," explains Blackburn, who would assume the leadership of Columbia-Nashville in 1980. "And that's what's expected and that's how you're paid, actually. So it changes the whole dynamic of things. So in the 70s, where fifty-thousand units was 'wow, that's okay' to all of the sudden it was like 'you're crap,' the whole mindset changed."

From where Blackburn stood, the new culture demanded market research. He needed to know which consumers to court in order to maintain the sales deluge that Nelson had uncorked, so he hired a consultant. He found "a Jewish guy from Brooklyn," says Blackburn, "who didn't know anything about country music. He didn't know Johnny Cash from Creedence Clearwater Revival, which is why I hired him. You don't get any kind of bias."

After crunching his numbers, the consultant discovered two things: one, that Nelson was an anomaly, his music appealing to older Americans who loved his songs and younger fans who identified with his hippie image; and two, that the record-buying market, mostly young people, craved young artists with a steeped-in-country sound. Country radio had already made these conclusions and cited them to urge the recording industry to harvest the Randy Travises and George Straits of the world.

Unfortunately for Cash, the consultant's research tracked waning interest among active record buyers in him and other CBS-Nashville stars, such as George Jones, Merle Haggard, Johnny Paycheck, Marty Robbins, and Lynn Anderson. So, Blackburn signed Ricky Skaggs, Rodney Crowell, Rosanne Cash, and others who helped fortify what became known as the new traditionalist movement.

The new realities of the recording industry frustrated artists like Cash. When they saw new artists raking in one-million-dollar advances, they pined for the same money. But Cash, who earned $500,000 advances, could never have hoped for more, says Blackburn. "Back into the economics: cassettes were selling retail for ten bucks. And wholesale would have been five. You sell to K-Mart at five. So five bucks at fifty-thousand, that would have been 250,000 [dollars] you'd generate.

And out of that, you got to pay artist royalties, publishing. You got to pay your overhead; [a big advance for an aging artist] doesn't work."

In the studio, the fallout from the emphasis on youth was even more devastating for Cash, who had become so reliant on other's songs for his material. The songwriting community, which ten years before had scrambled after Cash, was now leaving him to his fishing in Hendersonville. "Cash wasn't getting the good songs," says Blackburn, "and we weren't getting the good songs for Cash. I'd get a song in for Skaggs or Ricky Van Shelton, whoever we have who was popular at the time. And if you'd say, 'Let me give that song to Johnny Cash,' they say 'no' because they wouldn't get the revenue." Cash could still draw from the wells of Billy Joe Shaver, Kris Kristofferson, and Rodney Crowell (who had married Rosanne in 1979 and regularly plied him with his material), but there's little question that the top Nashville songwriters were passing him by.

With young songwriters out of his reach, Cash surrounded himself with young producers and musicians, knowing that they too might hold the keys to revitalization. In the late 1970s, he welcomed Jimmy Tittle, a young bassist and guitarist who had performed his apprenticeship with Merle Haggard (and who would soon become another Cash son-in-law when he married Kathy Cash). Tittle joined Cash on the road, played behind him in the studio, occasionally produced sessions, and into the final years suggested repertory. He was a link to a younger world. Another link was Marty Stuart, who slipped into the Cash fold in 1979, after six years playing mandolin with Lester Flatt's band (Flatt had died on May 11, 1979).

Of the young blood Cash recruited, no one would be closer to him than Stuart. All of twenty-one when he signed up for his hitch with Cash, Stuart became a personal confidante, a musical advisor, and a son-in-law when he married Cindy Cash in 1983. Stuart had tread among music giants and other show business folks since the age of thirteen, so it wasn't long before he'd acquired a comfort with Cash that amazed some band members who'd never grown close to him and filled others with jealousy.

A brash young man from Philadelphia, Mississippi, Stuart had met Cash when he tagged along with a friend who was delivering a guitar he'd made for the superstar. The friend dropped off the box at Jack Clement's, where Cash was hanging out, and before long Stuart, Clement, and Cash fell into a jam session. Soon thereafter,

Stuart wheedled Cash's phone number from Clement and called to ask him if he'd sing on a bluegrass album that he was producing for Curley Seckler and the Nashville Grass, a variation on Lester Flatt's last band. Cash agreed, and it wasn't long before Stuart returned the favor. Stuart was on the last night of a tour with Doc Watson when Bob Wootton summoned him and his guitar to Des Moines, Iowa, where another Cash tour was in full bloom.

"When I got to the show I didn't see him," says Stuart. "So I was standing on stage [set to play], and he walked out and said, 'Hello, I'm Johnny Cash,' and we went to town. And that was it. But after that I lay in bed that night, after doing the show and meeting all the people, going, 'This really is more about the soap opera and the legend these days than it is about Folsom Prison and making music like that.' And it took a lot of thought on my part to go, 'This is a great job and any kid ought to be happy to have the job, but it's not going to be about the music as much as it's going to be about personalities and legends. But while I was there, whether it was as a son-in-law or a band member or a friend, I experienced and saw just about every type of human behavior, and I experienced about every emotion a human being could have. To hang out with that show and him and June and the whole size of that machine, that whole magnitude of that whole environment, man, it was worldwide. It was huge. Huge."

If touring with Cash was a lesson in celebrity star power, then it was also a tutorial in showmanship. Cash, observed Stuart, could easily match a song with its audience: "Ragged Old Flag" at the Kansas State Fair, "Guess Things Happen That Way" in rockabilly-mad Stuttgart, Germany, and "Highway Patrolman" in Johnstown, Pennsylvania. "He knew who his audience was before he even walked out," says Stuart.

One April night in Texas, Stuart witnessed the headliner unleash a song whose power not even he could have predicted. At an Amway Convention in Dallas (one of Stuart's first gigs with Cash), the singer performed Billy Joe Shaver's "I'm Just An Old Chunk of Coal," which Cash had recorded for his *Believer Sings the Truth* album, a gospel set that Columbia had refused to release. "I thought, 'Amway. Oh God,'" recollects Stuart. "We walked out there and it was like being at a rock-and-roll show. These people were crazy, these Amway people. It was like this whole cult, and we had no idea that there was this level of intensity. Well, he just pulled out 'I'm Just An Old Chunk of Coal But I'm Gonna Be a Diamond Someday.' Well, when we got through, the applause went on for like two minutes. He pulled up his collar and said, 'Do it again.' So we did it the second time, and the place kept coming apart even more. He looked at me and said 'I think we've got us one here.' And we did it a third time. I've never seen it happen, only that one time. And, he just wouldn't quit. We were just all puffed up. 'We had got us a hit.'" On the next show in another town, Cash brandished the song again, but the ferocious applause had stayed back in Dallas. The Cash camp soon found out that Amway salespersons aspire to Diamond status in their organization. "I'm Just An Old Chunk of Coal" seemed tailor-made for them, a hit with them, but not for Cash.

Stuart took part in the Great Eighties Eight, a configuration Cash organized in an attempt to energize his road ensemble for the new decade. In the end, however, the band came off as a bunch of black-clad white men jiggling around the stage. In Stuart's view, the new band only served to drown the pure Johnny Cash sound. "He had horns on stage and a synthesizer," says Stuart. "Me and the Tennessee Three was just kind of covered up. When they'd send everybody off the stage except Johnny Cash and Fluke and Bob and a bass player, [they] would do 'I Walk the Line' and the place would come apart. The vision would come back, the thing that made me fall in love with him when I was a kid. And I'd say, 'J.R., here's where it's at with your sound: they want to see Johnny Cash. Why don't you drop all your Vegas bells and whistles, even if it means firing me, and go back to your deal?' And he never got around to it while I was there."

Even when Cash turned to the stripped-down set in his concerts, however, something was different. Marshall Grant was not there to play bass. Cash had discharged him in 1980, severing ties with the only other person who'd shared in the sweaty Memphis birth of the boom-chicka-boom. The reasons given for Grant's dismissal are foggy, and records of a lawsuit that Grant initiated in the early 1980s that might have cut through that fog were sealed after Grant accepted an out-of-court settlement. Former band members hint at a wide range of factors, not the least of which was a clash between two titanic egos: Cash, the star, and Grant, the star maker. Grant believed he'd helped write the classic songs, helped create the original sound, and kept the singer physically alive when Cash couldn't do it for himself. In any case, Grant retreated to his ranch in Hernando, Mississippi, and Cash reboarded his tour bus with a new bass player, first Joe Allen (who years before wrote "Pick the Wildwood Flower" for Cash) and then Jimmy Tittle.

Although some personnel came and went, Cash maintained the Great Eighties Eight structure well into the new decade. The composition of his studio band, though, was hardly static. He was still in hot pursuit of the next breathtaking song, and if that meant recording with members of the Wrecking Crew on the West Coast, A-list players in Nashville, or his own band, he tried it.

In 1983, Cash mounted another charge toward success when he paired again with Brian Ahern, the impetus behind Anne Murray's emergence in the early 1970s and wife Emmylou Harris's great albums later in the decade. For a few months, before their sessions in April of 1983, Cash had been living with Bruce Springsteen's "Johnny 99" and "Highway Patrolman" from the New Jersey rocker's *Nebraska* LP of 1982, and he planned to record them when he and Ahern got together in the studio. According to Cash, Columbia was hardly pleased: "The record people kept saying, 'You don't want to do a Springsteen song!' I said, 'Yeah, I do.' I even went to New York and talked to the president of the company about it. He said, 'I don't want to hear you do Springsteen, I want to hear you do Johnny Cash.' I said, 'But I gotta do these two songs, they feel so right for me.'"

The notion of recording Springsteen was intriguing, the veteran circling back to the music of a man whom he had influenced. It presaged the pairing of Cash with young rock artists that worked so well in the award-winning American Recordings formula of the 1990s. But before there was Rick Rubin, who fostered the American Recordings formula, there was Brian Ahern, whose unconventional vision, observed Stuart, seemed likely to shake Cash from his paralysis. "We were just in awe [of Brian]," says Stuart. "Maybe it was because he was married to Emmylou and everybody else wasn't. But Brian was a very eccentric character. He had a true love and knowledge for music across the world, all different genres. I think that was the common bond there."

The Aherns and the Cashes had become comfortable with one another back in 1979 when Ahern was preparing to produce *Silver* and the couples vacationed together in Jamaica. But when Ahern showed up in Hendersonville to discuss songs for the Los Angeles sessions, Stuart noticed a pronounced unease between producer and singer. "We went to the cabin [near Cash's house] (which later became a studio) and had dinner with Brian," recounts Stuart. "All the ladies brought dinner over from the main house. We were sitting there, and John was sweating and twitching. Brian sat down; he was quiet and nervous. And John came out of nowhere with a hatchet. And Brian was sitting there at the end of the table, and [John] just threw it right over his head and, 'Bam!,' it found its mark in the cabin wall, and it threw Brian completely off. And I just kept eating. I thought, 'That's pretty good shooting right there.'"

Cash's bizarre outburst could only have exacerbated the tension Stuart sensed and foreshadowed the mealy album that Cash and Ahern would ultimately release. It also augered another strange episode that came up as their sessions approached; the scene around Hendersonville was getting even weirder. Tittle was miffed that he'd be staying home while only Stuart would be following Cash to California for the recording dates. He felt that if he was good enough for the road, he should be let into the sessions, and his displeasure at it all deepened as he and Cash chugged beer and wine at the house in Hendersonville. If June were home, says Tittle, drinks and tempers never would have been uncorked, but June, he says, was in the hospital. To make matters worse, Cash's daughter Kathy was angry with her father over a picture she'd painted for him that she'd seen stowed in the garage.

As the alcohol nudged dark thoughts toward the open, Tittle uttered something so offensive that neither he nor Kathy will repeat it today. "It was really ugly," allows Kathy. "And I saw fire in Dad's eyes."

Cash leaped up and said, "What did you just say to me?" Tittle repeated himself, and Cash said "Son, you need to go to bed right now. If you don't, I think we're fixin' to have some trouble."

The night descended into an alcohol-fueled barrage of accusations that abated only when Tittle and Kathy followed Cash's orders and retreated to the bedroom. The next day Cash confronted his son-in-law. "I never have shot anybody," said Cash, according to Kathy, "but I came as close last night to shooting you as I have anybody in my entire life." He demanded written apologies from Tittle and Kathy, although Tittle recalls that the healing really came when he fetched a parcel of pills from Cash's own Dr. Nichopoulus. "We didn't talk to him for several days. He went to L.A. to start working on this record, and he called. And he said, 'James'—he started talking about cars—'why don't you all lease a Mercedes?' Or something like that. He said, 'I'm out here in California working on this record. Would you go down to Dr. so-and-so's office for me, I've already talked to him. You go back there and tell him I want this, this and this, and send them out here to me.' And that was his apology and my apology to him. In other words, score me some drugs and we'll be friends again."

For Kathy's part, she initially refused to write a letter of apology: "I said, 'I didn't do nothing, but I'll write one.' Dad said, 'Yeah, you got mad at me.' I said, 'Well, no, I didn't get mad. I was asking you why the painting I had made for you was in the garage. It really hurt my feelings that I had taken these art classes and won an award, and the painting I did for you is in the garage.' He said, 'Well, go get it. I didn't know it was down there.' I went and got it, and he said, 'I don't have any control over who puts what where. This'll stay in my office.' I said, 'Okay.' So he wanted an apology for that. I questioned him on that. But that was just a wild night. It was horrible."

When Cash regained his senses, he issued a ban on alcohol in the house. "He saw what it created," says Tittle.

Meanwhile, the project that would become *Johnny 99* was suffering from Cash's straying interest. He said years later that Ahern had "played producer" with him, dominating the choice of songs and stealing his emotional investment in the whole affair, but Cash's dependency probably was more to blame. Stuart observed that the sessions were too Hollywood, with celebrities stopping by, and that Cash appeared more interested in polishing a curious persona he'd created for himself after many recent performances of "God Bless Robert E. Lee," a tribute to the confederate leader that Ahern brought him. Colonel Reuben Rivers, a Civil War veteran Cash claimed to be descended from, possessed him during his L.A. stint. He purchased a massive blue wool overcoat from an Army surplus store, and he stitched onto it Civil War–era buttons that he and Stuart had purchased from the Pony Express Gun Shop in the San Fernando Valley. In subsequent weeks, whenever he unveiled "God Bless Robert E. Lee" in concert, he'd don his long dark coat for the faithful audience and swim in the fantasy of Reuben Rivers.

Cash and Ahern included the song (composed by Mack Vickery and Bobby Borchers) in *Johnny 99*, but it and most of the other songs were hopelessly disconnected from each other. They could have built the album around the two Springsteen numbers, which glistened, but instead "Highway Patrolman" and "Johnny 99" became the album's only redeeming songs. The man who personified the country-music concept album in the 1960s had made an album so disjointed that each number seemed cut from a different time and studio. "Once again," says Stuart, "we fell prey to trying to find something that worked instead of having the confidence in knowing that what we were doing was working." The set tanked in the market, and of the three singles released, only two made the country charts. Ironically, the odd one out was one of the album's best, "Johnny 99."

"Dad was a little scared," says Kathy. "He was losing his record sales. He was kind of thinking this might be his last shot."

"Everybody was desperate," adds Tittle.

The continued decline in Cash's fortunes during the 1980s coincided with his worsening addiction to painkillers and other prescription medication. The resulting missed shows and canceled sessions recalled the 1960s, when amphetamines and barbiturates virtually ruled his life. Nobody, though, talked about the creative force of drugs in Cash's 1980s, as some had in the 1960s. Age and fatigue had long since diminished the drugs' perceived utility in that area. Cash consumed them to ward off the mindlessness of incessant touring; the pressures of presiding over a sprawling corporation of family, staff, and band members; and the pains of numerous physical maladies that afflicted him. But most of all, he consumed the pills for the same reason he consumed stacks of candy bars in Jack Clement's studio and plates of ham and biscuits in June Carter's kitchen. "He liked drugs because they made him feel good," says Tittle. "He liked them. You know, sometimes you have a lot of depression, health issues that you don't know about, and you just want to feel better, whatever it is. If it's three or four beers, if it's a handful of pills, if you feel different than you did before you took them, that's enough. Of course, he was predisposed to addiction. There was no drinking one beer or taking one pill, none of that. Total excess. I've seen him hopped up and do great shows. But it catches you. It finally catches you. But I think that it was simple, he's been quoted saying that, and I agree with him, we've talked about it, we shared pills. He liked them because they made him feel good."

Everybody around Cash in the 1980s saw the prominence of drugs in his life, but publicly Cash admitted only to experiencing the temptation rather than the actual use of drugs. As far as the general public was concerned, Cash had kicked his habit in the 1960s. Numerous visits to rehabilitation centers in the late 1970s and 1980s stayed out of the news, and when he entered the Betty Ford Center in December of 1983, the media was told that the star was merely attempting to avoid an addiction to medication prescribed during recent illnesses.

The truth would come out later, of course. When Cash published his second autobiography in 1997, he confessed that addiction had hampered him throughout the 1980s, particularly in 1983 when he turned to painkillers after an ostrich that inhabited an exotic animal farm he owned attacked him and broke five ribs. The bizarre episode, (which surely left many wandering about Cash's choice of pets), with the drug use that surrounded it, was as pitiful an example of Cash's decline as any from the 1960s. Still, even in 1997, Cash's testimony described a man who had sunk to his lowest in the 1960s, only to be pulled up and redeemed by God. His later temptations were euphemistically cast as evidence of the continuing battle between the carnal and the spiritual that raged in every man.

In a way, drug use became Cash's convenient sin, the one that made for a great redemption story but that had no visible victims other than himself. As long as the drug-obsessed media focused on his addiction, the story functioned as a smoke screen. Cash rarely had to deal publicly in any substantive way with questions about extramarital affairs he engaged in during the 1970s and 1980s or with the pain that he'd brought upon his wives, daughters, friends, and band members. If reporters needed drama and degradation for their Johnny Cash stories, tales of drugs always filled the bill.

Just as few knew about the private suffering Cash had caused Vivian in the 1950s and 1960s, almost nobody saw the difficulties June confronted in the decades after Cash resumed his drug use. In the wake of Grant's discovery of Cash's consumption backstage in 1976, June again put on the warrior's mask. With Grant, she schemed to intercept the incoming pills, find the hidden ones, shoo the suppliers, confront the user, and chase away the girlfriends. All of this remained out of public view until 1980 when June published her first memoir, *Among My Klediments*, which hinted at the torment seeping back into her and her husband's life. Among the tributes to her husband as a great man, she encrypted the story of Cash's relapse and her frustration in a poem about and dedicated to Grant. She wrote, "For twenty years the man leaned upon his bass/The terror around took him every place/But like a tree planted there/He joined the girl within her prayers . . . ." The twenty years would cover the time from the early 1960s when June first worked with the Cash show right up to the present.

Although June went as far as to draw up divorce papers and even left Cash a time or two for brief periods, she clung to her marriage. "I give her credit for that because it had to be hard," says Tittle. "Even when I started with him in '82, he was rocking and rolling, staying up all night, doing weird things. A few shows got canceled. She was always the rock. She was the one that could make a statement, and people would believe it. Management and people like that always tried to make up a bunch of lies about what was going on, but June tried to keep it real as much as possible. And when he'd come around, he'd have all this remorse and guilt, and she'd still be there."

The closest June came to actually ending their union, in Tittle's estimation, was during a Las Vegas engagement in the mid-1980s. Cash had ordered a supply of pills from a physician in town who, says Tittle, supplied Elvis in the 1970s. By show time, he was firmly in the pills' grip. When Cash stepped before his packed house singing "Folsom Prison Blues," he was at least a verse behind the band's pace. "In other words," explains Tittle, who was playing bass, "he might be singing a chorus and we're playing a verse. He has no idea. He can't hear us. He's totally not there. It's something you can't correct. The band can't change and catch up to him because it's like his timing is way off. His words are falling in places that are unbelievably wrong. It's got to be obvious to everybody."

When "Folsom Prison Blues" collapsed into a heap of miscues and off-kilter rhythms, Tittle stepped up to his boss and suggested he bring June and the Carter Family on while he took a rest. Cash lumbered off, leaving behind him a silent stage and an arrested audience. "He knew something was wrong," says Tittle. Pianist Earl Poole Ball struck up an instrumental while everybody waited for June or Cash or the nightclub manager to appear. Five minutes passed. And then June came out and told the fans they were "witnessing history."

"It sent a shiver through my spine," says Tittle. "I thought, 'She's talking about divorcing him, right now.'" She spoke with grim determination, and she spoke it publicly. "It was clear what she meant. That was a low point for me. Fluke actually cried, and so did I. We teared up on stage." The seasoned showwoman who'd been through blazes with Cash, marched the Carter Sisters and the band into their regular set.

Meanwhile, backstage, Cash drank coffee and received an injection of stimulants. And then he stepped toward the stage. "He came out like nothing had happened," continues Tittle. "No apologies. Boom! Right back into it. They loved him. They absolutely loved him. That's what I thought was sad. And then I thought, 'This is pretty powerful. Nobody else could get away with that shit. They just loved that they got to see him, and he wasn't even there.'"

June stewed for a while, contemplating the end of her marriage, but she was soon back playing counselor, comforter, and mother, convincing Cash to cancel the Vegas stand and return home for rest and reassembly. They abandoned Vegas and in the process Tittle saw that June was preserving Cash until the next sober moment, when the J.R. Cash she could live with returned.

~

June found herself reliving the nightmare of the 1960s, but in the intervening years, her relationship with her husband had evolved in a way that made his flaws easier to bear. Perhaps it wasn't evolution, and the sort of business partnership that helped her compartmentalize his bad behavior and defined aspects of their relationship had been there since the very beginning. Whether it had begun in 1961 or developed by the 1980s, Hugh Waddell, a publicist and assistant to the Cashes in the 1980s and 1990s, saw that their merger transcended any hurt they caused each other. "At that point," explains Waddell, "they had come to the realization that they were both in it for the long haul. They had been through a lot of those times when they pushed each other's envelope."

Simply put, the Cash-Carter union was bigger than the marriage and any damage they could do to it. They were a public entity—June the faithful wife, stage foil, and show partner, and Johnny, the strong husband in the story of Christian marriage and family, around which he built his image in the 1970s and 1980s. The union served each other's needs. It also made it easier for June to tolerate Cash's drugging and made it easier for Cash to accept June's demands for the limelight and her sensational spending that had become legendary in the Cash-Carter circle.

Indeed, as Rosanne Cash observes, "basic human-to-human love" existed between them. They shared romantic and tender moments together, routinely watching evening television in their pajamas or motoring off on Old Hickory Lake in their boat. But they also relished their time apart from each other, when June could indulge her shopping and Johnny could go off by himself. After tours, for example, Cash's routines allowed for a day or two at home with June in Hendersonville, but then he would flee to his Bon Aqua farm west of Nashville until the next job demanded his return. "That was very, very important to him," explains Waddell. "There was this huge black 'do not disturb' sign when he went to

Bon Aqua. Unless there was something incredibly important, you left him alone." Elements of June and Cash's at-home separation also marked their concert tours together, as they inhabited separate hotel rooms, sharing only a living room if a suite was available to them.

While the partnership appeared to depend on maintaining a distance, it also relied on Cash keeping secure June's place next to him in the public eye. June's ire was as likely to be stirred by television directors who pushed her into her husband's shadow or other such slights as it was by Cash's peccadilloes. That's why Cash urged his employees to work as hard for her as they did for him and always made room for her and her singing sisters in his spotlight. "He wasn't concerned about launching a new career for June," says Waddell. "But—and I'm not trying to be disrespectful—it was to pacify her . . . because when June was upset, the whole organization shook."

She had always desired more of the spotlight than she got, often protesting that she deserved more attention because she'd given up a potentially lucrative career in acting to remain with Cash. It's uncertain how much fame she would have garnered without him, and if anybody was giving up career opportunities for the sake of the union, it was Cash. In the late 1980s, foregoing a possible jolt to his career, he refused to tour with the popular Hank Williams Jr. because the organizers had not invited June. And, says Jimmy Tittle, she was as big a reason as any for the end of the Johnny Cash network television specials in the late 1980s because producers came to see her featured parts in the shows as a liability. Cash, mindful of June's ego and his desire for peace at home, championed her, even as television executives and concert promoters dismissed her.

A member of the production crew on one of Cash's last network television specials recalls Cash flying to June's defense like an irate hawk when a director denigrated June and her talent on the set when he thought the Cashes weren't listening. But June's hairdresser, who was in the room with the director, heard the attack and reported every word to Johnny. "He said some really bad, stupid things that were wrong anyway, but, I mean, he said them," said the staffer, who wishes to remain anonymous. "And Johnny came up to me, and he said, 'You've got your headset on. Did you hear what he said?' I said, 'No, John. I didn't.' He said, 'You're not covering for [him], are you?' I said, 'John, if I said I didn't hear it, I didn't hear it." I said, 'Hear what?' I said, 'I don't know what I'm supposed to hear.' And I thought he must've said something about John. So, the next thing I knew, [the director] was fired. But John went straight to [the executive producer] and said, 'It's him or me.'"

Cash's love for June and loyalty to her inspired his defense of her, but so did the value he placed on her role in his career. As well as being the faithful wife in the Christian story Cash told about himself, few could deny that she had helped keep him straight when she could and often compensated for his shyness. On television talk shows when the embarrassing questions about his drug use cropped up, she'd step in with her exuberant comic presence and save her husband the discomfort of rehashing again the jagged story of his life. On stage, she filled the gaps and blew in fresh air, like the Folsom show in 1968 when the mere sight of her had dissolved a mood that had become so heavy. Losing June surely would have set Johnny adrift in his personal and professional world.

Although June might have become unmoored, too, Rosanne surmises that she never would have left the marriage to die in the first place. "As much as I know that she loved my dad," says Rosanne, "she also loved being Mrs. Johnny Cash and she loved combining the two names. That was incredibly seductive to her, and I can't imagine that she would have given that up easily."

Tittle declares that the night in Vegas was Cash's worst on-stage showing ever (although Grant, who saw the 1960s version, might disagree). But Tittle and his wife, Kathy, along with June, were about to witness off-stage misery beyond comparison.

Shortly after a brief November tour of Great Britain and the unheralded release of the single "Johnny 99" in 1983, doctors in Nashville operated on Cash's hand, which had been lacerated while he flailed about during a hallucination in England. Doctors also found internal bleeding and scheduled surgery to remove Cash's duodenum and parts of his stomach, intestine, and spleen. They had all been destroyed by years of pill taking.

Worried about an insufficient supply of painkillers in the hospital, Cash stowed away a pharmacy's supply behind the television in his room. After the operation, he grabbed a whole card of Valium and stuffed it down in the dressing of his stomach wound. The card melted into the wound. His body sucked the substance straight into the bloodstream and mixed it with the morphine that the doctors had already given him. He descended into oblivion, emerging two days later beset by hallucinations and making ludicrous demands.

Late one night during his hospital stay, Cash telephoned Kathy, who was pregnant with her son James Dustin, and asked her to bring down a six-pack of beer. She wisely rebuffed the request. "He said, 'Are you telling me no?'" she recounts, "I said, 'Yes, I am.' [He said,] 'Well, why would you do that? You're only four miles from here.' I said, 'Dad, if you want to kill yourself, you are not going to do it with my help. I am not bringing beer down there, and I can't believe you would even ask me. I am six months pregnant and you are asking me for beer in the hospital when you have more drugs than you need in your system.' He said, 'Well then, just forget it. I'll call Marty.' I said, 'Go ahead.' So I called Marty real quick, and I said, 'Dad's fixin' to ask you to bring some beer down there, and don't you dare even think about it.' He said, 'Man, I wouldn't do that.' So he went down there, but he didn't take any beer, and by then Dad was flying already."

After a hallucination that released army commandoes and flying buildings into his mind's eye, Cash's family members confronted him. They mounted an intervention that would deliver him on December 20, 1983, to the Betty Ford Center in Rancho Mirage, California, and cap one of Cash's worst years ever. "We just said, 'Look, you're killing yourself. This is ridiculous,'" says Kathy. "I brought [the beer] up to him at the intervention. I said, 'You got really pissed off at me for not bringing you a six pack of beer.' I said, 'What's wrong with this picture, Dad?' Then I said, 'You damn near kill yourself by sticking pills in your bandage.' And all of us just said enough is enough. Then he said, 'If I'm going to be straight, then everybody's going to be straight.'"

It was just like Cash to have the last word after his family heaped years of their frustrations on him. But in the due course of time, others around Cash did treat their drug addiction. Unlike Cash, some of them beat it.

15

BRANSON

The worried scowl on Ray Cash's face rarely lightened, despite the riches his son Johnny had accumulated and shared freely with him and his other sons and daughters. Ray and Carrie moved to Hendersonville in the early 1970s, where Johnny installed them in a house near his own. But even in old age, the Arkansas farmer could not be happy with his son or the life his son had given him.

Johnny Cash remained ever-faithful, lifting his father up in concert, on television shows, and on records as an example of the flinty American character that had carried a generation through war and depression. "My daddy's a patriot and gave me a sense of history and a strong love for my country," he once told an interviewer, echoing the tribute that he gave his father time and time again. For Ray's part, he smiled when old Dyess folks who wheeled up the road to Hendersonville raved about J.R.'s good fortunes, but he seldom offered up hearty compliments of his son.

Instead, Ray would acidly remark that his famous son deserved the six-dollar-an-hour wages of a laborer; after all, he'd say, Cash charged twelve dollars for a two-hour show. When the family gathered to watch Cash's television appearances, Ray could only manage to say that ol' Johnny was back on the tube acting like a big shot. When Cash delivered a new car to him, Ray scoffed at the extravagance. And the gift of a new big-screen television overjoyed Carrie, but Ray could only remark that the picture projected too high off the ground. "I never saw Grandpa hug Dad, ever," says Kathy Cash. "Every time Dad left the house, Grandma would hug him and say, 'I love you son, I love you baby.' But Grandpa never did. He'd just sit there. Dad would say, 'Bye Daddy' and he'd say, 'See you later.' Grandpa knew he had power over him. He used it. He was intimidating, and he liked it. What did he say to Dad one time? 'You are too big for your britches.'"

Kathy reckons that her grandfather, whose successes were few, resented his son's victories. "I do think that it was the fact that Dad had really made it, made it big," she says. "And he made more money than Grandpa could even imagine. I think he was humiliated in some weird way instead of being proud. You would be proud of your children if they accomplished something like that. Grandpa wasn't. He just took that as a big slap in the face."

And no matter the amount of cold indifference Ray communicated or the number of insults he delivered, Cash never protested. His reactions were often tearful, or, as Rosanne once observed, nothing more than timid silence. One day in her teens, she was sitting next to her grandfather in a car while her father drove. As Ray was wont to do, at one point he uttered something demeaning about black people, which pricked Rosanne's progressive sensibilities. "Well," she responded, "we're all the same underneath the skin, Grandpa." Ray's creased face reddened. He barked in her face and jabbed her with his elbow, as she shrank into the car's soft upholstery. Rosanne's father, at the wheel, drove on. "He saw it, but he didn't say anything," says Rosanne. "But it hurt him so much. He brought it up over the years. It was hard to see his dad do that to his own child. It just brought back a lot [of bad memories] for him." And, she adds, the scene illustrated Cash's utter and childlike helplessness in the face of his father's invective.

By 1984, Ray's health was failing and his venom draining; he succumbed to partial blindness and was often confined to bed. As he weakened, his children and grandchildren sat by his bed and sang gospel songs. Cash (when he was in town) brought his father a drink every day, "not because he wanted his dad to get sloppy drunk," says Jimmy Tittle, "but to say, 'Hey, you've earned it. You deserve it. Go ahead.'" To the end, honoring the fifth commandment, Cash served up his loyalty.

Ray Cash died on December 23, 1985, from complications related to Parkinson's disease. The sense of guilt, fear, and inferiority that he'd instilled in his son, however, remained.

~

In the summer before Ray's passing, Cash had found himself atop the country singles chart for the first time in almost ten years. This time, he got there as one-fourth of the country-music supergroup, The Highwaymen, with Waylon Jennings, Kris Kristofferson, and Willie Nelson.

Cash, of course, was the godfather of the quartet. He set the stage for the Outlaw movement that had lifted Jennings and Nelson to international fame in the 1970s and mentored Kristofferson in the late 1960s and early 1970s. But in 1985, Nelson was the superstar, endorsing the group with his easy vocals and independent spirit. He and Jennings, who also was still a chart contender in the mid-1980s, were the wings that briefly lifted the flailing legend. "[Cash] was way down the road in his journey," says Marty Stuart, a behind-the-scenes player in The Highwaymen saga. "And, once again—I hate to beat an old dog to death—but it just wasn't clicking. And I think he was up for trying anything. I think Columbia was suggesting anything they could think of to make all of this make sense because it was beginning to look real bad on everybody. Everybody was trying and nothing was coming of it. And America was just tired of it. It was over with. It did run its course. But what do you do with a guy like that? You keep trying."

The four country stars had gathered in Montreux, Switzerland, in November of 1984 to tape a Johnny Cash Christmas special for CBS-TV. And every night after taping, they gathered with June and Stuart in Cash's suite for rounds of joyous guitar pulling. Joining the crew as well was producer Chips Moman, who was handling sound for the show. Back home, Moman was producing Willie Nelson's gold albums and, as of late, some less-distinguished cuts with Cash. So when he saw his two charges meshing so well in Montreux, he proposed that they record a duet album in Nashville.

Cash and Nelson really didn't know each other (although their rebellious images would have suggested a long and storied relationship), but in the spirit of rejuvenating Cash and throwing two legends together to see what might percolate, Moman secured Rick Blackburn's commitment to the project and scheduled session time. However, what seemed to be inspired in Montreux fizzled in Nashville.

"Yet another trail," bemoans Stuart. "After about two days, there was nothing. We did 'I Still Miss Someone' and two or three things, and it was just laying there. The voices were too different to be doing duets."

The notion to salvage the duets by inviting Kristofferson and Jennings to join Cash and Nelson was inspired by the camaraderie at Montreux, but just as influential in the union was a song Stuart dug up from the catalog of Glen Campbell's publishing company. Longtime Campbell banjoist Carl Jackson had been telling Stuart about "The Highwayman," a Jimmy Webb composition so timeless and majestic that Jackson believed it would fit Cash like an old leather belt. When Stuart finally listened to the chilling tale of a traveler's continual reincarnation, he sensed its unmistakable allure and knew immediately with whom to pair each of its four stanzas. "I told John, 'You should take the last verse; it's the cool one,'" he says.

Nelson took the first stanza, a shrewd decision as the superstar's supple yet weathered voice gave the song immediate cache. It became one of the song's sterling bookends, calling to mind an authentic western desperado. In contrast, Kristofferson's and Jennings's parts, the middle verses, merely kept the song moving. The final verse, Cash's, is the other sterling bookend, filling out the final minute with enough verve and grit to launch the highwayman into his intergalactic incarnation: *I fly a starship/Across the universe divide. . . .*

"I remember [Cash] played it over and over and over in the bus," says Stuart. "He knew he had one. We all knew it. It was kind of the payoff to a lot of dead-end projects." "The Highwayman" galloped to number one in 1985 along with the accompanying album, a sluggish collection that contained a few of Nelson and Cash's duets from the initial sessions with Moman.

The colossal success of "The Highwayman" single and album spawned numerous tours and two more albums, but the four men never again mustered together the commercial success of their first outing. Often the songs that played to their legendary personas, like "Born and Raised in Black and White" and "Songs that Make A Difference," came off as bloated, and the pressure to give each star adequate limelight left the albums sounding half-baked and directionless.

As "Highwayman" boiled on the charts and another Cash collaboration (this one in Memphis with Carl Perkins, Jerry Lee Lewis, and Roy Orbison) garnered reams of major press coverage, Cash the solo artist could catch none of the updraft. He remained weighted down by unimaginative production, uninterested label executives, personal problems, and a growing pessimism. His 1985 album *Rainbow*, patched together from various sessions with Moman while Cash also worked on a duet album with Jennings, illustrated Cash's flagging hopes. "Even a blind pig gets a grain of corn once in a while," wrote the exasperated singer in the album's liner notes. "So who knows, maybe I'll sell hundreds."

Released in the buzz of "Highwayman" and *Class of '55* (Cash's Memphis reunion with Perkins and company), *Rainbow* collected lukewarm reviews and sparse sales. One of Nashville's influential critics, Alanna Nash, heard in the album a seasoned entertainer who had "improved so much through the years in intonation and in the nuances of expression." Yet she also discerned a detachment from the common folk and outcasts he sang about on the album.

In a story all to familiar to Cash by 1985, *Rainbow* unraveled in the market, failing to reach the charts or birth a hit single. It was his last solo album for Columbia, the end of a long fall from the top.

As Rick Blackburn marked his fifth year at the helm of Columbia-Nashville in 1985, he and the Cash camp began chatting about the next contract renewal. Cash's people were seeking a greater up-front payment per album, like the younger artists were collecting, but Blackburn protested, citing Cash's abysmal solo sales. Meanwhile, as the talks progressed in fits and starts, Cash poked around the industry to learn what his competition's contracts looked like, first calling on daughter Rosanne whose career was riding an uptown train. Her "I Don't Know Why You Don't Want Me," number one in 1985, was on track to a Grammy award when he telephoned to talk about the royalty rate she received from Columbia. "That to me was really significant," she says. "That is not something my dad would've talked about. He said, 'What's your royalty rate?' I said, 'Uh . . . I'm not sure. Maybe eleven [percent].' And he said, 'Okay.' He didn't say anything about it. When I hung up, I thought, 'Oh man. He's really upset. He would never [complain]. Never. Never. Never. But I knew he was really upset."

In the spring of 1986, Cash's contract with Columbia quietly expired while negotiations plodded on. But then, according to Blackburn, the Dutch recording giant Polygram Records entered the mix, holding out the promise of a one-million-dollar advance. These developments were followed by a revealing conversation between Blackburn and *Nashville Tennessean* music reporter Robert Oermann. Chatting in Blackburn's office about reorganization at CBS, Oermann asked about Cash's status with the company. Two days later on July 16, 1986, Oermann reported that Blackburn would not be renewing the country-music pioneer's contract. Speaking to me almost twenty years later, Blackburn insists that he had not yet shut the door in Cash's face. "My plan was to go out and sit at the lake and say, 'Look, how do we make this work?', those kind of conversations which John would have," he says. "But if [Polygram] is going to give him one million, I'm going to have to advise him to take it. The bottom line was I didn't have a plan as to how to turn that thing around, to go from fifty-thousand units to one million."

Touring in Canada when the news reached him, Cash struck back, attacking Columbia's integrity and spouting frustration that the label had broadcasted his departure without consulting him. Manager Lou Robin announced that he was negotiating with other labels, and Stuart (who had just been signed by Blackburn) stormed in protest through Columbia's Nashville office. "We had a hit," says Stuart, "and they were cueing up my second single, they were going to put a bunch of money behind it. And when I heard [about Cash], I walked in the office and told Blackburn what I thought, arrogant little punk that I was. I went downstairs to my buddy, Joe Casey, who was the promotions guy. He was sitting there, and he was on the phone, and he hung up the phone and said, 'Well, I don't know what you just did, but congratulations, you just killed your career here.' And they pulled my second single, and gave the song—it was called 'Crime of Passion'—to Ricky Van Shelton. And it started his career."

Stuart could see the hurt burrowing into his aging hero, but, he says, Cash remained statesmanlike, letting his admirers in the industry rise to his defense and blast Columbia. Cash had often commented to his band members during the declining Columbia years that there was nothing wrong with him that a hit couldn't cure, but in 1986 he must have wondered if there would ever be another hit. After twenty-eight years, Cash had lost the record company affiliation that had given him a world stage and indulged his musical whims and convictions, from the concept albums and hymns of the 1960s to *The Gospel Road* and *The Rambler* of the 1970s. Now Columbia hungered only for multimillion-selling records, saving little room for those who fell short, whatever their history with the label had been.

~

Despite the upheaval in Cash's recording world, the stories he told in song dwelled (as they traditionally did) on men and women dealing with defining circumstances such as death, loneliness, guilt, temptation, and confinement. Although Cash rarely wrote anymore about such themes himself, he clung to them, determined to be the one who brought them to American audiences. A few people who knew Cash at the time tell me that he had lost his artistic vision in the 1980s, but I'm convinced that his vision remained intact, weathering personal and professional downfalls and disappointments. He always knew what he wanted to say. What was lost was Cash's own expression of his vision; he relied mostly on other songwriters to give him the words and a revolving door of producers to tell him how to say them. No longer an inventive creator or the obstinate owner of his recording sessions, Cash now relied on his legend to carry him—the old songs, memories of the old fire, the visage of an American patriot, and remnants of the bad-boy cloak.

During the 1980s, Polygram did business in Nashville under the guise of its subsidiary Mercury Records. Home to the surging Kathy Mattea, The Statler Brothers, and Tom T. Hall, the label nonetheless bowed to the real titans of the Nashville recording world: MCA, Capitol, RCA, and Columbia. But Polygram had newly pledged to fund the label into greater prominence in country music. Former Columbia executive Dick Asher ran Polygram, and to bolster the Nashville operation, he hired Steve Popovich, another graduate of Columbia Records who'd been in the late 1960s and early 1970s a critical piece of the label's promotional mechanism, as well as an unofficial advisor to Clive Davis on all things Nashville. In the aftermath of Davis's removal, Popovich had inaugurated the Cleveland International label with Columbia money and brought the world the rock-and-roll curiosity Meat Loaf.

Asher and Popovich knew Cash, which naturally couldn't have hurt in Mercury's courtship of the legend. Popovich had first met Cash in the mid-1960s when the young promotion man worked the Cleveland area. The country king was sparking through Akron, Ohio, at his cockiest, uninhibited on the high of drugs and fame. But in 1986, Popovich drove out to meet Cash in Hendersonville and saw that misfortune had cut him down. "He was despondent," says Popovich. "We were sitting in his office, and I remember saying to him, 'John, I really believe in you. Our company believes in you. We feel, with the right record, that we can help support what you're trying to do here and get some strong records, some hit records.' I always felt that he was one of the top five visible people in music. And that's half the battle: getting people to know who you are."

Cash agreed to sign, reluctantly it appeared. At the signing ceremony on August 21, 1986, recalls Popovich, Cash was visibly uneasy, like a young groom uncertain about commitment. Cash had brought Waylon Jennings to lean on, and he sheepishly presented Popovich, who was a big polka music fan, with an accordion that he'd recently purchased at an auction.

After four years striking shale with big league producers like Billy Sherrill, Chips Moman, and Brian Ahern, Cash entrusted his first Mercury outing to Jack Clement. It fitted a pattern of turning to Clement when he needed a jolt. With the bearded eccentric, Cash knew he had an accommodating partner, comfortable studio environs, and the possibility of another "Ring of Fire." In 1982, though, he had teamed with Clement on the tepid *The Adventures of Johnny Cash*, which adhered to what had become a predictable Cash formula: songs by writers such as Billy Joe Shaver, a hymn, and a song cowritten by Cash, none of which anybody would confuse with "Folsom Prison Blues."

The first album for Mercury was different. *Johnny Cash Is Coming to Town* was intriguing from the very first cut, "The Big Light," an energetic, Cashian rumble written by Elvis Costello. Cash had met Costello in 1979 through Costello's friend and producer Nick Lowe, who was at the time married to June's daughter Carlene. Oddly, "The Big Light" came to Cash not through Costello nor even Lowe. Rather, a Michigan radio man who was emceeing a Cash show in Grand Rapids pointed the singer to Costello's new album *King of America* and its befitting "The Big Light." Indeed, the song melded completely with Cash's booming baritone and the big, roaring sound Clement built around it.

The album flourished as few Cash albums had in the preceding ten years, blessed with consistency of sound and seasoned with the delicious balladry of Bobby Braddock and Charles Williams's "The Night Hank Williams Came to Town," Guy Clark's "Let Him Roll," and Cash's own "Ballad of Barbara" (which he originally included on 1977's *The Last Gunfighter Ballad*). It also boasted Cash's swaggering performances of Merle Travis's "Sixteen Tons" and Guy Clark and Jim McBride's "Heavy Metal (Don't Mean Rock and Roll to Me)." Critics who had praised the legend's 1980s albums with fingers crossed behind their backs appeared relieved to be able to freely praise Cash. "Cash actually sounds like he was able to stay awake in the studio for this recording session . . . ," wrote reviewer Bob Allen in *Country Music.* "But it is the delightfully eclectic collection of songs here as much as it is Cash's relaxed, sometimes almost casual, renditions of them or Clement's intriguing—if occasionally over-indulgent—production, that makes this album so listenable."

The critics continued to spout fond words, and Mercury promoted as promised, but the market refused to be moved. Had the label released "The Big Light" as a single and worked the Costello connection more, perhaps *Johnny Cash Is Coming to Town* would have sold more, but the album and its two singles floundered on the charts. Popovich believed the album deserved a better showing. "But," he adds, "we hit a brick wall with radio because it was the new, young [acts who were valued]. As Blackburn said—and a lot of people got pissed off about it—'The torch has been passed to a new generation.' That was the feeling at the time and it permeated everything. It was a brick wall. And it wasn't like the company had a lot to spend. We did some videos for 'Let Him Roll,' and 'Sixteen Tons,' [but] that was before [Country Music Television] was a factor, really. So it was very tough. I forget what we sold initially on 'The Night Hank Williams Came to Town' or *Johnny Cash Is Coming to Town.*" Popovich may not have wanted to remember.

When Allen needled Clement for his "overindulgence" in the studio, he was hardly the first around Nashville to do so. Clement's florid production drew as many wisecracks in the musical community as Minnie Pearl's failed fried-chicken shops. A ting-a-ling here, a jingle there, a choral flourish before the chorus, a blast of horns after the verse, such were the trademark elements of Jack Clement, modeled first in the snappy Cash productions of the 1950s. In the 1960s, Clement came into his own, incorporating the fabulous mariachi horns on Cash's "Ring of Fire," which he produced without credit, before building a sweet and frothy sound around the slightly twangy Charley Pride.

Many charged Clement with overproduction and still do to this day. But Clement himself grins about his little embellishments as if they were dashes of salt to bring out the taste. "Well, a lot of times I put too much echo on things, and maybe I still do," admits Clement. "I liked [the essential sound], but I liked something to go with it. I wanted to hear some ringing and cymbals, and other stuff."

A few young rebels who hovered about Johnny Cash's sessions in the 1980s and early 1990s turned their noses up at the ringing and the jingling. Tittle, Stuart, and Clement's engineer David "Ferg" Ferguson shared a different vision of Cash's sound on records. Together they began a quest to save Cash by chipping away at the candy coating that Clement added to Cash's recordings. They believed Cash sounded best with the sparser production of the basic tracks they always recorded before Clement tinkered with them, so they attempted to erase the boss's kazoos, saxophones, and tambourines. "I knew the power of 'Run Softly Blue River' or 'Don't Take Your Guns to Town' [and what I felt] the first time I ever heard 'Folsom Prison Blues,'" says Stuart. "I knew the power that ragged-assed sound had on me. And to try to gloss that up and turn it into a Hallmark card was mostly more than I could bear."

Cash himself never seemed to mind the bells and whistles. Although he and Clement argued from time to time, he trusted the producer's intuitions and often let his ideas prevail.

The young crusaders were not so accommodating. After the sun set over the stumpy Nashville skyline, Stuart, Tittle, and Ferg would steal away from their homes and slip into the studio to rework a particular track they'd labored on during the day, so they might, says Stuart, "turn it into how it ought to sound." Peeling away the steel guitars and trombones from Cash's vocal track, they preserved Fluke Holland's drum track while adding their own handiwork. "I'd play Luther's part and Tittle would play bass," continues Stuart, "and we'd turn it back into a Tennessee Three record for our own enjoyment and to prove to ourselves that this will happen again."

When the sun rose, the men fled the studio and returned home. Their fantasy of returning Cash to his roots satisfied them in their early morning sleep, but it was only a fantasy. When the songs they meddled with at night appeared on albums, they were again laden with Clement's decorations.

And what did Cash himself think of Stuart and company's interventions? "He was receptive," says Stuart. "He was totally receptive. He got it, but he was also respectful of his producer, and he and Cowboy were already on this other trail. But we kept making these pirate tapes, and I'd slide them to him or just play them. He couldn't help but listen, because it was good. I just kept promoting the original vision of simplicity."

The faint optimism that accompanied Cash's Polygram deal rapidly faded as Cash's second album for the company, *Waters from the Wells of Home* (an unsteady clutch of duets produced by Clement), tanked. Cash's musicians observed the refreshing air of Clement's studio replaced by assembly-line-like ardor. Recording projects clumsily plodded along or ceased altogether because of Clement's interminable tweaking and Cash's dwindling desire to record for an ambivalent public. Two years into the Mercury marriage, Cash often appeared to be going through the motions. "He kept his session dates," says Tittle. "He worked, but Cowboy had him doing vocal [takes] to the point that John just had to say, 'I ain't doing anymore vocals.' So, he had the ethic. I'm sure there were moments of clarity when he was doing a song, but I think there were times when he said, 'Let's get this son of a bitch over with. I want to go to my farm, go hide, and get out of here.'"

In later years, Cash honorably took responsibility for losing his zest in the studios, but he always held Polygram responsible for its role in his reduced fortunes, accusing it of failing to promote his albums and of blind subservience to demographic trends. He wasn't altogether unjustified in pointing the finger at Polygram. Popovich saw, too, that from the beginning of Cash's tenure, the company was generally ambivalent to Cash and the entire country-music roster. He knew trouble lurked ahead when Polygram sales representatives and branch managers attending an artists showcase at the Opryland Hotel stood in the back of the ballroom and chatted while the singers, including Cash, performed. Disgusted, Popovich surveyed the scene and remembered that Columbia officials never would have tolerated such rudeness. "Here's our first big reintroduction of our Nashville company, and they could've cared less is the feeling I got," complains Popovich. "And it was just like, 'Hey man. I don't need this grief. It's not fair to the artist.' I took it as a genuine lack of interest in what we were doing."

Concern about Cash's rejection in the marketplace took a back seat in late 1988 when all eyes again turned to Cash's health. After a powerful wave of nausea almost felled him in early December, doctors examining him discovered two blocked arteries around his heart and immediately scheduled surgery. Cutting vessels from the singer's chest and leg to use in creating a bypass around the blockage, surgeons safely carried Cash through the ordeal. But there was no time for rest.

No sooner was Cash's chest sutured than pneumonia filled his lungs, a threat as serious as the heart blockage. Reflecting on the dramatic turn some five years later, he said he'd reached his lowest point yet. "I was layin' [there], three doctors and June around my bed," he recounted, "and one of the doctors said, 'He's not gonna make it.' I tried to smile, I tried to laugh . . . but I had this tube down into my lungs and I couldn't move my mouth. All I could do was just roll my eyes, but I was tryin' to laugh, because I knew I wasn't gonna die."

The saga of his hospital stay was one of those stories (like those about his 1967 recovery attempts) that Cash spun different ways, depending, one supposes, on his audience or his state of mind. When he related the near-death story in his 1997 autobiography, he described wanting very much to die. In the hospital, slipping away into what he called the "essence of light," Cash believed he was nearing the end and the beginning. "I've never felt such utter joy," he wrote. But then he was yanked back to this world. Reluctant to let go of the light, he pleaded to be released again.

Cash recovered slowly. Although he told the press in January of 1989 that he hoped to be on the road within a month, his pain scuttled any such notions. It grounded him until March, when he emerged for a Highwaymen session and a handful of shows. His return, however, only marked the beginning of twelve more months of health problems.

In the May after heart surgery, while on tour in Europe, Cash landed in a Paris hospital with chest pain, strangely described to the press corps as a pulled ligament. For the next few months, onstage and offstage, he often appeared ashen and drawn, and concert reviewers commented on the throat problems that plagued his performances. Then, just before Thanksgiving of 1989, he again sought treatment for addiction at the Cumberland Heights Alcohol and Drug Treatment Center in Nashville. The visit was inevitably and euphemistically described as preventative.

The worst of Cash's renewed battles with health problems began with dental surgery after his two-week detox in Nashville. A dentist removed an abscessed tooth in January of 1990, but a cyst developed after surgery and had to be scraped away. Unfortunately, the story didn't end there. In March, Cash broke his weakened jaw, and subsequent surgeries to mend it were barely successful and inflicted irreparable damage to the nerve endings around the bone. The ordeal left the bottom half of his face permanently disfigured. Subsequent photographs of Cash revealed a jaw that appeared to have a life of its own, jutting out as it did from the right side of his face. He spent the remainder of his life hampered by the pain of the nerve damage, and although he publicly said that the rush of performing was the only antidote, privately he complained that singing actually inflamed his jaw. "When I go out [on stage], I'm pretty much in pain for the entire performance," he told a theater manager. "My jaw feels like it's on fire for the entire performance."

The theatre manager to whom Cash revealed his nerve troubles oversaw the Wayne Newton Theater in Branson, Missouri. There Cash had taken temporary refuge from the grueling road that punished his battered body and pointed him to venues that were more often than not half full. In Europe, fans young and old swarmed to the Man in Black's shows, but in America, they were losing interest in him.

Branson glistened like an oasis in the eyes of country stars like Cash, Nelson, and Haggard, whose record sales were faltering and who after decades on the road relished the prospect of the road coming to them. In Branson, a weighty country or pop star could license his name to a theater owner and play everyday to the busloads of tourists and curious Missourians from the Ozarks who spilled into town and hopped from showplace to showplace to see their favorite fading stars. Visitors took in as many as five shows a day, grazing from the entertainment as if it were the all-you-can-eat buffet that was part of their package tours.

Banjo virtuoso and *Hee-Haw* star Roy Clark was first among country stars to hammer down stakes in Branson, tapping into an anxious well of mostly retired men and women with pension checks to burn and time on their hands. Word spread, and soon artists such as Moe Bandy, Mel Tillis, and Ray Stevens (who didn't have legend to fall back on) limped into Branson and found one more hearty breath of audience appreciation. It wasn't long before the line of moribund country and pop personalities joined the convoy into town. If they didn't put their own name on a theater, they set down for extended stints while the established stars vacationed or ventured back out on the road to face those who couldn't or wouldn't sojourn to Branson.

In the late 1990s, as Nashville finally pulled back many of the fans it lost to Branson and Las Vegas edged toward renaissance, Branson's allure waned. It became *de rigueur* in country-music culture to compare the town to a lamprey sucking up vitality and creativity. Where Nelson used to sing "Nashville was the roughest" in his anti-establishment anthem "Me and Paul," he began inserting "Branson was the roughest." Taking the cue, Cash likened the town to an alien starship that vacuumed up dazed performers, deprogrammed them, and regurgitated them. One might conclude from his retrospective assessment of Branson that he'd been bound, gagged, and taken there by gunpoint. "The whole situation for me was disappointing, because it was *not* what I wanted to do with my life," he said "I wanted to go out and perform for people and do something new. . . . But Branson didn't work out for me."

However, Cash attempted to make Branson work for him in 1991, when he joined the rush to town and agreed to attach his name to Cash Country, the brain-child of California developer David Green. Green envisioned a sprawling entertainment complex built around a twenty-five-hundred-seat theater. At sixty years old and sixty-five years old, respectively, their marriage finally settling into relative peace, Cash and June were ready for what amounted to a working retirement. They moved to Branson as soon as Green unleashed his bulldozers and carpenters on the building project. But like many of Cash's endeavors in the late 1980s and early 1990s, the Branson dream fizzled. Green, who had no experience in developing entertainment projects, filed for bankruptcy in 1992, leaving only the shells of various buildings. In 1993, Cash's lawyers won a $1.6 million settlement from the developer. Not long afterward, the empty buildings burned to the ground.

But Lou Robin wasn't long in finding Cash another Branson host, signing his client to do fifty shows in 1993 at the Wayne Newton Theater, the town's largest venue. Seeking to start over after a highly publicized bankruptcy, Wayne Newton had found a kingdom in the Ozarks. He was perched above the din of Branson's main drag, the Shepherd of the Hills Parkway, and quartered in a palatial apartment on the premises. The apartment, which amounted to Newton's dressing room, was off-limits to Cash when Mr. Las Vegas was out of town. The country music legend, direct heir to the traditions of Jimmie Rodgers and Hank Williams, had to settle for more modest backstage accommodations, a small space with cinder-block walls.

The modest dressing room in the theater seemed to bother Cash little. He and June were living in a comfortable house surrounded by water in nearby Blue Eye, Arkansas, and rarely stuck around the theater any longer than it took to do the show. He enjoyed fishing and boating in the nearby lakes and puttering about the bluff on which his house stood.

Cash enjoyed work far less. The Wayne Newton Theater manager observed that Cash appeared more ambivalent with every new show; the star would dutifully show up, but his mind appeared to be elsewhere. The disinterest marred the concerts. His sets were often disjointed, and the quality of the Carter Family segment of the show had plummeted as Helen and Anita Carter struggled with health problems. Seemingly bored with the task at hand, Cash often rambled on to his audiences about victorious moments in his past, such as the ABC television show or filming *The Gospel Road*. June, who was herself also wont to ramble, was the governess who finally corralled her preoccupied husband. "Press on," she'd implore. "Press on."

On a good night, fifteen hundred of the venue's three thousand seats were filled. It was not unusual, though, for Cash to arrive and learn that only three or four hundred tickets had sold.

In late November of 1993, with Newton again on hiatus, Cash was on duty for the Thanksgiving Day crowd. He woke that morning to a persistent snowfall that during the night had descended on the worn hills around Branson. The storm intensified by afternoon, and although the audience would have numbered only two hundred or so, the theater manager periodically checked the weather reports and reckoned that conditions weren't bad enough to keep the patrons away. Mindful of the extra time the Cashes would need to make it in, he called them hours before showtime to confirm that the show would indeed go on.

When the Cashes arrived two hours before showtime, the weather had markedly deteriorated, prompting management to cancel the show. The young theater manager, only in his mid-20s, dreaded Lou Robin's reaction, but he wandered off anyway to find him. At the moment, though, Robin was nowhere to be found. The manager would have to break the news to Cash, who by now was on stage, perched on a stool, running through some songs with a couple of band members.

Cash listened to the nervous young man. "No problem," he calmly replied, easing off the stool. He lurched over to his guitar case, unsnapped it, and placed the guitar inside of it. "Thanks," he intoned as he left the silent auditorium. He bundled his long black coat around him and stepped into the snowy night.

FIVE

~

ONE MORE RIDE
1994-2003

16

DRIVE ON

The pitiful Branson period accentuated the difficult days that spanned from 1988 to 1993. After the bypass surgery in 1988 and the ensuing hiatus from touring and recording, Cash's bank balances were dwindling. He was forced to fire employees and sell the publishing rights to his songs, an act akin to selling his own children (or at least Cash thought so), and rely on Lou Robin to heat up the concert circuit again. "He was in pretty rough shape financially," remarks Jimmy Tittle. "I mean, Lou basically said, 'Hey, we got to work.' And Lou worked him. He kept [the money] coming in." Complicating Cash's recovery was the turbulence in his court. Some of his children and stepchildren were weathering drug abuse and broken marriages, while his obstinate road family was a source of constant headache. It drained and frustrated him to have to preside over the drugging, feuds, petty jealousies, run-ins with the law, and firings of some of the bandmembers and crew, although June and Robin often ran interference. Still, a part of him must have pined for the 1960s, when he was too stoned to know or care about the squabbles in his midst, problems that Marshall Grant and Saul Holiff confronted instead.

In March of 1991, Cash's mother, Carrie, died, taking with her the unwavering support that had stabilized him, particularly in his youth. And then, shortly after his opening at Wayne Newton's in 1993, his brother Roy passed. Roy was the other encourager who had endorsed the vision Carrie had for her son. He had inspired the younger brother with his own poetry, stirred his imagination with his band the Delta Rhythm Ramblers, and brokered the union of Johnny Cash and the Tennessee Two.

Embittered by the sting of his father's tongue and belt, and perhaps also by the hand injuries that stilled his guitar playing, Roy Cash nonetheless followed his brother's career like a giddy cheerleader from the very beginning. "Johnny in his mind was going to be king," asserts Roy Cash, Jr. "And my dad was really caught up in it. He enjoyed being the brother, and it didn't take him long in a conversation of any kind anywhere before somebody knew that." Clinging to his old dream of playing music, Roy lived vicariously through his famous sibling. When he retired from Chrysler in Memphis in 1980, he and his wife, Wandene, moved to Hendersonville, where he worked as a security officer at the House of Cash offices, raising and lowering the American flag each day as cars sped by on the stretch of highway named for Johnny Cash.

When Marty Stuart encountered Roy around Hendersonville the first few times, he pegged him as a grouchy, chain-smoking, ex-mechanic up from Memphis. But then he spotted some of Roy's verse framed on the wall of Cash's cabin. There was beauty in it, "true elegance," recalls Stuart. "It never showed later in life, in the version of Roy that I knew. But, I kind of came to [the] conclusion that Roy might have been the one that everybody saw as the artistic one in the bunch to begin with."

When Roy died, his children returned his body to the cemetery surrounded by cotton fields in Bassett, Arkansas, and laid him to rest steps away from Jack's grave. Cash, standing between the headstones of his brothers, surely encountered emotions and memories as vivid as the deep green cotton crop nearby: the pain and guilt tied to Jack's death, the punishment his father inflicted on the family, the message of faith that Jack carried, and the creativity that Roy exemplified. And who could gauge the inevitable loneliness? Only he, Reba, and Louise now remained of the Cashes who had hobbled out of Cleveland County and into the arms of hope. "The memories were strong and in his heart right then," says son John Carter who stood near his father at Roy's funeral. "There's no doubt."

Recalling the Cash family's rapid return to the cotton fields after Jack's funeral, Cash was back on the road within days of Roy's burial. He was tackling an ambitious summer tour before returning to the Wayne Newton Theater in time to greet the autumn.

The rapid succession of deaths in Cash's family that accompanied his own maladies and career disappointments dampened his spirit, but it would be unfair to say that he'd been left emotionally destitute. On the contrary, he found victories and joys to balance the bad times: the birth of grandchildren, a comfortable friendship with Billy Graham, and industry and civic awards too numerous to list. Delightful, too, were his days and nights at his Cinnamon Hill retreat in Jamaica, an eighteenth-century estate he had purchased from a friend in the mid-1970s. Frequently, he escaped to its warm air to watch and listen to the time pass, gather family and friends, and host celebrities ranging from Tom T. Hall to Paul McCartney.

Cash's Bon Aqua farm in Hickman County, Tennessee, about an hour southwest of Nashville, was his local Cinnamon Hill. Friends describe it as his refuge from the travails of celebrity, arguments with June, and distractions of modern life. His daughters remember it as the setting of their reacquaintance with him. Cindy Cash, who joined the caravan of Cash offspring moving to Hendersonville from California in the late 1970s, says she rediscovered her long-absent father in the solitude of Bon Aqua. "He taught me how to shoot a gun out there," she says. "He taught me how to bait a hook out there. He taught me how to find arrowheads. I still have the first arrowhead I ever found with him. When we were looking, I found a perfect arrowhead. I'll never forget how proud he was that I found that. He was teaching me about slate, which rocks you can make an arrowhead out of and which you can't. I [was] in my 20s, but we didn't have that kind of quality time when I was little."

Cindy saw her father at his silliest at Bon Aqua, a mischievous side that she'd never seen much of before. She remembers the aftermath of one of their shooting lessons in particular. They had just sat down in the farm house after firing their Colt .22 pistols in the fields. "He said, 'Let's see who can get the straightest line of six bullets in a row in the ceiling,'" recalls Cindy. "I said, 'Yeah right, Dad.' I thought he was kidding. He goes, 'I'll go first.'" Boom! A tiny hole appeared in the plaster above. Cindy reminded him that there was a room upstairs. "There's nobody here except me and you," he replied. Boom!

"And he shot all six bullets in a line. He said, 'It's your turn now.' I was just sitting in a chair, and he was in the corner of the room in a recliner. There were six bullet holes and six more right beside them. And my line was straighter than his line, and he did not like that. He goes, 'I taught you too good.' June would have had a heart attack."

Away from the spotlight, Cash obviously delighted in the absurd, but he also basked in aspects of his life that approached the very definition of normalcy. Eschewing the cloistered life that Elvis Presley led in Graceland before he died in 1977, Cash walked in the world. His tall body could be seen hunched over drawers of nuts and bolts in the Hendersonville hardware store, sifting through albums in the Nashville Tower Records store in search of a Bill Monroe collection, and seeking out the latest Tom T. Hall cassette tape in K-Mart. Cash stopped in at the local diners, trolled the aisles of sporting goods stores, and even went to the movies without renting out the entire cinema.

When the notion seized him, he sauntered over to Jack Clement's studio with shenanigans on his mind. Harking back to his wild early days on the road, he once set loose a cage full of chickens in Clement's backyard. Shocked and amused, the producer asked Cash if the chickens would just fly away, but the singer assured him that banishing the fowl would not be so easy. Clement discovered pretty soon that Cash had either fibbed or didn't know anything about chickens. "Within a week or so them chickens were in all the trees around here, way the hell up there," grumbles Clement, gesturing toward his backyard. "They could fly. We had to set up traps and catch the chickens, clip their wings. And they started laying. On a good day we'd get seven or eight eggs. Well the chickens finally . . . the dogs would get out and get them. And finally it got down to one ol' lonesome chicken out there." From time to time, Cash got itchy and recruited Clement for a road trip, picking up his Memphis friend and motoring off down into the heat of Alabama or up to southwestern Virginia to knock around June's old home place, which the Cashes owned.

On the rare instances Elvis ventured out of Graceland alone, the Memphis Mafia squawked in alarm as if it were a prison break, but up in Nashville, Cash flew freely, often without June. When he wasn't hanging out with Clement, he might be fishing with John Carter, strumming old folk and western songs in his grandchildren's classrooms, or tending to a vegetable garden outside his home. Roy Cash, Jr., who in 1963 had begun a distinguished career in the U.S. Navy, tells me that in 1985 Cash attended his elevation to captain in Norfolk, Virginia, and doggedly stayed in the background. Roy's mother, Wandene (who used to fetch coffee for Johnny when he and the Tennessee Two practiced at her house in the beginning) had just died, so Cash had brought Roy Sr. to Norfolk, in hopes of cheering up his newly widowed brother. When reporters got wind of the super-star's presence, he insisted that his comments be quoted within the context of Roy's promotion. "This is Captain Cash's show," he told them.

During the visit, the new captain led his uncle onto his own personal boat, brought him out into the Chesapeake Bay, and took him along the waterfront to see the hulking naval vessels anchored there. Cash, the lover of American history who in the 1980s and 1990s would play Abraham Lincoln, Frank James, and Davy Crockett in made-for-TV-movies, marveled at the U.S.S. Sumter and U.S.S. Nashville that swayed in the waves. On that day, he was proud Uncle J.R., riding on the boat in the shadows of his tall nephew, the new captain. "He thoroughly enjoyed doing stuff like that," says Roy. "And he did not want to be the center of attention."

For almost ten years stretching from the mid-1970s to mid-1980s, Cash pur-sued, abandoned, and pursued again a novel he'd begun writing based on the life of the apostle Paul. In his former life as Saul of Taurus, Paul violently persecuted early Christians on behalf of the Jewish authorities until he experienced God on the road between Jerusalem and Damascus. He had set out from Jerusalem to weed out Christians from the Damascus synagogues, but God blinded him with light and ordered him to complete a different mission in Damascus. Within days, Paul's voice echoed the gospel through the places of worship. This was a man in whose story Cash must have taken comfort. After all, if God could embrace an avowed and bloodthirsty enemy of his son Jesus Christ, he'd make a place for Johnny Cash. It seems evident also that in Paul's journey, Cash glimpsed his own.

The novel, which proved to be another facet of Cash's marvelous artistry, had its genesis in a battery of correspondence Bible courses that he had undertaken in the mid-1970s, a pursuit that ultimately led to an associate degree of theology from the Christian International School of Theology in 1977. Magnetized by Paul's teaching, Cash came to revere the apostle. Paul, he said, became his hero. Filled with passion to create a novel about his hero, he nonetheless found the writing process arduous, and throughout the early 1980s, the manuscript often languished in his closet as he wrestled addiction, health problems, career concerns, and marital woes. "I decided that I had taken on more than I could handle," he wrote, referring to the process. "The love of writing was gone. I even forgot most of what I had written. After all, seven years had gone by since I had started it. I've changed my mind, I thought. I can't write a novel. Why did I ever think I could? I resented the obligation I had saddle myself with."

Cash refocused on the novel, he said, in the wake of his stretch at Betty Ford in late 1983 and early 1984, stuffing the dog-eared pages into a bulky leather saddle bag and attending to it when time allowed. He wrapped it up soon after his father's 1985 passing. If Cash still saw his career as a ministry in 1986 when *Man in White* was published, then the book was a substantial witness. But it also read like an autobiography, his identification with Paul so strong that the connection cropped up on virtually every page. Secondary characters resembled people in his own life, such as June and Jack, and the plot line tracked his own life's path.

Cash painted a man who, in the throes of his anti-Christian crusade before his conversion, questioned his standing with God, whom he believed he was serving in his denunciations and killing. "He had always strived to please God," related Cash in his narrative. "Still he always felt that he hadn't done enough, that he fell short of fulfilling God's wishes in his tribute to him. He never found perfect peace in any accomplishment." Cash had expressed similar sentiments about his own achievements as he bottomed out in the 1960s, often wondering why God allowed him to live and, more, enjoy a fruitful career.

In the novel, Cash's Paul sees only stone black as he's cast down on the road to Damascus, much as Cash himself groped in the nothingness of intense addiction. "He lay on the hard ground of the Damascus Road," wrote Cash of his hero, "thinking he was dead, that he had been cast into everlasting darkness." After Paul's startling moment on the road to Damascus, he holed up in a room for three tortuous days where, per Cash's telling, scenes from his murderous past rose in his mind like blood-red moons, only to be followed by soothing glimpses of a future in service of the Lord. Were these three days like the ones Cash had spent in his empty Hendersonville home in the fall of 1967 attempting to escape from drugs? Cash certainly had lived the torture of transformation, physical and spiritual, and he injected it into his rendering of Paul's journey from anti-Christian to apostle.

Cash's faith was a rock during the bad times, and his gospel-oriented projects, such as *Man in White*, were his redemptive accomplishments throughout years of commercial disappointment and personal failings. In 1979, he unveiled a double-album set titled *A Believer Sings the Truth*, which he said was his "dream gospel album." Produced by Jack Clement and flavored with uplifting takes on various gospel songs, including Rosetta Tharpe's and Cash's own, Columbia nonetheless had refused to release it, leaving Cash to lease the masters to a small record company, where lack of distribution and promotional muscle guaranteed its consignment to oblivion.

When he saw his record company's ambivalence to his gospel recording, first Columbia's and then Mercury's, he took his message of the gospel to other media. Along with his and June's regular appearances on the crusade rostrums with Billy Graham, Cash recorded an audio version of the Bible for commercial release, dedicated a portion of most every concert appearance to a gospel music-segment, and revisited *The Gospel Road* concept. He returned to Israel in the early 1990s with June and John Carter to videotape reflections and music for *Return to the Promised Land*, a sloppily produced television project that never made it to television. It sadly illustrated the neglect that his career was suffering at the time.

Although such pursuits barely peeped next to the booming secular successes of his early career, it never occurred to Cash not to pursue them. Gospel projects were imbedded in his vocation. And while many observers probably scoffed at what they viewed as his hypocrisy, his preaching the Word only to tumble back into his sins of the flesh, Cash refused to be deterred, leaning as he did on the reassuring preaching of Paul. Indeed, Paul (in Phillipians) passionately urged Christians to be as "innocent and pure as God's perfect children," but he also knew that, man being what he is, sinners would inevitably be God's mouthpieces on earth. The spiritual treasures glisten in clay pots. And to that knowledge the rumpled and redeemed Cash must have clung.

In 1972, while Cash was quartered in Las Vegas for a week-long stretch at The Hilton International Hotel, news spread across the nation that the gospel-infused singer had issued an altar call from the stage, offering the men and women who had come to see him the chance to dedicate or rededicate their lives to Christ. The story was cast as if Cash was suffering from a God complex. Though he later denied the report, there was little question that Cash believed his shows could be a vehicle for bringing people closer to the God. In fact, during that era, he talked about mounting a Johnny Cash Crusade and was uninterested for a time in any projects not directly linked to his Christian mission. In 1990, safely distanced from the Vegas brouhaha of 1972, Cash got serious about his conviction. He asked Reverend Jack Shaw of Johnstown, Pennsylvania, to join him on the road to minister to the spiritually hungry in his concert audiences and, one guesses, to prop him up through his own struggles.

As tall as Cash but with a placid face and reassuring voice, Shaw was some ten years in the ministry when he accepted Cash's call. Like Cash, he also had fumbled his way through a wayward young adulthood before a troubling episode jarred him. On Christmas Eve in 1974, he'd come home drunk and morose and shot himself with a .38 caliber pistol. Although he had done no serious harm to himself, he had bled profusely in front of his distraught wife and children. Within five years, he'd be sharing the story with audiences around the nation, hoping that the redemption he experienced after that utterly hopeless moment might inspire people to turn to Christ.

By the time of Shaw's suicide attempt, he had met Cash several times. The Pennsylvanian owned a steeplejack company, and while working on a church in New Orleans in the early 1960s, he encountered the singer for the first time after one of his shows. A few years later, Shaw caught up to the singer again, this time in Johnstown, where Shaw moonlighted in a country band that often opened for visiting stars. He'd not been hired to play on Cash's show in Johnstown that night, so it seemed his contact with Cash would again go no further than the quick hello Cash offered backstage. But later in the evening, recalls Shaw, as he spirited across the parking lot clutching a brown package close to side, a muffled figure called out to him for the darkness. "I heard the voice say, 'What do you have under your coat, Jack?' And I looked, and it was Johnny Cash. I said, 'Nothing.' And he said, 'Don't lie to me now.' So I said, 'Well, it's a bottle of whiskey.' He said, 'What are you going to do with that?'" Shaw explained to the gaunt star that he always brought a bottle for the local disc jockey who was emceeing the show, to stay in his good graces. But

Cash implored him not to waste the booze on such bribery. He invited Shaw on the bus and uncapped the bottle, and with Carl Perkins sidled up next to them, the three set into draining it. Perkins, a mellow drunk, was talking about music with Shaw, but Cash was sailing on whiskey river. "John had this bowie knife," continues Shaw, "and he was starting to feel the whiskey. He was throwing it to the back of the bus, saying he could hit a frog at forty paces with the bowie knife. He stuck it in the cabinet. It was just really weird."

Their next encounter wasn't as weird as it was cosmic; Shaw would say ordained. It was 1975. Cash was off the booze and pills, while Shaw (two years from his rededication to Christ) was still wrestling with them. Shaw had just left a bar and was crossing an intersection in his car when Cash's Dodge camper lurched to a stop, its bumper almost hitting the ground. Shaw looked up to the cab of the camper to see Cash in a red flannel shirt, fumbling with some directions. Suffering from back spasms after a long drive in from New England, Cash was trying to find his hotel. Shaw led him there, and later that night, the two of them played songs in the dressing room before Cash's show.

Six years would pass before they saw each other again. In the meantime, Shaw established a ministry and traveled and shared his rededication story and his vision to build a hospital in Africa. He also dreamt regularly of standing in front of a large picture window talking to Johnny Cash.

In 1981, Shaw found himself in Nashville feeling a quiet but persistent urge to visit the House of Cash in Hendersonville. Knowing that Cash had forgotten him, he succumbed to the pull anyway and drove to Hendersonville, where he met Carrie Cash, who managed the small museum and gift shop in the House of Cash building. Shaw told her about his pristine 1932 arch-top Martin guitar, one that he knew Cash would love to see. "She said, 'I know he would,'" he remembers. "'You go down to where he is, and tell him you got that guitar.' I said, 'And I bet they'll let me in, too.' She said, 'You tell him his mother sent you.'" Indeed, the mention of her name opened the door to Jack Clement's studio, where Cash and his band were rehearsing for an upcoming tour.

It was an all-too-familiar scene in Cash's world, a stranger appearing backstage or on the lane in front of his home or in the parking lot behind a studio, always with some purpose in mind. He or she might be pitching songs, looking for a recording deal, spinning a hard-luck story, or merely seeking a moment in his midst. Shaw, like many others before and after him, felt that God was leading him to seek out Johnny Cash.

At Clement's, Shaw reintroduced himself to Cash, who listened in earnest as the visitor described every inch of the 1932 guitar that was resting in its case back in Johnstown. Every time the rehearsals broke to rest, Cash wandered back out of the studio to Shaw and talked with him, expressing interest in seeing the guitar. He consented when the minister offered to bring it backstage when the tour visited the Stanley Theater in Pittsburgh, some fifty miles from Johnstown.

When Shaw departed from Cash and made his way back to Pennsylvania, one gleaming memory struck him again and again. In Clement's offices, he and Cash had stood and talked in the daylight that shone through a large picture window.

After the Pittsburgh meeting, where Shaw gave Cash the guitar as a gesture of admiration, Cash invited Shaw and a bluegrass band Shaw had formed to open an upcoming show at the Carter Fold (a rustic, nooklike amphitheater at Hiltons, Virginia, that June's cousins Joe and Jannette Carter operated). Cash then asked Shaw and the boys to finish the tour with him, and the bond between the singer and the minister solidified. At the tour's conclusion, Cash wrote down his private telephone number and asked Shaw to call him everyday.

Throughout the 1980s, as Cash was taken up in a vicious tide of career setbacks and personal maladies, Jack Shaw was a sturdy tether to his faith. On the phone—they usually connected around seven o'clock in the evening—or when Shaw visited in Nashville, their conversations rarely strayed from the spiritual: they dissected Bible verses, analyzed various religious faiths, and discussed gospel songs that Cash was recording or adding to his concerts. No matter how hard Cash's times were, says Shaw, his determination to understand God's true plan for him always came through. "I believe he knew he had had a strong call of God in his life," he says. "I'm not sure he figured out exactly in his mind what to do with it. But he sure tried to do everything, I believe, that he felt God wanted him to do. He'd probably be the first to recognize that we fail miserably no matter how hard we try, but God doesn't necessarily look at whether we hit the target. I think he looks over our shoulder at what we're aiming at. And I think John always did aim for the bullseye. He fell short. . . . He would admit that."

Through the years of telephone chats and Shaw's prayerful support during crises, Cash adopted the minister as something of a spiritual advisor, a role Jimmy Snow had played in the early 1970s and Billy Graham might have played had he not been the world's busiest evangelist. Cash trusted Shaw and seemed to believe their similarities were evidence of God's hand in the relationship. Along with checkered pasts, they each had children succumbing to drug addition and had lost brothers in horrible accidents, but Cash also believed Shaw's name itself was tell-tale. "His name is *Jack*," he solemnly declared when telling friends and family about his new friend.

Shaw recalls Cash telling the story of his brother Jack's faith, witness, and death, on a Missouri road one morning in the 1990s. While Cash drove, his wrist hanging over the steering wheel, Shaw commented that Jack's nascent ministry must have powerfully influenced him. "All these years it did," replied Cash. "It carried me a long way. And now I have you."

It was in 1990, during an intermission at a college show in Pennsylvania, that Cash cornered Shaw (who'd come from Johnstown to visit), and asked him to travel with him in the role of staff spiritual advisor and minister to the hungry in his audiences. The Holy Spirit, proclaimed Cash, was asking him to propose it. As Cash saw it, in every show before he and June sang a gospel set, he would announce that there was a minister of the gospel in the house who after the show would counsel anybody with addictions or family problems or advise folks who might be searching for God's purpose in their lives. Shaw would stand on the floor with the audience and receive anybody who wanted to talk.

"So we did that," says Shaw. That first night in Pennsylvania, the preacher redirected a suicidal woman back to her psychiatric treatment and comforted an older woman plagued by her alcoholism. "We prayed and the tears ran down and got mascara on her sweater," recounts Shaw. "God touched her. I know He did."

Whether Cash would admit it or not, placing Shaw at the disposal of his audience was tantamount to an altar call. This time, though, unlike in Vegas in 1972, there was no skeptical press to confront him about it. There was little press of any kind. He merely plugged his friend into his own vision of what the Johnny Cash Show could mean to God's kingdom.

From 1990 until Cash gave up touring in 1997, Shaw followed him around the world, leading Bible studies and prayer meetings for the band and road crew and waiting in the wings while Cash invited his faithful to meet with him. The Man in Black would joke to his audience that they need not pay Shaw a dime.

~~~~~~

Three years into Shaw's work with Cash, he accompanied the troupe to Branson, where like everybody he observed Cash's spirit crumple with every show. "It was testing time for him," explains Shaw. "But John had a lot of faith in himself. The purpose of his life—I know that *he* knew—was music. It was artistic ability and writing. And religion was the mainspring. His faith in God was the essential part of it all, [along with] his mother's strong faith and his prayers."

Still, no amount of faith in God or himself could pluck Cash from the gloom into which he often fell, and Shaw frequently found himself trying to shake Cash out of it. The minister would liken Cash's career to scaffolding. "I kept telling John that usually eighty percent of the work is getting up to where the work needs to be done," says Shaw. "In other words, building scaffolding to get up to go and leaf a cross or to replace it or to take something off a steeple and put it back might take a month, but once you get up there and do the work, that 's what it was all for. I said, 'Your life has been like that. It's been a lot of experiences, some good, some bad, some in between, some dark, some in the light, but it's been scaffolding that God's erected for the lily work that's going to take place here in the last part of your life. I believe the years ahead are going to far outshine anything that you've done so far. As glorious as some of it has been, I believe the best years are ahead.'"

~~~~~~

A turnaround, to everyone's surprise, came in the form of a thirty-year-old record producer named Rick Rubin, whom Cash's manager Lou Robin didn't know but, after some investigation, had discovered was as hot a producer as any working in the music business. Rubin owned the label American Recordings, and his acts included the Beastie Boys, Slayer, and The Black Crowes. Perhaps such a line-up gave Robin the impetus to schedule a meeting. Cash himself was skeptical, but he was also without a recording contract, his Cash Country had disintegrated, and the only major commitment on his horizon lay at the Wayne Newton Theater in Branson. He met Rubin after a show in Santa Ana, California, on February 27, 1993.

Perhaps one other reason Cash agreed to the meeting was another taste he'd gotten, earlier that same month, of being courted by the young and hip. While he was in the midst of an Irish tour, the rock band U2 invited him to a Dublin studio to record "The Wanderer," a prodigal-son theme written by Bono and the rest of the band. With Cash on lead vocals, the cut would appear on the band's *Zooropa* album in the spring of 1993. It portended the relationship that Cash would soon forge with the new rock world, as well as the opening of his career's fourth and final chapter: 1994–2003.

Many an outsider surely chuckled at the Johnny Cash–Rick Rubin arrangement, a brittle country-music king wed to a Long Island–raised thrash-and-rap producer who hid behind black shades and a Methuselahic beard. How could the child of Jimmie Rodgers and Roy Acuff find bliss with a man who listed AC/DC's *Highway to Hell* among his favorite albums?

As it turned out, there was harmony in their incongruence. From May to December of 1993, Cash and Rubin traded song ideas for a new album and met occasionally in Rubin's Los Angeles home to hear how those songs sounded in Cash's voice. Rubin's was no home studio in the conventional Nashville sense, where a home studio often meant a soundproofed room in the basement or, as in Cash's case, an outfitted cabin adjacent to his house (which had replaced the House of Cash studios). Cash was bemused as he sat in Rubin's living room amid a tangle of recording equipment, running through songs with his guitar at his own pace while the barefoot Rubin reclined on the floor with his dogs to listen. There were no clocks, no album deadlines, no recording executives pressing their faces to the window looking for the radio hit.

Cash reeled off dozens of takes while Rubin sat back and watched. Cash visited Jimmie Rodgers songs, dragged out some of his own chestnuts, and experimented with a handful of writers new to him, such as horrorcore icon and ex-Misfits frontman Glenn Danzig, Dire Straits guitarist Mark Knopfler, and folk singer Loudon Wainwright III. These were days not unlike those of the Sun years, he'd say, likening Rubin to his first producer. "He was a lot like Sam, actually," observed Cash of his first encounters with Rubin. "We talked a lot about the approach we were going to take, and he said, 'You know, we are not going to think about time or money. I want you to come out as much as you can.'"

It's clear just by reviewing the list of demos Cash laid down with Rubin in 1993 that the new producer was letting Cash explore, like Phillips had, but Rubin was also letting him get comfortable before trying anything too radical. Despite recording Danzig's "Thirteen" and Tom Waits's "Down There by the Train," entirely new material to Cash that made the final edit of the first album with Rubin, the sixty-one-year-old dug deeply into his old bag, sorting through Kris Kristofferson, Billy Joe Shaver, A.P. Carter, country standards, and traditional hymns. From a repertory standpoint, the collaboration seemed at first surprisingly conservative. But when the album emerged, it proved to be a substantial departure from the collections Cash had turned in over the previous decade. Yes, he had delved into new songwriters, but he'd been doing that in earnest and with little luck for twenty years. This time around, though, he had tacked to an album four new songs of his own: "Let the Train Blow the Whistle," "Drive On," "Redemption," and "Like A Soldier." Few albums from the previous twenty years had contained so many of his compositions. That, and the fact that one of those songs was a riveting Vietnam drama ("Drive On"), spelled victory for Cash.

Few critics and buyers zeroed in on the reawakening of Cash's songwriting prowess when Rubin released *American Recordings* in 1994. Perhaps they found the instrumentation more startling: Cash was singing with only his own acoustic guitar providing accompaniment. There was no throbbing bass, no surging background vocals, and—deafening in its absence—no charging boom-chicka-boom rhythm. Cash had fantasized about such a recording for years. Inspired by Marty Robbins, who used to close the *Grand Ole Opry* serenading the audience with only his guitar in support, Cash envisioned an album of love songs that he'd call *Late and Alone*, but he either never pushed the idea or Columbia and Mercury shunned it. Perhaps the concept smacked of Cash as lounge singer *a la* Frank Sinatra, too distant from the patented image and sound.

If there was any commercial risk in Cash releasing a solo acoustic album, Rubin more than compensated for it by dipping into the ever-roiling well of Cash's image or more accurately, images. Looking past the patriot and preacher and into the darkness below the country-music-king, Rubin collared the bad-boy image, the Cash of Folsom Prison, the Cash who abused drugs and mistreated women, the Cash who might have shot your uncle just to watch him die.

Although that side of him had never completely subsided—journalists had never stopped mentioning it and the news reports of relapses and rehabs confirmed it—Cash had not really traded on it for years. It had served him as he rose after the *Johnny Cash At Folsom Prison* album, but in the glow of his happy television show and *The Gospel Road*, he had shed Lucifer's cape.

But Lucifer's cape made for compelling packaging. The American Recordings marketing staff could sell it. Young fans had lapped up Rubin's other acts in part because they connected with the edge in their music, the voices (some aimless, some focused) that told them to fight the power and to flout conventions. Not all alternative, metal, and rap artists spoke this language, but among those who did, Cash seemed a plausible godfather. Rubin cast Cash as the avatar of darkness and rebellion. The album cover framed him as a solemn and bad dude, ready to wield a sawed-off shotgun. The song that Cash and Rubin chose to promote the album was "Delia's Gone," an old murder ballad that Cash had first recorded in 1961. In 1993, Cash updated the lyrics, throwing in references to submachine guns and showing that just as he was the bridge between country and rock in the 1960s (as *The New York Times* had proclaimed back then), he was a link between traditional American folk and gangsta rap in the 1990s.

The requisite video produced in tandem with "Delia's Gone" followed Cash as he ties up model Kate Moss, throws her in a pit, and shovels dirt over her porcelain face. When some priggish critics charged misogyny, Cash responded that the song wasn't anti-women, it was anti-Delia. MTV pulled it, but who in the Cash-Rubin camp cared? The video had already incited a buzz, as had Cash's prerelease appearances at vogue clubs and South by Southwest in Austin, Texas, the musical convocation that always had its fingers in the just-ready-to-boil cauldron of hot music. *American Recordings* was off to the races.

As if on cue, the media threw up a cheer such as Cash had not heard since the release of *Johnny Cash At Folsom Prison* in 1968. Scores of newspapers and magazines gave the album a stout thumbs up, including the all-important *Rolling Stone*, which hailed a ruddy centurian back from conquests in the provinces. "In Rubin's ruthlessly unadorned, dry-as-dust settings, Cash moves with stoic fury. His voice is the best it has sounded in more than 30 years (think 'I Walk the Line,' think 'Ring of Fire'), and he sings with a control reminiscent of Hemingway's writing. Not a feeling is flaunted, not a jot of sentimentality is permitted, but every quaver, every hesitation, every shift in volume, every catch in a line resonates like a private apocalypse."

Only a handful of media critics strayed from the message as American Recordings had delivered it. Journalist Patrick Carr, writing in *Country Music*, seemed peeved that so many were just now discovering Cash's cool, and Chris Dickinson, who would soon assume the editorship of *The Journal of Country Music*, quipped in the *Chicago Reader* that Cash had been born again, "only this time to an audience that wore crosses not as Christian symbols but as fashion accessories." Dickinson dismissed the album as a marketing gimmick to coax a few more miles from a rusted black Cadillac. "At this late date, considering the enormous body of his work, it's probably unfair to expect Cash to have many new ideas in him," she wrote. "Covering songs by such disparate songwriters as Glenn Danzig, Kris Kristofferson, and Leonard Cohen serves as a masterful marketing tool by generating plenty of press, but 'Why Me Lord' and 'Bird on A Wire' were done far better by the original artists. These ultimately tired choices hardly constitute a reason for the alternative crowd to wet its collective pants."

Dickinson saw the killing in "Delia's Gone" as nothing but a carny's hook to snag the kids of gangstadom and the purists among the hip who, she said, "believes 'real' country must hew to the Appalachian dead-baby school of songwriting." Indeed, "Delia" with its unflinching depiction of a murder and Kate Moss video wooed its intended audiences, but in doing so, it also toyed with Cash's entrenched fans' notions of who he was. For so long, he'd done everything he could to shroud himself in light and patriotism, so who could blame the blue hairs and knobby-kneed greasers if they (like Dickinson) scratched their heads and wondered if the old boy was playing dress up. But perhaps that's what they wanted all the time: Cash back in black, the tortured highwayman who loomed outside Folsom, who sang "I Walk the Line" with anguished authority in 1956, and who embodied their fantasies and fears of the dark side.

In any case, whether one beheld American Recordings as charade or revelation, who could deny the satisfaction of Cash's return to the front page and prime time? "Let's hear it for Rick Rubin," exclaims Marty Stuart, who admits to skepticism of the American gambit, "for seeing something there that was raw enough and real enough and hip enough in his eyes to bring it on. I'm not personally a big fan of all those American recordings. I think some of them are, you know, just there. There's no comparison to me between the American recordings and [Folsom], but at the same time it gave him an outlet; it told me what was on his mind. He absolutely threw his—as Waylon said—sugar-getter away, and he sang great songs for the most part on those American recordings. But if it took somebody that was in Rubin's tradition to make him hip again to a new audience, wonderful. Wonderful. Sure, there was a risk there. But Johnny Cash was the kind of guy that once you get him through the door, he didn't need no help. He took care of that, he kicked it up. Once you kick the door down for him, he took care of the risk himself. The risk became yours."

Nobody publicly considered the possibility that the supporting cuts from the album might be overshadowed by the hype surrounding the video for "Delia's Gone," but many listeners probably did miss the better example of Cash's abilities as they pondered the slain vixen. Take "Drive On," for example. It was a number that beat much closer to Cash's soul and artistry but that, like many songs cut during Cash's American years, was obscured by a hipper song placed out front to gather the masses.

"Drive On" dwells on a Vietnam veteran who, although haunted by his wartime past, finds a way to survive to the next day in an ungrateful America. It may have been the best song Cash had written since the tender and evocative "Flesh and Blood" of 1970, and it certainly embodied the Cash themes and sentiments as well as his approach to songwriting. Just like in the early 1950s when he had assembled "Folsom Prison Blues" after seeing a movie, he penned "Drive On" after reading John Del Vecchio's *The 13th Valley*, about a soldier's harrowing tour of duty in Southeast Asia. As clear and direct as a newspaper headline, Cash's verse magically summoned the loneliness in being the knowing one among the unknowing and identified with the astonishing and innate ability of man to compartmentalize the horrors of war.

Cash seemed to know when a sentiment deserved a song, and in this case he felt so strong the impulse of Del Vecchio's theme of survival that it also became a personal credo. "There are all these great expressions that men had in Vietnam," he explained to *Rolling Stone*, "and one of them is 'Screw it. Don't mean nothing. Drive on.' Meaning, if it isn't life threatening, don't worry about it. Since I had my sixtieth birthday, I've been using that expression a lot. I'm trying to learn that I can't sweat the little things the way I used to do. So what if I've got a broken jaw? It could be worse. Could be a broken back. Screw it. It don't mean nothing. Drive on."

The shining moment for "Drive On" wasn't on the radio because radio didn't play Johnny Cash, and it wasn't in the press because "Delia's Gone" seduced most writers' attention. Rather, it glowed on a VH-1 cable-television show that paired Cash with Willie Nelson for an acoustic evening of song-swapping, the unparalleled unplugged program. Recorded in front of a live New York audience in 1997, some three years after the song's release on *American Recordings*, Nelson's superior guitar picking and pocketful of country classics appeared to give him an edge with the audience. Either that or Nelsonites had just come out in greater numbers that day. As the stentorian men alternated songs, Nelson at one stage cruised on an overwhelming string of self-penned gems ("Funny How Time Slips Away," "Crazy," and "Night Life"), while Cash chose to interject numbers from his lower shelf, appealing songs, but virtually unknown compared to Nelson's standards. Cash could have unholstered "Folsom Prison Blues" or "Ring of Fire" and easily seized back the show, but instead he launched into a pounding take of "Drive On." In doing so, he summarily reminded the audience of his towering authority, over Nelson and over all comers. The utter seriousness of war and desperation trumped Nelson's pain of love and heartbreak, stilling the audience and delivering the show and its audience back to Cash's bosom. Nelson followed with his honky-tonk classic "Me and Paul," but in the wake of "Drive On," it was like water after wine.

American Recordings returned Cash to the country-music album charts. It also netted the legend his first solo Grammy Award (for Best Comtemporary Folk Album) since 1969's "A Boy Named Sue."

On the road, Cash percolated again as he played to the audiences that had flung him back onto the charts. He sold out downtown rock clubs, and in the auditoriums, showrooms, and theaters, where the empty seats had been multiplying, he watched the crowds return again. Concert critics found an invigorated veteran and, like many of their counterparts who wrote about albums, seemed incapable of issuing a bad review. Even Chris Dickenson, who had laid waste to *American Recordings*, gulped in awe when she encountered him in 1994 at Chicago's Bismarck Club. "Halfway through he sat alone on a stool and accompanied himself on guitar, and even 'Delia's Gone' rang with a true heaviness missing from his recorded version," she wrote. "Never mind that some in the audience laughed at several of the more gruesome lines; it seemed like a nervous response at being faced with Cash's unadulterated in-person rendition."

Cash smiled when he saw the young faces in the crowd, heard their whoops and hollers, and realized that many out there actually knew his new songs. It may have felt even better to be on a circuit that coursed widely around Branson. Driving out of the Missouri town for the last time with Jack Shaw, a palpable sense of relief filled the car. "When we left, he wasn't too fond of going back to Branson," recounts Shaw. "He didn't care if he ever went back. I said, 'We'll forget it, if it takes a week.' He said, 'It'll take about an hour, Jack.'"

17

UNCHAINED

By 1994, Marty Stuart had receded somewhat from Johnny Cash's world, having seven years earlier left both Cash's daughter Cindy and the Cash band to jack up a solo career that seemed infused all at once with Lester Flatt, Lefty Frizzell, and James Brown. Cash didn't hold a grudge about Stuart's departure, though. And he knew that if anybody embodied how country music could reach the future while still clutching the tassels of Frizzell, Hank Williams, and Johnny Cash, it was John Marty Stuart. Stuart above most could probably tell where Cash's Rick Rubin material stood along a country road. So, in early 1994, as Cash and Rubin were hammering down the final details of *American Recordings*, Cash summoned Stuart to his office for a private listening session.

Gingerly taking up the guitar in his hands, Cash coughed weakly and bore down on the strings. There was a sadness to the scene; the man who once handled repertoire and recording with absolute self-confidence and zeal was checking his compass against Stuart's. "I sat at the House of Cash," recollects Stuart, "and he sang me what we know now as that *American Recordings* record. He sang me every song as I was sitting on the couch in his office. And I could tell that he'd done this for four or five other people, looking for [affirmation] or getting his act together for what he was going to do at The Viper Room. He was getting himself ready. He got through, and I said, 'I can't see nothing wrong with this: this is as pure as it gets. I think it resets country music's clock. It absolutely takes it back to a new beginning, setting it up for the twenty-first century. In some way, it can parallel what the Carter Family and Jimmie Rodgers did at Bristol.' I said, 'Country music needs that, and in broader terms, American music could use it too.'"

The Carter Family and Jimmie Rodgers at Bristol? Stuart was invoking some mighty and unparalleled titans in that one breath, but in his enthusiasm there may have been some truth. Country music's godhead figure going acoustic and again harking back to themes rooted in religion, rural life, personal struggle, and the growth of a nation was something like Hank Williams rising from his grave to chastise the wayward music industry.

The country music industry couldn't ignore the gravity of Cash's statement, particularly when it became apparent that people were buying it. It's not that *American Recordings* herded country music back to the hills of southwestern Virginia. Sony, BMG, MCA, CMT, and country radio (all of the teen-targeting country music institutions) were too deeply mortgaged to the pop-oriented megastars of the day to let that happen. But Cash's new album did call attention to a yearning in America for plain-spoken music that was imbued by country music tradition but not necessarily bound by it. It had all the markings of alternative country, the movement that attracted enthusiasts, writers, and musicians from the pop, rock, and country worlds who yearned for the purer elements of country music. These fans embraced *American Recordings* as fervently as any of the grunge, metal, or rap kids who seemed to be the album's intended audience.

To the extent that Cash set up country music for the twenty-first century, as Stuart theorized, he did so by legitimizing and renourishing country music's roots, the themes and instrumental simplicity that birthed the genre. He granted them status once again just as country music seemed hopelessly consigned to the power ballads of Garth Brooks and Reba McEntire. And if the mainstream industry failed to take notice, at least the fringes listened, heartened now that the Man in Black had finally spoken. Not until the *O Brother, Where Art Thou* soundtrack of 2000 was there a statement louder than Cash's *American Recordings* declaring that America wanted its music back.

Though he was beckoned in the final hours before the *American Recordings* release and merely asked for his opinion, Stuart would play a more substantive role in Cash's second collaboration with Rick Rubin (finding himself more involved in a Cash project than he'd been since the late 1980s). Work on the album that would become *Unchained* had already begun when Stuart tumbled into the picture. Cash and Rubin had resolved to stick with the same song formula, trying a host of rock and country covers, a few Cash originals, and some spirituals. And they had decided that one solo acoustic album was enough. This one would be recorded with Tom Petty and the Heartbreakers and to up the hip factor, the cameo support of Flea of the Red Hot Chili Peppers, as well as Lindsay Buckingham and Mick Fleetwood of Fleetwood Mac. With so much California cool wafting into the L.A. studio where *Unchained* would be recorded, Cash needed a hand to hold. "He knew that he could look at me without saying one word, and I knew what he was thinking," says Stuart. "I think I was probably just a comfort factor to him inside a new world."

Cash had not intended to bring Stuart with him, but a chance meeting on an L.A.-bound airplane put the partnership in motion. "I was on the way to California to do something, sitting in the front end of the airplane," says Stuart. "And when I got on, I didn't notice who else was on the airplane. And when the flight landed in L.A., I stood up. Well, there was J.R., and I said, 'What are you doing?' He said, 'What are *you* doing?' I said, 'Sitting three seats away from you and not knowin' you're there.' I said, 'You need to work on your charisma.' And we were at baggage claim, and he said, 'How long are you going to be out here?' And I said, 'A day or two.' And he says 'Well, I'm going to the studio with Rick Rubin and Tom Petty. Why don't you come play some guitar?' And I know him well enough to know to go. Whether [I was] a leaning post or a guitar player or whatever, it was just the right thing to do. So, I rearranged my schedule for a few days, and we did those records."

Playing guitar with the Heartbreakers for two weeks before he had to leave on a tour, Stuart immediately noted the distance between Nashville and L.A. Producers and executives in Music City urged Cash to hew to his boom-chicka-boom, but Rubin, noted Stuart, figured Cash transcended boom-chicka-boom and blocked all the hallways back to the old formula. When the band was looking for a way into Soundgarden's "Rusty Cage," a song Cash had initially found to be ill-fitting, it might have been easier to lapse into the boom-chicka-boom rhythm. But Rubin roughed out a new structure for Cash, rising from his producer perch and chanting with decided rhythm the opening line: *You wired me awake/And hit me with a hand of broken nails. . . .*

Taking Rubin's cue, acoustic guitarists Stuart and Campbell built a track around the cadence of the producer's recitation and in doing so gave Cash and the rest of the band access to the song. If Cash couldn't absolutely absorb the essence of the lyric (which was why he wasn't cozying to "Rusty Cage"), he could, says Stuart, "wiggle" in the bold rhythmic borders envisioned by Rubin and spelled out by Stuart and Campbell.

The idea that Cash wasn't one-hundred percent in tune with the lyrics he sang seems a serious contradiction to Cash's artistry, but it certainly was not so in relation to Cash's sense of showmanship. Despite his image as a kind of dark reservoir of song where interpretation and inner feeling were indistinguishable, Cash knew he was a hawker of songs, his own as well as others. Keenly aware of the potential power of his dramatic delivery, he opened himself to the Soundgarden and Beck numbers that Rubin set at his feet. In the 1960s, he'd gone to the folk community in a similar frame of mind. "It was just a different set of writers saying a different set of words, but [Cash's was] a timeless voice applied to it," remarks Stuart. "He was cool. He got it. 'Rusty Cage' is just a new model vacuum cleaner. And he was cool enough to unplug the old one and just plug in the new one and go with it."

Unchained was full of new appliances. The title track, brought to him by Jimmy Tittle, moaned like a slave's spiritual, and Beck's "Rowboat" teased out Cash's penchant for destruction, playful and otherwise. He also ripped through two of his Sun oldies, "Country Boy" and "Mean-Eyed Cat," and resurrected four tunes moldering in the country canon: "Sea of Heartbreak," "Kneeling Drunkard's Plea," "I Never Picked Cotton," and "I've Been Everywhere."

There was focus on this project, real studio work sessions, unlike Cash had experienced in more than twenty years. In the 1980s and 1990s, Cash had recorded here and there between tours and TV commitments, nailing down two or three songs at a time before an album finally came together. It was a rudderless voyage, says Jimmy Tittle. "It never felt like, okay, here's our idea, here's what we're going to do, here's a concept, here's a group of songs that are going to be on that album." Even *American Recordings* was more assembled than achieved, songs picked like choice timber from dozens of songs recorded over more than seven months. On the other hand, *Unchained* rose like an Amish barn, exuding commitment, cooperation, and fun. "John, I felt, was like a kid in a playground," says Stuart of Cash's attitude on the sessions. "He knew he was on to something. I think everybody knew something good was happening."

Upon *Unchained*'s release in November of 1996, the critics again roared. Typifying much of the clamor, the *Los Angeles Times* praised a singer who had dared to modernize in a way that conformed to his essence: "Cash, sticking close to the gospel sounds and spiritual concerns that have always flowed though his music, confronts hard issues of mortality and never blinks. His singing, defiant and tender, rumbles right through to the marrow, excavating from every lyric an avenue to the essential truths about human experience."

Unchained may ultimately prove to be one of the great Cash albums, a splendorous journey through the American songbook taken while Cash's voice remained supple in its grim and weary sort of way. Its identification with Cash's legacy at the heart of its appeal, *Unchained* sold the themes of hard labor and humankind's darkness and proved to be an excellent band album. Petty and the other musicians buoyed Cash's voice with intensity and abandon not seen since the original Tennessee Three (with Carl Perkins loading the cannon) volleyed Cash songs against the hard walls of Folsom Prison.

The productivity of the *Unchained* sessions had tested Cash's stamina. His voice, endlessly vibrant on the album, belied the strain of those days in L.A. when he tired easily, seeking a chair at the close of the day, often when the boys around him were still rumbling. Rubin described the lapse in a 2004 radio interview: "We'd be in the studio working, and he would get dizzy, or he would be unable to sing and have to lay down for a while. And some days, he wasn't able to sing, and he would just not be himself, not be himself at all."

Cash made a career of evading himself, his malleable self, but Rubin wasn't alone in sensing that something was amiss. Daughter Rosanne saw her father more prone to sobbing, and she gauged her father's faltering against the persistent pain of his jaw and the increasing amounts of mind-numbing medication he consumed to cope with it. When Cash attended Rosanne's wedding to producer John Levanthal, on the eve of a European tour in late April of 1995, the pain and its prescriptions, she recalls, were scrambling his mind. "He kind of left the wedding a little bit early," she says, "and John and I went to Italy for our honeymoon and we're sitting out on the terrace of the hotel our first day there, and I get the *International Herald Tribune* or something. And I pick it up, and I see Johnny Cash." She read that after one date at London's Royal Albert Hall during which Cash had relied on extended interludes by the Carter Sisters and John Carter Cash (who was now often on tour with him) to carry the show, Cash had cancelled his tour because of facial pain. "It didn't say it was due to drugs, but I knew it was," she continues. "I had that same feeling that I had when I tore the [Ku Klux Klan letter] in half when I was nine. I was so angry with him."

A few months later, Rosanne gently confronted him. "I said, 'Dad, don't disappear,'" she remembers. "'We know you're in pain, but please try not to. Your family wants you to stay. We really need you.'"

According to Rosanne, after the scotched European tour, pain medication wrapped around Cash's mind like a viper, squeezing ever tighter with every year that passed. He became difficult to engage, she says. Although there were moments of absolute engagement, more frequently after 1995, he could seem fit for aggressive psychiatric treatment. One such incident occurred in 1997 (in the wake of *Unchained*'s release) when Cash, June, and Rosanne met for lunch at the Plaza Athénée, Cash's favorite lodging in Manhattan. Rosanne, husband John, and her two daughters had come up from their home in Chelsea. "We were sitting at the lunch table and I could tell he wasn't quite right," says Rosanne. "And he started hallucinating at the lunch table, and he said something about the black puppies in the room. And I said, 'Dad, there's no puppies in the room.' 'Yes, you know, you see them.' And then he was pouring his juice, and it would just fall into his lap and everything. . . .'" Wiping the juice from his lap, Cash excused himself to use the bathroom. Perplexed and worried at the same time, Rosanne asked June what was happening. Looking back, she speculates that June refused to admit that her husband was abusing again, for she offered no straight answer, only a look of perplexity that mirrored her stepdaughter's. "It was the pain meds," concludes Rosanne. "And then he called me the next day, and he said 'I'm so embarrassed to think what my daughter thinks about me right now.' I said, 'It's not me Dad. I don't think anything bad about you. But your granddaughters might want to know what's going on.' So it was kind of like that until his death. He would be lucid, and then he would kind of drift off."

While Rosanne observed pain killers boggling her father's mind, Cash himself could feel a vicious uncoiling inside, something that was more insidious than the facial pain and addiction. That something, he later wrote, became alarmingly evident in October of 1997 while visiting New York City: "There I was, proceeding down Madison Avenue in a perfectly normal manner, when I looked up for some reason and my next step was backwards. It was completely involuntary; it happened without any intention or control on my part. It was very weird."

Weird, yes; but it was hardly surprising. Cash had visited the doctor over the summer, complaining of strange sensations and exaggerated body movement that seemed to be his normal tics multiplied by one hundred. The doctors diagnosed Parkinson's disease, but he chose not to inform the public or many of his family members, deciding to simply ignore it until the symptoms advanced.

Carrying on with his summer agenda, a tour of Europe followed by a brief swing through New England, he felt his energy reserves draining with devilish speed. He took to traveling on the tour bus more often, as it was increasingly difficult and exhausting to negotiate airport lines, transfers, and fans constantly seeking his time and autograph. Finally, after a private appearance at Ford's Theater in Washington, D.C., where Lincoln was assassinated, he gathered his band and crew together to tell them he and June had decided to phase-in their retirement. It was September 16, 1997. By 2000, they told their employees, they would only be working special engagements.

Their plan was optimistic, however. On the doorstep of November, the road in front of them snapped up like a recoiling tape measure. A brief western tour, scheduled before he was to start promoting his new autobiography, found him in decline. Lyrics to classic songs eluded him, but, his creativity still beating, he hid the lapses by making up new lines. And despite magnetizing a reviewer in Albuquerque on October 2nd, after the first show of a two night stand at L.A.'s House of the Blues on October 3rd, W.S. Holland left the stage shaking his head. "There's something wrong with that boy," the drummer muttered to Earl Ball. "He never played 'Folsom' like that before." Slowly, Cash made concessions; he shortened his sets and, uncertain of his step, asked technical director Jay Dauro to lay down colored tape from the dressing room to the stage.

Although Cash appeared reasonably healthy at a taped television interview in Nashville on October 22nd, on October 23rd, a reviewer attending Cash's Knoxville, Tennessee, concert found the balladeer's timing off-kilter and noted that he uncharacteristically ignored calls for an encore, leaving the confused audience waiting ten minutes in raised houselights. "Every night, that last tour was a prayer," says Cindy Cash, who was singing solos and duets with her father on the show. "Please just let him get through this song."

Two days later, in Flint, Michigan, Cash's problems spilled out into the sunlight. Cindy fretted from the moment they took the stage. Her father was swaying, she noticed, and he almost tumbled over as he stooped down to retrieve a guitar pick he had dropped. When Cindy took a bow with Cash before leaving the stage, he stumbled again. "I thought he was going to pass out," she says. "And he thought he was going to pass out, and that's what scared me because I could see the fear in his eyes."

Normally after her bow, Cindy would charge off stage, rush out the door, and board the tour bus, but that night she waited at the side of stage, keeping a motherly eye on her father and wishing he'd leave the microphone. "I was frightened," she says, "and I was like, 'C'mon Dad, just end it. You don't have to do this.'" When he finally said good night, she waited to grab his arm and support him, but as Cash lumbered toward her, his entourage enveloped him and elbowed her aside. She recalls her frustration: "Push me away from my dad when I think there's something wrong with him? I really thought I was going to hit someone that night. I was trying to say, 'Dad, what can I do for you? Are you okay? Do you want my arm?' Whenever he got to a point like that, sometimes he just wanted somebody in his family real close by. It scared him to be sick, and I couldn't get to him. I remember feeling like, 'I just want to help my dad. Get out of the way.'"

The Flint press reported that Cash had admitted his Parkinson's to his fans that night, and that they had giggled, perhaps thinking that the star was joking. "It ain't funny," he replied on stage to the audience's titters. "It's all right. I refuse to give it some ground in my life." His defiance was admirable, but his disease would soon be stealing all the ground it wanted. After a television appearance in New

York to plug his autobiography (this is probably when he started walking backwards), Cash issued a press release confirming his diagnosis and canceling shows for the remainder of the year. A few days later, in another release, he added that the actual diagnosis was Shy-Drager syndrome, a disease related to Parkinson's.

Back in Nashville in early November, Cash entered Baptist Hospital for evaluation and treatment, only to fail dramatically as pneumonia and blood poisoning engulfed him. "I spent ten days and nights unconscious," he recounted later. "I was in such bad shape that for my first couple of nights on the ventilator, my doctor, Terry Jerkins, didn't know whether I'd live until dawn. On the tenth night, . . . she told God that she and medicine had done all they could, it was in His hands now, and she spent the whole night praying." June put out a call through the Johnny Cash website asking for prayers for Johnny that night. By morning, he said, he stirred; within days, he was receiving visitors.

Marshall Grant, up from Mississippi, called June intending merely to convey his good wishes, but Cash insisted his old bass player stop by to visit. Although memories of their bitter parting in 1980 had faded, Grant hadn't seen him in years. They had only spoken on the telephone. "When I walked in the room and he was lying in bed with his horn-rimmed glasses on, trying to read the paper, I couldn't believe what he looked like," says Grant. He was pale, emaciated, and, as far as Grant could tell, not long for the world.

Band members whom Grant met while in Nashville proposed that Cash's setback was temporary, that they would be back on the road by the spring. But Grant could only shake his head. The next trip that they would all take together, he told them, was to the cemetery.

Cash was discharged in early December, enfeebled by his disease and unsure what the future held. Family feared that if the disease didn't take him, inactivity would. "He was the definitive restless person," says Rosanne. "When he had to stop traveling because of his illness, all of us, all of his children, were frozen in fear of what was going to happen to him. We could not imagine him not traveling. I mean it was a huge thing for him to kind of assimilate into his life that he wasn't going to travel."

But Cash assimilated, and as his body slowly healed (mocking Marshall Grant's grim predictions), he negotiated a comfort with retirement, stating frequently that he couldn't imagine returning to the two-lane black top. Anxious to avoid another devastating bout with pneumonia, he and June quartered themselves in the warm climate of Jamaica before Christmas of 1997, a trip they would make for the next five years whenever the chill of winter began to crackle in the Nashville air.

～～～

The summer of 1998 found the Cashes back in Tennessee mourning the death of June's sister Helen who passed on June 2nd. Later in the month, Cash broke out for a few moments for a surprise appearance at a Kris Kristofferson tribute at the Ryman Auditorium, spontaneously appearing onstage to help his old friend sing "Sunday Morning Coming Down." But most of the time, Cash remained out of public view, flying up to New York to visit with Rosanne, dropping in on Jack Clement, and tending to the grapes at Bon Aqua. Across every threshold, he dragged his disease, and as fall moved in to push the stubborn sticky heat from Nashville, Cash lay in a hospital bed snared once again by pneumonia. Doctors released him after ten days, but he was soon back again; he remained hospitalized for most of October.

Returning to enforced recuperation and jetting to Jamaica once the doctors gave him the green light to travel, Cash welcomed Marty Stuart to Cinnamon Hill. Stuart was at work on his hillbilly opus *The Pilgrim* and, tapping the fading legend's voice of authority, planned to record Cash reading some dramatic lines for the album's conclusion. He found Cash under duress but in good spirits. "It was shaky," says Stuart. "He was still able to get on a golf cart and go around and swipe golf balls on the golf course to give to Jamaican kids. (He'd swipe golf balls from the rich golfers at that country club and give buckets full of them to Jamaican kids, so they could sell them back to the golfers.) And he was still in good voice, his mind was right on the money. But he was good. June was good. You could see him getting shaky, but there was nothing to be completely alarmed about."

During Stuart's visit, Cash repeated that he was happy away from the road, happy not to have to be Johnny Cash so often. And Stuart believed he might have been telling the truth. "He was sitting there with his glasses on, his belly out, and his shirt unbuttoned and a pair of shorts and he was picking flowers for June," he recalls. "And it reminded me of that scene with Marlon Brando at the end of the *The Godfather*, when he was out in the garden where he actually died in that movie. But he looked like the godfather to me, a well-seasoned oak tree enjoying the sunshine of what was left of his days. And, you know, there was just this countenance of wisdom around him, there was a halo of wisdom and goodness about him."

~

Cash's daughters were not so comforted. Although they agreed that retirement had grown on their father, they struggled with his drift away from the present. They were concerned that the cocktail of medication for his syndrome, for the diabetes he was now living with, and for a dozen other maladies, was exacerbating his affliction. One family member quipped that he'd been given chlorpromazine, an anti-psychotic drug, for the hiccups. Rosanne never knew what to believe about his medication, whether he was taking what he needed or gulping down some more for the road. Cognizant of the pitfalls of medicating an addictive personality, she suspected the latter.

"This is so complicated," she ventures, shifting in a wooden chair at her kitchen table some seventeen months after her father's passing. "I've spent the last ten years going through this in my head, angry that he's using, that it's beyond what he needs for the pain. And then realizing how much pain he's in and going, 'Poor guy, let him take whatever the hell he wants to take.' Angry because he can't show up emotionally and then realizing that he's struggling with so many things going wrong with his body that you go, 'Okay, whatever he needs.' All of us went back and forth like that for years. Talking to his doctors—ugh—I can't even tell you how many times. I talked to his doctor on the phone: 'What is he taking? Does he really need this? How are you keeping a check on it?'"

And she says she never got satisfactory answers. "I mean you have the lengthy conversations about what checks and balances are in place," she explains, "except that his tolerance is so enormous that she has to order extra doses just so he can get some pain relief. It's this constant kind of *feeling it through*, juggling it. And us really not knowing. And then one of my sisters would call: 'I really think Dad is using too much.' Blah, blah, blah. It was constant."

~

In April of 1999, Cash was well enough to take part in a remarkable television tribute on cable television that included appearances, live and taped, by Bruce Springsteen, U2, Emmylou Harris, and other top musicians. A performance by hip-hop's Wyclef Jean had to be one of the most electrifying. Starting into a riveting take on "Delia's Gone," which highlighted the yoke that linked Cash to rap and hip hop, Jean then juiced up an electric rap that shouted out to "Folsom Prison Blues" and everything else cool about Johnny Cash. Jean in five minutes had accomplished what Cash's occasional covers of Rosetta Tharpe's spirituals and television appearances with Ray Charles had not: establish Cash's connection with the black entertainment world. The only thing more stirring that night was Cash's appearance to sing "Folsom Prison Blues" and "I Walk the Line." He walked confidently on stage, draped in black. Except for his thinned hair and some swelling in face, he looked road ready. The songs appeared to take the audience back in time, making them forget that Johnny Cash really couldn't be theirs anymore and that he'd just emerged for a spell to thank them and say that he was doing all right. In their places behind him were Marshall Grant, back after nineteen years, and Fluke Holland, who had remained until the last date. It was a glorious night. It was also the last performance Cash would share with any audience of consequential size, for he was tired.

Activities such as the television special were precisely what stemmed Cash's slide, however. Having tasks to focus on seemed to pull him up. Just when the visits to specialists and stays in hospitals (punctuated only by forays to Wal-Mart and the local ice cream parlor) seemed too much to bear, an offer to contribute to a movie soundtrack or some other recording would arrive in the mailbox.

Cash rarely refused. To work was to live. He contributed performances to the film soundtracks *We Were Soldiers* and *Dead Man Walking* as well as albums paying tribute to the Louvin Brothers and Hank Williams. However, he reserved the bulk of his fading energies for Rick Rubin, who in 2000 helped Cash complete his third American album, *Solitary Man*.

Like its predecessors, *Solitary Man* hit the marketplace in a hail of publicity, only this time, it was Cash's return from a four-year recording hiatus that uncorked the storm. Most critics applauded him (in fact seemed unwilling out of respect to do anything but). Only a scant few ventured a hand in protest. Ben Ratliff, writing in *Rolling Stone*, was one. He noted that *Solitary Man* was "one Rick Rubin-built cover album over the line" and pined for more assertive production: "I can't believe I'm making this complaint of a country record—they're usually so overproduced—but Rick Rubin's work is too timid," he wrote. "Mostly, the shy combos of guitar, fiddle and accordion, or Benmont Tench's subliminal contributions on keyboards, make up the kind of severe meal that one is forced to think of as 'tasteful.'"

Despite Ratliff's cry for more production, he and others refrained from remarking on the singer's diminished vocals, which although courageous and often poignant, were difficult to absorb. Husky and panting, they reminded listeners of Cash's mortality. An infusion of more instrumental backing (a welcome addition to most any Cash album) may have helped Cash as he limped through performances such as "Before My Time," his own awkward composition, and the mirthless "I See A Darkness," written by Will Oldham.

Repertoire was a mixed bag, too. Cash tackled Tom Petty's "I Won't Back Down" to document his resistance to disease, one supposes, and Neil Diamond's "Solitary Man." Rubin's production on both sparkled, despite criticism to the contrary; the only problem was Cash's performances added nothing new to either. Both songs were so well known among rock and pop audiences that any artist would have had difficulty with the proverbial "making it his own." They seemed to have been chosen mostly because of their proximity to Cashian themes. On the other hand, Cash and Rubin redefined U2's "One" and Nick Cave and Mick Harvey's "The Mercy Seat." The warts of love discussed in "One" and the exploration of the condemned's mind in "The Mercy Seat" were rambles that sat easily with Cash. He performed them with aplomb.

The contrast between "Won't Back Down" and "One" revealed where Rick Rubin went wrong and right, respectively, in pairing Cash with postmodern material, whether for marketing purposes or artistic reasons. When Rubin could prod his musicians toward a new arrangement that turned the song inside and out and offer a lyric that Cash could feel (or learn to feel), the results could be staggering.

Solitary Man deserved more skepticism than the critics would allow. Nonetheless, the album confirmed that the most uneven of Johnny Cash projects could prove more interesting than those of the competition.

Rosanne was just happy that her father kept up his work with Rubin. To turn away from recording, she feared, would have spelled the end. "It made the arc of his decline so much slower," she argues. "I think Dad would have gone down like a forty-five degree angle without Rick. In fact, I know he would have. That's why I always felt so grateful to Rick."

~

While Cash continued to haltingly create, June used the void created by his slackened activity to pursue a variety of artistic projects that being Johnny Cash's wife and touring partner had not allowed. She had called it "walking in the wake of Johnny's fame," this subservience to her husband.

In 1999, she released her second solo album, *Press On*. She had released the first one, *Appalachian Pride*, in the 1970s, but it had been submerged in the deluge of her husband's popularity. In contrast, *Press On* garnered the kind of mass-media attention normally reserved for a new Johnny Cash project. Cash contributed vocals, but his role was marginal. The album gave June a spotlight, the likes of which she had not enjoyed since marrying him. A mix of Carter Family favorites and her own co-written songs, it captured a Grammy for Best Traditional Folk Album of 1999.

A dozen or so competing albums probably were more deserving of the Grammy than *Press On*, but it was as if the recording industry was thanking June, acknowledging that she'd sacrificed so much in order to sustain Johnny Cash over some thirty-five years. When a reporter asked the seventy-year-old woman if she'd be touring to support the album, she recited a theme that over the decades had been arduously hewn. "If we go back on the road, we will go together," she said. "I'll go where he goes, and he'll go where I go."

~

18

THE GLOAMING

In 2003, June Carter released her third solo album. Another mix of Carter Family standards and her own originals, *Wildwood Flower* would bring her two additional Grammys: Best Female Country Vocal Performance and Best Traditional Folk Album. She recorded much of the award-winning album at her homeplace near Hiltons, Virginia, where she and Cash still performed on the odd occasion for small crowds at the Carter Fold.

June and Cash also sang together on *Wildwood Flower*'s "The Road to Kaintuck," written by June and her sister Helen and recorded by Cash in 1965, and "Temptation," an old pop song enshrined by Bing Crosby in the 1930s. Their union was heartwarming. Who wouldn't admire the couple for practicing their craft into old age together? But it was heart wrenching, too: both voices had deteriorated so much that one wondered where they found the wind for the next verse.

A few video files burned on the *Wildwood Flower* CD were equally alarming. June, always so willowy, had ballooned because of a heart condition. And in one sequence recorded on a porch, Cash—slouched on a bench off to the side— appeared lifeless while June sings. There is only comfort in June's attitude. She had lost none of her spunk, filling the room (or the porch as the case may have been) with her ebullience and good nature. Sitting like an Egyptian queen among her court of musicians, an assistant fanning her, she poked fun at her husband and playfully scolded her son, the producer. What a contrast it was to the duo's appearance on Pete Seeger's *Rainbow Quest* some thirty-five years earlier, when Cash's celebrity and amphetamine-agitated unpredictability dominated the stage while June's bashful chirps (added only when asked for) hid her razor wit and jolly stage demeanor. Subdued by his disease in 2002, Cash girded the spotlight, while June delighted in it.

Cash's disease, it turned out, was not Shy-Drager syndrome after all. In 2000, doctors revised their diagnosis to autonomic neuropathy, a broad collection of symptoms that encompassed disorders of the nervous system and atrophy of body tissue. His doctor told him that his diabetes had marshaled the army of symptoms, though one couldn't help but wonder if his long history of drug abuse was also a contributor. The neuropathy also enabled the frequent onsets of pneumonia, which landed him back in the hospital again and again.

But Cash pressed on, scoffing at the suggestion of a link between his drugs and his illness. He trained his sights on his next album, despite his rapidly fading sight and increasing difficulty walking. In August of 2002, after recording for *Wildwood Flower* had wrapped up, he was hospitalized again, for what Lou Robin said was an allergic reaction to either prescription drugs or something he ate.

American IV: The Man Comes Around, though, was well on its way to completion. It appeared that despite the detachment that Rosanne witnessed and the lethargy that dogged him, Cash could still rally his spirits and concentration for recording. He did so while suffering quietly, remarked Rick Rubin in a 2004 interview. Tapping his family's stoicism, Cash marginalized his disease for the benefit of his work, his public, and, one might guess, his sanity. "One of his qualities," said Rubin, "was that he would never really talk about . . . pain or if he wasn't doing well, so we never really knew other than when it got so bad that he would say, 'I can't sing anymore now. I have to lay down for a little while,' or, you know, 'I think that's all I can do for today.' He wasn't someone who complained or really shared what was going on physically with him[self]. . . . He was used to living in pain and being in pain and he didn't really complain about it. The only time he would ever discuss it was when it was so overwhelming that it got in the way of what he was trying to do."

Released in November of 2002, *The Man Comes Around* notched Cash's decline. He had withered markedly since *Solitary Man*; time and disease had dried and cracked his voice. But most Cash fans had heard parched vocals on *Solitary Man*, so the diminished quality of Cash's voice on his latest endeavor should have come as no surprise.

What may have been surprising to some was Rubin and Cash's selection of material. They seemed to be constructing a soundtrack to Cash's demise, and an awkward one at that. Cash indulged in a brand of morbid rumination that other singers might have allowed in the September of their years, just not Johnny Cash. There were John Lennon and Paul McCartney's "In My Life" and the traditional "Streets of Laredo" and "Danny Boy," which Cash had not enhanced when he first recorded it in 1964. Rubin and Cash added to the list Glenn Frey and Don Henley's "Desperado," a burdensome song in anybody's hands, which Cash (with vocal help from Henley) could not elevate. Cash had no business recording these light rock ballads, as out of step with his vocal and interpretive abilities, not to mention his image, as they were.

In 1970, producers, critics, and likely Cash himself would have laughed at the suggestion of such repertoire, but in 2002, Cash appeared incapable or unwilling to mount an end run. In fact, the choice of repertoire is certainly another indication (long true) that Cash no longer owned his stage as he had in the 1960s, when he alone decided the music to record and how to record it. In *The Man Comes Around*, there were echoes of the 1980s, when Cash subjected his recording career to the winds of Nashville. Alarm bells should have clanged when he and Rubin recorded "First Time Ever I Saw Your Face," a piece of musical stained glass in Gordon Lightfoot's and Roberta Flack's earlier airings, but an arduous dirge in Cash's. There was a reason that Cash had not recorded that song, as well as "MacArthur Park" and "I Write the Songs," in the 1960s and 1970s; they lay far away from the grasp of his expressive powers.

The flagship cut on *The Man Comes Around* (at least from a marketing perspective) was "Hurt," written by Trent Reznor and recorded under Reznor's Nine Inch Nails moniker in 1994. In the American Recordings genealogy, "Hurt" was in a family with "Rusty Cage," "One," "The Mercy Seat," "Personal Jesus" (also from *The Man Comes Around*), and other songs that Rubin had taken from modern rock and magically recast for Cash's voice. It also became the lenses through which many viewed Cash's deterioration, thanks mostly to an accompanying video by Mark Romanek, who had directed videos for MTV stars such as Michael Jackson and Lenny Kravitz. "Hurt" appears to dwell on a man's physical and emotional erosion and the emptiness of the material world around him, and it features vivid allusions to drug addiction. Initially Cash hesitated to record it, as he did on occasion whenever Rubin nominated songs from his side of the aisle. But this time even John Carter Cash, who looked out for his father's interests in the studio and chimed in with production assistance, paused. "I was a little wary about it," he said in an interview with *Vanity Fair*, "because I sort of cut my teeth on Nine Inch Nails, so to speak. The aggression and the hopelessness of it seemed almost like a little too much."

When the album lumbered into stores in November of 2002, "Hurt" was aboard, but it was not until Mark Romanek's video debuted in early 2003 that the song became a testimonial on the impending death of Johnny Cash. The theme of the video itself is decline, Cash's decline, as images of a young vibrant star collide with the feeble and unsteady senior of 2002. Shots of the House of Cash offices and museum, shuttered and in disarray, pound with the beat of the music, accentuating Cash's condition. Shaking in a later scene, Cash lifts a goblet of wine and pours it over an elaborate feast spread out on a banquet table. Is Cash in his song snubbing the materialism of this earth, Reznor's "empire of dirt"? Or is the banquet table the table of the last supper? The images flash as Rubin's arrangement intensifies, building to a dramatic close. Those images of the aged Cash now alternate with clips of Christ's crucifixtion from *The Gospel Road*. Is Romanek, and Cash in his complicity, comparing the singer's suffering to Christ's? It is a plausible interpretation and one that may have disturbed Cash if he gave much thought to it.

If ever there was an example of the music video's power to dictate the interpretation of the music it was Romanek's "Hurt." It turned Reznor's "Hurt" into a documentary on Cash's mortality, stirring chatter from Memphis to Madrid about Cash's illness and raising a thorny question about the marketing of Cash's final album. Had Cash, Rubin, and company stepped beyond merely framing Cash's frailty and chosen songs and video that exploited it instead?

"I don't know," chimes Marty Stuart, who contributed his guitar playing to *The Man Comes Around*. "I think what meant the most to him was to create to the very end: create, create, create, because he was a true artist. And when I heard 'First

Time Ever I Saw Your Face' and some of those kind of songs, I'm going, 'Oh, what are we up to here guys? What are we up to?' I didn't know if we were just trying to pile up a bunch of songs to sell later or what."

Cash's family and management struggled with the original cut of the video, which they believed portrayed Cash as nearly destitute in his infirmity. Only after Lou Robin's aggressive lobbying did Romanek recut the maudlin production. To Rosanne, who did not see the original cut, the video was startling nonetheless. "I wasn't aware of the video until it was done. And then June told me afterwards they re-edited it. I heard that it was being done, and that it was going to be very intense. And then my Dad's secretary sent all of us kids a copy, and I didn't watch it. My sister called and said, 'Have you seen the video?' I said, 'No.' And she said, 'Be really careful.' I said, 'Really?' She said, 'Yeah.' So, I didn't want to watch it because we were already in that space of years of intense anxiety about my dad's health and this fear that he was going to die at any moment. Back and forth to the hospital, you know, just that whole roller coaster. So, the next trip down, in January 2003, Dad said, 'Have you seen the video?' I said, 'No.' He says, 'Well, come on in the office. I'll show it to you.' So he and June and I went in, and they showed it to me. Of course I was just sobbing. June was just sitting there kind of just patting me. And then she says, 'Well, it was much worse, but we took some things out.' But they were not affected. They had an artist's eye to the end."

Unfortunately, like "Drive On" by "Delia's Gone" on the first *American Recordings*, the album's best example of Cash's art was buried by the clatter over "Hurt." It was the title track, Cash's own "The Man Comes Around." Encased in Rubin's magnificent production, Cash's lyrics ponder apocalyptic rejection and acceptance discussed in the final book of the New Testament. It is probably the most riveting religious composition from Cash's pen: *Will you partake of that last offered cup/Or disappear into the potter's ground?* And it is another example, the last one, of his dogged desire to spend his secular capital making his gospel music, his testimony. "It's the culmination of a lifetime of that vision," notes Rosanne Cash.

Drawing from a dream in which the Queen of England told him that he was "like a thorn tree in the whirlwind," Cash traced the phrase to the Old Testament book of Job and then proceeded to build a song around it. Cash mined the book of Revelation for the theme of his apocalyptic story and gleaned other verses from the Bible for spice. He even reached back to his hero Paul, who in Acts had recalled the Lord whom he condemned, holding up a mirror to his tyranny: "Saul . . .," the Lord pleaded, "It hurts *you* to kick against the goads." Cash in his song made it *kick against the pricks.*

Cash first took "The Man Comes Around" into his Hendersonville studio with Marty Stuart, who was toting Luther Perkins's Fender Esquire guitar, and another guitarist. Together, the musicians unfurled a gentle yet insistent evocation of the rhythm that Cash, Perkins, and Grant had created in 1955. The cadence would be glossed over when Rubin finally processed it in Los Angeles, but the rough cut was a return to Cash's essence, at least the essence as he had known it in the Sun recording studio in Memphis. As the guitars smartly throbbed behind him, Cash stepped into their rhythm, bouncing from each beat as if it were a springboard. For one last time, Cash became one with his instrumentation, as he sang his song, from his heart. "I knew what we were doing," says Stuart. "I knew how special it was because that's the last time, that right there, check me down, that the original vision of Johnny Cash and the Tennessee Two passed before a microphone." Indeed, if there is an omega to the alpha that was "I Walk the Line," it is "The Man Comes Around."

Tellingly, the liner notes Cash wrote for *The Man Comes Around* in August of 2002, two weeks before a hospitalization, made no mention of "Hurt." Instead, it was his title track that raced his heart. "I wrote and recorded 'The Man Comes Around' early in this project," he wrote, "and for three or four months I recycled that song, over and over, until I'd have to get up out of bed, and turn on the radio. It worked for a while, but my inner playback system always went back to 'The Man Comes Around.'"

Unfortunately, few other playback systems harked back to "The Man Comes Around." It became a stepsibling to "Hurt," and when the album itself was named for Cash's song about God, the title subverted Cash's original intent. The Man became Cash. Those who criticized as sacrilege Cash's cover of Depeche Mode's "Personal Jesus" may have found more fodder in the album title.

———

June appears in the "Hurt" video standing on a small stairway overlooking her gray and drawn husband. She gazes at him, obviously worried, on the brink of tears. June becomes the "sweetest friend" who in Reznor's narrative must be "hurt" by the protagonist. Cash appears unfazed by his own poor health and the song's hopeless sentiment. It falls to June to show the emotional response to death and self-destruction, she who so often shouldered the weight of her husband's spiritual lapses and physical weakness.

Few watching the video in early 2003, however, would have guessed that June's death lurked so much nearer to that moment than Cash's. Family members had noted slips in her certain step as early as 2001, but engrossed in concerns about Cash's well-being, they gave them little thought. "For me it had been a year or longer that she would get real spacey and weird," recalls Jimmy Tittle. "She'd say things, and you'd go, 'What's she on?' She did her album [in 2002], and had a hard time remembering things. We thought she had dementia or Alzheimer's. That's what we thought it was. So it was obvious. She still had a sweet nature. She never was mean, ever."

Rosanne points to Anita Carter's death on July 29, 1999, in tracking the start of June's decline. "She was so down after Anita died," she says. "Usually she was so up. She would always bounce back, and even though she was using a fair share of pain medication herself, she was just kind of charming and [always] getting everything together. But after Anita died, you could tell that she was depressed and distracted and not her usual self." It didn't help, says Rosanne, that both of June's daughters, Rosey and Carlene, were hard into drugs and were constant sources of controversy in the family. "That was really, really painful to her. Guilt, fear, anxiety, grief."

Almost two years after Anita's death, on June 23, 2001, the Cash and Carter clans gathered in southwestern Virginia for what Cash called "grandchildren's week," a celebration that Cash had devised for the progeny to honor June. "We had two nurses with us," recounts Rosanne, "and they would help [Dad] move around and take his meds. He was pretty sick by that time. His diabetes was really up, as well as everything else he was dealing with, the circulatory problems. There was a lot going on, and Rosey showed up that week. It was so stressful. She was so awful. But he did a beautiful, beautiful thing that week. He wrote this thing, this very elaborate thing on this card, this page that each grandchild had to read to June. And it was the exact same thing, so it became like this mantra about 'to the lady Grandmother.' It was beautiful. He was very, very, very sweet that week."

June, though, was very philosophical that week. Abloom in a cotton dress and large slouching sun hat, she pulled Rosanne close to her and told her how happy she had been with Cash. For a moment, it was as if June was saying goodbye, but Rosanne dismissed the thought, chalking it up to June's unconventionality.

In April of 2003, an ambulance rushed June to Baptist Hospital, a cement monolith just blocks from Music Row in Nashville. She was suffering from heart failure, but doctors managed to stabilize her, and after a few days, they sent her home to Hendersonville. But the drama was far from over. At home for only twelve days, she was dispatched back to the hospital, where doctors detected a valve problem that was denying oxygen to her blood, the probable explanation for the mental confusion that Tittle and others had witnessed in June over the preceding year. She consented to valve replacement surgery, but appeared to be losing hope. Although she endured the surgery and showed signs of a promising recovery, June confided to Kathy Cash her belief that she was near the end.

Early in the morning on the day after surgery, June went into massive cardiac arrest and was placed on a respirator. Her brain was no longer functioning. On May 12, her husband allowed the respirator to be removed. And, like Jack Cash, she lingered for days.

Cash remained close, shuttling back and forth between the hospital and home, and finally quartering himself in a suite upstairs from her room. During the nights he stayed in the hospital, he struggled to sleep because of his worrying, so every few hours, a nurse would push him in his wheelchair down to her side. "It was gut-wrenching," says Tittle.

On May 15, while Cash and his children and stepchildren gathered near, June died as evening fell over Nashville. The town that she had first embraced in the 1950s, long before her husband found peace there, paused and remembered one of its own. She had sent tongues wagging in the 1960s with her affair with Cash, but she had ultimately garnered respect for sustaining her famous husband and for her royal status as a daughter of country music.

In the first of many reminders of June's generosity that cropped up immediately after her death, Cash directed their accountant to the hospital room where their children were gathering to grieve and commune. He arrived an hour after she passed. "[He] handed out checks to all the children that were substantial because June's wish was she didn't want anybody to worry about anything immediately after her death because they had enough sorrow and things to worry about," says Tittle. "That was amazing. [The accountant said], 'June wanted you to have this;

she didn't want you to worry about what you were going to wear to the funeral or how you're going to get there.' I mean, isn't that sweet?"

Amid the wailing of children and the firm hands of comfort pressing on his shoulder, Cash took calls of condolence and listened blankly to the reassurances of friends. Cash dreaded life and home without June's formidable feminine presence. She had brought order and comfort to his world. Now, devoid of her joyous howls and the graceful clatter that followed her through each room, the house on the lake was bound to grow silent.

Despite the stunning effect of June's death, Cash insisted on visiting the funeral home to make arrangements for her services and internment. He couldn't see the caskets in the showroom, as his vision was rapidly fading, but he brushed his swollen hands along their silky interiors, repeating in a gravelly murmur that his baby needed a soft resting place. At the funeral, he could barely speak, nodding his head and whispering thanks to those who stopped to console him. Nobody believed he would survive June's death.

Cash, though, could see a way to the light. He knew that to live he must work. Otherwise, he'd find the days too excruciating to endure. He instructed John Carter to assemble some musicians and warm up the consoles at the cabin studio. "After June passed away," says Marty Stuart, "the microphone was his place of business."

Cash tackled dozens of songs and experimented with new sounds, allowing John Carter to bring in Mac Wiseman for a bluegrass timbre and letting loose Marty Stuart's guitar for a blues flavor that no Cash recording had ever exhibited. At the same time, it was plainly evident that somebody hadn't given up on mashing sappy good-bye songs into Cash's hands. Tittle recalls Tommy Cash suggested "My Way," but in Marty Stuart's telling, Rick Rubin pitched the idea just before Cash was to record at Stuart's house. "[Cash] came over to record here, brought all the gear in," says Stuart. "John Carter came in and said, 'Uh, Dad, Rick wants you to try 'My Way.' And John said, "My Way"? What for? Why "My Way"?' 'I don't know [replied John Carter]. 'He just thinks it's a good idea.' And so I started almost like an Orbison kind of beat. But what we were so proud of was we got about halfway through the verse and the chorus. And every one of us were so proud of ourselves for not knowing the song."

Drooping in a wheelchair, his face gaunt from grief and illness, Cash may have felt satisfaction in forgetting "My Way." It was harmless rebellion, rejecting the ballad that had escorted his rival Elvis Presley into death. Cash and company turned from the failed "My Way" and in the ensuing weeks tried a marvelous assortment of material, including Larry Gatlin's "Help Me," Bruce Springsteen's "Further On (Up the Road)," and the spiritual "There's Ain't No Grave Gonna Hold My Body Down." When the takes drained him and he needed rest, Cash reclined his fragile body on a nearby sofa before staggering back to try again. Did anybody note the parallels with Jimmie Rodgers's final session in 1933, when, plagued by tuberculosis, the Singing Brakeman had turned often to a cot sitting in New York's Victor Studios?

When John Carter had no sessions scheduled, the days at home gnawed at Cash. He wept for June, virtually every thought riddled by her memory. He told the children to take what they wanted of her jewelry and vast antique collection, but he wanted pictures, blown up so he could see them, and letters written in June's hand, as if they were lifelines to her.

~

It often fell to Cindy Cash to see to many of her father's small wishes. In June, she had come up from her home near Jackson, Mississippi, for a short visit, but she ended up remaining in Hendersonville for much of the three months before her father's death. "He would not let me leave," she says. "I was only going to stay for a couple of weeks, and I ended up not leaving at all. Everyday he would say, 'You're not leaving, right?' He was like a little boy again."

At her father's behest, Cindy had the cover of June's *Wildwood Flower* album painted on the elevator in the house. And as his eyesight worsened, she bought fluorescent tape to mark routes around the house and the armrests of his wheelchair, which were proving difficult obstacles when he tried to sit. She stuck large letters and numbers on objects and entrances that he could no longer see very well. By August, she says, he was virtually blind. "Finally one day I said, 'Dad, look at me,'" she recalls. "And he said, 'What?' Like something was wrong. I said, 'Just look at me.' And I was sitting in front of the window in his office, and he was at his desk, and he goes, 'Okay.' And he's just looking. And I said, 'What do you see when you look at me? What does your actual vision see when you look at my face?' He says, 'I see the shape of your head, and then I see a light around it and that's all.' I said, 'You can't see my eyes anymore? You can't see my features?' And he goes, 'No, honey.'"

Cindy remembers just one moment of visual clarity during the entire time of her stay in Hendersonville. She and Cash's sister Reba had taken him to the cemetery to visit June's grave. Cindy and Reba sat him in a golf cart, and a cemetery employee drove them the short distance to June. While Cash strained to see the ground, Cindy sighed, relieved that her father couldn't see the marker and be plunged more deeply into sorrow. "Well his eyes must have come into focus," she says, "because you could see the instant that he read that stone and saw her name because he started hollering to her, 'I'm coming baby. I'm coming.' I said, 'Dad, don't say that. You're not leaving me.' He turned to apologize to me, but then he's like, 'But I *am*. I'm coming to heaven.' And he knew she was waiting for him."

Back in his office, the pictures of June's warm face around him, he would grieve. He picked up the telephone and pretended to talk to her. At night, his darkness was filled with her elusive image. He dreamt that she was calling him, that she was next to him. Sleeping alone in their room disquieted him, so he moved to a small hospital bed in his small book-lined office. There his daughters could hear his muffled sobs. "I would think I heard him calling me or something," says Cindy, "and I would go in there and he would be, 'I miss her.' Just like a child. He would talk to her. It was just devastating."

Inevitably, his spirits collapsed as the sun fell. The gloaming, he'd say, invoking the Scottish term for evening, was the hardest part of the day. It was the hour when she had passed. He'd stare out the office window, absorbing what he could discern of the shimmering of the setting sun on the lake.

~

Praying for sleep yet unable to find it on his own, he relied on his daughters to soothe him and bring him rest. Kathy was often by his side at the gloaming. "He wanted to go to sleep," she says, recalling one restless night. "He said, 'Baby, talk to me until I go to sleep.' So I talked to him, and he said, 'Tell me a story.' I said, 'Once upon a time there was a daddy that would not go to sleep.' We were talking like that. He got to laughing, and then finally he closed his eyes, and I thought he was asleep so I just sat there, looking out the window and watching him. And I started crying, thinking about how sad he was and how quiet the house was, and I eased myself up out of the chair, and he popped his eyes up and said, 'Where do you think you're going?' I said, 'I thought you were asleep.' He said, 'No. That doesn't happen near like I wish it would. Just sit here with me.' So I sat there another hour at least until he was snoring and sound asleep."

Rosanne took her turn with her father in the evenings when she was in town, but she also joined him in the mornings, the early mornings, at four or five o'clock, when he rose for coffee. They sat in the dim light of his office and chatted on topics mundane and significant. In the morning, he'd wake with a clarity that slowly drained as the day wore on and the nurses arrived to shave him, dress him, help him in the bathroom, and administer his pills. "We had some beautiful conversations in the last few months of his life," says Rosanne. "I mean deep, some of the best conversations of my life, things I'll always treasure, where he would say something to me that was so meaningful. Then you think, 'He was probably on thirty medications at that point.' And, yet, he could still come out."

In my interviews with Rosanne, she twice returned to a conversation she had with her father about the baptism of her son, Jake. It seems to her to be the redemptive moment in what she has come to call the "horrible, horrible summer" between June's death and Johnny's. Her Jewish husband, John Levanthal, understandably resisted her wishes to have their son baptized in an Episcopalian church in Manhattan. But after long discussions, Leventhal relented with the caveat that he not attend the ceremony. The caveat was to Rosanne almost as bad as not baptizing their child at all. She stewed about it for months, took it to her minister, but never thought to broach the dilemma with her father, until the summer of 2003. "I told him the whole situation," explains Rosanne. "I said, 'What would you do? This is really important to me and we're at an impasse.' And he was just so thoughtful. The first thing he said was totally not what you would expect him to say. He said, 'I understand how John feels.' This is a man who's Southern Baptist. He said, 'I really understand that. He has respect for his father, and as a Jew, this is not something that's part of his experience that he could understand or accept. You have to go to him and ask him if he really is okay with you doing it apart from him. And then if he is, you have to just let that go, that need to have him there, and go ahead and do it.' I thought, 'I waited years to ask him, and he gives me the perfect advice.'"

As Rosanne surely must have realized when her father imparted his advice, letting go was central to his philosophy. It had pulled him through years of guilt and disappointments, personal and professional. When his sins threatened to complicate or burden his journey, he invoked God's promise of forgiveness and let them go. His prescient advice to Rosanne was his personal creed, his mental-health remedy. How else had this man coped with the pain he'd inflicted on himself and others, as well as the commercial rejection in the 1980s and 1990s that had left him playing to half-empty houses and bereft of a recording contract? A different philosophy may have driven him from music, indeed, from life. "Drive on, it don't mean nothin'," he'd written in 1993.

Little more than a month after June's demise, his desire to feel close to her led him back to Hiltons, Virginia. On June 21st, the day before June's birthday, Cash emerged from the house they owned and ambled to the Carter Fold, where he performed for a thousand people. "I don't know hardly what to say tonight about being up here without her," he whispered. "The pain is so severe there is no way of describing it. It really hurts."

Two weeks later, he returned to the same stage. Helped from a black Mercedes into a wheelchair and pushed to the rustic boards, he interrupted a local bluegrass band to perform once again. His face seared red and bristly gray hair combed back, he stilled the crowd with a seven-song set before handing back the stage to the featured band. "I tell you," one of the pickers remarked afterward, "when he sat down and strummed that guitar and started talking and started to sing, it was Johnny Cash down to the ground."

Back home in Hendersonville a week later, Cash received his first wife. According to Rosanne, she was seeking his permission to write a book based on the volumes of letters the two had exchanged during Cash's air force years. Encamped in Nashville for a week or so, Vivian visited with Johnny on three or four separate occasions. They had never lost touch, hearing news about each other through their daughters, reuniting at the weddings of children and grandchildren, and catching up backstage if she happened to attend a show in California. She had never completely let go of him, and now more than thirty years after their divorce, she was so much more grounded in herself. No longer the gawky, unsure woman Cash left at home while he toured and gallivanted, she approached him firmly and with some regret. "I guess on an unconscious level she wanted to say good-bye," says Rosanne, "or to get some kind of resolution. I'm sure that, somewhere in her unconscious, she knew that he was going soon. And she always said then afterwards what a good meeting that it was and how glad she was that she went. So I guess that was very important for them. For her anyway. I don't know how my dad felt about it."

Cash was actually happy to see Vivian. They took pictures with Cindy. Vivian tried to comfort him, and he endorsed her book.

~

In the wake of Vivian's visit, worries about Cash's medical treatment became high drama as Rosanne and Kathy loudly protested his care. His daughters suspected that his doctor was snarling him with useless medication and hospitalization. Intense discussions erupted while the emaciated Cash looked on, helpless to gain much voice in the matter. About the only aspect of his care that he refused to suffer quietly were the hospital stays. Doctors ordered him to stay put in the hospital after June's death, but he had shirked their orders after a day, checking himself out and speeding back to Hendersonville.

In early August, Cash was back in the hospital again, this time in the intensive care unit. But he was still bucking hospitalization. Kathy dutifully paid a visit, and two hours after returning home, she got a call from her bedridden father, who should not have had access to a phone in the ICU. He admitted that he'd ordered a nurse to bring him one. Kathy says he was just desperate to leave. "He said, 'I need you to come bust me out of here,'" she recounts. "I said, 'Dad, I can't do that. You're in the ICU. You can't just leave. You're hooked up to all that stuff.' He said, 'No. You got to bring me a Snicker's Bar, a Coke, and some crackers and peanut butter and bust me out of here.' It was so sad. I hung up and just started crying."

Later in the evening, Kathy appeared in her father's room with a bag of crackers and peanut butter and Diet Coke and found a patient still intent on escape. Hobbling herself after a recent hernia operation and a chronic tremor disorder that could have only come from her mildly spastic father, she was in no condition to spirit her father out of downtown Nashville. "I said, 'There's no way you and I are going to sneak out of here.' He just laughed, and he said, 'Well, as long as I have company, that's all I care about. I'm just so tired of being here.' I said, 'I know you are. We'll get you out of here.' I lay in the recliner and slept next to him all night. He kept waking up, and we'd watch CNN, and we'd talk a little bit."

~

Throughout the summer, Kathy Cash reported Cash's doctor to state medical authorities, but it seemed borne of desperation and even Cash questioned her. Rick Rubin, who had dispatched a faith healer to lay hands on June during her final hours, persuaded a sports physician named Phil Maffetone to treat him. A believer in the power of wholesome foods and skeptical of medication, Maffetone cut the Snickers and Cokes from Cash's diet and prescribed an ambitious exercise regimen.

Ordering Cash to cast off the clunky diabetic shoes that steadied him when he tried to walk, Maffetone had him walking better than he had in months. The doctor also escorted Cash through aquatic therapy in Cash's swimming pool, chiropractic care, and muscle-toning exercise. "We walked into the bedroom one day," explains Kathy, "and Dad's walking across the room. He said, 'Look at me. Look at me. No walker, no crutches, no nothing, no wheelchair.' We were so excited."

The treatment buoyed Cash. He believed he'd be able to attend the MTV Music Awards in New York, where the video "Hurt" was to be presented as a nominee for video of the year. He envisioned his body walking across the stage of Radio City Music Hall to accept the award, should he be victorious. Planning past New York, he had also booked air passage to Los Angeles and rented a house there so that he could return to another round of recording with Rubin after the awards.

The optimism notwithstanding, Cash still seemed adrift and unusually reliant on his daughters, who as a troika had come to replace June as a source of strength, aid, and comfort. (Daughter Tara visited, too, but she lived with her family in the Pacific Northwest and could only leave her small children for short periods.) Rosanne, like her sisters, observed that he could be childlike when faced with uncertainty. In the midst of promoting her *Rules of Travel* album, she was trying to visit biweekly, but Cash would have preferred more frequent visits. "I had been there for two days, and he thought I was leaving the next morning," she recalls. "And I said, 'No, Dad. I have to go back today.' His face just fell like a child's. And he said, 'I'm so disappointed I'm not going to have coffee with you in the morning.' And I had to take him by the shoulders, literally, and say, 'Dad, now remember, I would be really disappointed too if I knew I wasn't going to see you in two weeks, because you're coming up for the MTV awards, remember? 'Oh yeah,' [he repeated]. 'I remember. I'm coming up for the MTV awards.' It was so . . . like a four-year-old."

～

Cash's office booked rooms at the Plaza Athénée in anticipation of the awards and even sketched out who would ride in whose limousine from hotel to ceremony. But it was all for naught. Out of deference to the legend's ill health, MTV informed Lou Robin days before the show that his video had not been chosen. It would win for cinematography only.

Robin contacted Cash with the bad news, and Cash, knowing Rosanne was anticipating his arrival, called her to relay the message. Her reaction must have made him wince. "I went ballistic on the vote," she exclaims. "I said, 'I'm going to firebomb their offices, Dad. I have no respect for them. They are over with me. This is the most disrespectful thing I've ever seen.' I went and just flipped out on the phone for a minute, and he didn't say anything. And then when I finished, he said, 'Well.' That's all he said. Like, you can't do anything about this."

In all likelihood, Cash would not have made it to New York even if the plaudits were his. On Monday, August 24th, doctors admitted him to the hospital with peritonitis, and he remained there until September 9th. Kathy Cash doubts the diagnosis, citing Maffetone's belief that it was a drug reaction that resembled the symptoms of an abdominal disorder.

On September 11th, Cash slouched in his office, having bid goodbye to Cindy, who had left to spend a few days with her mother in California. He was in the midst of a session with Maffetone, who was staying in a hotel on Johnny Cash Parkway. They were saying little; then Cash turned to Maffetone and said, "It's time." Figuring that Cash was ready to end their session and go to a recording session, he left Cash and returned to the hotel.

Later that afternoon, Kathy was startled by a telephone call from Cash's niece and office manager Kelly Hancock, who said Cash's nurses had just called the ambulance because her dad was in "bad shape." As Kathy arrived at Baptist Hospital to find her father in the emergency room receiving harried resuscitation, Rosanne headed for the airport in New York. Cash's brother and sisters and their spouses gathered in the ER waiting room, while the doctors relocated the wispy Arkansas gentleman to the intensive care unit. Stabilized but entangled in yards of tubes and hoses, Cash reclined while John Carter, Kathy, and Rosanne prayed with him and reassured him. "He knew we were there," recounts Kathy. "But he couldn't talk. He was struggling, and he was squeezing our hands, and you could tell he was kind of panicking." Around midnight, John Carter plodded up to the eighth floor to lie down, while Rosanne and Kathy nestled in recliners in a glass-walled room across from where Cash was fitfully resting. They could see their father.

Both daughters had dozed off when Kathy heard a nurse say that her father's doctor was on her way to his room. Kathy bolted up and queried the nurse, who advised her to wake her sister and find her brother. Rosanne lurched from a deep sleep, and the nurses roused John Carter from his bed upstairs. The siblings gathered around their father, hugging him, kissing him, and telling him it was okay if he left them. "We didn't want him to be in pain anymore," says Kathy. After ten minutes, he was gone. The nurses looked at their watches. It was 2:00 a.m.

~

A little more than two years later, as Hollywood's Johnny Cash story shimmered on movie screens across America, Marshall Grant slept and dreamed in his home in Hernando, Mississippi. It was fifty-one years after picking up a bass, twenty-five years after Cash fired him, and six years since he reunited with Cash on a New York stage. Grant's night travels took him, as they do every night, to the early days. Cash and the Tennessee Two rumble on stage, their hair greased back, sweat glistening on their faces, spotlights glancing off the steel microphone stands and polished wood of the singer's guitar. "It's always good dreams," says Grant after another night. "We go out and do shows. We do everything and have so much fun. He's not wiped out. That's one good thing about my dreams. My dreams are all of J.R. It's never about this guy they called Johnny . . . and I can live with that."

~

NOTES

INTRODUCTION

"I want a place": Author interview with Kathy Cash Tittle, 17 August 2004.

In life, I am told: Ibid.

Songwriter, musician, and former Cash son-in-law: "Words on Cash," http://www.tennessean.com (September 12, 2003).

Irish rocker Bono: Jason Fine, ed. *Cash*. (New York: Crown Publishers, 2004), 208.

"I have unshakable": Kurt Loder, "Johnny Cash: The Final Interview," *Record Collector* (September 2004).

In his lifetime: The financial ledgers of Johnny Cash's former manager Saul Holiff (made available to me courtesy of Jonathan Holiff) reveal that Dial Books paid Cash $6,250 for his participation in the biography *Winners Got Scars, Too: The Life and Legends of Johnny Cash* (1971).

CHAPTER ONE: DELIVERANCE

"Cotton went down": Christopher Wren. *Winners Got Scars, Too: The Life and Legends of Johnny Cash*. 1971. (New York: Country Music/Ballantine Books, 1974), 29.

"[Dave] hated grandpa": Author interview with Kathy Cash Tittle, 22 September 2004.

Perhaps to burn fear into the boy: Ibid.

Many decades later: Ibid.

"Men would stop him": Ibid.

For that reason: Cindy Cash. *The Cash Family Scrapbook* (New York: Crown Publishers, 1997), 11.

As Cash himself later explained: Johnny Cash. Interview. *Ralph Emery: On the Record with Johnny Cash.* Network Enterprises, Inc. 1997. To confuse the matter of Cash's given name further, the Cash family's local newspaper announced the February 26, 1932, birth of "John R." Perhaps Ray placed the notice. *Cleveland County Herald* (March 9, 1932).

Long after the Depression: Author interview with Cash Tittle.

His son, who was preparing: "Jim Lindsey, 45, Commits Suicide,": *Cleveland County Herald* (July 19, 1933).

"We heard that we could buy twenty acres": Wren, 34.

The *Cleveland County Herald* detailed: "Cash Loses Heavy in Blaze on Farm," *Cleveland County Herald* (November 14, 1934).

"Sometimes Moma would cry": Johnny Cash with Patrick Carr. *Cash: The Autobiography* (New York: Harper San Francisco, 1997), 15.

"It was a nicer house": Wren, 39.

One colonist said: Author interview with Everett Henson, 11 August 2004.

"Several months ago": A. Aaron. Memo to Wendall Lund. 19 February 1936. (Works Progress Administration, NA, RG 69).

Another believed that Dyess colonists: Author interview with Henson. Henson is referring to his mother here.

"There are quite a few": Ibid.

"Those same officials": Ibid.

And nobody knew: Author interview with A.J. Henson, 11 August 2004.

"There are and will be": Aaron. Memo to Wendall Lund.

A farmer from Clay County: Ibid.

"There was a man": Ed Salamon, "Johnny Cash Tells the Stories Behind His Greatest Hits," *Country Music* (July/August 1980).

"He had opened all the doors": Ibid.

"I got to remembering": Ibid.

"He was a strict disciplinarian": Author interview with A.J. Henson.

Ray's hand and harsh tongue: Author interview with Roy Cash, Jr., 16 August 2004.

"It was a stray": Cash with Carr, 237.

He'd use the few dollars: Author interview with Milton Stansbury, 19 October 2004.

"I . . . loved the stories": Holly George-Warren, "Growing Up Country," *The Journal of Country Music* 19: 1 (1997).

He also played: Cash with Carr, 74.

"I drifted into": Roy Cash, "Wild Western Outlaw," *The Colony Herald* (May 29, 1936).

"He was one of the nicest": Author interview with Stansbury.

"Jack was my protector": Johnny Cash. *Man in Black*. (New York: Warner Books, 1976), 30.

CHAPTER TWO: GUILT

Later he recalled: Cash, 31–32.

"Jack was trying": Author interview with Stansbury.

"Someone knows": Ibid.

"There was a neighbor": Nick Tosches, "Chordless in Gaza: The Second Coming of John R. Cash," *The Journal of Country Music* 17:3 (1995).

J.R.'s eldest daughter: Author interview with Rosanne Cash, 3 March 2005.

"Grandpa always kind of blamed": Author interview with Cash Tittle.

He accentuated the regret: Cash, 40–41.

Such unanimous: Author interview with A.J. Henson.

"He was devastated": Author interview with Rosanne Cash, 7 July 2004.

The next day: Cash with Carr, 27.

"This is why I'm here": Author interview with Stansbury.

"He fitted in well": Author interview with A.J. Henson.

"He was the best friend": Author interview with Stansbury.

"He was a really good teacher": Ibid.

"When we'd be picking": Louise Cash. Interview. *Johnny Cash: The Man, His World, His Music*. Sanctuary, 2005.

"He was more visionary": Author interview with A.J. Henson.

"He was the one": Ibid.

"We used to get": Author interview with Stansbury.

"He walked to our house": George-Warren, *The Journal of Country Music*.

"We weren't a musical bunch": Author interview with A.J. Henson.

It could have been another vein of influence: Ibid.

A schoolmate remembers: Ibid.

"I was at Jesse's": Johnny Cash, liner notes, *American Recordings*, American Recordings, 9 45520-2, 1994.

"No one would": Author interview with Stansbury.

CHAPTER THREE: DREAMS

"I don't know": Author interview with A.J. Henson.

"We didn't pay much attention": Author interview with Stansbury.

"God has His hand": Johnny Cash, liner notes, *Silver*, Columbia, JC 36086, 1979.

On May 19, 1950: Christopher Wren in his biography stated that Cash performed "Drink to Me Only with Thine Eyes" at his high school graduation, and other sources have echoed Wren. The program from the ceremony merely states that Cash is to perform a "special." In 1973, Cash stated on a recording that he sang "Drink to Me Only with Thine Eyes" at the 1949 high school graduation in Dyess. The reference to the song and performance is on the Cash album *Personal File*, Sony Music, 2006.

Stansbury had graduated: Author interview with Stansbury.

For months before: Author interview with Roy Cash, Jr., 11 October 2004.

Stansbury recalls: Author interview with Stansbury.

"Grandpa just said bye": Author interview with Cash Tittle.

Recalling neighbors' and friends' experiences: Author interview with Stansbury.

"Here I was": Author interview with Cash Tittle.

Fed up with the monotonous work: Wren, 75.

Many young recruits also believed: Author interview with Nesbit Bowers, 17 May 2005.

After seven months: Author interview with Bill Craig, 1 June 2005.

"He was nice looking": Author interview with Joyce Criswell, 29 September 2004.

Cash did have his father's beat-up Ford sedan: Cash, 54–55.

After a few: Author interview with Cash Tittle.

Cautious eyes were always trained: Author interview with Bowers.

Cash was among the elite: Author interview with Craig.

"Those planes would fly in": Ibid.

He most always collared the sound: Ibid.

"We would catch": Ibid.

It was nothing: Ibid.

Sauntering like John Wayne: Author interview with Dwayne Mueller, 27 May 2005.

"All he could talk": Author interview with Bill Carnahan, 9 March 2006.

The farm boy from Dyess: Author interview with Cash Tittle.

Cash found an apartment: Author interview with Carnahan.

Her mother drank: Author interview with Cindy Cash, 13 October 2005

Cash hinted: Cash, 60.

In Zurich on a three-day pass: Author interview with Mueller.

The promise of reunification: Author interview with Craig.

"This happened every day": Ibid.

"One night . . .": Wren, 81–82. Some who served with Cash question his story of throwing a typewriter out the window, claiming that there were no windows in the attic room where the radio operators worked. However, at least two former radio operators whom I interviewed recall that there were windows in the room. Bill Craig remembers a window near Cash's position: "The window was certainly big enough to throw a typewriter out and you wouldn't even miss it. So that could have happened." Author interview with Craig.

Bill Craig, who roomed with Cash: Author interview with Craig.

"The three of us": Ibid.

"I was locked there": Kenny Berkowitz, "No Regrets," *Acoustic Guitar* (June 2001).

He told his protégé: Author interview with Marty Stuart, 19 September 2003.

Privately, he told manager Lou Robin: Author interview with Lou Robin, 16 February 2004.

Not until Cash re-recorded: Author interview with Bruce Jenkins, 24 February 2004.

"At the time": Tim Perlich, "Johnny Cash: Hard-living Legend Finds Youthful Alternative to Nashville Grind," *Now Magazine* (November 21–27, 1996).

CHAPTER FOUR: MEMPHIS

"When I went": Wren, 83.

"I'd be at home": Wren, 84.

"I had this funny little feeling": Nick Spitzer interview with Marshall Grant, 11 July 2005.

"[Cash] had an": Author interview with Grant, 10 July 2003.

"You ought to": Ibid.

"We went back": Ibid.

Marshall scrawled the: Ibid.

"The sound of Johnny Cash": Ibid.

At the end: Author interview with Cash, Jr..

The boys tried: Ibid.

Roy Jr. recalls: Ibid.

With the boys: The exact dates of Cash and the band's KWEM broadcasts are not documented, but a reference in the show to the opening of the movie *Apache* staring Burt Lancaster in Memphis suggests that the KWEM broadcasts may have begun as early as August of 1954. If this is so, Cash, Perkins, and Grant had moved quickly from their initial meeting to make their name known to the Memphis radio audience.

Cash recalled: Wren, 91.

The show aired: Author interview with Marshall Grant, 18 January 2006. According to Grant, the three musicians met disc jockey Dick Stuart (a.k.a. Poor Richard) at KWEM. Stuart would be the group's first agent, booking them into tiny venues in and around Memphis.

"Black people": Margaret McKee and Fred Chisenall. *Beale Black and Blue: Life and Music on Black America's Main Street* (Baton Rouge and London: Louisiana State University Press, 1981), 75.

Like any country: Richard Wright. *Black Boy* (New York: Harper Perennial, 1993), 270-271.

"He would talk": Peter Guralnick. *Last Train to Memphis: The Rise of Elvis Presley* (Boston: Little Brown, 1994), 61.

"You didn't get": John Braven, liner notes, *Bootin': The Best of the RPM Years*, Ace Records, CHCHD 694, 1998.

"It became a fight": Peter Guralnick, "John R. Cash: I Will Rock 'n' Roll with You (If I Have To)," *Country Music* (July/August 1980).

"He was timid": James D. Kingsley, "Mr. Phillips Met the Appliance Salesman at 706 Union Ave.," *Memphis Commercial Appeal* (c. 1970).

"There was something": Sam Phillips. Interview. *Ralph Emery: On the Record with Johnny Cash*. Network Enterprises, Inc., 1997.

"It has borne": Kingsley, *Memphis Commercial Appeal*.

"We couldn't change": Author interview with Grant.

Billing his new artists: Many have assumed that Phillips hastily labeled the band "Johnny Cash and the Tennessee Two" upon the release of the first single, but a broadcast of Cash's KWEM radio show released by Sony in 2005 indicates Cash and the band were using the appellation as early as 1954.

CHAPTER FIVE: FAME

"John came by": Wren, 98–99.

From the summer: Author interview with Cash, Jr., 16 August 2004.

And the concert: Author interview with Grant.

"The family was": Author interview with Cash, Jr.

Nervous and sad: Author interview with Rosanne Cash, 3 March 2005.

Roy doubted Vivian: Author interview with Cash, Jr.

"I'm fixin' to": Steve Turner. *The Man Called Cash: The Life, Love, and Faith of An American Legend*. (Nashville: W Publishing Group, 2004), 56.

Cash told Ben A. Green: Ben A. Green, "Johnny Cash Achieves 'Life's Ambition,' Wins Opry Hearts," *Nashville Banner* (July 16, 1956).

"Finally, he told": Steve Pond, "Johnny Cash," *Rolling Stone* (December 10–24, 1992).

With Nashville reporter: Green, *Nashville Banner*.

That night Cash: Ibid.

"He'll be every bit as good": Ibid.

"A lot of people": Pond, *Rolling Stone*.

"I really liked": Cash with Carr, 157.

"I can't remember": June Carter Cash, liner notes, *Johnny Cash: Love God Murder*, Sony Music, C3K 63809, 2000.

Davis represented: Author interview with Don Davis, 22 February 2005.

"It just about drove me crazy": Ed Salamon, "Johnny Cash Tells the Stories Behind His Greatest Hits," *Country Music* (July/August 1980).

"I was making": Author interview with Grant, 10 July 2003.

"I heard it": Johnny Cash. Interview. *Fresh Air*. WHYY-FM, 1997.

It was Phillips's art: Author interview with Jack Clement, 3 June 2004.

"It was the seat-of-the-pants kind of thing": Ibid.

"It wasn't that he wasn't interested": Ibid.

"He was a lot more": Jack Clement. Interview with John Lomax III. Country Music Foundation Library and Media Center's Oral History Project. 13 May 1978.

"Cash loved it": Author interview with Clement.

"Everybody around": Ibid.

"Everything was based": Author interview with Grant.

"Constantly, Johnny": Marion Keisker. Interview with Jerry Hopkins. Mississippi Valley Collection, University of Memphis. Undated.

"Finally Cash came": Hank Davis, liner notes, *Johnny Cash: The Sun Years*, Charly Records, Sun Box 5, 1995.

"She knew that": Author interview with Cash, Jr., 11 October 2004.

CHAPTER SIX: CALIFORNIA

"He used to get crazy": Author interview with Billy Walker, 6 August 2001.

"It was a thing": Larry Linderman, "Penthouse Interview: Johnny Cash," *Penthouse* (August 1975).

"When John got out": Author interview with Marshall Grant, 3 July 2003.

"Like everybody else": George Riddle. Interview. *Bravo Profiles: Johnny Cash,* Hallway Group Productions, 2001.

"John had this thing": Author interview with Jimmy Tittle, 17 August 2004.

"Stew had a lot": Author interview with Grant, 18 January 2006.

"Like I say," Author interview with Clement.

"There were so many things": Peter Guralnick, "John R. Cash: I Will Rock 'n' Roll with You (If I Have To)," *Country Music* (July/August 1980).

But the A&R man: Author interview with Ken Nelson, 18 September 2005.

The singer agreed: In addition to Columbia, Cash was apparently also courted by Lew Chudd of Imperial Records, which at the time was home to Ricky Nelson, Slim Whitman, and Fats Domino. In a letter to Cash, manager Bob Neal revealed that Chudd had offered Neal a five-thousand-dollar bribe in attempt to lure Cash. Bob Neal. Letter to Johnny Cash. 4 September 1959 (Saul Holiff Collection, courtesy of Jonathan Holiff).

"I looked Johnny straight in the eye": Colin Escott with Martin Hawkins. *Good Rockin' Tonight: Sun Records and the Birth of Rock 'n' Roll.* (New York: St. Martin's Press, 1991), 26.

Sam exploded: Author interview with Clement.

"I got as much": Ibid.

"It used to be": Wally George, "Strictly Off the Record," *Los Angeles Times* (November 15, 1958).

Bob Neal had been told: Neal. Letter to Johnny Cash. The letter from Neal to Cash details Neal's discussions with Bobby Brenner. In an interview with me, Brenner had no memory of pointing Neal to Lee Cooley but conceded that he may have done so. Author interview with Bobby Brenner, 18 January 2006.

A magazine journalist who visited: "Write Is Wrong," *Time* (February 23, 1959).

"We heard about the flood waters": Salamon, *Country Music.*

"I was fighting": Author interview with Grant.

Travis's consumption: Cash with Carr, 161.

"She urged me": Cash with Carr, 145.

Either way: Author interview with Grant, 3 July 2003.

The singer streaked: Author interview with Jim Malloy, 3 June 2004.

"He came in": Ibid.

"Let me tell you something": Ibid.

"I thought it was a good record": Robert Hilburn, "Nothing Can Take the Place of the Human Heart: A Conversation with Johnny Cash," *Rolling Stone* (March 1, 1973).

CHAPTER SEVEN: J.R., JOHN, JOHNNY

Grant oriented Holland: Maxine Brown documents her romance with Cash in her book *Looking Back to See: A Country Music Memoir* (Fayetteville: University of Arkansas Press, 2005), 177.

"He just sat on the stool": Author interview with Marshall Grant, 10 July 2003.

Variety found the film "clumsy": *Variety Film Reviews, 1907–1980, Volume 11.* (New York and London: Garland Publishing, 1983).

Cash had been forced: Nat C. Recht. Letter to Johnny Cash. 11 July 1962 (Saul Holiff collection, courtesy Jonathan Holiff).

Cash and Neal's: Neal, Letter to Johnny Cash.

"We had a terrible argument": Author interview with Saul Holiff, 13 July 2004.

"So I guess you put all those things together": Ibid.

"I'm like a mystery guest:" Author interview with Holiff, 14 July 2004.

"I decided that I had to": Ibid.

"It was a terrible shock": June Carter Cash. *Among My Klediments* (Grand Rapids, Mich.: Zondervan, 1979), 82.

"Once we were in Albuquerque": Carter Cash, 82–83.

"Ring of Fire" framed: Ben Ratliff, "June Carter, a Fixture in Country Music, Dies at 73," *TheNew York Times* (16 May 2003).

"She and I fought a lot of battles": Author interview with Grant, 3 July 2003.

It was, he says, the promise: Author interview with Grant, 18 January 2006.

He'd watch June return home: Author interview with Davis,.

"June got mad": Author interview with Loretta Lynn, 13 February 2002.

CHAPTER EIGHT: BALLADEER

"I got a lot of credit": Hilburn, *Rolling Stone.*

"He liked that": Author interview with Saul Holiff, 13 July 2004.

"I could only whisper": Cash, 85.

"Mr. Cash came highly endorsed": Robert Shelton, "Troupe of Country Musicians Gives Program at Carnegie Hall," *The New York Times* (May 11, 1962).

"I invited him": Hilburn, *Rolling Stone.*

"He was pretty suave": Author interview with Ramblin' Jack Elliott, 1 March 2005.

"It might have been": Ibid.

"He wasn't looking": Peter La Farge. "Johnny Cash," *Sing Out!* (May 1965).

Robert Shelton of *The New York Times*: Robert Shelton, "Symbolic Finale," *The New York Times* (August 2, 1964).

"To find Newport so warm": Robert Shelton. *No Direction Home: The Life and Music of Bob Dylan.* 1986. (New York: Ballantine Books, 1987), 297.

His girlfriend at the time: Elizabeth Thomson and David Gutman, eds. The Dylan Companion. 1990. (New York: Da Capo Press, 2001), 78.

"John wanted to go over": Author interview with Elliott.

Cash's handiness with a car engine: Ibid.

"Bob played us a couple": Ibid.

He turned to Elliott: Ibid.

According to Cash's notes: Johnny Cash, liner notes, *Johnny Cash Sings Ballads of the True West*, Columbia Records, C25 838, 1965.

Elliott learned the aged narrative: Author interview with Elliott.

"I followed trails": Cash, *Johnny Cash Sings Ballads of the True West.*

"I was never a cotton farmer": *Pete Seeger's Rainbow Quest: Johnny Cash and Roscoe Holcomb.* Shanachie Entertainment Corporation. 2005.

"We were heading towards Waterford": Author interview with Holiff.

"He came off the road": Author interview with Rosanne Cash.

"Dad quit coming home": Author interview with Cash Tittle, 17 August 2004.

"All of a sudden": Ibid.

Cash gazed down: Ibid.

~

CHAPTER NINE: SELF-DESTRUCTION

"The whole thing": Author interview with Bill Walker, 2 June 2004.

When Sam Phillips called: Cash, 123.

"The plumbing didn't work": Cash, 122.

Dressed in patent: "Singer Cash Bailed Out," *San Jose News* (October 6, 1965).

"Money from the sale": "Arrest Exposes Johnny Cash's Negro Wife," *The Thunderbolt* (January 1966).

"And that meant contacting newspapers": Author interview with Holiff.

In the months after: John Garabedian, "Singer Johnny Cash Fights the Voice of Hate," *New York Post* (October 6, 1966).

In fact, press accounts: "Hate Groups Gun for Johnny Cash in A Racial Error," *Variety* (October 5, 1966).

"He wrote me": Author interview with Rosanne Cash.

"I don't pretend": Dixie Deen, "Everything Ain't Been Said," *Music City News* (January 1966).

"They say what is wrong": Ibid.

"He stayed in pretty good shape": Wren, 178.

"I think they're billing it": Dixie Deen, *Music City News*.

"He was very, very, very strung out": Author interview with Holiff, 15 July 2004.

"There were pills": Ibid.

"There was something about him": Author interview with Grant, 10 July 2003.

When Holiff struck a deal: Lucky Moeller. Letter to Saul Holiff. 2 October 1967 (Saul Holiff collection, courtesy Jonathan Holiff).

"Your professional behavior": Saul Holiff. Telegram to Johnny Cash. 6 May 1967 (Saul Holiff collection, courtesy Jonathan Holiff).

"We were on a tour": Author interview with Holiff.

"He was as unique": Author interview with Don Reid, 4 June 2003.

Ray wondered: Author interview with Holiff.

The final settlement: Stanley Williford and Howard Hertel, "Singer Johnny Cash Pays $82,000 to U.S. in Fire Case," *Los Angeles Times* (3 July 1969).

He struggled: Author interview with Bob Johnston, 30 October 2003.

Holiff took Cash: Saul Holiff. Letter to Johnny Cash. 31 October 1967 (Saul Holiff collection, courtesy of Jonathan Holiff).

"John had gotten to where we couldn't": Author interview with Grant, 18 January 2006.

"This is a nice album": Peter Reilly, "Entertainment," *Hi Fi/Stereo Review* (January 1968).

"The thing about Johnny": Author interview with Wornall Farr, 4 October 2003.

Throughout their tempestuous relationship: Author interview with Grant.

Grant is one of the story's detractors: Ibid. Marshall Grant may not be alone in his doubt of Cash's Nickajack Cave account. Steve Turner, an authorized biographer, wrote skeptically about the story in his 2004 biography, and Christopher Wren never mentioned it in his 1971 biography. On the other hand, daughter Rosanne Cash accepts the cave story: "The cave was significant," she says "The cave in a way really was a turning point, even if it didn't happen the next day. It's what led him to [sobriety]. . . . The cave was the window to get there." She adds her belief that her father's transformation was also primarily fueled by self-survival: "I can't say what percentage was June and what percentage was a guy whose self-survival instincts came to the surface and he said, 'I've got better things in me and I want to survive. I have a mission to fulfill that I can't fulfill when I'm screwed up all the time.' I'm *certain* that that was in my dad, that that sense of his own mission and his own purpose in his life was coming up. Maybe it was framed by love and lust and this woman wanted him to get straight. Or maybe [June's threats to leave him] came first and then as he started to get his head clear, he saw that he had a mission and that he had to get straight for it. I'm certain that was in there somewhere." (Author interview with Rosanne Cash, 9 March 2006.)

Cash was "in obvious distress": Hugh Waddell, ed. *I Still Miss Someone: Friends and Family Remember Johnny Cash* (Nashville: Cumberland House, 2004), 272–273.

He wrote that June had threatened: Johnny Cash. Letter to Saul Holiff. 21 October 1967 (Saul Holiff collection, courtesy of Jonathan Holiff).

"We could still see": Carter Cash, 86.

"They kept him off": Author interview with Grant.

"There wasn't five days": Author interview with Grant, 3 July 2003.

CHAPTER TEN: FOLSOM

"The Beatles were making": Robert Palmer. *Rock and Roll: An Unruly History*. (New York: Harmony Books, 1995), 110–111.

So Columbia courted: Author interview with Tom Noonan, 8 October 2003.

"Bob is middle aged": Michael Zwerin, "Jazz Journal," *The Village Voice* (September 19, 1968).

Don Law, who boasted: Don Law. Interview with Douglas Green. Country Music Foundation Library and Media Center's Oral History Project. 14 May 1975.

Although Law would continue: Evidently, Columbia Records asked Cash's opinion about the decision to replace Law. I don't know Cash's reaction, but I do know that manager Saul Holiff urged Cash to support Johnston, believing Johnston would stand up to Cash and bring fresh ideas. "However, the time is ripe for a change," wrote Holiff, "and it should be *now*. Saul Holiff. Letter to Johnny Cash. 29 December 1966 (Saul Holiff collection, courtesy Jonathan Holiff).

Marshall Grant sized him up: Author interview with Grant, 3 July 2003.

"He was a wild man": Author interview with Don Reid, 3 June 2003.

"Rather than go": Clive Davis with James Willwerth. *Clive: Inside the Record Business*. 1974. (New York: Ballantine Books, 1976), 258–259.

He wrote in his liner notes: Author interview with Frank Jones, 8 October 2003.

When Cash raised the idea: Marshall Grant claims that a major factor in Columbia's decision to record Cash at Folsom State Prison was its inability to get Cash in the studio for proper recording sessions. Author interview with Grant, 18 January 2006.

"Bob Johnston believed me": Johnny Cash, liner notes, *Johnny Cash At Folsom Prison*, Columbia Records, CS-9639, 1968.

Cash had visited Folsom: Author interview with Earl Green, 15 October 2003.

"While we were there": Bob Garcia, "Johnny Cash at Folsom," *Open City* (July 12, 1968).

"He was a terrific writer": Author interview with Green.

"He said, I'm going out": Author interview with Bob Johnston, 30 October 2003.

"See, that album appealed": Author interview with Noonan.

Richard Goldstein of *The Village Voice*: Richard Goldstein, "Pop Eye," *The Village Voice* (June 6, 1968).

Little more than a year later": Richard Goldstein, "Johnny Cash, 'Something Rude Showing,'" *Vogue* (August 15, 1969).

Rolling Stone editors appeared to be: "The New Bob Dylan: A Little Like Johnny Cash?," *Rolling Stone* (April 6, 1968).

"At the end of the Newport Folk Festival": Jann Wenner, "Country Tradition Goes to Heart of Dylan Songs," *Rolling Stone* (May 25, 1968).

"When he proposed": Author interview with Grant.

At the wedding reception: Ibid.

"The times when I was so down": Linderman, *Penthouse*.

"The main reason for doing this": Garcia, *Open City*.

"The songs in that old book": Johnny Cash, liner notes, *My Mother's Hymn Book*, American Recordings, B0002362-02, 2004.

In a letter he wrote to himself: Cash, 154.

"If you listen to Luther's work": Author interview with Grant, 3 July 2003.

He was like a brother: W.R. Morris, "Legend Credits Guitarist Established Sound," *Music City News* (May 1979).

There was more: Hugh Waddell, ed., 274.

"The two of them": Author interview with Grant, 18 January 2006.

CHAPTER ELEVEN: OVATION

"John was trying to help Carl": Author interview with Grant, 3 July 2003.

Perkins remained: Cash's deference to Perkins' former fame was replicated in relationships with other friends and peers who toiled in Cash's shadow. In 1973, upon learning he was to play the main showroom of the Sahara Tahoe Hotel in Lake Tahoe at the same time Roy Orbison was booked into the hotel's lounge, he worried that Orbison might feel "uncomfortable" with the contrast. At Cash's behest, his sister and office manager Reba Hancock wrote Saul Holiff asking him to alert Orbison's agent of the coincidental bookings. Reba Hancock. Letter to Saul Holiff. 30 March 1973 (Saul Holiff collection, courtesy Jonathan Holiff).

Robert Wootton played country music: Bob Wootton. Interview. *Restore Radio*, WYGG-FM, 2 April 2004.

When he reached the big flatbed truck: Ibid.

When June summoned Wooton: Ibid.

As winter rain lashed outside: Ralph J. Gleason, "Johnny Cash at San Quentin," *Rolling Stone* (May 31, 1969).

"It was surprising": Author interview with Johnston.

A black man: Ralph J. Gleason, "Johnny Cash at San Quentin," *San Francisco Chronicle* (February 26, 1969).

"The new Johnny Cash at San Quentin": Robert Hilburn, "Cash at Finest in 'Quentin' Album," *Los Angeles Times* (June 29, 1969).

The many stories: Author interview with Davis.

"He put them in a large leather toilet kit": Author interview with Holiff, 14 July 2004.

Columbia's marketing people: Author interview with Ron Alexenburg, 22 October 2004.

"I never liked television": Marion Simon, "Smart Money Says Johnny Cash Is the One to Watch This Year," *National Observer* (June 2, 1969).

The producers would have preferred: Ibid.

"I finally convinced": Author interview with Stan Jacobson, 15 June 2004.

Bill Walker recalls: Author interview with Walker.

"The opening number": Author interview with Jacobson.

"One underground columnist: James Stoller, "Riffs," *The Village Voice* (June 12, 1969).

"I wanted [the] network to call me": Tom Dearmore, "First Angry Man of Country Singers," *New York Times Magazine* (September 21, 1969).

"Well, Dylan got a standing ovation": Author interview with Jacobson.

"Another thing I entertained": Stoller, *The Village Voice* (June 12, 1969).

"The show on the whole": Louise Sweeney, "Johnny Cash on TV: Dylan Returns A Call," *Christian Science Monitor* (June 14, 1969).

"I'll continue to do it": Unpublished notes of Jerry Hopkins, 27 September 1969. Mississippi Valley Collection, University of Memphis.

"Perhaps many of the down-South country folk": Tom Dearmore, *The New York Times Magazine* (September 21, 1969).

"We walk out": Author interview with Holiff, 15 July 2004.

"He told me": Author interview with Jacobson.

Cash was touring Australia: Author interview with Walker.

Recently, a baby boomer: Author interview with Morley Bartnoff, 30 November 2004.

⌒

CHAPTER TWELVE: THE GOSPEL ROAD

When a reporter asked him: Linderman, *Penthouse*.

"The Cash performance": Louise Sweeney, "'A Gunfight': at Last A Classic Western," *Christian Science Monitor* (August 28, 1971).

"The [venue's] typical season": Author interview with Holiff.

At the time Robin and his company: Author interview with Lou Robin, 20 August 2003.

"I was probably at the highest point": Author interview with Holiff, 14 June 2004.

"The past couple of years": Leslie Keating, Johnny Cash: 'What I'll Tell My Son about Drugs . . . God . . . Love,'" *Coronet* (December 1970).

"He started traveling": Author interview with Holiff, 15 June 2005.

"Starting in late '68": Author interview with Grant, 3 July 2003.

"From the time John Carter was born": Author interview with Rosanne Cash, 3 March 2005.

"The man who was clean": Ibid.

"I have never known a greater man": Waddell, ed., xii.

"When it came time to leave": Author interview with Jack Shaw, 25 May 2005.

The couple was ultimately lured: Charles P. Conn. *The New Johnny Cash* (Old Tappen, N.J.: Fleming H. Revell Company, 1973), 36–37.

"We'd thought about making a kind of travelog": Peter McCabe and Jack Killian, "Interview with Johnny Cash," *Country Music* (May 1973).

Cash would call it: Johnny Cash, "Gospel Road: A Dream," *Music Journal* 31:7 (1973).

Holiff, draped for the role: Author interview with Holiff.

Although Cash noted the political hat: McCabe and Killian, *Country Music*.

Initially, Elfstrom himself: Richard Maschal, "A Man 'for the People,'" *The Washington Post* (February 16, 1973).

"I had about a 30-minute meeting": McCabe and Killian, *Country Music*.

A chilly winter's rain: Maschal, *The Washington Post*.

The president of Gardner Webb: Ibid.

"We were really trying": Author interview with Holiff.

Despite widespread media coverage: Kenneth L. Woodard, "A Country Jesus," *Newsweek* (January 29, 1973); George Vecsey, "Cash's 'Gospel Road' Film Is Renaissance for Him," *The New York Times* (December 13, 1973).

But Cash never blinked: Johnny Cash. Interview. *Mornings with Siegel*. WLAC-TV. 20 August 1975.

Tellingly, *Rolling Stone*: Robert Hilburn, "Nothing Can Take the Place of the Human Heart: A Conversation with Johnny Cash," *Rolling Stone* (March 1, 1973).

Despite the carelessness: Author interview with Cash, Jr.; Author interview with Holiff.

A despondent serviceman: Conrad J. Ward, "The Day I Met Johnny Cash," *Family Weekly* (October 31, 1971).

On a cold December morning: Author interview with Cindy Cash.

In front of the sentators: U.S. Cong., Senate, Subcommittee on National Penitentiaries of the Committee on the Judiciary, *Parole Legislation*, 92nd Cong., 2nd Sess., S. 2383, S. 2462, S. 2955., S. 3185., S. 3674. (Washington, D.C.: GPO, 1972), 82–83.

"But it was a mistake": Author interview with Grant, 10 July 1973.

"I said to John": Ibid.

"He lived": Johnny Cash. Interview. *Johnny Cash: The Solitary Man Interview with Tim Robbins*. The American Recording Company. 2000.

~

CHAPTER THIRTEEN: LEGEND

"The tour was relentless": Author interview with Rosanne Cash.

"He loved [touring]": Ibid.

"[Columbia] thought it was the way to go": Patrick Carr, "Cash Comes Back," *Country Music* (December 1976).

The *New York Post*: "A Man Called Cash," *New York Post* (December 8, 1969); Jack Newfield, "My Back Pages," *The Village Voice* (December 25, 1969).

A disgruntled reader: R. Padilla, letter to the editor, *Broadside* (August/September 1969).

Critic Richard Goldstein: Bill C. Malone. *Don't Get above Your Raisin': Country Music and the Southern Working Class* (Urbana and Chicago: University of Illinois Press, 2002) 244.

While the fading leader banged out: Jeannette Smyth, "The Grand Ole Opry Ain't Po' No Mo,'" *The Washington Post* (March 18, 1974).

Rosanne, who served as a production assistant: Author interview with Rosanne Cash.

Wayne Kemp, a prolific songwriter: Red O'Donnell, "Copter Caper Gives Writer Kemp . . .," *Nashville Banner* (April 24, 1976).

Kemp planned to record: Author interview with Davis.

"We were at the House of Cash": Author interview with Grant.

"It's like everyone shared": Carr, *Country Music*.

Cash spoke to journalist Patrick Carr: Ibid.

"Jack Clement is always around": Ibid.

"He called me": Author interview with Clement.

By the time they left New York: Larry Butler, who frequently produced, played piano, and wrote for Cash, is listed as the producer for *Gone Girl*.

Clement and Howard: Patrick Carr, "Johnny Cash's Freedom," *Country Music* (April 1979).

"It's awfully important": Ibid.

"He got to where he'd come over": Author interview with Clement.

"We were playing this show": Author interview with Grant, 3 July 2003.

"I always gave this little countdown": Author interview with Grant, 18 January 2006.

~

CHAPTER FOURTEEN: ADDICTION

"There was this element": Author interview with Rosanne Cash, 7 July 2004.

Pianist Earl Poole Ball: Author interview with Earl Poole Ball, 18 September 2005.

Nelson's 1978 success: Author interview with Rick Blackburn, 21 January 2005.

Yetnikoff's command: Ibid.

From where Blackburn stood: Ibid.

When they saw new artists: Ibid.

"Cash wasn't getting the good songs": Ibid.

"When I got to the show": Author interview with Marty Stuart, 21 September
2004.

"He knew who his audience was": Ibid.

One April night: Ibid.

"He had horns on stage": Ibid.

"The record people": Bill Flanagan, "Johnny Cash, American," *Musician* (May
1988).

"We were just in awe": Author interview with Stuart.

"We went to the cabin": Ibid.

Tittle was miffed: Author interview with Tittle, 17 August 2004.

"It was really ugly": Author interview with Cash Tittle.

Cash leaped up: Ibid.

"I never shot": Ibid.

"We didn't talk": Author interview with Tittle.

For Kathy's part: Author interview with Cash Tittle.

"He saw": Author interview with Tittle.

He said years later: Flanagan, *Musician*.

Stuart observed: Author interview with Stuart.

"Once again": Ibid.

"Dad was a little scared": Author interview with Cash Tittle.

"Everybody was desperate": Author interview with Tittle.

"He liked drugs": Author interview with Tittle, 23 September 2004.

Numerous visits: "Johnny Cash Enters Betty Ford Drug Center," *The Washington
Post* (December 21, 1983).

For twenty years: Carter Cash, 89.

"I give her credit": Author interview with Tittle.

Although June went: Marshall Grant is my source regarding June's contemplation
of divorce. Author interview with Grant, 18 January 2006.

"In other words": Author interview with Tittle.

"He knew something": Ibid.

"It sent a shiver": Ibid.

"He came out": Ibid.

"She stayed with him ": Ibid.

"At that point": Author interview with Hugh Waddell, 1 May 2006.

Indeed, as Rosanne observes: Author interview with Cash, 9 March 2006.

"That was very, very important": Author interview with Waddell.

"He wasn't concerned": Ibid.

In the late 1980s: Author interview with Hugh Waddell, 14 July 2005; Author interview with Tittle.

"As much as I know": Author interview with Cash.

Late one night: Author interview with Cash Tittle.

"We just said": Ibid.

CHAPTER FIFTEEN: BRANSON

"My daddy's a patriot": Linderman, *Penthouse.*

Instead, Ray would acidly remark: Author interview with Cash Tittle, 22 September 2004.

"I never saw": Ibid.

"I do think": Ibid.

One day in her teens: Author interview with Rosanne Cash, 10 March 2006.

As he weakened: Author interview with Tittle, 22 September 2004.

"[Cash] was way down the road": Author interview with Stuart.

"Yet another trail": Ibid.

When Stuart finally listened: Ibid.

"I remember [Cash] played it": Ibid.

His 1985 album: Johnny Cash, liner notes, *Rainbow,* Columbia Records, FC 39951, 1985.

One of Nashville's influential critics: Alanna Nash, "Johnny Cash: Weathering the Storm," *Stereo Review* (March 1986).

"That to me was really significant": Author interview with Rosanne Cash, 7 July 2004.

But then, according to Blackburn: Author interview with Blackburn.

Two days later: Robert K. Oermann, "Reporter's Aim Was in Wrong Direction," *The Tennessean* (July 21, 1986).

Speaking to me: Author interview with Blackburn.

Touring in Canada: David Zimmerman, "'Man in Black' Fires Salvo at Record Label, *USA Today* (July 18, 1986).

Lou Robin merely announced: William C. Trott, "Johnny Cashiered," United Press International (July 17, 1986).

"We had a hit": Author interview with Stuart.

"He was despondent": Author interview with Steve Popovich, 15 July 2004.

At the signing ceremony: Ibid.

Rather, a Michigan radio man: Jack Leaver, "Reaction to Johnny Cash's Death Hits the Local Scene," *Grand Rapids Press* (September 13, 2003).

"Cash actually sounds": Bob Allen, "Record Reviews," *Country Music* (September/October 1987).

Popovich believed: Author interview with Popovich.

"Well, a lot of times": Author interview with Clement.

Tittle, Stuart, and Clement's engineer: Author interview with Stuart.

"I knew the power": Ibid.

After the sun set: Ibid.

"He was receptive": Author interview with Stuart, 20 January 2006.

"He kept his session dates": Author interview with Tittle, 23 September 2004.

Disgusted, Popovich surveyed: Author interview with Popovich.

"I was layin'": Tosches, *The Journal of Country Music*.

When he related the near-death story: Cash with Carr, 259.

In the May after surgery: "Johnny Cash Hospitalized in Europe," Associated Press (May 4, 1989).

Then, just before Thanksgiving: "Johnny Cash Checks Back into Alcohol, Drug Treatment Center," *Lakeland (Fla.) Ledger* (November 26, 1989).

"When I go out": Author interview with Kent Underwood, 15 February 2005.

"The whole situation': Barry Hoskyns, "Johnny Cash: A Law Unto Himself," *Mojo* (December 1996).

Green, who had no experience: Leon Frederick and Patricia Bates, "Cash Country Latest Celebrity Attraction for Branson, Mo.," *Amusement Business* (May 6, 1991).

The Wayne Newtown theater manager: Author interview with Underwood

He woke that morning: Author interview with Underwood.

CHAPTER SIXTEEN: DRIVE ON

"He was in pretty rough shape": Author interview with Tittle.

"Johnny in his mind": Author interview with Cash, Jr., 16 August 2004.

When Marty Stuart encountered Roy: Author interview with Stuart, 21 September 2004.

"The memories were strong": Author interview with John Carter Cash, 29 July 2005.

"He taught me": Author interview with Cindy Cash.

Shocked and amused, the producer: Author interview with Clement.

Roy Cash, Jr., who in 1963 Author interview with Cash, Jr.

Paul, he said: Johnny Cash. *Man in White: A Novel.* (New York: Harper and Row, 1987), 5.

"I decided that I had taken on more": Ibid.

"He had always strived": Cash, 50.

"He lay on the hard ground": Cash, 120.

In 1979, he unveiled a double album: Patrick Carr, "Cash Lives," *Country Music* (March/April 1989).

On Christmas Eve: Author interview with Shaw.

But later in the evening: Ibid.

Their next encounter: Ibid.

He also dreamt: Ibid.

In 1981: Ibid.

After the Pittsburgh meeting: Ibid.

On the phone: Ibid.

"His name is *Jack*": Ibid.

"All these years": Ibid.

It was in 1990: Ibid.

"It was testing time": Ibid.

"I kept telling John": Ibid.

How could the child of Jimmie Rodgers and Roy Acuff: A 2004 magazine article listed *Highway to Hell* among Rubin's favorite albums. Russell Hall, "Producer's Corner," *Performing Songwriter* (July/August 2004).

"He was a lot like Sam": Robert Hilburn, "Important Music Comes from the Gut," *Los Angeles Times* (April 25, 1994).

When some priggish critics charged: Author interview with Cash Tittle, 17 August 2004.

"In Rubin's ruthlessly unadorned, dry-as-dust settings": Anthony DeCurtis, "Recordings Their Way," *Rolling Stone* (May 19, 1994).

Journalist Patick Carr: Patrick Carr, "Cash Has Always Been Cool," *Country Music* (July/August 1994); Chris Dickinson, "Cash Conquers, *The Chicago Reader* (September 16, 1994).

"At this late date": Dickinson, *The Chicago Reader*.

"Let's hear it for Rick Rubin": Author interview with Stuart, 19 September 2003.

"There are all these great expressions": Pond, *Rolling Stone*.

"Halfway through, he sat alone": Dickinson, *The Chicago Reader*.

"When we left": Author interview with Shaw.

~

CHAPTER SEVENTEEN: UNCHAINED

Gingerly taking up the guitar: Author interview with Stuart, 21 September 2004.

"I sat at the House of Cash": Ibid.

"He knew that he could look at me": Author interview with Stuart, 19 September 2004.

"I was on the way": Author interview with Stuart, 21 September 2004.

Playing guitar: Ibid.

Taking Rubin's cue: Ibid.

"It was just a different set": Ibid.

"It never felt like, okay, here's our idea": Author interview with Tittle.

"John, I felt, was like a kid": Author interview with Stuart.

"Cash, sticking close": Richard Cromelin, "Johnny Cash: Unchained," *Los Angeles Times* (November 3, 1996).

"We'd be in the studio": Rick Rubin. Interview. *Fresh Air*. WHYY-FM, 16 February 2004.

Daughter Rosanne saw her father: Author interview with Rosanne Cash, 3 March 2005.

A few months later: Ibid.

One such incident: Ibid.

"There I was:" Cash with Carr, 400.

Cash had visited the doctor: Ibid.

He took to traveling: Author interview with Poole Ball.

"There's something wrong": Ibid.

Although Cash appeared reasonably healthy: Wayne Bledsoe, "Cash Performs Show in the Middle of Two Worlds," *The Knoxville News-Sentinel* (October 24, 1997).

"Every night": Author interview with Cindy Cash.

"Her father was swaying": Ibid.

Normally after her bow: Ibid.

The Flint Press: "Cash Cancels Book, Concert Tour," *The Seattle Times* (October 28, 1997).

"I spent ten days": Cash with Carr, 400.

Marshall Grant, up from Mississippi: Author interview with Grant, 18 January 2006.

Band members whom Grant met: Ibid.

"He was the definitive restless person": Author interview with Rosanne Cash, 7 July 2004.

Across every threshold: "Johnny Cash Back in Nashville Hospital," *Seattle Post-Intelligencer* (October 15, 1998).

"Stuart was at work": Author interview with Stuart.

During Stuart's visit: Ibid.

One family member: Author interview with Cash Tittle.

Rosanne never knew what to believe: Author interview Rosanne Cash.

This is so complicated: Ibid.

"I mean you have the lengthy conversations": Ibid.

He noted that *Solitary Man*: Ben Ratliff, "Cash, Back," *Rolling Stone* (October 26, 2000).

Rosanne was just happy: Author interview with Rosanne Cash.

She had called: Gina Arnold, "She Walked the Line for You Johnny," *The Scotsman* (Edinburgh, Scotland) (May 20, 1999).

"If we go back": Arnold, *The Scotsman*.

<hr />

CHAPTER EIGHTEEN: THE GLOAMING

In 2000, doctors revised: Johnny Cash. Interview. *Larry King Weekend*. CNN. 29 December 2002.

In August of: 2002 "Johnny Cash in Hospital," *The Cincinnati Post* (August 27, 2002).

He did so while suffering quietly: Rick Rubin, *Fresh Air*.

"I was a little wary": David Kamp. "American Communion," *Vanity Fair* (October 2004).

"I don't know": Author interview with Marty Stuart, 19 September 2003.

Cash's family and management: Author interview with Rosanne Cash.

"I wasn't aware": Ibid.

"It's the culmination": Author interview with Rosanne Cash, 10 March 2006.

He even reached: Cash, 126.

"I knew what": Author interview with Stuart.

"I wrote and recorded": Johnny Cash, liner notes, *American IV: The Man Comes Around*, American Recordings, 440 077 083-0, 2003.

"For me it had been a year": Author interview with Tittle.

"She was so down": Author interview with Rosanne Cash, 3 March 2005.

"It didn't help": Author interview with Rosanne Cash, 7 July 2004.

Almost two years: Author interview with Rosanne Cash, 3 March 2005.

Although she endured: Author interview with Tittle.

"It was gut-wrenching": Ibid.

In the first of many reminders: Ibid.

Despite the stunning effect: Author interview with Cash Tittle.

"After June passed": Author interview with Stuart.

Tittle recalls: Author interview with Tittle, 17 August 2004; author interview with Stuart.

In June, she had come up: Author interview with Cindy Cash.

"Finally one day": Ibid.

Cindy remembers: Ibid.

"I would think": Ibid.

"He wanted to go": Author interview with Cash Tittle.

Rosanne took her turn: Author interview with Rosanne Cash.

It seems to her to be the redemptive moment: Ibid.

"I don't know": "Johnny Cash Heals His Aching Heart," *Detroit News* (June 26, 2003).

"I tell you": Ralph Berrier, Jr., "'Man in Black Will Be Missed By Fans, Family, Friends in Roanoke, *The Roanoke Times* (September 13, 2003).

According to Rosanne: Author interview with Rosanne Cash.

Cash was actually happy: Author interview with Cindy Cash.

Kathy dutifully paid a visit: Author interview with Cash Tittle.

"We walked into the bedroom": Ibid.

"I had been there": Author interview with Rosanne Cash.

"I went ballistic": Author interview with Rosanne Cash, 7 July 2004.

Kathy Cash doubts: Author interview with Cash Tittle.

On September 11th: Ibid.

Later that afternoon: Ibid.

"He knew we were there": Ibid.

Both daughters had dozed off: Ibid.

A little more than two years later: Author interview with Grant.

BIBLIOGRAPHY

REFERENCE

Bogdanov, Vladimir, Chris Woodstra, and Steve Erlewine, eds. *All Music Guide to Country*, 2nd ed. San Francisco: Backbeat Books, 2003.

Botkin, B.A., ed. *A Treasury of American Folklore*. New York: Crown Publishers, 1944.

————. *A Treasury of Southern Folklore*. New York: Crown Publishers, 1949.

————. *A Treasury of Western Folklore*. New York: Crown Publishers, 1975.

Cantwell, David, and Bill Friskics-Warren. *Heartaches by the Number: Country Music's 500 Greatest Singles*. Nashville: Vanderbilt University Press/Country Music Foundation Press, 2003.

Guralnick, Peter, and Ernst Jorgensen. *Elvis Day By Day: The Definitive Record of His Life and Music*. New York: Ballantine Books, 1999.

Kingsbury, Paul, ed. *The Encyclopedia of Country Music*. New York: Oxford University Press, 1998.

Lewry, Peter. *I've Been Everywhere: A Johnny Cash Chronicle*. London: Helter Skelter, 2001.

Lomax, John A., and Alan Lomax, eds. *American Folk Ballads and Songs*. New York: Dover Publications, reprinted, 1994.

————. *Cowboy Songs and Other Frontier Ballads*. New York: MacMillan, 9th printing, 1952.

McCloud, Barry, ed. *Definitive Country: The Ultimate Encyclopedia of Country Music and Its Peformers*. New York: Perigree, 1995.

Meade, Guthrie T., Jr. with Dick Spottswood, and Douglas S. Meade. *Country Music Sources: A Biblio-Discography of Commercially Recorded Country Music*. Chapel Hill: University of North Carolina Press, 2002.

Shelton, Robert, and Burt Goldblatt. *The Country Music Story: A Picture History of Country and Western Music.* New York: Bobbs-Merrill, 1966.

Smith, John L. *The Johnny Cash Discography, 1984–1993.* Westport, CT: Greenwood Press, 1994.

———. *The Johnny Cash Discography.* Westport, CT: Greenwood Press, 1985.

Stambler, Irwin, and Grelun Landon. *The Encyclopedia of Folk, Country and Western Music.* New York: St. Martin's Press, 1984.

Variety Film Reviews, 1907–1980. New York and London: Garland Publishing, 1983.

Whitburn, Joel. *Top Country Albums, 1964–1997.* Menomonee Falls, WI: Record Research, Inc., 1997.

———. *Top Country Singles, 1994–1993.* Menomonee Falls, WI: Record Research, Inc., 1994.

———. *Top Pop Singles, 1955–1993.* Menomonee Falls, WI: Record Research, Inc., 1994.

———. *Top R&B Singles, 1942–1988.* Menomonee Falls, WI: Record Research, Inc., 1988.

Workers of the Writers' Program of the Works Projects Administration. *Arkansas: A Guide to the State.* New York: Hastings House, 1941.

WPA Guide to Tennesee. Knoxville: University of Tennessee Press, 1986.

GENERAL

Allen, Bob. *George Jones: The Saga of an American Singer.* Garden City, NY: Dolphin Doubleday, 1984.

Bearss, Edwin C. *Steele's Retreat from Camden and the Battle of Jenkins' Ferry.* Little Rock: Arkansas Civil War Centennial Commission and Pioneer Press, 1967.

Biographical and Historical Memoirs of Northeast Arkansas. Chicago: The Goodspeed Publishing Co., 1889.

Booth, Stanley. *Rhythm Oil: A Journey through the Music of the American South.* London: Vintage, 1999.

Brown, Cecil. *Stagolee Shot Billy.* Cambridge: Harvard University Press, 2003.

Brown, Maxine. *Looking Back to See: A Country Music Memoir.* Fayetteville: University of Arkansas Press, 2005.

Bufwack, Mary A., and Robert K. Oermann. *Finding Her Voice: Women in Country Music, 1800–2000.* Nashville: CMF/Vanderbilt Press, 2003.

Cantwell, Robert. *When We Were Good: The Folk Revival.* Cambridge, MA: Harvard University Press, 1996.

Cash, Cindy. *The Cash Family Scrapbook.* New York: Crown, 1997.

Cash, Johnny with Patrick Carr. *Cash: The Autobiography*. New York: HarperSanFrancisco, 1997.

Cash, Johnny. *Man in Black*. Grand Rapids, MI: Zondervan Press, 1975.

———. *Man in White: A Novel*. New York: Harper and Row, 1986.

Cash, Rosanne, ed. *Songs without Rhyme: Prose by Celebrated Songwriters*. New York: Hyperion, 2001.

Cavanaugh, Peter C. *Local DJ: A Rock 'N' Roll History*. Xlibris Corporation, 2001.

Charles, Ray with David Ritz. *Brother Ray: Ray Charles' Own Story*. New York: Da Capo Press, 2003.

Clark, Georgia H., and R. Bruce Parham. *Arkansas Counties and Local Histories: A Bibliography*. Fayetteville: Bicentennial Committee, Mullins Library, University of Arkansas, 1976.

Cleaver, Eldridge. *Soul on Ice*. New York: Delta, 1968.

Cochran, Robert. *Our Own Sweet Sounds: A Celebration of Popular Music in Arkansas*. Fayetteville: University of Arkansas Press, 1996.

Conn, Charles P. *The New Johnny Cash*. Old Tappen, NJ: Fleming H. Revell Company, 1973.

Conrad, David Eugene. *The Forgotten Farmers: The Story of Sharecroppers in the New Deal*. Urbana, IL: University of Illinois Press, 1965.

Cooper, Daniel. *Lefty Frizzell: The Honky-tonk Life of Country Music's Greatest Singer*. Boston: Little, Brown, 1995.

Davis, Clive with James Willwerth. *Clive: Inside the Record Business*. New York: Ballantine Books, 1976.

Dawidoff, Nicholas. *In the Country of Country: A Journey to the Roots of American Music*. New York: Pantheon Books, 1977.

Dickerson, James. *Goin' Back to Memphis: A Century of Blues, Rock 'n' Roll, and Glorious Soul*. New York: Schirmer, 1996.

Doggett, Peter. *Are You Ready for the Country?* New York: Penguin, 2001.

Dylan, Bob. *Chronicles: Volume One*. New York: Simon and Schuster, 2004.

Eberly, Philip K. *Music in the Air: America's Changing Tastes in Popular Music, 1920–1980*. New York: Hastings House, 1982.

Edrington, Mabel F., ed. *History of Mississippi County, Arkansas*. Ocala, FL: Ocala Star Banner, 1962.

Einarson, John. *Desperados: The Roots of Country Rock*. New York: Cooper Square Press, 2001.

Eng, Steve. *A Satisfied Mind: The Country Music Life of Porter Wagoner*. Nashville: Rutledge Hill Press, 1992.

Escott, Colin with Martin Hawkins. *Good Rockin' Tonight: Sun Records and the Birth of Rock and Roll*. New York: St. Martin's Press, 1991.

Farber, David, ed. *The Sixties: From Memory to History*. Chapel Hill: University of North Carolina Press, 1994.

Fine, Jason, ed. *Cash*. New York: Crown Publishers, 2004.

Govoni, Albert. *A Boy Named Cash*. New York: Lancer Books, 1970.

Green, Douglas B. *Singing in the Saddle: The History of the Singing Cowboy*. Nashville: Country Music Foundation Press and Vanderbilt University Press, 2002.

Grissim, John. *Country Music: White Man's Blues*. New York: Coronet, 1970.

Guralnick, Peter. *Last Train to Memphis: The Rise of Elvis Presley*. Boston: Little, Brown, 1994.

Haggard, Merle with Peggy Russell. *Sing Me Back Home: My Life*. New York: Times Books, 1981.

Halberstam, David. *The Children*. New York: Random House, 1998.

Hemphill, Paul. *The Nashville Sound: Bright Lights and Country Music*. New York: Simon and Schuster, 1970.

Heylin, Clinton. *Bob Dylan: A Life in Stolen Moments*. New York: Schirmer Books, 1996.

Hobson, Archie, ed. *Remembering America: A Sampler of the WPA American Guide Series*. New York: Columbia University Press, 1985.

Horstman, Dorothy. *Sing Your Heart Out Country Boy*, 3rd ed. Nashville: Country Music Foundation Press, 1996.

Howard, Jan. *Sunshine and Shadows*. New York: Richardson and Steirman, 1987.

Hoye, Jacob, ed. *VH1's Greatest Albums*. New York: Pocket Books, 2003.

Irwin, Jim. *The Mojo Collection: The Greatest Albums of All Time*. Edinburgh, UK, 2001.

Jennings, Waylon with Lenny Kaye. *Waylon: An Autobiography*. New York: Warner Books, 1996.

Jones, George with Tom Carter. *I Lived to Tell All*. New York: Villard, 1996.

Jones, Margaret. *Patsy: The Life and Times of Patsy Cline*. New York: Harper Collins, 1994.

King, B.B. with David Ritz. *Blues All Around Me: The Autobiography of B.B. King*. New York: Avon Books, 1996.

Kingsbury, Paul. *The Grand Ole Opry History of Country Music*. New York: Villard Books, 1995.

Kingsbury, Paul. *Vinyl Hayride: Country Music Album Covers, 1947–1989*. San Francisco: Chronicle Books, 2003.

Kramer, Daniel. *Bob Dylan*. New York: Citadel Press, 1967.

Laird, Tracey E.W. *Louisiana Hayride: Radio and Roots Along the Red River*. New York and London: Oxford University Press, 2005.

Leibovitz, Annie. *American Music*. New York: Random House, 2003.

Malone, Bill C. *Country Music USA* (Revised Edition). Austin: University of Texas Press, 1985.

————. *Don't Get above Your Raisin': Country Music and the Southern Working Class*. Urbana and Chicago: University of Illinois Press, 2002.

Mandrell, Barbara with George Vecsey. *Get to the Heart: My Story*. New York: Bantam Books, 1990.

Marcus, Greil, ed. *Rock and Roll Will Stand*. Boston: Beacon Press, 1969.

Marsh, Dave, ed. *For the Record: Sun Records*. New York: Avon Books, 1998.

McKee, Margaret, and Fred Chisenhall. *Beale Black and Blue: Life and Music on Black America's Main Street*. Baton Rouge and London: Louisiana State University Press, 1981.

Miller, Bill. *Cash: An American Man*. New York: Pocket Books, 2004.

Miller, Stephen. *Johnny Cash: The Life of An American Icon*. London: Omnibus Press, 2003.

Moneyhon, Carl H. *Arkansas and the New South: 1874–1929*. Fayetteville: University of Arkansas Press, 1997.

Morthland, John. *The Best of Country Music*. Garden City, NY: Dolphin, 1984.

Murray, Albert. *Stomping the Blues*. New York: Da Capo Press, 1976.

Nelson, Willie with Bud Shrake. *Willie: An Autobiography*. New York: Simon and Schuster, 1988.

Noles, Randy. *Orange Blossom Boys: The Untold Story of Ervin T. Rouse, Chubby Wise and the World's Most Famous Fiddle Tune*. Anaheim Hills, CA: Centerstream Publishing, 2002.

Palmer, Robert. *Deep Blues*. New York: Viking, 1981.

————. *Rock and Roll: An Unruly History*. New York: Harmony Books, 1995.

Perkins, Carl, and David McGee. *Go, Cat, Go!: The Life and Times of Carl Perkins*. New York: Hyperion, 1996.

Porterfield, Nolan. *Jimmie Rodgers: The Life and Times of America's Blue Yodeler*. Urbana: University of Illinois Press, 1979.

Pugh, Ronnie. *Ernest Tubb: The Texas Troubadour*. Durham, NC: Duke University Press, 1996.

Quain, Kevin, ed. *The Elvis Reader: Texts and Sources on the King of Rock and Roll*. New York: St. Martin's Press, 1992.

Sanjek, Russell (updated by David Sanjek). *Pennies from Heaven: The American Popular Music Business in the Twentieth Century.* New York: Da Capo Press, 1996.

Sculatti, Gene, and Davin Seay. *San Francisco Nights: The Psychedelic Music Trip, 1965–1968.* New York: St. Martin's Press, 1985.

Self, Philip. *Guitar Pull: Conversations with Country Music's Legendary Songwriters.* Nashville: Cypress Moon Press, 2002.

Shelton, Robert. *No Direction Home: The Life and Music of Bob Dylan.* New York: Ballantine Books, 1987.

Snow, Jimmy with Jim and Martie Hefley. *I Cannot Go Back.* Plainfield, NJ: Logos International, 1977.

Sounes, Howard. *Down the Highway: The Life of Bob Dylan.* New York: Grove Press, 2001.

Stuart, Marty. *Pilgrims: Sinners, Saints, and Prophets.* Nashville: Rutledge Hill Press, 1999.

Thomson, Elizabeth, and David Gutman, eds. *The Dylan Companion.* New York: Da Capo Press, 2001.

Tucker, David M. *Arkansas: A People and Their Reputation.* Memphis: Memphis State University Press, 1985.

Turner, Steve. *The Man Called Cash: The Life, Love, and Faith of An American Legend.* Nashville: W Publishing Group, 2004.

Unterberger, Richie. *Eight Miles High: Folk-Rock's Flight from Haight-Ashbury to Woodstock.* San Francisco: Backbeat Books, 2003.

———. *Turn! Turn! Turn!: The '60s Folk-Rock Revolution.* San Francisco: Backbeat Books, 2002.

Van Ronk, Dave with Elijah Wald. *The Mayor of MacDougal Street: A Memoir.* New York: Da Capo Books, 2005.

Waddell, Hugh, ed. I *Still Miss Someone: Friends and Family Remember Johnny Cash.* Nashville: Cumberland House, 2004.

Wald, Elijah. *Escaping the Delta: Robert Johnson and the Invention of the Blues.* New York: Amistad, 2004.

Whayne, Jeannie M. *A New Plantation South: Land, Labor, and Federal Favor in Twentieth-Century Arkansas.* Charlottesville: University Press of Virginia, 1996.

Wilentz, Sean, and Greil Marcus, eds. *The Rose and the Briar: Death, Love and Liberty in the American Ballad.* New York: W.W. Norton and Company, 2005.

Williams, Hank, Jr., with Michael Bane. *Living Proof: An Autobiography.* New York: Putnam, 1979.

Wolfe, Charles, and Kip Lornell. *The Life and Legend of Leadbelly*. New York: Harper Collins, 1992.

Wren, Christopher. *Winners Got Scars Too: The Life and Legends of Johnny Cash*. New York: Dial Press, 1971.

Yetnikoff, Walter with David Ritz. *Howling at the Moon: The Odyssey of A Monstrous Music Mogul in An Age of Excess*. New York: Broadway Books, 2004.

Zwonitzer, Mark with Charles Hirshberg. *Will You Miss Me When I'm Gone: The Carter Family and Their Legacy in American Music*. New York: Simon and Schuster, 2002.

ALBUM LINER NOTES

Alden, Grant, and Peter Blackstock. *Exposed Roots: The Best of Alt. Country*. K-tel International, 1999.

Cash, Johnny. *American Recordings*. American Recordings, 1994.

———. *American IV: The Man Comes Around*. American Recordings, 2002.

———. *Gone Girl*. Columbia Records, 1978.

———. *My Mother's Hymn Book*. American Recordings, 2004.

———. *Johnny Cash At Folsom Prison*. Columbia Records, 1968.

———. *Johnny Cash Sings Ballads of the True West*. Columbia Records, 1965.

———. *Rainbow*. Columbia Records, 1985.

———. *Unchained*. American Recordings, 1996.

Cash, June Carter. *Johnny Cash: Love God Murder*. Sony Music, 2000.

Costello, Elvis. *Almost Blue*. Rhino Records, 2004.

Davis, Hank. *Johnny Cash: The Sun Years*, Charly, 1995.

Escott, Colin. *Johnny Cash: The Man in Black, 1954–1958*. Bear Family Records, 1990.

———. *Johnny Cash: The Man in Black, 1959–62*. Bear Family Records, 1991.

———. *Johnny Cash: The Man in Black, 1963–69 Plus*. Bear Family Records, 1995.

Kienzle, Rich. *Chet Atkins: Galloping Guitar*. Bear Family Records, 1993.

———. *The Best of Merle Travis*. Rhino Records, 1990.

Simmons, Sylvie. *Cash: Unearthed*. American Recordings, 2003.

FEDERAL RECORDS

Farmers Home Administration, NA, RG 96.

U.S. Department of Commerce and Labor. *Thirteenth Census of the United States: 1910*. Population. Washington, DC, 1912.

U.S. Department of Commerce. *Fourteenth Census of the United States: 1920.* Population. Washington, DC, 1922.

―――. *Fifteenth Census of the United States: 1930.* Population. Washington, DC, 1932.

Works Progress Administration, NA, RG 69.

～

MASTER'S THESIS

Hayden, David. "A History of Dyess, Arkansas." MA Thesis, Southern Illinois University, 1970.   ～

DIRECTORIES, INDEXES, JOURNALS, MAGAZINES, AND NEWSPAPERS

Billboard, 1955–2003.

Cleveland County (AK) Herald, 1932–1976.

The (Dyess) Colony Herald, 1936.

The Dyess Eagle, 1938.

Journal of Country Music, 1971–2005.

Los Angeles Times, 1957–2003.

Memphis Commercial Appeal, 1932–2003.

Memphis City Directory. St. Louis: R.L. Polk and Co., 1954–1960.

Memphis Press Scimitar, 1932–1984.

Nashville Banner, 1956–1998.

New York Times, 1951–2003.

Ross Reports on Television, 1956–1962.

Television Index, 1963–1966.

The Tennessean (Nashville), 1969–2003.

The Washington Post, 1951–2003.

～

INDEX